PROMISES OF THE GOOD LIFE

Social consequences of
private marketing decisions

The Irwin Series in Marketing

Consulting Editor   Gilbert A. Churchill
University of Wisconsin, Madison

104476

PROMISES OF THE GOOD LIFE

Social consequences of
private marketing decisions

S. PRAKASH SETHI
*The University of Texas
at Dallas*

1979

RICHARD D. IRWIN, INC.   Homewood, Illinois   60430
Irwin-Dorsey Limited   Georgetown, Ontario   L7G 4B3

Cover: David Smith, "Voltron XVIII." New York
State, The Governor Nelson A. Rockefeller
Empire State Plaza Art Collection.

© RICHARD D. IRWIN, INC., 1979

ISBN 0–256–02230–5
Library of Congress Catalog Card No. 78–70945
Printed in the United States of America

1 2 3 4 5 6 7 8 9 0 ML 6 5 4 3 2 1 0 9

Dedicated to the memory of

RAYMOND A. BAUER

the late Joseph C. Wilson Professor of Business Administration,
Harvard Business School

a dear friend, an intellectual and a scholar, who was also a social activist. He believed that business had a social responsibility beyond its narrow economic function and worked all his life to bring about greater harmony between business and other social institutions.

Preface

Marketing activities by business firms, large and small, historically have been subject to greater public scrutiny and regulation than any other area of business activity. This results principally from two factors. First, the pricing function is one of the critical elements in the maintenance of competitive markets and therefore is subject to governmental scrutiny. Second is the nature of marketing function itself: it is the closest link between the manufacturer and the ultimate consumer.

Elements of the marketing mix, such as pricing, product design, product safety, advertising, consumer information, warranties, and after-sale service, have the effect of personalizing a company to the public. Consumers come into contact with a firm through its marketing activities. When they are unhappy or dissatisfied, they seek relief through withholding future patronage or through pressure for further governmental regulation, as well as through judicial remedies. This has resulted in the formation of new agencies such as the Consumer Product Safety Commission (CPSC); greater activism on the part of the existing agencies, such as Federal Trade Commission (FTC); and an ever-increasing stream of new laws, regulations, and court decisions affecting virtually all aspects of marketing activity.

"Consumerism" is one catch-all term that describes the sum total of tensions and conflicts between buyers and sellers in the marketplace. There is an increasing awareness on the part of consumers about product-related safety hazards. Consumer groups have also emerged as a political lobby. Furthermore, most modern products have become increasingly complex, with attendant higher malfunction or failure rates and a decline in after-sale service. Last but not least, there has been a failure on the part of marketers to realize that marketing does not mean just selling; it means satisfying a consumer need with a product that delivers according to customers' reasonable expectations and marketers' implied and specific promises. All these factors have combined to increase the schism between buyers and sellers where mutual harmony and an identity of interest should exist, according to the tenets of the new marketing concept.

To the extent that companies have been unable or unwilling to stem the tide of increasing dissatisfaction in the marketplace, the consumer has increasingly resorted to nonmarket mechanisms to achieve satisfaction. Examples are the FTC's advertisement substantiation programs; truth-in-lending laws, unit pricing, information disclosure, pricing policies, and product warranties; CPSC's rule-making powers in establishing product safety standards and product recall requirements; and FDA's requirements for product testing, safety, and labeling. Furthermore, the courts have been consistently broadening the scope and applicability of various laws and relief remedies, thereby creating significant uncertainties for marketing executives as to the possible adverse implications of their otherwise normal marketing decisions. Notwithstanding, it should be noted that public interest groups and corporate critics believe that the remedies currently available to the consumer are woefully inadequate and that more stringent measures and regulations are required.

This book is intended to serve a threefold purpose:

1. To bring to the attention of the student and practitioner of marketing the various facets of the conflict that arises among the suppliers, marketers, and consumers of goods in the marketplace. The definition of the problem is seen not only from the viewpoint of the firm, but also from the viewpoint of the consumer and the state.

2. To demonstrate the fact that all marketing activities of individual firms have second-order effects that extend far beyond the boundaries of the parties to the immediate exchange. Quite often their effects are far more pervasive in their collectivity than visualized by individual firms when making simple transactions. If the private sector continues to ignore these second-order effects, the consequences could be serious not only for individual firms, but for the entire social system.

3. To develop an understanding among various producer and consumer groups of the need to develop new mechanisms for resolving disputes and to keep expectations within reasonable bounds. For in the final analysis, if either producers or consumers succeed in driving the other group to the point where it chooses to withdraw from the negotiating process and opts for a third-party resolution, the calamity would be the market system itself—a prospect which is none too desirable from either party's point of view.

The cases and issues presented in the book relate to real situations and problems. The emphasis is not on the right or wrong decision as made by the various parties involved, but on an analysis of the sources of the problems, the often conflicting and erroneous perceptions of various parties as to others' motives, strategies, and tactics, and how solutions that have been traditionally effective turn out to be inappropriate in a changed economic and sociopolitical environment. It is hoped that a careful examination and analysis of these issues will lead the professional marketer and the marketing student into developing new approaches that will be more cognizant of the changed reality and also reinforce the old adage that the consumer is king.

This book would not have come into being without the subtle persuasion and overt encouragement of my friend, David A. Aaker of the Graduate School of Business, University of California, Berkeley. Not only was he responsible for planting the idea for the book in my mind, but he was also instrumental in its eventual completion through careful review of the manuscript that went a long way toward sharpening the focus of the issues involved.

In the development of the book, I was assisted by three graduate assistants, Sandra Segal, Paul Tiffany, and Christopher Miller. Not only did they carry out library research, they also assisted in the preparation of initial drafts of various case studies. In particular, Ms. Segal was responsible for the work on the cases of Pharmaceutical Industry (B), U.S. Product Safety Commission, Children's Television Advertising and Programming, and Marketing of Infant Formula Foods in Less-Developed Countries cases. Mr. Tiffany worked on the cases of Omnivest Corporation, The Commodore Corporation and the Mobile Home Industry, the Trouble Lights, and General Electric and Matsushita Electric Corporation of America. Mr. Miller contributed to the case of Pharmaceutical Industry (A). Robert N. Katz, Graduate School of Business, University of California, Berkeley, collaborated and jointly wrote the Acme Markets case. Their assistance and contributions are gratefully acknowledged.

My wife, Donna, was responsible for the onerous chore of reading and correcting the galleys and page proofs; it was a job she performed painstakingly. She has my gratitude.

The typing of the various drafts of the manuscript was primarily done by Patricia Murphy at the School of Business, University of California, Berkeley. Her careful and speedy work and knack for picking up errors significantly contributed to the timely completion of the manuscript. Her assistance is appreciated.

I am also grateful to Prentice-Hall, Inc., and D. C. Heath & Co., for their permission to reprint material from my two books, namely, *Up Against the Corporate Wall* and *Advocacy Advertising and Large Corporations.*

April 1979 **S. Prakash Sethi**

Contents

PART I

ELEMENTS OF MARKETING MIX AND THEIR IMPACT ON SOCIETY

SECTION A
PROMOTION
AND PRICING

1 Pharmaceutical (prescription drugs) industry (A)

Promotion and pricing practices

*Given its commercial role of advocacy, promotion remains neverthe-
less an essential function within the health care system by bringing
needed information to health professionals. Not only the outflow of
data and materials from pharmaceutical companies, but the daily feed-
back from the professionals leads to improved products and services.*[1]

Pharmaceutical Manufacturers Association

*One has to be blind, deaf, and dumb, to lock his office if he wishes to
avoid being deluged with direct mail advertising, visits by detailmen,
and more recently, heavy promotion in "throwaway" unsolicited journals which, for the most part, serve as advertising vehicles. I have no
objection to ethical promotion of products, but the matter is out of
hand.*[2]

Dr. Calvin Kunin

The pharmaceutical industry is one of the most profitable and growth-
oriented industries in the United States and the world. Total sales in the
United States in 1974 were $10.493 billion; worldwide sales of drugs at the
retail level were approximately four times that amount.[3] Between 1963 and

---

[1] Pharmaceutical Manufacturers Association, "General Overview of Function and Value
of the Pharmaceutical Industry Promotional Activities," in U.S. Congress, Senate, Committee on Labor and Public Welfare, Subcommittee on Health, *Examination of the Pharmaceutical Industry* (Washington, D.C.: U.S. Government Printing Office, 1972–73), part 6, p. 2432.

[2] Calvin Kunin, statement in U.S. Congress, Senate, Select Committee on Small Business,
Subcommittee on Monopoly, *Present Status of Competition in the Pharmaceutical Industry*
(Washington, D.C.: U.S. Government Printing Office, 1967), part 2, p. 714.

[3] Pharmaceutical Manufacturers Association, *Prescription Drug Industry Factbook '76*,
p. ii; and "Profits in Pills," *The Economist*, June 5, 1976, p. 62.

3

1970, the ethical drugs industry grew at a 60 percent higher rate than manufacturing in general. During this period, the dollar sales of all manufacturing increased by 49.8 percent, while the pharmaceutical industry's sales increased by 81.9 percent.[4] Sales of ethical drugs in the United States in 1972 amounted to $22.50 for every person in the United States. In that same year, every man, woman, and child spent an average $97.45 on alcohol, $60.50 on tobacco, and $40.40 on papers and books.[5] (See Appendix to this chapter.)

DIMENSIONS OF THE PROBLEM

The growth of the industry and its contributions to public health and welfare not withstanding, it is beset with many problems and public discontent over its promotion and pricing.

Estimates of the amount of money drug companies spend on promotion vary according to different sources. The industry spends approximately 20 percent of its sales revenues for all types of promotion activities in the United States. A Social Security Administration analysis found that in 1971 the prescription drug industry spent over $1 billion on all promotion in the United States.[6] The figure breaks down as shown in Table 1–1. In contrast, total research and development spending in the United States by the pharmaceutical industry amounted to slightly less than $700 million in 1973.[7]

A statement by the Pharmaceutical Manufacturers Association (PMA) offered slightly different figures. The drug marketing research firm of Professional Market Research of Philadelphia estimated that in 1974, promotional expenses totaled $715 million. The same statement asserted that in 1973, $824 million was spent on research and development (R&D) of human and veterinary pharmaceuticals. Of this figure, $698 million was for

TABLE 1–1

Purpose	$ million
All costs associated with detailing, including free samples	$700
Professional journal and direct mail advertising	167
Other promotional expenses such as films, pamphlets, seminars, plant tours, convention displays, and entertainment	150
Institutional promotion	3

---

[4] A. T. Sproat, *A Note on the U.S. Prescription Drug Industry*, part I (R), Harvard Business School, No. 6-373-136 (1972), p. 1.

[5] *Key Facts about the U.S. Prescription Drug Industry 1974*, Pharmaceutical Manufacturers Association, p. 3.

[6] Milton Silverman and Philip R. Lee, *Pills, Profits, and Politics* (Berkeley and Los Angeles: University of California Press, 1974), pp. 54–55.

[7] Ibid.

expenditures in the United States. In 1974 total R&D expenditures were budgeted to reach $930 million.[8]

The rising cost of health care in the United States has created tremendous pressure from government agencies and public interest groups for the purchase of drugs by generic name, the least expensive source. The impact of such a policy on the earnings of the drug companies could be significant. The industry has fought such initiatives through the courts, in the legislatures, and in the mass media. It argues that such policies are shortsighted because they will adversely affect the industry's ability to engage in R&D and bring out new products, and will also not guarantee uniformly superior product quality. There is a great deal of price disparity among different retail outlets, cities, and countries that is difficult to account for in terms of differences in services. Critics also argue that drug companies use patent protection to charge monopoly prices. (See Appendix to this chapter.) When this advantage is combined with heavy promotion of brand name products during the protected period, it is all but impossible for the generics to make any dent in the market share of the brand name products. This results in consumers' paying unnecessarily high prices. The poor and the elderly are most affected by such practices because they cannot afford to buy a sufficient quantity of drugs. The drug industry disagrees with this argument.

ISSUES FOR ANALYSIS

Promotion plays an important role in the marketing activities of a consumer product industry, and the pharmaceutical industry is no exception. At the same time, one cannot ignore the possible abuses of promotional activities where such promotion may cause overuse or misuse of ethical drugs, thereby leading to consumer health hazards and wasteful expenditures. The questions for analysis include these:

1. What is the nature and extent of drug promotion by the pharmaceutical industry? What criteria might one use to determine whether the volume of promotional activities is adequate or excessive?
2. How might one evaluate the informational content of promotional material distributed by various firms in the pharmaceutical industry?
3. To the extent that all promotional copy is subject to regulation by the FDA, could the industry be blamed for disseminating inaccurate, insufficient, or misleading information?
4. Since physicians and pharmacists—the prime targets of industry promotion—are professionals and experts in their fields, one would expect them to be better equipped to evaluate any information received from the manufacturer. Under these circumstances, shouldn't they

---

[8] Pharmaceutical Manufacturers Association, "Questions and Answers About the U.S. Prescription Drug Industry," revised June 1975, pp. 5, 7.

share any blame for receiving and accepting product-related information in a manner and form that is inadequate for their purposes? What roles should these groups play in improving the information content of ethical drug promotion?

5. What measures need be taken by the industry, government, and other groups to improve the quality of ethical drug promotion and also discourage excessive drug usage and usage for unindicated purposes?

In terms of pricing policies:

1. How valid are critics' arguments about the high prices for brand name prescription drugs?
2. If price relief is justifiable, what is the best method for obtaining such relief? Should the drug companies be relied upon to control drug prices at the retail level? What are some of the adverse consequences that are likely to follow such a course of action?
3. What role should the physician, the druggist, the consumer, and the FDA play in ensuring that prescription drugs are available to users at the lowest possible prices? How well have these groups performed this function in the past?
4. What are the relative merits of the various arguments for and against the use of generic versus brand name drugs?

THE RATIONALE FOR DRUG PROMOTION

Studies have shown that the profits of drug companies increase in proportion to their promotional expenditures. One study found that companies which spent $50 million in 1966 had an average rate of return of 29.2 percent between 1961 and 1965; companies which spent between $10 million and $50 million had an average rate of return of 19.7 percent; and companies spending less than $10 million earned 17.3 percent.[9]

The pharmaceutical industry believes that drug promotion is a necessary and important part of the practice of medicine. Drug companies stress their dedication to the informational and educational aspects of promotion. According to the drug companies, promotion provides doctors with necessary and valuable information about new drugs and treatments, and also provides a channel (particularly through detailmen) for doctors to make their experience with the drugs known to drug manufacturers. Searle stated that marketing and sales activities were essential to the discovery and development of new methods for improving patients' well-being.[10]

Drug companies use the bulk of their promotional funds for detailing,

[9] U.S. Senate, Present Status of Competition, part 5, p. 1637.

[10] For a general discussion of this issue, see Pierre R. Garai, "Advertising and Promotion of Drugs," in Drugs in Our Society, ed. Paul Talalay (Baltimore: Johns Hopkins Press, 1964), pp. 189–202.

as this is the most influential aspect of drug promotion (see Part B, "The Detailman," in Case 4). However, the other areas of promotion also influence the physician's prescribing habits. A 1958 study by Ben Gaffin and Associates asked doctors what source of information led to prescribing the last new drug they had adopted. According to this study, direct mail advertising has the second largest effect on physicians. Surveys have shown that the majority of doctors read this material: a 1960 study showed 69 percent of physicians gave at least minimum attention to all sorts of direct mail; a 1971 study reported that of 5,000 internists, 86 percent either occasionally (54 percent), frequently (21 percent), or always (11 percent) read mail advertisements.[11] Medical journals may influence doctors both through their articles and their advertising. Several studies found that the majority of doctors at least skimmed some journals, and only a minority were critical of drug company advertising. A 1971 study of 5,347 internists found that 75 percent read the drug advertisements in journals, and 80 percent of these found the advertisements helpful.

Free samples is another method of influencing physicians. The Gaffin study showed that 10 percent of the physicians surveyed were led to prescribe a new drug by samples. A study in 1960 found that 82 percent of the physicians surveyed saved the samples they received, and over 96 percent at least looked at them.

The *Physician's Desk Reference* (PDR) is also influential in forming doctors' prescribing patterns. The Audits and Survey Company found in 1960 that 91 percent of the physicians in their survey kept PDR in or on their desks, and 53 percent of the busiest physicians used PDR at least once a day. PDR was found by a 1960 PMA study to be the second most preferred source of information on new drugs; a 1968 study found that 61 percent of physicians felt that PDR was the most frequently used source of prescribing information.

Critics sometimes claim that the selling aspect of promotion outweighs the informational aspect. Drug companies agree that selling and merchandising are a major part of promotion; in fact, if they did not try to sell, they would not have a business. But since doctors would not use products about which false statements had been made, accurate, balanced information is essential. In addition, advertisements for drugs must comply with FDA regulations, and drug companies state that all drug promotion is reviewed by their medical and legal staff.[12]

A spokesman for Pfizer suggested that some of the critics' complaints about the merchandising aspect of promotion stem from a confusion between selling a "multiple source pharmaceutical" such as a generic drug,

---

[11] Russell R. Miller, "Prescribing Habits of Physicians: A Review of Studies on Prescription of Drugs," *Drug Intelligence and Clinical Pharmacy* 8 (February 1974): 81–89.

[12] U.S. Senate, *Examination of the Pharmaceutical Industry*, part 3, pp. 793–1209, 988; Pharmaceutical Manufacturers Association, "General Overview," pp. 2452–64.

and a "single source pharmaceutical," which can be bought only from one company. Although selling the first type of drug requires many promotional techniques, including price competition, selling single source drugs depends primarily on providing the doctor with enough information. Pfizer claimed that because of an increase in the production of innovative drugs, the company had tripled the number of MDs and PhD scientists in their pharmaceutical marketing organization from 12 in 1968 to 37 in 1973.

Drug companies assert that this need for highly skilled people to research and communicate the technical information needed to sell drugs is one reason for the high cost of promotion. Because in addition in the drug industry the entire burden of promotion is carried by the manufacturer, drug companies feel that they do not spend an unusually large amount of money on promotion. Although critics also claim that promotion adds to the price of drugs, the pharmaceutical industry asserts that competition makes mass production possible, which leads in turn to lower production costs.[13]

DIFFERENT PROMOTIONAL METHODS: WHAT THEY ARE AND THE CONTROVERSIES THEY CREATE

Detailing

Detailing, as the major form of promotion, has been the subject of the most controversy. It is discussed in depth in Part B, "The Detailman," (Case 4).

Journal advertising

The amount of money spent on journal advertising is second only to that spent on detailing. A 1970 estimate of gross advertising revenues for the four journals carrying the largest amount of paid advertising found $11 million for *Medical Economics,* $9 million for *Modern Medicine,* $8 million for *Medical World News,* and $7 million for *Journal of American Medical Association (JAMA).* Only one nonmedical journal had as much paid advertising in that year.

There are three types of medical journals: scientific society journals, journals published by official state and national medical organizations, and "throwaway" journals.

Scientific journals are paid for by subscribers, and their circulation is generally small. They include the *Journal of Laboratory and Clinical Medicine, Endocrinology, Circulation Research,* and *American Journal of Physi-*

---

[13] For a general discussion, see Harry Dowling, *Medicines for Man* (New York: Knopf, 1970), pp. 121–36; Silverman and Lee, *Pills, Profits, and Politics,* pp. 48–80; Pharmaceutical Manufacturers Association, "General Overview," pp. 2452–64.

ology. The second type of journal is the national and state medical society publication. These include *JAMA, New England Journal of Medicine,* and *California Medicine.* These journals receive a great deal of advertising. Advertising in *JAMA,* for example, contributes $14 million to the American Medical Association (AMA), about 43 percent of total AMA income. A 1974 survey of doctors found that *JAMA* had the highest overall readership of the wide range of journals considered. The third type of journal is the throwaway publication, including *Medical World News, Current Therapeutic Research, Medical Economics,* and *Modern Medicine.* Most of these journals are privately owned and completely supported by advertising. One journal, *Medical Tribune,* is owned and run by the McAdams advertising agency. Some journals are subsidized in part by the sale of reprints of articles to drug manufacturers. Although critics claim that this subsidizing of journals by drug companies or advertising agencies biases them, editors of these journals have often asserted that the drug advertising has no influence on editorial policy.

The majority of journals do not screen or review advertising in any way. The FDA may review drug advertising only after it appears in print.

According to the drug companies, journal advertising is one of the most efficient ways of quickly and inexpensively reaching the doctors with the news of new and important products. The advertisements of new products not only inform the doctors of their existence, but also provide the details about dosage, function, and so on, necessary for prescribing the drug long before such information is available elsewhere. Journal ads also serve to remind the doctor about the value and availability of older drugs, as well as providing prescribing information and other reference material. (See Exhibits 1–1 to 1–4 for a variety of medical journal advertisements.)

The information in the journal ads is carefully screened and monitored. According to the drug industry, new advertising is reviewed by a team of medical and legal experts. In the Senate hearings, Eaton Laboratories, for example, claimed that all advertising was "carefully reviewed and approved by our editorial, medical, legal and marketing staffs for quality of content, medical accuracy, legal compliance, and professional standards." In addition, all advertising must meet FDA requirements. These requirements include general guidelines covering the kind of data and claims which can or cannot be used, and specific guidelines covering particular claims, indications, clinical data, and restrictive wording. Advertisements must adhere to the FDA-approved package insert, and must contain certain parts of it. According to the drug companies, very few "remedial ads" have been ordered by the FDA to correct misleading advertising (see Exhibit 1–5).[14]

---

[14] U.S. Senate, *Examination of the Pharmaceutical Industry,* part 3, pp. 1203, 1266; Pharmaceutical Manufacturers Association, "General Overview," p. 2458.

Motrin®
ibuprofen
a clinical update

Efficacy and tolerance of Motrin confirmed by further studies and by experience in more than 5,000,000 patients with rheumatoid arthritis or osteoarthritis

Update: Efficacy

Motrin (ibuprofen) is comparable to indomethacin as well as to aspirin Controlled studies in patients with rheumatoid arthritis have shown that Motrin is comparable to indomethacin in reducing joint inflammation and pain.

Earlier studies had shown Motrin to be comparable to aspirin in controlling signs and symptoms of rheumatoid arthritis and osteoarthritis.

Motrin improves functional capacity.... reduces disease activity The anti-inflammatory action of Motrin has been demonstrated by reduction in joint swelling, pain, and duration of morning stiffness, and by reduction in disease activity as assessed by both the investigator and the patient.

Motrin's anti-inflammatory activity has also been confirmed by improvement in functional capacity, evidenced by increased grip strength, delayed onset of fatigue, and a decrease in the time required to walk 50 feet.

Motrin is indicated for acute flares as well as long-term symptomatic treatment of rheumatoid arthritis and osteoarthritis. The safety and effectiveness of Motrin have not been established in patients with Functional Class IV rheumatoid arthritis.

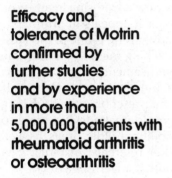

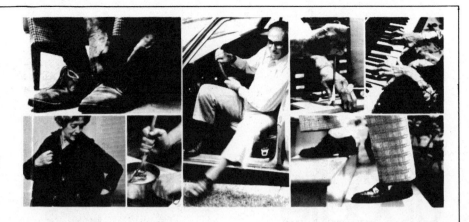

Update:
GI and CNS tolerance

Better GI tolerance than aspirin or indomethacin
Controlled studies have shown that the incidence of milder gastrointestinal complaints with Motrin (ibuprofen) is about one half that observed with equally effective doses of indomethacin.

Earlier controlled studies established that the overall incidence of gastrointestinal complaints with Motrin is about one half that reported with equally effective doses of aspirin.

Gastrointestinal bleeding, sometimes severe, has been associated
with Motrin, aspirin, indomethacin, and the other nonsteroidal antiarthritis agents.

It is not definitely known whether Motrin causes less peptic ulceration than aspirin. However, in a study involving 885 patients with rheumatoid arthritis treated with either Motrin or aspirin for up to one year, there were no reports of gastric ulceration with Motrin, but there were reports of frank ulceration in 13 of the aspirin-treated patients (statistically significant, p < .001).

Fewer CNS side effects than indomethacin
In clinical studies of patients with rheumatoid arthritis, Motrin has been shown to be associated with a statistically significant reduction in CNS side effects.

in rheumatoid arthritis
and osteoarthritis
for long-term symptomatic treatment
and acute flares

Motrin 400 mg TABLETS
ibuprofen, Upjohn

anti-inflammatory...analgesic...well tolerated

Upjohn

Please see last page of this advertisement for a brief summary of prescribing information.
© 1976 THE UPJOHN COMPANY

EXHIBIT 1-1 *(continued)*

Motrin®
ibuprofen
a clinical update

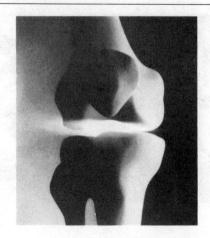

Motrin is well tolerated by most patients with rheumatoid arthritis* or osteoarthritis

Motrin is not contraindicated by a history of gastrointestinal complaints. However, gastrointestinal distress, including occasional bleeding, has been reported in patients taking Motrin.

Motrin may be well tolerated in some patients who have had gastrointestinal side effects with aspirin. These patients should be carefully followed for signs and symptoms of gastrointestinal ulceration and bleeding when treated with Motrin.

Motrin and relief of morning stiffness Motrin has been demonstrated to reduce the duration of morning stiffness. Because most patients can take Motrin without food, Motrin may be taken on arising without waiting for breakfast. If gastrointestinal complaints occur without food, Motrin may be taken with milk or other foods with no appreciable decrease in absorption.

Motrin and the older patient Use of Motrin is not restricted by advanced patient age. Because **fluid retention has occurred** with Motrin, as it has with other nonsteroidal antiarthritis agents, Motrin should be used with caution in patients with marginal cardiac compensation.

*The safety and effectiveness of Motrin have not been established in patients with Functional Class IV rheumatoid arthritis.

Motrin
ibuprofen, Upjohn

Indications and Usage
Treatment of signs and symptoms of rheumatoid arthritis and osteoarthritis during acute flares and in long-term management. Safety and efficacy have not been established in Functional Class IV rheumatoid arthritis.

Contraindications
Individuals hypersensitive to it, or with the syndrome of nasal polyps, angioedema and bronchospastic reactivity to aspirin or other nonsteroidal anti-inflammatory agents (see WARNINGS).

Warnings
Anaphylactoid reactions have occurred in patients with aspirin hypersensitivity (see CONTRAINDICATIONS).

Peptic ulceration and gastrointestinal bleeding, sometimes severe, have been reported. Ulceration, perforation and bleeding may end fatally. An association has not been established. Motrin should be given under close supervision to patients with a history of upper gastrointestinal tract disease, only after consulting ADVERSE REACTIONS.

In patients with active peptic ulcer and active rheumatoid arthritis, nonulcerogenic drugs, such as gold, should be tried. If Motrin must be given, the patient should be under close supervision for signs of ulcer perforation or gastrointestinal bleeding.

Precautions
Blurred and/or diminished vision, scotomata, and/or changes in color vision have been reported. If these develop, discontinue Motrin and the patient should have an ophthalmologic examination, including central visual fields.

Fluid retention and edema have been associated with Motrin; use with caution in patients with a history of cardiac decompensation.

Motrin can inhibit platelet aggregation and prolong bleeding time. Use with caution in persons with intrinsic coagulation defects and those on anticoagulant therapy.

Patients should report signs or symptoms of gastrointestinal ulceration or bleeding, blurred vision or other eye symptoms, skin rash, weight gain, or edema.

To avoid exacerbation of disease or adrenal insufficiency, patients on prolonged corticosteroid therapy should have therapy tapered slowly when Motrin is added.

Drug interactions. *Aspirin* used concomitantly may decrease Motrin blood levels. *Coumarin:* Bleeding has been reported in patients taking Motrin and Coumarin.

Pregnancy and nursing mothers: Motrin should not be taken during pregnancy or by nursing mothers.

Adverse Reactions
Incidence greater than 1%
Gastrointestinal: The most frequent type of adverse reaction occurring with Motrin is gastrointestinal (4% to 16%). This includes nausea*, epigastric pain*, heartburn*, diarrhea, abdominal distress, nausea and vomiting, indigestion, constipation, abdominal cramps or pain, fullness of the GI tract (bloating and flatulence). **Central Nervous System:** Dizziness*, headache, nervousness. **Dermatologic:** Rash* (including maculopapular type), pruritus. **Special Senses:** Tinnitus. **Metabolic:** Decreased appetite, edema, fluid retention. Fluid retention generally responds promptly to drug discontinuation (see PRECAUTIONS).
Incidence: Unmarked 1% to 3%; *3% to 9%.

Incidence less than 1 in 100
Gastrointestinal: Upper GI ulcer with bleeding and/or perforation, hemorrhage, melena. **Central Nervous System:** Depression, insomnia. **Dermatologic:** Vesiculobullous eruptions, urticaria, erythema multiforme. **Cardiovascular:** Congestive heart failure in patients with marginal cardiac function, elevated blood pressure. **Special Senses:** Amblyopia (see PRECAUTIONS). **Hematologic:** Leukopenia, decreased hemoglobin and hematocrit.

Causal relationship unknown
Gastrointestinal: Hepatitis, jaundice, abnormal liver function. **Central Nervous System:** Paresthesias, hallucinations, dream abnormalities. **Dermatologic:** Alopecia, Stevens-Johnson syndrome. **Special Senses:** Conjunctivitis, diplopia, optic neuritis. **Hematologic:** Hemolytic anemia, thrombocytopenia, granulocytopenia, bleeding episodes. **Allergic:** Fever, serum sickness, lupus erythematosus syndrome. **Endocrine:** Gynecomastia, hypoglycemia. **Cardiovascular:** Arrhythmias. **Renal:** Decreased creatinine clearance, polyuria, azotemia.

Overdosage
In cases of acute overdosage, the stomach should be emptied. The drug is acidic and excreted in the urine so alkaline diuresis may be beneficial.

Dosage and Administration
Suggested dosage is 300 or 400 mg t.i.d. or q.i.d. Do not exceed 2400 mg per day.

How Supplied
Motrin Tablets, 300 mg (white)
Bottles of 60
Bottles of 500
Motrin Tablets, 400 mg (orange)
Bottles of 60
Bottles of 500
Unit-dose package of 100

Caution: Federal law prohibits dispensing without prescription.

NIM-1

in rheumatoid arthritis and osteoarthritis
for long-term symptomatic treatment and acute flares

Motrin 400 mg TABLETS
ibuprofen, Upjohn

anti-inflammatory...analgesic...well tolerated

Upjohn

The Upjohn Company, Kalamazoo, Michigan 49001 U.S.A.
J-5424-4   December, 1976

EXHIBIT 1–2

ANAEROBIC INTRA-ABDOMINAL INFECTIONS:
A MATTER OF MORBIDITY AND MORTALITY

Beware the breached bowel

Today, it is recognized that a majority of postoperative wound infections of the gastrointestinal tract are caused by contamination of the operative wound by endogenous organisms. When the bowel is opened by trauma, disease, or surgical manipulation, the organisms may gain access to the wound. Often, anaerobic fecal microorganisms are the cause of these infections. Even where visible spillage of contaminated bowel contents does not occur, the rate of sepsis in "clean contaminated" wounds is three times higher than in wounds contaminated only by bacterial fallout from the environment.

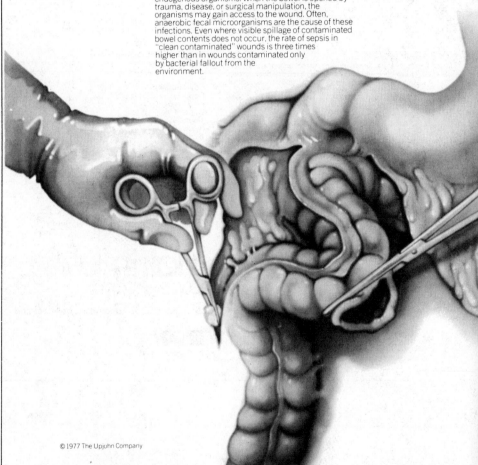

Summary Anaerobic fecal microorganisms are frequently implicated in the majority of postoperative abdominal wound infections. The major culprits are *Bacteroides fragilis*, clostridia species, and anaerobic cocci. Intra-abdominal anaerobic sepsis characterized by peritonitis and abscess formation usually starts between the seventh and tenth postoperative days. These intra-abdominal infections are associated with a particularly high incidence of morbidity resulting in hospitalization of patients for periods of 21 days to 80 days. As part of the total management of serious intra-abdominal infections, successful antibiotic therapy should incorporate antibiotics indicated and effective against the anaerobic as well as the aerobic pathogens that are present.

The anaerobic trilogy

In virtually all intra-abdominal infections, there is a recurring trilogy of anaerobes that are seen either singly or in combination, often mixed with aerobes.

This trilogy is composed of *Bacteroides fragilis*, clostridia species, and anaerobic cocci, particularly peptostreptococci and peptococci. In studies, *B. fragilis* has been isolated from 65% of intra-abdominal infections, clostridia in 60%, and anaerobic cocci in 32%.

In sepsis, the seventh postoperative day can be significant

The common wound infections caused by aerobic organisms typically develop clinical signs around the fifth to seventh postoperative day. Sepsis caused by anaerobic microorganisms occurs later in the postoperative period, usually between the seventh and tenth days. An intra-abdominal wound abscess that occurs weeks to several months postoperatively is almost always due to anaerobic microorganisms, often together with facultative bacteria.

Clinical evidence of infection important

The mere presence of aerobic or anaerobic bacteria in an operative incision is not synonymous with clinical infection. The differentiation between bacterial contamination and wound infection is a clinical decision. Evidence of wound sepsis includes wound tenderness that increases progressively in severity. Initially there is fever without spikes, but often spiking occurs in the afternoon or evening, returning to normal by morning. It is important to emphasize that a positive anaerobic culture without clinical signs is not an infection.

Clinical course of anaerobic infections

The first event in an anaerobic intra-abdominal infection is either generalized or localized peritonitis. If the patient survives early peritonitis, the usual progression is walling off of the infection, and abscess formation. These collections of pus can be located intraperitoneally, retroperitoneally, or within the viscera. Whether in the early peritonitis stage or in the later abscess stage, culture of purulent material yields anaerobes in the majority of cases. In fact, 90% to 96% of intra-abdominal infections occurring with bowel perforation have been reported to be associated with anaerobic bacteria.

Unusually high incidence of morbidity and mortality

The highest incidence of anaerobic wound infection (usually *B. fragilis* and gram-negative organisms such as *E. coli* may both be isolated) follows resection of the large bowel — 10% to 15%. An infection rate of 5% to 10% may occur after surgical procedures involving the biliary tract and small intestine, whereas the rate following gastric or duodenal surgery is somewhat lower. It should be borne in mind that these infection rates are for elective operations. However, in emergency surgery for perforated appendicitis, diverticulitis, or traumatic wounds of the intestine, the infection rate can approach 40%.

Moreover, unusually long periods of morbidity are generally associated with intra-abdominal abscesses. Periods of hospitalization ranging from 21 days to 47 days for patients with intraperitoneal abscesses and 57 days to 80 days for patients with retroperitoneal abscesses have been reported. Mortality rates have been reported to range from 2% for patients with abscesses complicating acute appendicitis to 100% in patients with undrained hepatic, pancreatic, or retroperitoneal abscesses.

The role of antibiotics in therapy

Marked reduction in morbidity and mortality in anaerobic intra-abdominal infections is possible with earlier diagnosis, adequate surgical drainage, and proper choice of antibiotics. Successful use of antibiotics in infections complicating intestinal surgery involves knowledge of the probable organisms likely to be found in various clinical settings, the susceptibility of these organisms to antibiotics, and the risk of the infection to the patient in any given set of circumstances. In general, antibiotic therapy for serious intra-abdominal infections, whether in the acute phase or in the chronic abscess stage, should include drugs to manage anaerobic bacteria as well as facultative and aerobic organisms.

For information on one antibiotic to consider in treating serious intra-abdominal infections caused by infectious anaerobes, please turn the page.

Upjohn

Upjohn

Therapeutic considerations...

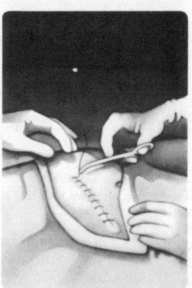

Anaerobic activity: Cleocin® PO₄ (clindamycin phosphate injection) has proved to be effective in a variety of serious intra-abdominal infections caused by susceptible anaerobic organisms including gram-positive cocci, and gram-positive and gram-negative bacilli. Specifically, the activity of clindamycin has been established in the following conditions: septicemia; serious intra-abdominal infections such as peritonitis and intra-abdominal abscess; serious infections of the female pelvis and genital tract such as endometritis, nongonococcal tubo-ovarian abscess, pelvic cellulitis, and postsurgical vaginal cuff infection; serious lower respiratory tract infections such as empyema, anaerobic pneumonitis, and lung abscess; and serious skin and soft-tissue infections caused by susceptible strains of bacteroides, fusobacteria, eubacteria, actinomyces, peptococci, microaerophilic streptococci, and clostridia.*

Since disc susceptibility testing with current methods is not reliable for anaerobes, *in vitro* dilution methods should be used to determine susceptibility to clindamycin.

Also of value in serious aerobic gram-positive infections caused by susceptible streptococci, staphylococci, and pneumococci. The use of Cleocin PO₄ in gram-positive infections has been investigated both clinically and bacteriologically. Because of the risk of colitis, as described in the WARNING box, before selecting clindamycin the physician should consider the nature of the infection and the suitability of less-toxic alternatives (e.g., erythromycin).

Indications include: serious lower respiratory tract infections such as pneumonia caused by susceptible staphylococci; serious soft-tissue infections such as deep abscesses and deep traumatic or surgical wound infections caused by susceptible staphylococci and streptococci; septicemia caused by susceptible staphylococci and streptococci; and acute hematogenous osteomyelitis caused by susceptible staphylococci. In many instances, the evaluated cases

*Clostridia are more resistant than most anaerobes to clindamycin. Some species, e.g., C. sporogenes and C. tertium, are frequently resistant to clindamycin.

have been secondary to massive wounds, surgery, or debilitating disease. With few exceptions, the organisms proved susceptible *in vitro* and were successfully eradicated from the clinical lesions.

Other therapeutic considerations:

1. Cleocin PO₄ (clindamycin phosphate injection) is clinically effective in serious infections caused by penicillin-resistant or penicillinase-producing staphylococci. However, staphylococcal strains resistant to clindamycin have been encountered, and susceptibility testing should be performed.

2. Cleocin PO₄ is useful in patients who are sensitive to penicillin. Clindamycin does not share antigenicity with the penicillins; however, hypersensitivity reactions have been reported with clindamycin therapy. If a hypersensitivity reaction occurs, the drug should be discontinued. Serious anaphylactoid reactions require immediate emergency treatment with epinephrine. Oxygen and intravenous corticosteroids should also be administered as indicated.

Thus, Cleocin PO₄ can fill a need for both penicillin-sensitive patients and those with serious infections caused by penicillin-resistant staphylococci.

As with all antibiotics, Cleocin PO₄ should be used with caution in atopic patients. Clindamycin has demonstrated cross-antigenicity with lincomycin.

Cleocin PO₄ should be reserved for serious infections where less-toxic antimicrobial agents are inappropriate, as described in the Indications section of the brief summary on the following page.

If significant diarrhea or colitis occurs during therapy, this antibiotic should be discontinued. (See WARNING box and summary of prescribing information on following page.)

EXHIBIT 1–3

EXHIBIT 1–4

ROCHE announces
<u>new</u> BACTRIM™

Each tablet contains 80 mg trimethoprim and 400 mg sulfamethoxazole.

a new type of antibacterial for a two-pronged attack against chronic urinary tract infections due to susceptible organisms

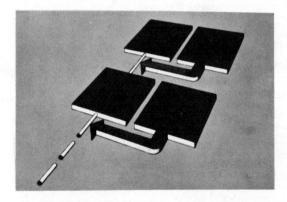

Please see the last two pages of this advertisement for complete product information.

EXHIBIT 1–4 (continued)

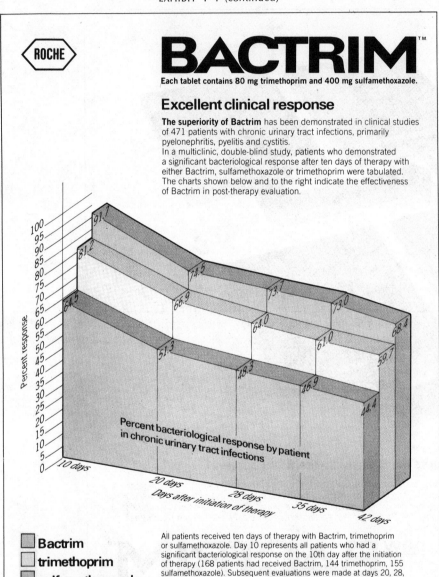

⟨ROCHE⟩

BACTRIM™

Each tablet contains 80 mg trimethoprim and 400 mg sulfamethoxazole.

Excellent clinical response

The superiority of Bactrim has been demonstrated in clinical studies of 471 patients with chronic urinary tract infections, primarily pyelonephritis, pyelitis and cystitis.

In a multiclinic, double-blind study, patients who demonstrated a significant bacteriological response after ten days of therapy with either Bactrim, sulfamethoxazole or trimethoprim were tabulated. The charts shown below and to the right indicate the effectiveness of Bactrim in post-therapy evaluation.

Percent bacteriological response by patient in chronic urinary tract infections

- **Bactrim**
- **trimethoprim**
- **sulfamethoxazole**

All patients received ten days of therapy with Bactrim, trimethoprim or sulfamethoxazole. Day 10 represents all patients who had a significant bacteriological response on the 10th day after the initiation of therapy (168 patients had received Bactrim, 144 trimethoprim, 155 sulfamethoxazole). Subsequent evaluations were made at days 20, 28, 35 and 42. Day 42 represents an arbitrary cutoff for reporting findings.

Please see the last two pages of this advertisement for complete product information.

proven clinical efficacy in chronic urinary tract infections due to susceptible organisms

Impressive long-term response even with obstructive complications

Bactrim has been proved significantly superior to its constituents in maintaining significant bacteriological response in cases with urinary obstruction – cases regarded as being notoriously difficult to treat. The chart shows the percentage of 276 patients who maintained this response for up to 42 consecutive days. (On day ten, 97 patients had received Bactrim, 85 trimethoprim, 94 sulfamethoxazole.)

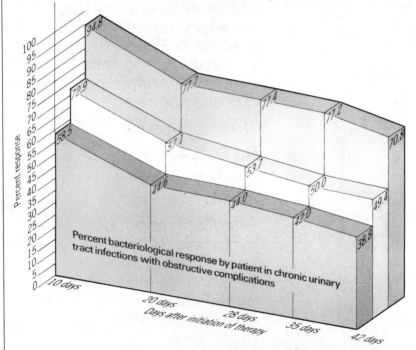

Percent bacteriological response by patient in chronic urinary tract infections with obstructive complications

new BACTRIM™

Each tablet contains 80 mg trimethoprim and 400 mg sulfamethoxazole.

for chronic urinary tract infections

EXHIBIT 1–4 *(continued)*

EXHIBIT 1–4 (concluded)

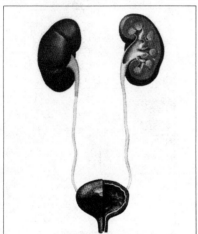

Complete Product Information:

Description: Bactrim is a synthetic antibacterial combination product, available in scored light-green tablets, each containing 80 mg trimethoprim and 400 mg sulfamethoxazole.

Trimethoprim is 2,4-diamino-5-(3,4,5-trimethoxybenzyl) pyrimidine. It is a white to light-yellow, odorless, bitter compound with a molecular weight of 290.3.

Sulfamethoxazole is N^1-(5-methyl-3-isoxazolyl)sulfanilamide. It is an almost white in color, odorless, tasteless compound with a molecular weight of 253.28.

Actions: *Microbiology:* Sulfamethoxazole inhibits bacterial synthesis of dihydrofolic acid by competing with *para*-aminobenzoic acid. Trimethoprim blocks the production of tetrahydrofolic acid from dihydrofolic acid by binding to and reversibly inhibiting the required enzyme, dihydrofolate reductase. Thus, Bactrim blocks two consecutive steps in the biosynthesis of nucleic acids and proteins essential to many bacteria.

In vitro studies have shown that bacterial resistance develops more slowly with Bactrim than with trimethoprim or sulfamethoxazole alone.

In vitro serial dilution tests have shown that the spectrum of antibacterial activity of Bactrim includes the common urinary tract pathogens with the exception of *Pseudomonas aeruginosa*. The following organisms are usually susceptible: *Escherichia coli, Klebsiella-Enterobacter, Proteus mirabilis* and indole-positive proteus species.

Representative Minimum Inhibitory Concentration Values for Bactrim-Susceptible Organisms (MIC — mcg/ml)				
Bacteria	Trimeth-oprim alone	Sulfameth-oxazole alone	TMP/SMX (1:20) TMP	TMP/SMX (1:20) SMX
Escherichia coli	0.05–1.5	1.0 –245	0.05–0.5	0.95– 9.5
Proteus spp. indole positive	0.5 –5.0	7.35 –300	0.05–1.5	0.95–28.5
Proteus mirabilis	0.5 –1.5	7.35 – 30	0.05–0.15	0.95– 2.85
Klebsiella-Enterobacter	0.15–5.0	0.735–245	0.05–1.5	0.95–28.5

Human Pharmacology: Bactrim is rapidly absorbed following oral administration. The blood levels of trimethoprim and sulfamethoxazole are similar to those achieved when each component is given alone. Peak blood levels for the individual components occur one to four hours after oral administration. The half-lives of sulfamethoxazole and trimethoprim, 10 and 16 hours respectively, are relatively the same regardless of whether these compounds are administered as individual components or as Bactrim. Detectable amounts of trimethoprim and sulfamethoxazole are present in the blood 24 hours after drug administration. Free sulfamethoxazole and trimethoprim blood levels are proportionately dose-dependent. On repeated administration, the steady-state ratio of trimethoprim to sulfamethoxazole levels in the blood is about 1:20.

Sulfamethoxazole exists in the blood as free, conjugated and protein-bound forms; trimethoprim is present as free, protein-bound and metabolized forms. The free forms are considered to be the therapeutically active forms. Approximately 44 percent of trimethoprim and 70 percent of sulfamethoxazole are protein-bound in the blood. The presence of 10 mg percent sulfamethoxazole in plasma decreases the protein binding of trimethoprim to an insignificant degree; trimethoprim does not influence the protein binding of sulfamethoxazole.

Excretion of Bactrim is chiefly by the kidneys through both glomerular filtration and tubular secretion. Urine concentrations of both sulfamethoxazole and trimethoprim are considerably higher than are the concentrations in the blood. When administered together as in Bactrim, neither sulfamethoxazole nor trimethoprim affects the urinary excretion pattern of the other.

Indications: Chronic urinary tract infections (primarily pyelonephritis, pyelitis and cystitis) due to susceptible organisms (usually *E. coli, Klebsiella-Enterobacter, Proteus mirabilis,* and, less frequently, indole-positive proteus species).

Important note. **Currently, the increasing frequency of resistant organisms is a limitation of the usefulness of all antibacterial agents, especially in the treatment of chronic and recurrent urinary tract infections.**

Contraindications: Hypersensitivity to trimethoprim or sulfonamides. Pregnancy and during the nursing period (see Reproduction Studies).

Warnings: Deaths associated with the administration of sulfonamides have been reported from hypersensitivity reactions, agranulocytosis, aplastic anemia and other blood dyscrasias. Experience with trimethoprim alone is much more limited, but it has been reported to interfere with hematopoiesis in occasional patients. In elderly patients concurrently receiving certain diuretics, primarily thiazides, an increased incidence of thrombopenia with purpura has been reported.

The presence of clinical signs such as sore throat, fever, pallor, purpura or jaundice may be early indications of serious blood disorders. Complete blood counts should be done frequently in patients receiving Bactrim. If a significant reduction in the count of any formed blood element is noted, Bactrim should be discontinued.

At the present time, there is insufficient clinical information on the use of Bactrim in infants and children under 12 years of age to recommend its use.

Precautions: Bactrim should be given with caution to patients with impaired renal or hepatic function, to those with possible folate deficiency and to those with severe allergy or bronchial asthma. In glucose-6-phosphate dehydrogenase-deficient individuals, hemolysis may occur. This reaction is frequently dose-related. Adequate fluid intake must be maintained in order to prevent crystalluria and stone formation. Urinalyses with careful microscopic examination and renal function tests should be performed during therapy, particularly for those patients with impaired renal function.

Adverse Reactions: For completeness, all major reactions to sulfonamides and to trimethoprim are included below, even though they may not have been reported with Bactrim.

Blood dyscrasias: Agranulocytosis, aplastic anemia, megaloblastic anemia, thrombopenia, leukopenia, hemolytic anemia, purpura, hypoprothrombinemia and methemoglobinemia.

Allergic reactions: Erythema multiforme, Stevens-Johnson syndrome, generalized skin eruptions, epidermal necrolysis, urticaria, serum sickness, pruritus, exfoliative dermatitis, anaphylactoid reactions, periorbital edema, conjunctival and scleral injection, photosensitization, arthralgia and allergic myocarditis.

Gastrointestinal reactions: Glossitis, stomatitis, nausea, emesis, abdominal pains, hepatitis, diarrhea and pancreatitis.

C.N.S. reactions: Headache, peripheral neuritis, mental depression, convulsions, ataxia, hallucinations, tinnitus, vertigo, insomnia, apathy, fatigue, muscle weakness and nervousness.

Miscellaneous reactions: Drug fever, chills, and toxic nephrosis with oliguria and anuria. Periarteritis nodosa and L.E. phenomenon have occurred.

The sulfonamides bear certain chemical similarities to some goitrogens, diuretics (acetazolamide and the thiazides) and oral hypoglycemic agents. Goiter production, diuresis and hypoglycemia have occurred rarely in patients receiving sulfonamides. Cross-sensitivity may exist with these agents. Rats appear to be especially susceptible to the goitrogenic effects of sulfonamides, and long-term administration has produced thyroid malignancies in the species.

Dosage and Administration: Not recommended for use in children under 12 years of age.

The usual adult dosage is two tablets every 12 hours for 10 to 14 days.

For patients with renal impairment:

Creatinine Clearance (ml/min)	Recommended Dosage Regimen
Above 30	Usual standard regimen
15-30	2 tablets every 24 hours
Below 15	Use not recommended

How Supplied: Tablets, containing 80 mg trimethoprim and 400 mg sulfamethoxazole—bottles of 100 and 500; Tel-E-Dose® packages of 1000; Prescription Paks of 40, available singly and in trays of 10. Imprint on tablets: ROCHE 50.

Reproduction Studies: In rats, doses of 533 mg/kg sulfamethoxazole or 200 mg/kg trimethoprim produced teratological effects manifested mainly as cleft palates. The highest dose which did not cause cleft palates in rats was 512 mg/kg sulfamethoxazole or 192 mg/kg trimethoprim when administered separately. In two studies in rats, no teratology was observed when 512 mg/kg of sulfamethoxazole was used in combination with 128 mg/kg of trimethoprim. However, in one study, cleft palates were observed in one litter out of 9 when 355 mg/kg of sulfamethoxazole was used in combination with 88 mg/kg of trimethoprim.

In rabbits, trimethoprim administered by intubation from days 8 to 16 of pregnancy at dosages up to 500 mg/kg resulted in higher incidences of dead and resorbed fetuses, particularly at 500 mg/kg. However, there were no significant drug-related teratological effects.

new

Each tablet contains 80 mg trimethoprim and 400 mg sulfamethoxazole.

for chronic urinary tract infections

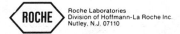

Roche Laboratories
Division of Hoffmann-La Roche Inc.
Nutley, N.J. 07110

EXHIBIT 1–5

Along with its informational role, several other aspects of drug advertising make drug companies feel this form of promotion is especially valuable. One is that journal advertising is the main support of many medical journals. Without journal advertising, according to PMA, the number of journals would decline, and "the open, diverse proliferation of medical opinion and information via journals would be drastically reduced." Another function of journal advertising is its relation to product innovation. Drug manufacturers claim there is a high correlation between the intensity of research and development and the intensity of advertising. This occurs both because advertising helps to support research and because the more innovative laboratories have more discoveries about which doctors should be informed.

Critics of the drug companies disagree with most of these claims. Their biggest complaint is that journal advertising is misleading, a criticism they support with examples of "Dear Doctor" letters and remedial advertisements ordered by the FDA. In 1966 there were 28, and in 1967 there were 27 of these letters. Critics also claim that journal ads help to create a need for drugs where none really exists. The promotional campaigns for psychoactive drugs and antibiotics are two examples.[15]

Free samples

A 1973 survey indicated that 20 major drug companies gave doctors more than 2 billion free samples of drugs in that year.[16] Whether requested or unsolicited, free samples are delivered to the doctor. Free samples may also be provided to pharmacists, hospitals, clinics, or other potential buyers or prescribers.

The AMA feels that the use of free samples should be restricted, but that under regulated conditions free samples can serve a useful purpose. Among the uses cited by the AMA are that free samples allow the doctor to begin medication of a patient immediately with a small amount of the drug. The doctor can then determine the effectiveness and the patient's acceptance of the drug before prescribing a larger amount for a full course of treatment. However, the AMA insists that "a drug sample should be designed to fulfill a legitimate medical need, and not simply to be an unneeded and costly promotion technique, because samples lend themselves to abuse and exploitation."[17] In Senate hearings, drug manufacturers and the PMA agreed with AMA's support of the use of drug samples.

Studies showed that over 90 percent of all physicians wanted samples, so PMA felt that any criticism of samples was due to the distribution of unsolicited samples. However, according to PMA, this problem had been reduced over the years. Total mail sampling volume declined from nearly 82 million samples in 1969 to 38 million in 1973. Mail sample expenditures

---

[15] For the views of the critics of journal advertising, see Dowling, *Medicines for Man,* pp. 121–36; Silverman and Lee, *Pills, Profits, and Politics,* pp. 48–80; U.S. Senate, *Examination of the Pharmaceutical Industry,* part 6, "Testimony of Sidney Wolfe," p. 2625; part 4, "Testimony of Roger J. Bulger," p. 1275.

[16] Harold M. Schmerk, Jr., "U.S. Doctors Got 2 Billion Samples: Senate Panel Says 20 Drug Concerns Gave Them in '73," *The New York Times,* May 3, 1974, p. 13.

[17] U.S. Senate, *Examination of the Pharmaceutical Industry,* part 4, pp. 1285, 1293, 1334.

also dropped from $25 million in 1969 to $14 million in 1973.[18] The individual drug manufacturers were generally in agreement with PMA about the importance of drug sampling and the decline of unsolicited samples. The drug companies also asserted that very few abuses occurred, and those which did were without their approval. Most companies had strict policies on drug sampling. Pfizer's pledge for detailmen said,

> In signing the following statement, I signify that I am fully aware of the importance of my strict control and responsibility in the handling and distribution of prescription legend drugs.
>
>> I will distribute starter samples . . . of prescription . . . drugs only to practitioners licensed by law to prescribe such drugs. . . .
>>
>> To the best of my ability I will attempt to determine whether the contacted physician can actually use samples of specific products before they are left with him. . . .[19]

Critics of free samples have cited many abuses of this practice. Free samples were often requested by doctors and pharmacists and then resold. Many samples would end up in a waste bin, where they might be found by children and lead to accidental poisoning. Doctors asserted that free samples encouraged doctors to dispense a drug with which they were not familiar and possibly to dispense an insufficient amount of a drug for a given condition. Other critics agreed with one doctor, who mentioned "the inherent lessening, no matter how small, of the characters of both the giver and receiver in any 'something for nothing' scheme."[20]

Gifts, premiums, and dividends

Drug companies also use premiums, gifts, dividends, and reminder items, ranging from small gimmicks to expensive grants, to promote a particular drug. A 1973 survey of 20 drug companies found that the cost of gifts and reminder items totaled more than $14 million for that year. A Social Security Administration analysis in 1971 discovered that the industry as a whole spent $150 million for such forms of promotion as films, pamphlets, seminars, plant tours, convention displays, and entertainment. The type and expense of gifts vary widely. For example, free gifts offered to medical students have been described as free medical bags, free drugs,

---

[18] Pharmaceutical Manufacturers Association, "General Overview," pp. 2422–30.

[19] U.S. Senate, Examination of the Pharmaceutical Industry, part 3, p. 856.

[20] F. J. Ingelfinger, "Toxic Mail," New England Journal of Medicine, May 2, 1974, p. 1019. For a general criticism of free samples, see U.S. Senate, Examination of the Pharmaceutical Industry, part 3, "Testimony of Bennet Wasserman," p. 721; "Testimony of Spencer King," p. 746; "Testimony of Douglas Patton," p. 758; "Testimony of Robert Perry," p. 767; part 4, "Testimony of Joseph Sargent," p. 1334; "Testimony of Robert Bulgar," p. 1293; Silverman and Lee, Pills, Profits, and Politics, pp. 48–80.

free baby food, free textbooks, free class steak parties and beer busts, free weekends in Manhattan, and part-time jobs as detailmen. Physicians have been offered cocktail parties, golf tournaments, golf balls, prescription pads, hospitality suites at medical conventions, and an unlimited supply of free drugs. Premiums for doctors who purchase various amounts of drugs include microwave ovens, color television sets, and wristwatches. Drug companies also give gifts in the form of grants to researchers or institutions, or financial support or sponsorship of conferences and symposia.[21]

As part of a drug company's promotional effort, detailmen are involved in giving free gifts or premiums to doctors. In the Senate hearings, a former Merck detailman described giving advertising pens, memo pads, paperweights, ash trays, desk blotters, and other paraphernalia; a former Eaton laboratories employee gave out tickets to sporting events, golf balls, and rain hats. Detailmen also managed the dividend programs. In bulletins to detailmen, Pfizer, for example, described its "Clinic Deal," which would give prizes to doctors who had accumulated "bonus points" by buying antibiotics. Other laboratories issued booklets filled with pictures of gifts and listing the number of points needed to "win" them. Parke-Davis offered a "Christmas Gift Book Awards" for points gained by buying their products.

The practice of gift giving has been justified by the drug industry on several grounds. One major defense is that the bulk of free gifts distributed are educational in nature. PMA asserts that drug companies provide doctors with reference books, teaching films, patient aids, and audio tape cassettes, as well as sponsoring symposia, seminars, meetings, and exhibits. This type of gift giving helps advance medical knowledge. Lederle and Ortho are especially emphatic on this point, stressing the educational and informational aspects of their promotional items. Pfizer maintains that when dividend and premium offers are not connected to the medical profession, such programs are used in special cases only to increase the use of a necessary drug. For example, Pfizer's 1973 "Polio Immunization Stocking Program," which offered prizes ranging from a book on "Care of the Well Baby" to an upright freezer for buying a certain number of dosages of polio vaccine, was started to encourage doctors to immunize children for polio because the number being immunized had dropped sharply.

Drug manufacturers also maintain that the gift-giving aspect of promotion has decreased in recent years. Pfizer discontinued premium offers to doctors after 1969. Although Searle Laboratories asserted that gifts to doctors had a place as "useful attention-getting devices of negligible cost," less than 1 percent of their total marketing budget was spent on this sort

---

[21] Schmerk, "U.S. Doctors Got 2 Billion Samples"; Silverman and Lee, *Pills, Profits, and Politics,* pp. 55, 76.

of activity. Instead, their marketing expenditures were used for various educational activities, including what Searle called "no-strings" support of medical meetings, conferences, and symposia.[22]

Critics of the use of free gifts and dividends agreed in general with a former Merck detailman, who said: "These types of gimmicks use personal gain as the basis upon which the physician will decide which injectable products to buy, or which drugs to prescribe." The AMA has agreed with this judgment; it has condemned gift giving irrespective of the size of the gift, and charged that acceptance of such a gift is unethical.

Direct mail advertising

A 1973 PMA estimate of industry expenditures on direct mail was $43.4 million. This form of promotion is similar to journal advertising and free sampling, and has been discussed in the same terms.

The drug companies feel that the use of direct mail advertising is useful and justifiable. PMA asserts that physicians receive very little direct mail; according to one survey, an average of four pieces per day in 1973.[23] A 1973 survey also cited by PMA reported that 54 percent of doctors surveyed read their direct mail, and a 1965 survey found that more than half of a national sample of physicians felt that pharmaceutical direct mail advertising was beneficial both to the physician and to the practice of medicine. PMA also emphasized the educational aspect of direct mail advertising, asserting that it can quickly get important new information to doctors, can provide extensive information not practical in space-limited magazine advertising, and may be one of the few sources of information for doctors who practice in rural areas. In addition, according to Roche, direct mail enabled specific types of information to be sent to specialists.[24] Many drug companies also repeated their claim that all drug advertising is subject to strict internal and external controls.

As in their criticism of journal advertising, some doctors criticized direct mail advertising as being inaccurate, misleading, and a waste of time to read. One doctor contended that "all those pretty, multi-colored, mini-syllabic blurbs with pictures and graphs [were] only slightly less insulting to the reader's intelligence than their television counterparts." Several doctors stated that the vast majority of the direct mail they received was weeded out and discarded by their receptionists. An additional criticism of direct mail was the staggering amount of such mail a doctor would receive daily. This bombardment was viewed by some doctors as an invasion of privacy.

---

[22] U.S. Senate, Examination of the Pharmaceutical Industry, part 3, p. 1255.

[23] Ibid., part 6, p. 2478.

[24] Ibid., p. 2481; part 3, p. 1142.

Physician's desk reference

A source of information to doctors which is less often recognized as a promotional method is the *Physician's Desk Reference* (PDR). PDR, published by *Medical Economics,* is a compilation of FDA-approved labeling (that is, the package inserts) for different drugs. Drug manufacturers purchase space for their product descriptions, and only those descriptions are included. The PDR is issued annually without charge to nearly all physicians. A 1974 report for the FDA found that 97 percent of physicians in the sample used this source an average of 7.5 times per week.

There is a great deal of support for PDR. The survey of drug information needs conducted by the FDA concluded that PDR was the most convenient drug information source available. PDR contained information on most drug items in use, and with updating bulletins issued regularly, it was relatively complete and current. Although PDR contains only a limited number of drugs, its publishers felt that trying to include all available drugs would make the reference book too large to use and would be "a victory of technique over purpose."[25]

Despite its popularity among physicians, PDR has been attacked by critics. One of the major complaints is that since PDR contains descriptions of only those drugs manufacturers have paid to include, other drugs and generic drugs, which there is no advantage in advertising (generic drugs are marketed by many companies under the same name), do not appear. In addition, although the drug descriptions are not FDA-approved, PDR's information is still limited. PDR cannot, for example, make statements about the comparative efficacy or relative toxicity of drugs.

PRICING

Drug prices are by far the most controversial item for industry critics. This criticism is almost universal, both in the United States and the rest of the world. Tables 1–2 and 1–3 provide various examples of drug pricing in

TABLE 1–2
COMPARATIVE INTERNATIONAL PRICES OF SELECTED BRAND NAME DRUGS, 1971
(in $ U.S.)

Drug	United States	Brazil	Ireland	Italy	New Zealand	Sweden	United Kingdom
Achromycin	5.34	4.22	3.42	10.87	13.78	13.89	5.04
Darvon	7.02	3.72	1.66	7.86	2.08	3.33	1.92
Declomycin	19.79	4.93	8.97	17.88	3.87	19.43	8.20
Polycillin	21.84	41.95	9.31	19.15	11.30	16.58	8.23
Terramycin	20.48	4.63	7.74	13.27	3.68	13.04	9.06
Thorazine	6.60	2.47	1.71	3.47	1.82	2.88	1.68

Source: Milton Silverman and Philip R. Lee, *Pills, Profits, and Politics* (Berkeley and Los Angeles: University of California Press, 1974), p. 336.

---

[25] Ibid., part 6, pp. 2723–33.

TABLE 1–3
COMPARATIVE WHOLESALE PRICES OF SELECTED BRAND
NAME AND GENERIC NAME DRUG PRODUCTS, 1972

Product	Price ($)	Price ratio
Reserpine: 1,000 .25 mg		
Serpasil (Ciba)	39.50	
Reserpine (Vita-Fare)	1.10	35.9:1
Pentaerythrotetranitrate: 1,000 10 mg		
Peritrate (Warner-Chilcott)	27.00	
Pentaerythrotetranitrate (Vita-Fare)	1.50	18.0:1
Tetracycline: 1,000 250 mg		
Achromycin (Lederle)	52.02	
Tetracycline (Interstate)	8.75	5.9:1
Penicillin G: 100 400,000 units		
Pentids (Squibb)	10.04	
Penicillin G (Midway)	1.75	5.7:1

Source: Milton Silverman and Philip R. Lee, *Pills, Profits, and Politics* (Berkeley and Los Angeles: University of California Press, 1974), p. 334.

the United States and European countries and show wide across-the-board variations.

These tables show several drugs and many prices. Table 1–2 shows how price can vary for the same drug across countries. Table 1–3 shows the variation that can occur in the price of a drug when it is dispensed under a brand name and when it is sold using a generic name. Table 1–4 shows the variation in the price of the same drug sold in different locations and under different brand names. In all these tables, note the variation in price over location, brand name, or brand versus generic name.

When a manufacturer or an industry is able to charge different prices to different groups of people for the same item, it indicates that pure competition, or a fair approximation of it, does not exist in that market. The manufacturer or industry is able to remove some of the consumer surplus and thus increase its return on sales. The fact that the pharmaceutical industry has the power to charge different prices, and uses this power, is not

TABLE 1–4
AVERAGE AND RANGE OF CONSUMER PRESCRIPTION PRICES, 1973
(product: Ampicillin: 20 250mg capsules)

Rx written for brand name	Supplier	Price		
		Lowest	Average	Highest
Pen A	Pfizer	$2.60	$4.19	$7.50
Totacillin	Beecham	2.00	4.21	9.88
Sk-Ampicillin	Smith Kline	3.00	4.59	7.50
Principen	Squibb	2.59	4.60	7.50

Source: "Resistant Prices," *Newsletter*, Council on Economic Priorities, N5-1, January 6, 1975.

in dispute between the industry and its critics. What is in dispute is the need for the high return provided by this power.

The industry states that it needs high profits because of its research and development activities. The drug industry in general spends more on R&D than any other industry segment in the United States, and the results of this research have had great impact on the health of millions of people. The introduction of new drugs not only saves the population from needless pain and suffering, but also saves the economy billions of dollars that might otherwise have been spent on health care. To maintain the momentum of this research, the industry states that it requires high profits:

1. The cost of the industry's R&D is very high and getting higher because of stricter FDA requirements for the methods used in putting new products on the market and the increased time between the discovery of a new drug and its actual use.
2. R&D in the industry is risky. Each year the industry tests some 150,000 substances, of which only about 15 will reach the market.[26]

High profits are also needed because of the reduced effective patent protection period. Generally, patents provide protection for 17 years and enable the manufacturer to reap the rewards of an invention. This protection allows for higher than normal profits, which can be invested in future R&D. In the drug industry, however, the time between when an entity is patented and when it is put on the market is increasing due to more stringent FDA requirements. The PMA states that the effective period of protection is now only 10.5 years, and thus, because of this reduced time period, profits should be high.[27]

Critics of the industry contend that although the industry may spend a large percentage of its revenue on R&D, it also has one of the highest returns on revenue and equity of any industry. Much of the industry's R&D efforts, they say, are directed not at significant breakthroughs, but at obtaining patent protection for drugs that are not needed or that are redundant. It is also pointed out that while R&D is very high, so is the amount of money spent on promotion, which has been around 16 to 20 percent of the sales dollar.

APPENDIX: A DESCRIPTIVE NOTE ON THE PHARMACEUTICAL INDUSTRY

Ethical (prescription) drugs constitute the bulk of the industry's sales. However, in the last few years there has been a shift toward greater

---

[26] *Key Facts about the U.S. Prescription Drug Industry,* p. 6.
[27] Ibid., p. 11.

diversification. This shift has been away from the industry's traditional concentration on low-volume, high-profit ethical drug products to mass merchandising of high-volume, low-profit and not necessarily drug products. American firms have also been expanding their overseas activities, partly in response to increased sales competition in the United States from foreign-based manufacturers. Foreign sales currently constitute more than 50 percent of Lederle's total sales. Comparable figures for other companies are: Merck, 45 percent; Pfizer, 52 percent; Eli Lilly, 36 percent; Richardson-Merrell, 45 percent; and Warner-Lambert, 42 percent.[1]

Total foreign sales of American firms in 1974 were $3.9 billion[2] and the United States had a net world trade balance in ethical drugs of $592,349,000 in 1974. In comparison, West Germany's ethical drug industry recorded net sales abroad larger than those of the United States.

Industry structure

The twenty largest firms accounted for 73 percent of industry sales in 1972. There were 756 drug manufacturing firms in the United States in 1972, down from 1,114 in 1958. One measure of the level of competition in an industry is the concentration ratio, which measures the percentage of sales held by the top four or the top eight firms. Figures produced by the PMA show that the concentration ratios for the industry are rather low compared to many other industries in the United States and that they have been constant over the years (Table A–1).

The problem with these figures, however, is the definition of the relevant market. One might want to consider the relevant market not as the total market but the market for each therapeutic class, or for each type of drug. If we look at the concentration ratios in different therapeutic classes (such as analgesics, analeptics, anesthetics, anti-infectives, diabetic therapy, and so on), the ratios appear quite different. According to PMA figures

TABLE A–1
CONCENTRATION RATIOS FOR FIRMS MANUFACTURING
PHARMACEUTICAL PREPARATIONS

	Number	Percentage of sales accounted for by		
Year	of firms	4 largest	8 largest	20 largest
1958	1,114	25	43	71
1963	1,011	22	37	71
1967	875	24	40	70
1972	756	25	43	73

Source: Pharmaceutical Manufacturers Association, *Prescription Drug Industry Factbook '76*, p. 36.

---

[1] "The Drug Industry's Clouded Future," *Business Week*, November 23, 1974, p. 65.

[2] Pharmaceutical Manufacturers Association, *Prescription Drug Industry Factbook '76*, p. ii.

in 1967, each of the top therapeutic classes had at least 14 firms involved in manufacturing, distribution, and marketing.[3] However, in hearings on the industry, it was pointed out that in 20 therapeutic markets, the sales of the leading five manufacturing firms ranged from 56 to 98 percent.[4]

If we look at the even narrower classification of drugs themselves, the concentration ratios get even higher. To cite an example, Hoffmann-La Roche accounts for 90 percent of all sales of tranquilizers in the United States with the sales of Librium and Valium. In fact, Valium represents 4 percent of all prescriptions written in the United States, while no other drug accounts for over 1 percent.[5] In the case of specific drugs, it was found that in 1958, of the top 51 drugs sold, which represented some two thirds of the total pharmaceutical drug sales in the United States, 27 had only one producer, 8 had two producers, and 10 had three producers.[6]

The product

There are currently over 7,000 ethical drugs on the market. Of these, 1,200 are of the single chemical entity type. The remainder are combination products made with various combinations of the single chemical entity drugs. Furthermore, the industry is constantly bringing out a new stream of drugs—single chemical entity products, combinations, and/or new dosage forms. In the last 20 years 715 new single chemical entities, 1,407 new duplicate single chemical entity drugs, 3,840 new combination products, and 1,820 new dosage forms have been introduced into the market. This represents a total of 7,782 new products with which physicians must acquaint themselves if they want to keep abreast of the remedies offered by the pharmaceutical industry.[7]

Faced with such a large number of new and old products, most physicians tend to restrict the drugs they commonly write prescriptions for to a relatively small number. In 1968 there were some 1.1 billion prescriptions written in the United States and of these, 67 percent were for 200 drugs and 85 percent were for 500 drugs. Out of the top 200 drugs, 119 were single chemical entities and 81 were combination products. Accord-

---

[3] A. T. Sproat, *A Note on the U.S. Prescription Drug Industry,* part I (R), Harvard Business School, No. 6-373-136 (1972), p. 4.

[4] U.S. Congress, Senate, Select Committee on Small Business, Subcommittee on Monopoly, *Competitive Problems in the Drug Industry, Summary and Analysis,* November 2, 1972, p. 30.

[5] "A Drug Giant's Pricing Under International Attack," *Business Week,* June 16, 1975, p. 51.

[6] U.S. Congress, Senate, Subcommittee on Antitrust and Monopoly of the Committee on the Judiciary, *Report on Administered Prices, Drugs.* Hearings held in 1959 and 1960, p. 10825.

[7] U.S. Congress, Senate, Subcommittee on Monopoly of the Select Committee on Small Business, *Competitive Problems in the Drug Industry,* part 2, February 19, 20, 26, 27 and March 13, 18, 25, and 26, 1969, p. 4300.

ing to the PMA, the average physician uses fewer than 50 prescription products in daily practice.[8]

Given the twin facts of a large number of products on the market and a small number used in the average physician's daily practice, it is in the interest of the manufacturer to sell products by brand name—that is, to persuade physicians to use a particular manufacturer's brand name when they write a prescription for a drug in a certain therapeutic class. The use of brand name products is central to the promotion activities of the industry. The industry justifies the promotion of brand names by claiming that these products are superior to their generic equivalents because of better quality control. The industry also argues that between 1967 and 1975 the rise in the cost of prescription drugs has been minimal (9 percent) compared with the increase in the consumer price index (61 percent) and medical care costs (69 percent). (See Exhibits A–1 and A–2.)

The argument against the physician's use of a brand name in a prescription is that it requires the pharmacist to fill that prescription with a specific drug from a specific manufacturer. This differentiates that manufacturer's product from all its equivalents. The result is that the patient gets the drug but at a higher price than if the pharmacist filled the prescription with an equivalent (generic) drug at a much lower price.

Research and development

The amount of money invested in research and development by the pharmaceutical industry is higher, as a percentage of sales dollars, than for any other industry in the United States. The absolute level of spending and expenditures as a percentage of sales have increased tremendously since 1950. In 1950 industry R&D was about $39 million, or 2.7 percent of sales. By 1975, R&D spending had increased to over $1 billion, some 11 to 12 percent of sales.[9] Note that these figures are for the United States pharmaceutical drug industry, and sales are worldwide sales for these firms. PMA figures show that of the total R&D budget, 81.3 percent is devoted to research for advancement of scientific knowledge and development of new products, and 18.7 percent goes for significant improvement and modification of existing products.[10]

Although dollars can measure the input to R&D, the usual measure of output is the introduction of new single chemical entity drugs in the United States. Between 1950 and 1974, input increased some 26 times, although there was an actual decline in the number of new drug introduc-

---

[8] Pharmaceutical Manufacturers Association, *Key Facts about the U.S. Prescription Drug Industry 1974*, p. 2; and *Competitive Problems in the Drug Industry*, part 2, p. 4300.

[9] Milton Silverman and Philip R. Lee, *Pills, Profits and Politics* (Berkeley and Los Angeles: University of California Press, 1974), p. 27; and Pharmaceutical Manufacturers Association, *Prescription Drug Industry Factbook '76*, p. ii.

[10] *Prescription Drug Industry Factbook '76*, p. 5.

EXHIBIT A–1

The Great Health Care Stakes

Odds favor higher medical care costs if prescription drug prices are arbitrarily cut. A gamble? Yes, considering the following:

Drugs markedly reduce the costs of hospitalization, surgery, psychiatry, intensive care, and other forms of health care. Examples:

1. Polio vaccines eliminated iron lungs, lengthy hospital stays, and saved thousands of potential victims.[1]
2. Since drugs to treat mental illness were introduced, the number of patients in mental hospitals has been more than cut in half: from 558,000 in 1955 to about 225,000 in 1974[2]
3. Antibiotics save millions of lives and billions of health care dollars[3]
4. Drugs that cure tuberculosis closed most sanatoriums[4]

The stakes are these: new drugs to fight cancer, viral infections, heart ailments, psychoses and other diseases. But—

- New drugs come only from research, a very sophisticated form of roulette.
- Most new drugs are discovered by U.S. research-oriented pharmaceutical companies[5]
- Their research funds come from current prescription drug sales.
- For every drug that's a winner, there are thousands of other promising chemical compounds that never make it to the gate.
- Cutting drug prices arbitrarily is a sure-shot loss for research investment.

What may be gambled away is much of the future progress in health care for the sake of short term savings.

Dr. Louis Lasagna, a leading clinical pharmacologist, puts it this way: "It may be politically expedient, for the short haul, to disregard the health of the United States drug industry, but its destruction would be a gigantic tragedy."[6]

One last point: Between 1967 and 1975, according to the U.S. Bureau of Labor Statistics Consumer Price Index, the cost of all consumer items rose 61%, and medical care costs increased 69%, while prescription drug costs increased only 9%.

1. Pharmacy Times, March 1976, pp 36-39.
2. "Health in the United States," U.S. Department of Health, Education, and Welfare, 1975, p. 40.
3. National Health Education Committee, "Facts on the Major Killing and Crippling Diseases in the United States," 1971, p. 5.
4. Lambert, P.D. and Martin, A. (National Institutes of Health), Pharmacy Times, April 1976, pp 50-66.
5. deHaen, Paul, "New Drugs, 1940 thru 1975," Pharmacy Times, March 1976, pp. 40-74.
6. Lasagna, L., The American Journal of Medical Sciences, 263.72 (Feb.) 1972.

 LEDERLE LABORATORIES,
A Division of American Cyanamid Company,
Pearl River, New York 10965

tions in the same period. In 1950 32 new drugs were introduced. This number increased until 1959, when 65 new drugs came on the market, and then began to decrease until in 1975 only 15 new drugs were introduced. Three reasons are generally given for this paradox of increasing R&D budgets and decreasing results. One, new discoveries are becoming harder and more difficult to find as the research moves further into unknown areas.

Three little words can save you medicine money.

Frequently when you're sick, nothing hurts as much as the cost of the medicine to help you get better. But there is a way you can save money on prescription drugs and medicine. By remembering three little words . . . "the generic name."

What do these words mean?

Simply this. Your doctor can write a prescription two ways. He can write the "brand name" or *the generic name* (pronounced jen-air-ic) of the drug. The difference is that prescriptions can cost a lot less if the doctor uses *the generic name.*

How come?

Most well-known advertised brands of anything cost more than unknown or store brands. You pay for the advertising that makes the "brand name" well-known. Brand name drugs also usually cost more. For example, one drug used to reduce high blood pressure costs drug stores about $4.50 under its "brand name," yet only 99¢ under its *generic name.* What's more, up to half of the most widely prescribed drugs (the top 50) are available under their *generic name.*

Here's what to do.

First, ask your doctor to write down *the generic name* instead of the brand name. Don't be afraid to tell him you need to save money on medicine. Second, tell your pharmacist that the prescription calls for *the generic name* at your request. Ask for the lowest-priced quality generic drug he or she can recommend.

You could tear out this message and wrap it around your finger to help you remember. Or you could keep thinking of the dollars you want to save. Either way, remembering three little words can save you lots of medicine money. Please remember *the generic name.*

Public Communication, Inc.

10203 Santa Monica Blvd., Los Angeles, California 90067
Citizen-supported advertising and research in the public interest.

Two, the cost of research has increased faster than prices in general. Three, the Food and Drug Administration has so increased the number of regulations and requirements that must be satisfied before a new drug can be marketed that it is becoming much more expensive to develop new drugs.

Although there is little debate about the decreased productivity of R&D (as measured by the number of new single entity drugs), there is some controversy about the direction and objective of industry research. According to an industry spokesperson:

> Constant striving for discovery and excellence has resulted from competitive rivalry in the marketplace. . . . From 1940 to 1966, an amazing total of 823 new single chemical entity drugs were introduced as prescription drugs in the U.S. The U.S. originated 502 of the 823 new weapons against disease and suffering in the last 27 years. Of the U.S. discoveries the laboratories of American manufacturers were responsible for 87 percent.[11]

However, foes of the industry claim that most research spending is not directed toward new products and product improvement but at getting around somebody else's patent in order to gain patent protection. Thus, although the number of new entities may have been great, the actual increase in therapeutic value has been small. Dr. Dale Console, former medical director for Squibb Laboratories, charged

> that doctors and the public are subjected to a constant "barrage" of new drugs, some of which are worthless and others of which have a greater potential for harm than for good. . . . that since so much depends on novelty, drugs change like women's hemlines. That more than half of the drug companies' research effort is directed towards products that are really not worthwhile but are pursued simply because there's profit in it.[12]

Given the debate over the aim of R&D in the industry, there is also a debate over the need for high prices and high profits in order to support a yearly R&D budget of over $1 billion.

SELECTED BIBLIOGRAPHY

Applied Management Sciences. *Final Report, Survey of Drug Information Needs and Problems Associated with Communications Directed to Practicing Physicians,* May 8, 1974. Prepared for FDA Bureau of Drugs, Contract No. FDA 72–301.

Cooper, Michael H. *Prices and Profits in the Pharmaceutical Industry.* New York: Pergamon, 1966.

Council on Economic Priorities. "In Whose Hands." *Economic Priorities Report* 4 (August–November 1973): 4–5.

---

[11] U.S. Senate, *Competitive Problems in the Drug Industry, Summary and Analysis,* p. 24.

[12] U.S. Senate, *Competitive Problems in the Drug Industry,* part 5, December 14, 19, 1967 and January 18, 19, and 25, 1968, p. 1867.

"Drugs: Prescription Prices." *Newsweek,* June 16, 1975, p. 71.

Funk, Edwin. "Yesterday, Today and Tomorrow in Drug Advertising." *Pharmaceutical Marketing and Media* 2 (March 1967): 13.

Garai, Pierre R. "Advertising and Promotion of Drugs." In *Drugs in Our Society,* ed. Paul Talalay. Baltimore: Johns Hopkins Press, 1964, pp. 189–202.

Pharmaceutical Manufacturers Association. *Patterns of Prescription Drug Use: The Role of Promotion,* undated.

"Profit in Pills." *The Economist,* June 5, 1976, p. 62.

Schwartzman, David. *The Expected Return from Pharmaceutical Research.* American Enterprise Institute for Public Policy Research, Washington, D.C., Evaluative Studies no. 19 (May 1975).

Sproat, A. T. *A Note on the U.S. Prescription Drug Industry, Part I (R).* Harvard Business School, 1972.

U.S. Congress, Senate, Select Committee on Small Business, Subcommittee on Monopoly. *Competitive Problems in the Drug Industry, Summary and Analysis.* Washington, D.C.: U.S. Government Printing Office, 1972.

U.S. Senate, Committee on the Judiciary, Subcommittee on Antitrust and Monopoly. *Administered Prices in the Drug Industry.* Washington, D.C.: U.S. Government Printing Office, 1973–74, parts 3–6.

Waite, Arthur S. "The Future of Pharmaceutical Drug Promotion." *Medical Marketing and Media* 6 (June 1971): 9.

Waxberg, J. "What Motivates a Physician to Try a New Product." *Medical Marketing and Media,* July 1973.

2 Warning: Cigarette smoking is dangerous to your health*

Clash between economic interests and public safety: Consumer freedom and government regulation

The further a man is removed from physical need the more open he is to persuasion—or management—as to what he buys. This is, perhaps, the most important consequence for economics of increasing affluence.
John Kenneth Galbraith,
The New Industrial State

In a widely televised January 11, 1964, broadcast, U.S. Surgeon General Luther Terry reported to the nation the conclusions of his advisory committee on smoking and health: Smokers have a 70 percent higher fatality rate from lung cancer than nonsmokers! The report warned that "cigarette smoking is a health hazard of sufficient importance in the United States to warrant appropriate remedial action."

Since the publication of the report, various government agencies and private groups have consistently imposed increasingly severe restrictions on the promotion and sale of cigarettes. These efforts have resulted in a total ban of cigarette advertising on radio and television, insertion of a warning label on all cigarette packages, and print advertising indicating that cigarette smoking was dangerous to the smokers' health. There have also been successful attempts to restrict smoking to designated areas in public buildings, mass transportation, and public recreation and entertainment facilities.

Notwithstanding all these efforts, the sale and consumption of cigarettes, after a temporary decline, appears to have resumed the secular upward trend.

---

* Revised and updated from S. Prakash Sethi, *Up against the Corporate Wall: Modern Corporations and Social Issues of the 70s* (Englewood Cliffs, N.J.: Prentice-Hall, Inc., copyright © 1971, 1974, 1977).

ISSUES FOR ANALYSIS

The issues raised by the case are multifaceted. They deal with the role of government and industry, and the rights of individuals. In addition, they deal with the economic and sociopolitical effects of a restriction on smoking on other industries and economic segments of the population.

1. To what extent should the various public agencies restrict the choice of people to consume certain products and assume the consequences of their personal actions? In other words, what is the rationale of government action? Should such an action be limited to dissemination of information only, or should the government assume the responsibility of protecting individuals from injuring themselves?
2. How much information and what type of information is necessary? What groups should this information be disseminated to, for how long, and by whom?
3. If protection from advertising is desired, what groups in the population should be protected, for how long, and by what method?
4. How should the tobacco industry in general and individual companies in particular conduct themselves, given the increasing and almost irrefutable evidence of the linkage between smoking and cancer? Should there be any self-imposed constraints on promoting certain kinds of cigarettes or promoting them to certain groups, such as teenagers?

Once the broad issues have been clarified, a careful analysis of the case should lead us to develop reasonable norms of behavior for the state, the industry, and the activist groups, and also to evaluate and monitor their future activities. In particular,

1. An analysis of the constitutional, political, and social arguments of a ban on the promotion of an otherwise legal product, in a specific medium, should be instructive for its broader implications.
2. An evaluation of the major effects of a ban on cigarette advertising in the broadcast media and warning labels in terms of their intended objectives should assist in the formulation of new strategies in the future.
3. An understanding of the activities of the tobacco industry during various phases of a changing external environment should be instructive in developing future industry responses to public pressure. It should also provide an indication of the extent to which the industry can be depended upon to regulate itself or act in other ways that may serve to better fulfill societal expectations.

HISTORY AND BACKGROUND

The surgeon general's report brought to a head the long dispute between health authorities and the tobacco industry. The antecedents linking smoking to cancer go back to 1900, when statisticians noted an increase in cancer of the lung. Their data are usually taken as the starting point for studies on the possible relationship of smoking to lung cancer, to diseases of the heart and blood vessels, and to noncancerous diseases of the lower respiratory tract. The next important date for comparisons is 1930, when definite trends in mortality and disease incidence became apparent. Since 1939 there have been twenty-nine retrospective studies of lung cancer and cigarette smoking.[1] In 1950, as research and statistical analysis became more competent, more evidence pointed to a definite relationship. Two American doctors, Graham and Wydner, concluded from their research that "excessive use of tobacco, especially cigarettes, seems to be an important factor in the induction of lung cancer."[2]

In 1954 Doctors Hammond and Horn, working for the American Cancer Society, issued their now-famous study which found that male cigarette smokers, smoking a pack a day, were sixteen times more likely to die of lung cancer than nonsmokers. This study caused a general health scare. In June 1956, at the request of the surgeon general, a scientific study group established jointly by the National Cancer Institute, the National Heart Institute, the American Cancer Society, and the American Heart Association reviewed 16 independent studies made in five countries over an 18-year period. The group's conclusion that there was a causal relationship between excessive cigarette smoking and lung cancer was officially supported by Surgeon General Leroy E. Burney in 1956 and 1959.[3] At the group's urging, President Kennedy established a commission to study the tobacco problem, and in January 1962 Surgeon General Terry and the commission were encouraged by a report called "Smoking and Health," issued by the Royal College of Physicians in Great Britain. It stated that a definite causal relationship between cigarette smoking, lung cancer, and other diseases did exist. Sufficiently motivated, the commission agreed to conduct a two-phase study consisting of (1) a review and evaluation of available data, and (2) recommendations for action.

In 1963 legal considerations emerged when the question of cigarette manufacturers' liability was raised in the case of *Green* v. *The American Tobacco Company*. A district court in Miami held that, although smoking was a cause of cancer, the company was not liable since it could not have foreseen the consequences. As a result, however, the industry began to give serious consideration to a warning on cigarette packages in order to limit companies' liability. In December 1963, the American Cancer Society issued the results of a survey of more than one million Americans. Its con-

---

[1] U.S. Public Health Service, Advisory Committee to the Surgeon General, *Smoking and Health* (Washington, D.C.: Government Printing Office, 1964), p. 33.

[2] "Cigarettes and Society: A Growing Dilemma," *Time*, April 25, 1969, pp. 98–103.

[3] *Congressional Quarterly 1964 Almanac* (1965), p. 246.

clusion was that "the evidence continues to pile up, and the burden of proof that there is not a causal relationship could soon shift over to the cigarette companies."

The surgeon general's report of 1964

As a result of its investigation, the president's commission reached the conclusion that "cigarette smoking is causally related to lung cancer in men; the magnitude of the effect of cigarette smoking far outweighs all other factors." The commission also found that the risk of developing lung cancer increased with the duration of smoking and the number of cigarettes smoked per day, and diminished with discontinuing smoking. According to the report, "the risk of developing cancer of the lung for the combined groups of pipe smokers, cigar smokers, and pipe and cigar smokers is greater than for nonsmokers, but much less than for cigarette smokers." In addition, the report stated that cigarette smoking was the greatest cause of chronic bronchitis in the United States and greatly increased the risk of death from that disease and from emphysema. For most Americans, cigarette smoking was a much greater cause of chronic bronchopulmonary disease than atmospheric pollution or occupational exposure. The report also concluded that cigarette smoking was related to cardiovascular diseases.

Reaction to the report

The tobacco industry, although somewhat defensive, was undeterred by the report. Through the Tobacco Institute, it repeated the old arguments: No causal relationship had been established between smoking and cancer; any ban against smoking would cause serious economic injury to a vital industry and unemployment to countless workers and farmers; a reduction in smoking would result in a significant decrease in federal, state, and local taxes; a ban would be an infringement of individuals' personal freedom. The industry then moved to back up its assertions that more research was needed. In February 1964, Dr. Raymond McKeon, AMA president, announced that six tobacco companies had given the AMA $10 million for research, without any restrictions whatsoever. In addition, all the companies began or intensified their own filter research.

On April 27, 1964, the major tobacco companies announced the formulation of a voluntary advertising code to become effective in January 1965. It outlawed any advertising that would appeal to those under 21, thus barring cigarette commercials before and after television programs designed for minors. It forbade any advertising that portrayed smoking as being essential to social prominence, distinction, success, or sexual attraction. The broadcasting industry also established codes to regulate cigarette advertising. The National Association of Broadcasters' television code board stated that cigarette advertising should not contain false claims and that neither programming nor advertising was to depict smoking as promoting health or as being necessary or desirable to young people. The industry agreed to subject itself to self-regulation, to be enforced by an independent administrator capable of leveling fines of $100,000 for infractions.[4]

The response of the tobacco industry to this change in its external environment seems typical of all industries faced with similar situations. It might be noted here that the cigarette industry in the United States is highly concentrated: six firms account for more than 99 percent of the total output—American Brands, Brown & Williamson, Liggett & Myers, P. Lorillard, Philip Morris, and R. J. Reynolds. Table 2–1 shows the ranking of various tobacco companies and their relative market shares.

The 1954 Hammond and Horn study brought about the first significant change in the otherwise relatively stable external environment of the industry. During this period, the industry displayed behaviors that reflected an uneasiness with the changed external environment, an unwillingness to accept the new situation, and an absence of a long-range strategy.[5] The next dramatic change in the external environment occurred with the publication of the surgeon general's report in 1964. By then it appeared that the tide of evidence linking smoking to cancer was too overwhelming to be summarily rejected. The cigarette industry's posture changed from calculated indifference to active defense. The strategies pursued by the industry following the publication of the report could be summarized as follows:

TABLE 2–1
ANNUAL SALE OF CIGARETTES AND RELATIVE MARKET SHARES, 1973–1974

Company	1973		1974*	
	Market share (percent)	Sales of cigarettes (billions)	Market share (percent)	Sales of cigarettes (billions)
R. J. Reynolds	31.3	180.3	31.5	185.9
Philip Morris	21.8	125.6	23.0	135.7
Brown & Williamson	17.6	101.4	17.5	103.3
American Brands	15.7	90.4	15.0	88.5
Lorillard	8.4	48.4	8.2	48.4
Liggett & Myers	5.1	29.4	4.7	27.7
All other	0.1	0.5	0.1	0.5
Total	100.0	576.0	100.0	590.0

* 1974 estimates are subject to revision.
Source: "A Deluge of New Cigarettes," *Business Week*, November 23, 1974, p. 115.

---

[4] "Smoking Scare: What's Happened to It," *U.S. News and World Report*, January 11, 1965, pp. 38–41.

[5] The reader should find it interesting to read the statements of various tobacco company executives in annual reports of this period. See also R. B. Tennant, "The Cigarette Industry," in *The Structure of American Industry*, ed. W. Adams (New York: Macmillan, 1961), 2nd ed., pp. 357–92; Lars Engwall, "Business Behavior: The Cigarette Case," *Marquette Business Review*, summer 1973, pp. 59–72.

1. Continue the pre-1964 strategies denying the existence of scientific proof linking smoking to cancer.
2. Use all political measures available to thwart legislative action that might restrict the promotion and sale of cigarettes.
3. Continue aggressively promoting the product to maintain profitability and also demonstrate that adverse publicity was not affecting sales.
4. Encourage other groups whose economic fortunes were closely linked to those of the cigarette industry to join the effort to forestall restrictions on the cigarette industry.
5. Institute self-regulation measures to meet the demands of critics and to promote the image of a responsible industry capable of putting its house in order.

The American Medical Association (AMA) came out with a feeble statement that more research was needed and that there was a need to "find how tobacco smoke affected health, and if possible, to eliminate whatever element in smoke may induce disease."[6] The first official government reaction came from the Federal Trade Commission (FTC), when it announced on January 18, 1964, that it was scheduling hearings for March 16 on the following proposed forms of regulation:

1. Cigarette packs and ads shall carry the warning "caution—cigarette smoking is dangerous to health and may cause death. . . ."
2. Ads and labels must not suggest that cigarettes promote health or well-being, are not dangerous, or that one brand is less harmful than another.
3. The "tar derby" or competitive safety claims will be resumed only when a manufacturer can support his claims with scientific evidence; tar and nicotine contents must be verified by testing procedures.[7]

The FTC subsequently announced proposed trade regulation rules to require a warning on cigarette packages and advertisements, the actual wording to be left to the manufacturers. FTC Chairman Paul Rand Dixon notified the House of the commission's decision and said that the labeling requirement would become effective January 1, 1965. The FTC dropped its regulation on the two other ad directives regarding claims of good health and statements that one brand may be less harmful than another. This loosening of control was the FTC's reaction to the creation of the industry's self-policing codes. There was so much opposition from the tobacco industry, however, that Chairman Dixon postponed the labeling requirement to July 1, 1965, so that the 89th Congress, which convened on January 4, 1965, would have time to examine the proposal.

Congressional reaction to the report and the FTC decision was mixed. Southern representatives from tobacco states fought to delay FTC requirements and introduced bills to provide funds for research on the effects of

---

[6] *Congressional Quarterly 1968 Almanac* (1968), vol. 23.

[7] *Congressional Quarterly 1967 Almanac* (1967).

tobacco on health. Congress quickly scheduled hearings on the matter of cigarette labeling and advertising regulation and health problems associated with smoking. The first hearings were held before the full House Committee on Interstate and Foreign Commerce in late June and early July 1964. Chairman Oren Harris noted that in 1963 70 million Americans bought tobacco products at a cost of approximately $8 billion, and that over $2 billion of this sum went to the federal government in taxes, over $1 billion went to state governments, and millions of dollars went to municipal governments.[8] These first hearings provided the staging ground for the formulation and articulation of the positions and strategies adopted by the various parties involved in the cigarette controversy.

CONGRESSIONAL HEARINGS, JUNE–JULY 1964

Basic positions

Three basic positions, all documented in the various hearings reports, were offered to the committee—those of the FTC, the tobacco industry, and the Department of Health, Education and Welfare (HEW).

The FTC's position.   Chairman Paul Dixon contended that the commission had authority to regulate cigarette advertising under Section 5 of the Federal Trade Commission Act, which authorizes the commission "to proceed against any actual or potential deception in sale, or offering for sale, of any product in commerce. . . . Such deception may result either from a direct statement concerning a product or a failure to disclose any material fact relating to such a product." Dixon stated that "the Commission had completed its consideration of the record in this proceeding and has determined that the public interest requires the promulgation of a trade regulation rule for the prevention of unfair or deceptive advertising or labeling of cigarettes in relation to the health hazards of smoking." The chairman, however, was more anxious that Congress take the initiative in such a politically sensitive and explosive area. He testified:

> I make it perfectly plain to you, we are a creature of the Congress. But until the Congress changes our basic responsibility I think we are dutybound to act. If the Congress passes a law removing this from our jurisdiction and vesting it somewhere else then we are relieved of that responsibility.

The tobacco industry's position.   Early in 1964 the Tobacco Institute set up a lobbying campaign utilizing the influence of Senator Earle C. Clements, former representative and Democratic whip under Lyndon B. Johnson. At the hearings, the industry's position was presented by Bowman Gray, chairman of the board of directors of R. J. Reynolds Tobacco Company, Winston-Salem, North Carolina. The industry opposed the FTC reg-

---

[8] U.S., Congress, House Committee on Interstate and Foreign Commerce, Hearings, *Cigarette Labeling and Advertising,* 88th Cong., 2d sess., 1964.

ulations regarding labeling and advertising for three reasons: (1) The FTC did not have the authority to issue such a trade regulation and the commission therefore acted unlawfully; (2) the matter was of such importance that it should be resolved by Congress and not by an agency: "the Commission's rule would not have preemptive effect, and the industry would be exposed to the possibility of diverse State and municipal laws"; and (3) "We oppose it because we believe the Commission's warning requirement is unwise, unwarranted and is not a fair factual statement of the present state of scientific knowledge." If, however, some action was deemed necessary, Gray said:

> We certainly do not think that any action should be taken by an administrative agency such as was taken yesterday by the Federal Trade Commission, and if any such action is to be taken, we believe it should be taken by the Congress and by no one else. The problem is national in scope; it is clearly not local. . . .
>
> Great care should be exercised before any action is taken which could seriously disrupt this important industry. . . .

Should Congress consider that a warning label was absolutely necessary, Gray emphasized the following points:

1. Any such legislation should make it absolutely clear that the congressional statute preempted the field. If there was to be a caution notice, it should be uniform and again nationwide in scope.
2. The required caution notice should be fair and factual. It should be phrased in a way that reflected the lack of scientific clinical and laboratory evidence of the relationship between smoking and health.
3. If a warning was to be required on the package, it certainly should not be required in cigarette advertising.

On April 27, the cigarette companies announced the Cigarette Advertising Code, thus supporting Gray's contention that the industry itself had taken action to meet criticisms. The tobacco companies were using the mechanism of a membership corporation, with each cigarette company as a member, and had asked for a clearance from the Antitrust Division of the Department of Justice. In a July 1, 1964, letter to the House Committee, Gray stated that the industry interpreted the Justice Department's reply as clearance to implement the voluntary code.

HEW's position. Surgeon General Luther Terry, testifying before the House committee, presented the position of the Department of Health, Education and Welfare:

> In summary, I would like to say that the Department of Health, Education, and Welfare recognized the major public health hazard caused by cigarette smoking. The Department believes that additional regulatory and nonregulatory action is required. . . . We must not use the need for further research as an excuse for lack of action. . . . With the overwhelming scientific evidence we now possess, I predict that the years ahead will constitute an era

of action in which we will make significant progress in reducing the burden of disease, disability, and untimely death imposed upon millions of our people by cigarette smoking.

The House commerce committee heard further testimony from a number of senators and representatives from tobacco-producing states. The committee felt that action taken by Congress would be based on the question of whether the surgeon general's report "can be absolutely depended upon as a matter of fact and not necessarily taken as the judgment of experts." The committee therefore heard a good deal of professional testimony. Dr. Thomas Burford, professor of thoracic surgery at Washington University, St. Louis, testified that there was "a large volume of good scientific evidence which tends to refute the rather hastily accepted premise that cigarette smoking is causally related to lung cancer." Dr. William B. Ober pointed out that saying that a large proportion of lung cancer patients have been "heavy cigarette smokers for 20 or 30 years or longer is quite a different matter [from saying] that a large proportion of those people who smoke heavily will develop cancer of the lung." He added that the "only really scientific statement one can make at the present time is that no one really knows what causes lung cancer."

Further hearings.   Further hearings were held before both the House and Senate Commerce Committees during the first session of the Eighty-ninth Congress, March 22 to April 1, 1965. The testimony in these hearings emphasized regulation of advertising. It was argued, on the basis of the proper role of government and the proper relationship between government and business, that it should not be the government's role to attempt to change the behavior of individual citizens. When an industry demonstrated a willingness to regulate itself, as the cigarette industry had through its voluntary code, government regulation represented undue interference with business and free enterprise. The government, furthermore, had no right to prohibit the advertising of a product that could be legally manufactured and sold. If action was considered necessary, a warning on the label and not in advertising would be the proper form. The label was the traditional and most effective place for hazard warnings. Testimony was also given on the nature and purposes of advertising in the cigarette industry. Advertising, it was argued, was a basic means of competition, and prohibiting it would restrict competition in the industry. The intent of cigarette advertising was not to encourage people to smoke, since half the people in the country were already smoking, but to encourage smokers to change brands—that is, to increase a company's market share. The industry was mature and had a mature marketplace. The aim, therefore, was selective and not primary demand.

Results of the hearings

Congress ultimately passed S.559, a bill introduced by Senate commerce committee Chairman Warren G. Magnuson, which required that all cigarette packages bear the label "Caution: Cigarette Smoking May Be Hazardous to Your Health." The bill provided for a uniform and overriding federal labeling requirement that was not expected to affect sales seriously. All action on control of advertising was suspended until July 1969. In its final form, the bill called for a fine of $10,000 for violations and required periodic reports from the FTC and HEW. The bill was strongly opposed by Republican John E. Moss, who stated that the warning was not sufficiently forceful to curb the smoking habit. Shortly before President Johnson signed the bill into law on July 27, 1965, eight senators, among them Robert F. Kennedy, urged a veto. They argued that S.559 was more beneficial to the cigarette companies than to the nation's health, especially as the companies themselves had admitted that the labeling requirement would have little or no effect on consumption. Despite the opposition, the bill was passed, and the FTC reluctantly canceled its regulations requiring a health warning in advertising. The agency did say, however, that it would continue to keep watch on cigarette advertising to make sure that S.559 was being obeyed and that fraudulent and misleading advertising was not being used.

During 1966, the federal agencies concentrated on research and on determining the effect of the 1965 law on smokers. Various bills and resolutions to set new requirements for cigarette labeling and advertising were introduced in Congress. The Senate commerce committee held three days of hearings on the development of a safer cigarette, but no further action was taken. The March 1966 cigarette price rise may have caused some smokers to consider quitting, but the government stepped in on grounds of inflation. President Johnson persuaded the cigarette companies to roll back the price increase, thereby posing the question: Which is the greater threat, inflation or the smoking peril?

The tar and nicotine derby

In March 1966 the FTC also ruled that companies could mention the tar and nicotine content of their cigarettes. The next month, P. Lorillard quit the industry ad council and rushed to market a new cigarette, TRUE, asserting that it would "deliver less tar and nicotine." This conflicted with the industry code, which required proof of health significance, and started a new "tar derby" of tar and nicotine claims. The conflicting claims were subject to much controversy, and in August the FTC decided to hold hearings on ways of uniformly measuring tar and nicotine content.

In November 1966, the Public Health Service issued a new report dealing exclusively with death-rate statistics. It showed that mortality rates went up with cigarette consumption. Starting in early 1967, various executive agencies released new findings, including data gathered by the surgeon general and a report that the 1965 law was having little effect on smokers. In January 1967, after the FTC hearings concluded, HEW Secretary Gardner endorsed a Senate commerce committee bill that would make cigarette firms disclose tar and nicotine content. The Tobacco Institute's position at this time was that "there is no valid scientific evidence demonstrating that either tar or nicotine is responsible for human illness."[9]

The FTC wanted the Senate bill to set up uniform testing methods. The bill requiring cigarette firms to print the tar and nicotine content of their cigarettes failed to pass Congress, but money was appropriated for the FTC to set up its own testing procedure and to report its findings. On February 28, 1967, President Johnson directed HEW to organize a committee to study lung cancer and cigarette smoking. The following summer, Kennedy M. Endicott, director of the Public Health Services National Cancer Institute, announced the organization of a ten-member commission to study lung cancer and smoking and the development of a safer cigarette.

That summer the new U.S. surgeon general, William H. Stewart, released a report summarizing the development of tobacco-related research since Surgeon General Terry's controversial report of 1964. Stewart said that over two thousand research programs completed since 1964 had given no evidence that conflicted with the 1964 conclusions.[10] The 1967 report concluded that the danger to males from all smoke-related illnesses increased with age, especially during the years from 45 to 54. In the 35- to 39-year-old age group, the deaths of one of every three men and one of every fourteen women were attributed to smoking. According to the report, women who smoked regularly had significantly higher death rates than those who had never smoked. The difference in the mortality rates between men and women was attributed to the fact that women were less exposed to cigarette smoking than men. Other information provided by the report showed that there was a downward trend in risk from disease and death for those who had stopped smoking.[11] Younger smokers showed undesirable respiratory symptoms and shortwindedness. Death rates were higher for those who started smoking early in life. As for diseases other than lung cancer, the report indicated that smoking was the most important cause of chronic bronchopulmonary disease in the United States and that it was significantly related to peptic ulcer.

The report was sent to Congress with a letter from HEW Secretary John Gardner outlining the department's recommendations for congressional action. He recommended that (1) action be taken to strengthen the warning label on cigarette packages by stating more specifically that smoking was hazardous to health, (2) that legislation be passed to require warning in advertisements, and (3) that both labels and advertising identify the tar and nicotine levels in cigarettes.[12] The conclusions reached in the surgeon

---

[9] "Tobacco," *Time,* August 1, 1969.

[10] *1967 Almanac,* p. 737.

[11] *Federal Register,* vol. 34, no. 28 (1969).

[12] *1967 Almanac,* p. 738.

general's report were also supported by a national survey conducted by the Public Health Service National Center for Health Statistics.

The effect on industry

But the law that was finally passed had little effect on the tobacco industry's sales. For the fiscal year ending June 1965, consumption was at a record level of more than 5.33 billion cigarettes. The U.S. Public Health Service also noted that although a million Americans were giving up smoking each year, they were replaced by 1.5 million new smokers, mostly youngsters.[13]

The Federal Trade Commission made a study on the effect of the first eighteen months of the act of 1965 on the smoking habits of Americans and on the advertising practices of the industry. Its report concluded that 82 percent of the respondents felt the current warning label (Caution: Cigarette Smoking May Be Hazardous to Your Health) was having no appreciable effect. In addition, despite the voluntary advertising code, the tobacco industry continued to represent smoking as an enjoyable and even healthful activity. Also, much of the advertising was done during prime broadcasting hours and consequently was reaching young people. Since industry regulation was proving ineffectual, the report recommended that cigarette advertising be banned from radio and television. In addition, it urged a stronger warning on cigarette packages: "Caution: Cigarette Smoking Is Dangerous to Your Health and May Cause Death from Cancer and Other Diseases." Funds were requested by the National Institute of Health for the development of a safer cigarette.

The Federal Communications Commission steps in

On June 2, 1967, the FCC ordered radio and television stations to allow time for antismoking advertisements. The seven commissioners said that their decision was based on the fairness doctrine, which states that the public should have access to conflicting viewpoints on controversial issues of public importance. This fairness doctrine, a basic principle of the broadcasting field, was made part of the Communications Act of 1959, although it was not applied to product advertising until 1967.[14]

Thus, stations running cigarette ads had to turn over a significant amount of free time to antismoking commercials—one antismoking for every three smoking commercials. Antismoking groups such as the American Cancer Society filled the air with effective anti-ads. After the ruling, the American Cancer Society distributed 8,900 antismoking commercials in 16 months.

---

[13] "Cigarettes and Society: A Growing Dilemma," *Time*, April 29, 1969, pp. 98–103.

[14] Federal Communication Commission Reports, "Television Station WCBS-TV," 2d ser., vol. 8 (May 19–August 4, 1967): 381–87.

The counter-ads were, in effect, the reverse of the cigarette ads. Instead of looking happy and vigorous, smokers were presented as miserable and unhealthy. A number of celebrities were used to advocate quitting smoking, and others refused to perform on programs sponsored by cigarette companies.

The person largely responsible for the FCC's application of the fairness doctrine to cigarette advertising was John F. Banzhaf III, a 28-year-old New York attorney known as "the Ralph Nader of the cigarette industry."[15] In January 1967, Banzhaf had filed a formal complaint with the FCC against WCBS-TV. The complaint maintained that the fairness doctrine required the station to give equal time to "responsible groups" to present the case against cigarette smoking. Although the FCC rejected the equal time contention, its June 3 ruling responded to Banzhaf's complaint. Banzhaf then formed two organizations. The first, ASH (Action on Smoking and Health), sponsored by noted physicians, raised more than $100,000 to conduct litigation on the fairness doctrine[16] and to enforce its application by monitoring TV stations and filing complaints against those failing to comply. The other organization, LASH (Legislative Action on Smoking and Health), raised funds and enlisted support for the congressional battles.

As the antismoking forces speeded up their efforts, the tobacco industry—through its major Washington lobby, the Tobacco Institute—continued to oppose them. In addition to carrying on its own research, the Tobacco Institute challenged the validity of almost every government study on smoking and health. The industry introduced the 100 mm cigarette—up to half an inch longer than the regular. In his speeches and writing, lobbyist Clements emphasized the industry's belief that the causes of lung cancer and heart disease were unknown and hence were not automatically related to cigarette smoking. In May 1967, bills were introduced in Congress by various senators, including Robert F. Kennedy, Warren G. Magnuson, and Frank E. Moss, to strengthen the Cigarette Labeling and Advertising Act of 1965. However, no new legislation resulted. On November 27, 1967, the consumer subcommittee of the Senate commerce committee made public the FTC tests giving tar and nicotine contents of 59 varieties of cigarettes. Senator Magnuson, chairman of the subcommittee, said: "This information will enable a smoker who is unable or unwilling to give up smoking to select the least hazardous cigarettes on the market." Individual companies had no comment.

Developments during 1968 also took the form of recommendations and warnings rather than legislation. On July 1, 1968, HEW Secretary Wilbur J. Cohen brought to Congress the surgeon general's 1968 *Supplemental Report on the Health Consequences of Smoking* and urged more strongly

---

[15] *The New York Times*, June 3, 1967.

[16] See *Banzhaf v. FCC*, U.S. Court of Appeals, D.C. Circuit, Case #21285, November 21, 1968.

worded warnings of the hazards involved in cigarette smoking. He also asked Congress to require warnings on advertisements.

ATTEMPTS TO BAN CIGARETTE ADVERTISING IN THE BROADCAST MEDIA

The FTC, although always in favor of regulating cigarette advertising, had consistently argued that the political and economic implications of such a regulation made Congress the proper initiating body. Congress, for the same reasons, was also reluctant. In a pressure play in 1965, the FTC announced that it would require a stiffer warning on cigarette packages unless Congress took action. This precipitated the 1965 act, which would expire on June 30, 1969. The FTC used the same tactic again in June 1968; in a 3 to 2 decision, it voted to ban all cigarette advertising from radio and television and strongly suggested to the Senate committee that Congress legislate on the matter. Later in the summer, the surgeon general's Task Force for Smoking and Health charged that the tobacco industry was encouraging death and disease with its advertising practices and that it was unwilling to face up to the health hazards of smoking.

On February 5, 1969, the FCC, in a 6 to 1 decision, moved to ban cigarette advertising from radio and television. Chairman Hyde indicated that the commission would be satisfied only with a complete ban and not with the voluntary restrictions. In defense of its legal power, the commission said: "In the case of such a threat to public health, the authority to act is really a duty to act"; it would appear "wholly at odds with the public interest for broadcasters to present advertising promoting the consumption of a product imposing this unique danger."[17]

The cigarette industry considered the decision arbitrary, and the National Association of Broadcasters charged that the FCC was outside its normal jurisdiction. Despite the heated reaction to the FCC proposal, however, there could be no actual ban without extensive hearings, and there remained the possibility of contrary legislation. Thus, the FTC and FCC made it clear that Congress would have to act.

The hearings by the interstate commerce committee began in April 1969, and it seemed that nothing had changed since 1965: The positions of the various parties were the same and their monotonously repetitious utterances were distinguished only by a new vehemence.[18] The broadcasting industry, impelled by economic considerations, unwillingly found itself an ally of the defensive cigarette industry. In an effort to generate public support, the tobacco industry circulated an article, "How Much Is Known

---

[17] "Move to Ban Cigarette TV Ads," *San Francisco Chronicle*, February 6, 1969. "A Move to Limit Cigarette Ads," *U.S. News and World Report*, February 17, 1969.

[18] U.S., Congress, House Committee on Interstate and Foreign Commerce, *Hearings, Cigarette Labeling and Advertising—1969*, 91st Cong., 1st sess. (1969).

about Smoking and Health?" by Dr. Clarence Cook Little, through paid advertising space in leading national magazines and newspapers. Dr. Little, a retired biologist, member of the National Academy of Sciences, former managing director of the American Society for the Control of Cancer (now the American Cancer Society), and a founder and former director of Jackson Laboratory for Cancer Research, supported the industry's point of view. The Council for Tobacco Research also argued that the cause of cancer had not yet been proved. In its booklet, *The Cigarette Controversy: Eight Questions and Answers,* the council raised some questions to strengthen its position:

1. If smoking does cause disease, why has it not been proven after 15 years of intensive research how this occurs?
2. Why, if smoking causes disease, has no ingredient found in smoke been identified as the causative factor?
3. The type of malignance for which smoking is most often blamed is "epidermoid" lung cancer. Have researchers ever produced this in animals with cigarette smoke? No.
4. Why do so many more men than women get lung cancer? If cigarette smoking is indeed the hazard it is said to be, the roughly six-to-one difference is most perplexing.
5. Why is it that lung cancer often does not occur in those parts of the lung which are exposed to the most smoke?
6. Do statistics prove that cigarette smoking is a cause of lung cancer, heart disease, emphysema, bronchitis, and other diseases? It is a cardinal principle that statistics alone cannot prove the cause of any disease.

The industry spokesman, Joseph F. Cullman, chairman of the executive committee of the Tobacco Institute, testified at the hearings and repeated the industry's arguments of no proved link between smoking and cancer. He contended that the 1965 Labeling Act had achieved its objective of informing the public concerning smoking and health, and he also took strong exception to the FCC's decision of June 2, 1967, regarding the application of the fairness doctrine, which gave a significant amount of free time to antismoking commercials on TV.

In presenting its position, the tobacco industry repeated its usual defenses. According to it, the warning "Caution: Cigarette Smoking May Be Hazardous to Your Health" reflected the extent of available scientific evidence, and the stricter warning proposed was unwarranted by the facts and punitive in spirit. Again the industry stressed the need for more research and not more regulation. The industry also voiced opposition to bills that would require a statement of tar and nicotine contents of cigarettes on all packages and in advertising. The industry was again supported by testimony of senators and representatives from major tobacco-producing states. The industry agreed that the FCC should be allowed to prohibit an advertiser from making false, fraudulent, or misleading claims, but it objected to the singling out of cigarettes for regulation. Congressman

Walter Jones of North Carolina said: "There were 18,000 alcoholics in the Veterans Hospitals of this nation, or one-fourth of the patient population. Where is the censorship of the beer and wine advertisements—is it to be next?" (p. 41). "Zeroing in from the other direction," said Congressman John J. Duncan of Tennessee, "the FCC could ban all commercials of cigarettes on radio and television, leaving the industry hopeless and helpless in reaching a multitude of potential customers. One does not have to stretch his imagination very far to see how crippled the industry might become" (p. 78). Other testifiers for the industry charged that the antismoking forces were being guided more by their own personal beliefs and emotions than by objectivity. As stated by Congressman Carl D. Perkins of Kentucky, "Tobacco has been impeached in passion but it has not been convicted in fact. Facts, cold, hard facts, are the basis upon which Congress should legislate" (p. 16).

The economic arguments against regulation were also presented. Representatives from the tobacco-producing states argued that the small farmer who depended on tobacco as a main cash crop would be seriously affected if the industry were restricted. Not only the 3 million men, women, and children connected with tobacco farms but numerous others would also be affected adversely, as Congressman Duncan pointed out in his testimony:

> Involved in this industry too are the people who transport the tobacco, the dealers and warehousemen, manufacturers of tobacco products, people who work in the tobacco plants, those who are involved in making the paper wrappers and boxes, the distributors of finished products, and the retailers. The U.S. tobacco manufacturing companies themselves employ over 100,000 people who receive aggregate wages exceeding $500 million a year. [p. 78]

As industry spokespeople indicated, severe restrictions on cigarette advertising and subsequent harm to the tobacco industry would create a huge labor problem. On the economic question, the industry was also quick to delineate the great amount of government revenue obtained from cigarette sales. In fiscal year 1967–1968, tobacco taxes reached an all-time high. On cigarettes alone, the federal tax was $2,066,159,000, state taxes $1,969,674,000, and municipal taxes $61,696,000—a total of $4,097,529,000 (p. 43). Of the $8.5 billion annual cigarette sales, each pack contributed an average of 16 cents in combined taxes, and proposals to increase tobacco taxes continued. The industry considered cigarette taxes to be a peril to the market and unjust, because no user secured any special benefit by paying the tax.[19]

Congressman John E. Moss of Cailfornia, who favored stricter antismoking legislation, introduced a bill calling for a stronger warning label on

---

[19] Frank Snodgrass, "Tobacco: A Very Big Industry with Very Few Defenders," *United States Tobacco Journal*, December 26, 1968.

packages and for a statement of tar and nicotine content to accompany every package and advertisement. Moss's bill was supported by the American Cancer Society. Dr. Baker of the American Cancer Society expressed the antismoking forces' view in criticizing the effect cigarette advertising was having on young potential smokers and smokers who were trying to quit:

> One of the worst things about cigarette advertising—particularly on television and radio—is the impact it seems to have on those who are making the effort to give up smoking. It is extremely tough for nervous, struggling, irritable men or women, trying to do what they know is best for them and their children, to be constantly invited by witty, expensive, alluring television commercials to return to their dangerous habit (pp. 309–311).

California Congressman Jerry L. Pettis was more concerned with the young smokers. His bill, HR 3817, would prohibit cigarette advertising between such hours as the FCC determined were most likely to influence children of school age. Pettis's bill would also give the FCC authority to regulate the total amount of cigarette advertising. Pettis stressed the fact that the economic considerations involved could not justify the acute medical problem at hand; even if a decline in cigarette sales caused a major dislocation in the economy, "the restricting of cigarette advertising is more than justified by the terrible death toll extracted by cigarettes." One of the most important speakers in favor of regulation was Surgeon General Stewart, who represented HEW and the Public Health Service. He testified that the 1965 act did not adequately inform the American public of the health dangers involved in smoking.

At the conclusion of the hearings, the House of Representatives passed HR 6543, which was a good deal weaker than the regulations to be imposed by the FTC and FCC. This bill reflected the strength of the southern members of the House and was referred to by Congressman Moss as a "disgraceful performance which served the tobacco industry rather than the public interest."[20] The bill was favorable to the industry because it extended until June 30, 1975, the preemptive clause of the 1965 act which prohibited local, state, or federal agencies from requiring any health warning in cigarette advertising. The warning label required by HR 6543 was: "Warning: The Surgeon General Has Determined That Cigarette Smoking Is Dangerous to Your Health and May Cause Lung Cancer or Other Diseases." This label, although stricter than the one then in use, was not as harsh as the one proposed earlier by the FCC: "Warning: Cigarette Smoking Is Dangerous to Health and May Cause Death from Cancer and Other Diseases." Another provision in the bill was that nothing, apart from the preemption clause, limited or restricted the FTC's authority in regulating

---

[20] "Ban on Warning in Smoking Ads," *The New York Times,* June 19, 1969.

unfair practices in cigarette advertising. It also required annual reports from the HEW secretary on the health consequences of smoking. In addition, it required annual reports from the FTC on the effectiveness of cigarette labeling and on current practices in cigarette advertising. Hearings before the Senate Commerce Subcommittee on Consumers were scheduled to begin on HR 6543 on July 21. Subcommittee Chairman Frank E. Moss, who threatened to filibuster the bill out of existence, predicted that discussion in the Senate would extend into the August recess.

INDUSTRY CONCERN FOR THE ADVERSE ECONOMIC IMPACT OF REGULATION

The effect of a ban on cigarette advertising would apparently have been greater on the broadcasting industry than on the tobacco industry. The tobacco companies spent about $245 million a year on radio and TV advertising. Cigarettes, the single product most advertised on television, accounted for up to 11 percent of television advertising time.[21] Some contended, however, that the "loss of cigarette commercials would hardly bring economic disaster to an industry already fat with profits."[22] They suggested that potential sponsors such as department stores, which had never used television in a big way, could possibly fill the gap, at least in the larger agencies. In addition, the advertising business could perhaps sell the $50 million worth of free time given to antismoking commercials, a procedure that would also certainly be welcomed by the tobacco industry. At this point, however, it was not entirely certain that these counter-ads would be discontinued. Although the larger agencies could probably withstand the blow created by the ban, the smaller ones, whose cigarette clients amounted to 40 percent of their total business, would lose much more.[23]

Although the effect of the antismoking campaign seemed small, it was disturbing to an industry that had no doubt counted on steady growth before the surgeon general's report in 1964. Perhaps because of this, industry members amplified their acquisition activities.[24] One company merged with a hotel and motel theater chain; another—with two recent food acquisitions—acquired a large transportation company. Still another, which owned a safety razor company, a shaving cream company, and a chewing gum company, became a distributor for an English candy firm. Other industries into which the cigarette companies branched included liquor, clothing, soft drinks, and pet food. Reflecting the trend, R. J. Reynolds and

---

[21] "Tobacco: Trouble from an Old Friend," Time, July 18, 1969.

[22] "Cigarettes and Society: A Growing Dilemma," Time, April 25, 1969.

[23] Ibid.

[24] "The Bill to Ban Cigarette Ads," San Francisco Chronicle, July 13, 1969.

American decided to drop the word "tobacco" from their corporate names.[25]

Diversification, the Tobacco Institute declared, would improve the growth potential of the industry; it was not the case that cigarettes were as hazardous as they had been depicted. For the big companies, at least, the diversification drive was started with the long run in mind. In the short run, a ban on radio and television advertising would freeze the market rather than cut down perceptibly on cigarette sales. Many new brands would be forced out of the market and the minor brands would become smaller and smaller. But the big brands would probably get bigger.[26] Although cigarette ad bans were in effect in Czechoslovakia, Denmark, France, Italy, Norway, Sweden, and Switzerland, people continued to smoke.[27] In Britain, despite the Labor government's broadcasting ban in 1966 and its magazine and newspaper ad ban in 1967, people continued to smoke cigarettes in record numbers. The cigarette companies would try to cut down on the harmful long-range effects by putting money into other advertising media such as print, which was protected by the First Amendment, and into games and coupons. Also, the more than $40 million not spent on television advertising could be used to alter the companies' profit picture.

Another path the cigarette companies would probably take if the market at home was substantially reduced would be to look to foreign markets to offset decreased domestic sales. Exports already accounted for some 26 billion cigarettes in 1968—an enterprise ironically supported by subsidies from the same federal government that restricted the industry at home. However, the bigger opportunities came through establishing plants overseas, arranging for foreign licensing agreements, and obtaining foreign affiliates and subsidiaries. Philip Morris already had plants in India, New Zealand, and Venezuela. Lorillard was established in Puerto Rico and was making progress in Luxembourg, Hong Kong, and South Africa.[28]

During the April hearings, the National Association of Broadcasters— composed of the 3 television networks, 400 independent television stations, and 6,272 radio stations—became apprehensive as federal action seemed near.[29] They thought about applying their airwave code (which bans liquor ads) to cigarettes, but did not want to eliminate cigarette ads altogether. One code revision would have banned physical smoking in

---

[25] "Bad News Can Mean Good Growth," *Forbes,* November 15, 1969, pp. 50–51; see also "Caution: This Meaning Is Hazardous," *Newsweek,* April 28,.1969, pp. 82–86; "Cigarettes and Society: A Growing Dilemma," *Time,* April 25, 1969.

[26] "No Smoking on the Air," *Business Week,* February 8, 1969, p. 36.

[27] "Showdown in Cigarette Advertising," *The New York Times,* Sec. 6, May 4, 1969, pp. 36ff.

[28] "Cigarettes and Society: A Growing Dilemma," *Time,* April 25, 1969.

[29] "Tobacco: Trouble from an Old Friend," *Time,* July 18, 1969.

ads, would have prohibited ads in or adjacent to children's programs, and would have eliminated all cigarette advertising between 4 and 9 p.m. with the exception of that in newscasts. On June 10, the day before the House was scheduled to vote on HR 6543, Warren H. Braren, a former employee of the NAB's television and radio code authority office in New York, charged that the broadcasting industry's self-regulation had become "nothing more than an industry defense mechanism designed to cover up selfish interests."[30]

On July 8, 1969, the Television Code Review Board of the NAB recommended that all cigarette advertising be eliminated from television by September 1, 1973. The NAB's Radio Code Board followed suit.[31] The broadcasting industry thus anticipated that the FCC would fix an arbitrary date for the cessation of advertising. On July 11, the FTC voted to recommend that Congress ban all cigarette advertising on radio and television. The FTC had called for strong health warnings in all smoking ads on radio and television, but the report to Congress was the first time it had agreed with the FCC that the ads should be banned. As it had previously, the commission also recommended that the stronger health warning be used.[32] The continued warnings pressured both the tobacco and the broadcasting industries into action, but the NAB's plan became virtually meaningless when, on July 22, 1969, the cigarette makers agreed to stop advertising on radio and television by September 1970 if granted immunity from the antitrust laws.[33] They also agreed to halt advertising any time after December 31, 1969, if broadcasters would cancel the current advertising contracts. In return for its concession, the tobacco industry received assurances that the government would delay for two years the requirement for a stricter warning on cigarette packages, and the FTC assured industry that if its broadcast advertising ended, the agency would suspend until July 1971 a plan to seek health warnings in other ads. The move by the industry seemed to reinforce the viewpoint that it would not really be hurt by a ban on broadcasting advertising.

On August 9, ABC rejected a proposal to let cigarette makers out of their contracts for cigarette commercials at the end of the year. ABC President Leonard H. Goldenson contended that it discriminated against broadcasting to ban smoking commercials while cigarette advertising continued in the print media. Following one of the earlier arguments of the tobacco industry, Goldenson stated: "If Congress is convinced that cigarette smoking represents a clear and present danger to the health of the American

---

[30] "Go Ahead for Bill Giving Cigarette Ads a Free Hand," *San Francisco Chronicle,* June 11, 1969.

[31] "New Move on TV Ads for Cigarettes," *San Francisco Chronicle,* July 9, 1969, p. 1; "Cigarette Ad Ban on Radio Urged," *San Francisco Chronicle,* July 10, 1969, p. 2.

[32] "Radio-TV Cigarette Ad Ban Proposed by FTC," *Los Angeles Times,* July 12, 1969.

[33] "Cigarette Makers Agree to Ban TV Ads in '70," *Los Angeles Times,* July 23, 1969.

public, then the only direct approach to the problem is to declare cigarettes an illegal product and to bar their advertising and sale in interstate commerce."[34]

THE ADVERTISING BAN COMES INTO EFFECT

After the broadcasting industry's offer to phase out cigarette advertising and the cigarette manufacturers' subsequent decision to voluntarily go off the air, the legislating of cigarette advertising lost its controversial nature. In March 1970, a House-Senate conference committee agreed to a cigarette bill which was signed by the president (who had not taken sides in the earlier controversy) and which became law on April 1.

The law banned cigarette advertising on radio and television on or after January 2, 1971 (instead of January 1) to allow the cigarette companies to take advantage of New Year's Day football game broadcasts.[35] Effective November 1, 1970, cigarette packages also carried the message, "Warning: The Surgeon General Has Determined that Cigarette Smoking Is Dangerous to Your Health."[36] In addition, the law gave the FTC authority to require, after July 1971, this or other health warnings in all cigarette advertisements after giving Congress six months' notice of its intentions.

In February 1970, Dr. E. Cuyler Hammond, vice-president in charge of epidemiology and statistical research for the American Cancer Society, and Dr. Oscar Auerbach, pathologist of the Veterans Administration Hospital, East Orange, New Jersey, and New York Medical College, reported to the American Cancer Society the results of their experiments on dogs taught to inhale cigarette smoke. The study found that healthy beagles inhaling unfiltered cigarette smoke twice a day for two and a half years developed lung cancer. Healthy beagles inhaling filtered cigarette smoke over the same period developed tumors in their lungs but no cancer. Beagles exposed to no cigarette smoke at all had no cancer and a lower death rate. The society pointed out that the experiment was the first in which lung cancer had been produced in a laboratory animal that inhaled smoke as people do, and that the study "effectively refutes" the contention that smoking and lung cancer are not linked. The society cautioned that filter cigarettes are not safe, and "at best only less damaging to lung tissue" than unfiltered cigarettes.[37] A spokesperson for the Tobacco Institute challenged the results of the study, contending that no parallel could be drawn "between human smoking and dogs subjected to these most stressful labora-

---

[34] "A Setback for Smoke Ad Ban," *San Francisco Chronicle*, August 9, 1969.

[35] "House, Senate Conferees Agree to Abolish Broadcast Cigaret Ads; as of Jan. 2, 1971," *The Wall Street Journal*, March 4, 1970, p. 4.

[36] "FTC Wants Tar, Nicotine Levels Disclosed in Cigaret Ads; Makers Doubt Authority," *The Wall Street Journal*, August 10, 1970, p. 9.

[37] "Smoking Dogs Show Cancer Link," *The Wall Street Journal*, February 6, 1970, p. 1.

tory conditions."[38] Indeed, in May 1970 the institute announced it would launch a major attack on the validity of the experiments.

EPILOGUE

Even the staunchest supporters of the antismoking campaign would concede that all the warnings on labels and advertising bans have had little effect on cigarette smoking (Table 2–2). Similarly, advertising expenditures, which registered a sharp decline in 1971 after the ban in the broadcast media, have started moving up (Table 2–3). A more disturbing trend has been the increase in smoking among young girls. For example, between 1970 and 1974, the percentage of young smokers showed a small increase, while that of young men actually decreased. However, the percentage of young girls smoking has sharply increased (Table 2–4).

The antismoking forces claim that all the publicity about smoking-related health hazards has resulted in more people smoking filter cigarettes. An estimated 10 million Americans, mostly men, have quit smoking. However, the population growth and a steady influx of new smokers had increased the ranks of smokers to 52 million at the end of 1973, from 50 million in 1964. Public health officials claimed that but for the adverse publicity, the number of smokers would have increased to 75 million.[39]

TABLE 2–2
OUTPUT AND CONSUMPTION OF
CIGARETTES IN THE UNITED STATES

Year	Output (billions)	Consumption (billions)	Consumption—18 years and over per capita
1962	535.5	508.4	—
1963	550.6	523.9	—
1964	539.9	511.2	—
1965	556.8	528.7	4,258
1966	567.3	541.2	4,287
1967	576.2	549.2	4,280
1968	579.5	545.7	4,186
1969	557.6	528.9	3,993
1970	583.2	536.4	3,985
1971	576.4	550.0	4,037
1972	599.1	566.8	4,043
1973	644.2	589.7	4,147
1974*	635.0	600.0	4,150

* Estimates, subject to revision.
Source: Compiled from *Tobacco Situation*, Economic Research Service, U.S. Department of Agriculture, Washington, D.C., March 1975.

[38] Ibid.

[39] "Decade of Warnings Fails to Cut Cigarette Smoking," *The New York Times*, January 11, 1974, p. 8.

TABLE 2–3
CIGARETTE ADVERTISING EXPENDITURES
($ millions)

Year	TV	Newspapers, magazines	Radio	Direct	Other	Total
1963	151.7	45.6	31.6	13.2	7.4	249.5
1964	170.2	45.2	25.5	14.6	5.8	261.3
1965	175.6	41.9	24.8	14.7	6.0	263.0
1966	198.0	43.4	31.3	17.9	6.9	297.5
1967	226.9	41.2	17.5	20.3	6.0	311.9
1968	217.2	44.6	21.3	21.6	6.0	310.7
1969	221.3	48.7	13.6	13.4	8.9	305.9
1970	205.0	64.2	12.4	16.9	16.2	314.7
1971	2.2	157.6	—	27.0	64.8	251.6
1972	—	159.2	—	22.9	75.5	257.6
1973	—	157.7	—	15.2	74.6	247.5
1974	—	—	—	—	—	252.6*

* Estimate.
Source: (1) *Statistical Supplement to Federal Trade Commission Report to Congress,* pursuant to the Public Health Smoking Act, dated December 31, 1973; (2) 1974 figures provided by *The Tobacco Institute Inc.,* Washington, D.C.

TABLE 2–4
TEENAGE SMOKERS

Sex	Age	Percent of applicable population
1970		
Boys	12–18	18.5
Girls	12–18	11.9
Total		30.4
1972		
Boys	12–18	15.7
Girls	12–18	13.3
Total		29.0
1974		
Boys	12–18	15.8
Girls	12–18	15.3
Total		31.1

Source: U.S. Congress, *Department of Labor and Health, Education, and Welfare Appropriations for 1976, Hearings before a Subcommittee of the Committee on Appropriations,* 94th Congress, 1st sess., part 3, 1975, p. 144.

And how are the various groups reacting to this state of affairs?

It appears that government agencies are not deterred by the failure of their earlier strategies to curb smoking and are proposing more of the same in terms of stiffer warnings and further curbs on promotion and sale of cigarettes. Thus, the Federal Trade Commission is proposing that present health warnings should be changed to read: "Warning: Cigarette Smoking

Is Dangerous to Health and May Cause Death from Cancer, Coronary Heart Disease, Chronic Bronchitis, Pulmonary Emphysema and Other Diseases."

There are also indications that efforts will be made in Congress to limit the tar and nicotine content of cigarettes.

The antismoking groups have been pressuring the Consumer Product Safety Commission to regulate the manufacture and sale of cigarettes on grounds of health and safety hazards.

The tobacco industry, bolstered by the reversal of declining trends in cigarette smoking, seems to have abandoned its defensive posture. The major tobacco companies have been directing their sales efforts away from low tar and nicotine cigarettes toward intensive promotion of "full flavor" and longer 120 mm cigarettes. For the first time, in 1975 advertising expenditures also seem to be rising. In all, twenty-seven new brands and brand extensions were introduced during 1974, and 1975 is also expected to be a banner year. Most of the new brands have been "full flavor," the industry euphemism for high tar and nicotine cigarettes.[40]

SELECTED BIBLIOGRAPHY

Annual Reports. American Brands, Inc. (1971–74), Liggett and Meyers Tobacco Company (1974), Philip Morris, Inc. (1974), R. J. Reynolds Tobacco Company (1971–74).

"Cigarette Advertising: Deceptive and Against the Public Interest." *Kansas Law Review* 17 (1969): 690.

Hamilton, James L. "The Demand for Cigarettes: Advertising, the Health Scare, and the Cigarette Advertising Ban." *Review of Economics and Statistics,* November 1972.

Little, Clarence Cook. *How Much Is Known About Smoking and Health?* New York Council for Tobacco Research, February 3, 1969.

Securities and Exchange Commission, Form 10-K. Philip Morris, Inc. (December 31, 1973, 1974), R. J. Reynolds Tobacco Company (December 31, 1974).

Tobin, Richard. "Cigarette Advertising and Federal Law." *Saturday Review,* March 13, 1971.

U.S. Department of Agriculture, Economic Research Service. Washington, D.C.: U.S. Government Printing Office, March 1975.

U.S. Department of Health, Education, and Welfare. *Patterns and Prevalence of Teen-age Cigarette Smoking: 1968, 1970, 1972, 1974.* Bethesda, Md.: Center for Disease Control, National Clearinghouse for Smoking and Health, Program Research Division, July 1974.

Wagner, Susan. *Cigarette Country.* New York: Praeger, 1972.

Whiteside, Thomas. "Selling Death: Cigarette Advertising in Magazines." *The New Republic,* March 27, 1971.

---

[40] "A Long Strong Pitch for Cigarettes," *Business Week,* April 14, 1975; "A Deluge of New Cigarettes," *Business Week,* November 23, 1974, pp. 114–16.

Omnivest Corporation*

3 Deceptive practices in the selling of real estate

> White collar crime is the most corrosive of all crimes. The trusted
> prove untrustworthy, the advantaged, disadvantaged. It shows the ca-
> pability of people with better opportunities for creating a decent life
> for themselves to take property belonging to others. As no other crime
> it questions our moral fiber.
>
> Ramsey Clark, former U.S. Attorney General

On December 16, 1975, a permanent court order prohibiting future
violations of numerous California laws dealing with deceptive practices
and misrepresentations in the subdivision and sale of land was entered by
agreement against 'Omnivest, a Los Angeles-based land sales company,
and its principal officers. It was based on these assertions by the company:

1. Omnivest and its related corporate entities comprised a multimillion
    dollar organization, and its officers had an excellent reputation for in-
    tegrity; Robert Calhoun has a record of success for over 25 years in all
    phases of real estate development and sales.
2. The company was seeking employees to be trained as real estate sales-
    persons, and they could earn specified amounts of money within a
    limited period of time after beginning employment with Omnivest;
    it was possible to become a millionaire working for Omnivest, even
    on a part-time basis.
3. The company would provide a complete training program, at no ex-
    pense to the new employee, preparatory to the employee's obtaining
    a real estate license.
4. The company would provide salespersons with thousands of qualified
    leads or prospects developed through major real estate advertising
    campaigns.

---

*The author is grateful to Mr. Randall P. Borcherding, Deputy Attorney General, State
of California, for his assistance in furnishing information on the legal proceedings in which
the Attorney General acted as counsel. The author is, however, solely responsible for the
content of this case.

5. The salespersons employed by the company could work close to home, with no requirement for travel; the company would provide an "immediate prestige car plan" and offered free Cadillacs, Lincolns, Mercedes, and Rolls Royces to its salespersons. The salespersons could also receive free trips including but not limited to a four-day vacation for two as well as a free trip to Hawaii for two.
6. Antelope Valley northeast of Los Angeles was a prime development area, with specific plans for the location of the world's largest airport, a rapid transit system, an ample water supply, and substantial population growth. Investment in Omnivest's land development program in this area should make an investor three to five times his or her investment in only five to eight years time.

Among the acts and practices enjoined in the permanent injunction were Omnivest's use of the following:

1. The company's use of such titles as "land investment consultant" for its salespersons to create an erroneous impression, in the mind of potential buyers, that such salespersons had a certain degree of expertise or qualification in the area of land development and sales.
2. The company's use of promotional material containing misleading and untrue statements as to the nature of the investments or real property being sold.
3. Deeds of trust offered to secure promissory notes of the company and sold by the company showing a certain stated value substantially more than the actual value of the land covered by the trust deed.[1]

In 1974 Omnivest went into Chapter XI bankruptcy proceedings, perhaps as a defensive move to lessen the effect of the state's civil action against the firm. While in bankruptcy, the company offered to rescind certain land sale agreements entered into with customers between 1970 and 1974. As part of the permanent injunction and final judgment, Omnivest was ordered to comply with the terms of this offer and to attempt to repay certain amounts, paid in by customers eligible for restitution and claiming it, out of future postbankruptcy earnings.[2] There appears, however, little prospect of any of Omnivest's investors receiving refunds; under the court-appointed bankruptcy receiver, the firm lost $760,000 on operations from July 1974 to February 1975, and any refunds to be paid out to former land purchase investors will more than likely be at a substantial discount, stretched out over many years to come.[3]

[1] *The People of the State of California v. Omnivest, et al.* Permanent Injunction and Final Judgment, pp. 10–14, Docket #C 90080, Filed December 16, 1975.
[2] Ibid., pp. 15–16.
[3] "Rescission Offer," correspondence of Omnivest to all of its investors, March 14, 1975. (Included in exhibits to *People v. Omnivest,* above.) This opinion is based on the author's own review and analysis of the facts of the case.

Sources familiar with the California land sales industry have commented that the lure of "easy money," that is, potentially large profits in a relatively short period of time, have been a powerful incentive to a number of firms in the past—not only the less well known operators like Omnivest, but also such respected corporations as Boise Cascade, Transamerica, and Dart Industries. In many cases, firms engaged in this industry and some of their sales personnel have chosen to ignore the letter of the law in their haste to turn a quick profit.

Cases such as Omnivest are not, of course, confined only to California. Since the 1960s there has been a proliferation of governmental legal action against "ripoff" land sale schemes that utilize deception or fraudulent practices and misrepresentations in the sale of relatively cheap land at many times its value. In March of 1975, the FTC filed complaints against two major land development and sales firms, AMREP and Horizon Corporation.[4] The former, once known as American Real Estate and Petroleum Corporation, was accused of "unfair and deceptive practices" in selling land at its subdivisions in Arizona, New Mexico, and Florida. Horizon Corporation was charged with similar activities at its huge Rio Rancho development in New Mexico. Among the charges made by the FTC in the combined 80 pages of complaint against the two firms was that the green grass shown in advertisements was actually paint, pine cones on trees were attached by wire, and Merv Griffin, the well-known television personality, did not really own the lot he was touting in a company brochure.

In comparison to these two giant firms (AMREP alone had sold lots to over 215,000 people), Omnivest was a minnow, selling to perhaps 5,000 customers since its founding in the 1960s. Yet a striking point to note in comparison is the similarity of marketing techniques adopted by all such firms: Whether large or small, whether selling land in California, Florida, or New York, no matter if the customer was a GI stationed in Germany or a working couple living in the Los Angeles suburbs, the product pitch remained fairly standard. The following practices were typical throughout the industry:

1.   Solicitation of potential customers at vacation and resort locales in both the United States and abroad. The customer, invited to a free meal with champagne and all the trimmings, was then given a full-blown pre-

---

[4] U.S. Federal Trade Commission, Complaint in the Matter of AMREP Corporation (Docket #9018); U.S. FTC, Complaint in the Matter of Horizon Corporation (Docket #9017); also see FTC News Release, "FTC Complaint Alleges Deceptive Practices by Land Sales Firm," March 17, 1975 (Washington, D.C.: Federal Trade Commission).

For further research into cases of fraud and deception in the sale of land and other forms of real estate, see the following: Leonard Downie, *Mortgage on America* (New York: Praeger, 1974); Robert C. Fellmeth (project director), *Politics of Land: The Nader Study Group Analysis of Land and Power in California* (New York: Grossman, 1973); Lynn Ludlow, "A Valley Where Only Money Blooms," *San Francisco Sunday Examiner and Chronicle*, March 23, 1974, p. A3; Albert Winnikoff, *Land Game* (New York: Lyle Stuart, 1970); Anthony Wolff, *Unreal Estate* (San Francisco: Sierra Club, 1973).

sentation of the land sales project, complete with a short film, glossy pictures, multicolored charts and graphs, and numerous glowing projections of future growth and rising land values. Potential buyers were invariably seated in small groups with a sales representative, often referred to as a "land consultant," and sprinkled among the tables were several shills. Following the formal presentation, the consultant would discuss project details with the customers, pointing out specific parcels that were available. The shills would be jumping up and shouting "I'll take parcel #535," or some such thing. These high-pressure tactics were designed to convince the customer to sign a sales contract right then and there, site unseen.[5]

2. The use of high-ranking political or public officials, either still in office or recently retired, as well as celebrities who were touted as investors in or "believers in" the project. Cooperating politicians often found a tidy sum contributed to their campaign by the land sales company.[6]

3. The use of numerous charts, graphs, maps, pictures, newspaper and magazine excerpts, and other props designed to convince the customer that this was a scientifically sound investment project, and that financial security was bound to be his or hers with the inevitable growth that the charts, and so on, supported; all he or she had to do was hold on for a few short years and then sell to the highest bidder among the many who would be eagerly vying for the property once its value multiplied.

4. The use of low down payments (usually well under 10 percent of the sale price) and easy monthly payments (around $25 to $75) so that a large percentage of the populace would be able to participate in the project and thus "own their own lot."

5. A high-pressure sales program that put a premium on "buying now," and that usually featured sales personnel trained to apply psychologically intimidating measures to customers to induce them to "get with" the smart investors, not to be a "sucker" like the masses who had no financial security, and to "show their intelligence" by purchasing a lot, right now, today, here, before the opportunity had passed.

6. In many cases, strong pressure on the salespeople themselves (recruited through newspaper advertisements promising gloriously successful careers) to purchase a lot, thus proving their "good faith" in the project and helping them to convince other customers of their sincerity. In fact, in some projects, such as California City in the desert north of Los Angeles, nearly 75 percent of the lots were sold to sales representatives who were continually being recruited throughout the state.[7]

---

[5] Leonard Downie, "The Great Land Rush," *Mortgage on America* (New York: Praeger, 1974), pp. 135–52.

[6] "FTC's Picture of 'Painted Desert,' " *San Francisco Chronicle*, March 15, 1975, p. 20.

[7] Wolff, *Unreal Estate*, p. 47.

ISSUES FOR ANALYSIS

The issues for analysis in this case are as follows:

1.   What are the objectives and characteristics of Omnivest's sales train-
     ing program? Given the nature of the program and its goals, what can
     one expect in terms of consumer service and accurate representation
     of facts?
2.   How do Omnivest's practices differ from the practices of industry
     leaders or a significant number of companies in the industry?
3.   Land sales companies employ twin marketing strategies of mass pro-
     motion and direct personal selling. In this sense, they are somewhat
     akin to the sellers of other high-ticket items, such as cars, boats, and
     the sellers of franchises. How are marketing techniques, including di-
     rect selling practices, different in these industries? In particular, *(a)* Is
     there anything in the nature of the product sold, or types of marketing
     strategies employed, that makes potential customers especially vul-
     nerable to deception and misrepresentation by the seller? In other
     words, how effective is the market mechanism in protecting consum-
     ers from fraud? *(b)* Are there any characteristics related to industry
     structure (concentration, size of leading firms in the industry, ease of
     entry) that lend themselves to the adoption of certain sales practices?
     If so, to what effect?
4.   How are industry practices currently regulated? Is the regulation ef-
     fective? What are some of the legal and other remedies currently avail-
     able to protect the unwary buyer? To what extent should the buyer be
     expected to assume the responsibility for his or her actions and bear
     the costs for his or her mistakes?

OMNIVEST AND THE INDUSTRY

Omnivest

The Omnivest Corporation in Beverly Hills, California, in business under
that name since 1972, sold approximately 5,000 lots at its projects in the
Mojave Desert that surrounds the northern and eastern expanses of the
Los Angeles basin. Its owner and principal operator, Robert M. Calhoun,
had gained his experience in the undeveloped speculative land sales business through the acquisition, subdivision, and sale of land in the Salton
Sea area in the desert east of San Diego in the 1960s. Mr. Calhoun thus
developed and refined his business practices in a period when the industry
was growing rapidly and attracting substantial new capital.

The rural and recreational land sales industry

The sale of rural or recreational land in the Sunbelt states has shown
phenomenal growth in the last decade. In 1970 there were more than

3,500 recreation land developers registered with the federal Department of Housing and Urban Development (HUD). In that year alone, they collectively sold 650,000 lots for a total sales price of $5.5 billion. The American Land Development Association, a Washington, D.C.-based trade and lobby group for the industry, counted over 9,000 members on its rolls.[8]

By the 1970s the industry had attracted large, nationally known, and well-financed firms. Companies such as ITT, Westinghouse, Boise Cascade, and Ralston Purina were systematically buying huge chunks of rural real estate, subdividing it into smaller parcels of anywhere from a quarter to five or more acres, and then peddling them to the public as "second home" sites suitable for vacations, retirement, or—as in most cases, even if implied rather than guaranteed—high return "investment" potential. Forbes Corporation, the owner of the conservative financial magazine *Forbes*, was selling five-acre "ranches" on its 168,000 acre property in Colorado; Boise Cascade had 29 different projects going at once throughout the country.[9]

Many small firms in the industry somehow managed to tie up huge tracts of land on highly leveraged terms. Horizon Corporation was developing 25,000 acres of "retirement" sites in the Adirondacks in New York state in the late 1960s; GAC (formerly General Acceptance Corporation) alone held 300,000 acres for development in the Cape Coral area of Florida; AMREP had a 100,000-acre operation under way near Alburquerque in New Mexico, and others in Missouri and Florida.[10] Land purchased at $100 per acre, as GAC did in Florida, was sold at the rate of $3,000 to $5,000 an acre following subdivision.[11] Only rarely did any of the developers invest heavily in expensive front-end costs such as site preparation or recreational amenities to improve the land. Moreover, generally accepted accounting principles allowed these firms to declare as revenue the full sales price of the parcels sold in the year they were sold, even though the cash flow from the sales was usually only a small fraction of the total price. This proved particularly attractive to the large publicly traded firms who were under constant pressure to produce income.[12]

Yet although their financial methods were often modern, in more cases

---

[8] Downie, *Mortgage on America*, p. 137.

[9] Wolff, *Unreal Estate*, p. 10.

[10] Ibid., chap. 1, and Downie, *Mortgage on America*, chap. 6.

[11] Downie, p. 143.

[12] The AMREP Corporation offers an interesting example of this practice. Their fiscal year 1971 Annual Report listed income from "homesite sales" at $44.8 million; yet cash flow from these sales included only the down payment, averaging 11 percent, or less than $5 million. Another lucrative source of income is the "finance charge," averaging 7.5 percent, which AMREP adds to the lot purchaser's monthly installment payment. Since the 11 percent down payment usually covers the seller's investment in the land, the "finance charge" is pure "gravy" to the seller: he collects this although nothing really has been financed. In 1971 AMREP showed "interest income on homesite sales contracts" of $4.8 million (*1971 Annual Report*, AMREP Corporation).

than not these large firms adopted the marketing techniques of the fly-by-night operators who had characterized the rural land sales industry in the past. The key to these promotions was a charismatic individual personality who could "con" the potential buyer with his or her sincerity and honesty —a throwback to the "medicine show" salesmen of the traveling vaudeville and circus performances. Respected firms that entered the land sales business in search of legitimate (albeit high) profits found themselves hiring these somewhat "shady" individuals to run their programs, since they were the only ones around with any experience. The result was a respectable company name sometimes unwittingly fronting for highly questionable business transactions. These old-hand operators were not the only ones doing business under the guise of a respectable publicly traded firm: Investigation by law enforcement agencies, as well as several local newspapers, revealed the possible presence of organized crime involvement in several land sales projects, especially in Arizona.[13]

The primary attraction for the larger new entries into the industry was the mass-market potential created by the increasing urbanization of the nation, a growth in consumer disposable income combined with more leisure time, and the inherent desire for land ownership. The land sales firms had indeed a very potent product to push. Yet what the large operators brought to bear, and what separates them from the smaller competitors of the past, was the introduction of mass-marketing techniques.

By the 1960s, a large percentage of the population had both a home and an income sufficient to allow for more than basic shelter. What was necessary to convert the public's age-old desire for land into mass demand— capable of generating mass profits—was the availability of relatively cheap sites and easy financial terms. Cheap land, however, was valued that way for a very sound reason: its economic potential was such that it could not command a higher price in the marketplace. Yet this proved to be the foundation of the new rural land sales industry. It would create a value where there was none by convincing the buyer that the future potential of the site was unlimited. Here was a challenge to modern mass marketing which the new giants of the industry understood, and they went at the task with a vigor unmatched in the past.

And, indeed, it did seem a highly effective strategy. The results were spectacular, and they produced a real growth industry. In California, for example, the number of rural land project lots sold in 1960–61 was 3,239; by 1970–71 the volume had grown to 37,865. This general trend was experienced in nearly all the major land sales areas. The only trouble was that various public agencies were soon forced to take action against these

---

[13] There were hints of such involvement in the August 1976 homicide case of investigative reporter Don Bolles of the *Arizona Republic* (Phoenix, Arizona); Bolles was investigating the involvement of organized crime in the state's multimillion-dollar land fraud scandals at the time of his murder. (See David Gelman, "Mightier Than the Sword," *Newsweek*, September 20, 1976, p. 84.)

companies. In nearly every case, the legal point of contention involved the marketing techniques used by the firm and its sales staff.

Marketing practices: Omnivest

The key to Mr. Calhoun's operations at Omnivest was the development of a high-pressure sales force, trained in all the accumulated wisdom he had acquired in the past, and which itself advertised the success of his methods. (Each sales representative was expected to purchase a lot in the project, and usually did.) The "bible" of Mr. Calhoun's techniques was the *Consultant's Manual,* which new salespeople were expected to memorize in large part. It detailed the specific ways of finding the customer, setting him or her up, and closing the deal.

A condensed version of this manual is reproduced below (the original runs to nearly 200 pages). The reader can draw his or her own conclusions regarding the nature of the personal selling program undertaken by Omnivest.

THE CONSULTANT'S MANUAL

Training & Operations Manual for the Licensed

Omnivest

Land Investment Consultant

Contents

This manual has been condensed from the original for the purposes of this case; no new material has been added, nor has the sequence of presentation been altered.

I. THE OPPORTUNITY

A. INTRODUCTION: A WORD ABOUT YOU . . . AND OMNIVEST

When searching out a company for a meaningful and profitable career, what are the vibrant, dynamic qualities you seek? They are many. SUCCESS, PERSONAL RECOGNITION, PLEASANT WORKING CONDITIONS, CAPABLE PROVEN MANAGEMENT, A LEADER IN THE INDUSTRY . . . plus an opportunity for personal and financial growth.

As you read the OMNIVEST SALES MANUAL you'll find these things are possible—and that success is a progressive realization toward predetermined goals.

B. THE OMNIVEST LAND INVESTMENT CONSULTANT

The OMNIVEST Land Investment Consultant enjoys a unique position within the field of real estate investment. Being in the business of selling an investment program that is based on predeveloped acreage situated squarely in the path of progress, the OMNIVEST Land Investment Consultant knows his clients will reap maximum benefits over a short period of years.

Besides selling an excellent product and providing a valuable service, the OMNIVEST Land Investment Consultant is representing principals who, for over a quarter of a century, have maintained an enviable reputation for both integrity and business acumen.

Moreover, the "MAN FROM OMNIVEST" can earn an income and enjoy a standard of living as high as any in the profession. They dress fashionably and drive the best automobiles and, just like their clients, they are assuring their own future security by astutely investing in land as they continue to prosper and grow.

No one ever accomplishes anything of consequence without a goal. We should also keep in mind that a man's ATTITUDE, not his aptitude, is the chief determinant of his success. With these thoughts in mind, let's establish simple compensation goals for your first year's sales with OMNIVEST.

FIRST YEAR INDIVIDUAL SALES GOAL BASED
ON ONE SALE PER WEEK
(average $10,000 for 50 weeks)

12% compensation on first 3 sales	$ 3,600
17% compensation on next 2 sales	3,400
20% compensation based on next 45 sales	90,000
Your Goal for First Year	$97,000*

* All earnings are based on the total of salesman's commissions.

C. CONSULTANT BENEFIT PROGRAMS

Always innovating and advancing, OMNIVEST takes pride and pleasure in making available to its Consultants an impressive array of valuable bonuses and benefits. . . .

We feel sure that as you read through the next several pages you will appreciate the privileged career position you have stepped into, and will be glad that you joined forces with OMNIVEST. We are!

1. Circle of influence program

To get a fast start at earning maximum income, take full advantage of the Circle of Influence Program.

This program provides a basic, proven procedure for contacting your personal friends and offering them a splendid opportunity . . . as well as your participating in excellent commissions for your services.

You supply your Director of Marketing with a completed Circle of Influence form. The company supplies you with: Introductory letters, Secretarial help, Postage, Surveys, Brochures, Photographs, Plus a host of other exciting, dynamic aids.

*   *   *   *   *

3. Tour compensation program

In view of the fact that, as an independent contractor, you normally would have to absorb your own operating expenses, here is a bonus benefit that we are especially proud to extend to you.

After you have toured a client and a sale is consummated, you will be eligible to receive a check from OMNIVEST to compensate you for tour expenses you incurred, in accordance with the following schedule:

Your Tour Compensation Will Be	If Your Investor's Down Payment Is At Least
$50	10%
25	5%

After the sale is closed, allow a few days for your investor's down payment check to clear the bank.

4. Prestige car program

DRIVE A CADILLAC, LINCOLN OR MERCEDES-BENZ!

An important aspect of your Land Investment Consultant image is a prestige automobile. Successful Consultants find that a current model prestige car enhances sales appeal and improves their effectiveness. OM-NIVEST provides every Consultant the opportunity to drive the most prestigious automobile available.

OMNIVEST will pay up to $200 per month toward the cost of your prestige car, as follows:

INITIAL PAYMENT (Company-approved leasing agency only): Upon taking delivery of your prestige car submit a copy of your lease contract* as proof of delivery.

The Company will then give you a check for up to $200 to apply toward your initial cost. The actual amount will be equivalent to one month's regular payment on your lease, subject to the $200 maximum.

SECOND PAYMENT: Contingent upon completion of *two* standard sales during your first month with the Company as a licensee.

SUBSEQUENT PAYMENTS: Contingent upon completion of *three* standard sales during any subsequent fiscal month.

CONTACT YOUR DM TODAY, AND TOMORROW YOU MAY BE DRIVING A CADILLAC, A LINCOLN CONTINENTAL OR A MERCEDES-BENZ, WHICHEVER YOU CHOOSE!

5. Special $1,000–$2,000 draw programs

. . . Upon completion of two standard sales† during your *first month* with the Company as a licensee, submit a $1,000 Draw Request form. You will receive a check for $1,000.

Upon completion of *three* standard sales during any subsequent fiscal month, you are eligible for a $1,000 draw subject to any debits to your account from the previous month's draw.

Upon attainment of at least $50,000 in cumulative volume and completion of *five* standard sales during any subsequent month with the Company as a licensee, you are eligible for a $2,000 draw subject to any debits to your account from the previous month's draw.

6. $600 a month salary plan

Financial security is assured to the successful Land Investment Consultant. OMNIVEST provides a guaranteed salary of $600 per month to its qualified licensed consultants. This is over and above your regular commissions and bonuses.

---

* The liability for any lease entered into under this program rests solely with the Consultant. OMNIVEST accepts no responsibility for making or guaranteeing payments to the lessor.

† The liability for any lease entered into under this program rests solely with the Consultant. OMNIVEST accepts no responsibility for making or guaranteeing payments to the lessor.

You will become eligible for this salary when you have been continuously licensed to OMNIVEST as a real estate salesman for a period of ninety days.

7. Help-a-friend program

IT'S AS EASY AS A–B–C! TO MAKE $750–$1,500–$3,000 OR MUCH MORE . . . HERE IS ALL YOU DO.

A.   Contact each one of your friends in person and invite him or her to investigate the outstanding "Passport To Prosperity" career positions available at OMNIVEST to both men and women, full-time or part-time, as professional LAND INVESTMENT CONSULTANTS. Stress to your friends that they need not give up their present jobs, and mention that there are no educational or experience requirements, as OMNIVEST will provide all the necessary training *tuition-free.*

B.   When you talk to each friend, tell him that you will use your influence to secure an appointment for him to be interviewed and then, *while in his presence,* you call us and set the appointment. Ask for your Director of Marketing by name. When your DM answers, say that you have a friend you'd like him to meet and possibly consider for one of our staff Consultant positions. Then ask him to please adjust his schedule to arrange a time to see you and your friend.

C.   Accompany your friend to the office at the appointed time—both of you dressed in proper business attire—and let your DM do the rest!

For your part in bringing OMNIVEST and the people you know together, here is how you will be compensated:

1.   FOR EACH OF YOUR FRIENDS WHO WE HIRE, YOU WILL RECEIVE $50 IN CASH!*

2.   UPON HIS FIRST SALE YOU WILL RECEIVE AN ADDITIONAL $100 IN CASH!

3.   UPON HIS SECOND AND ANY SUBSEQUENT SALE YOU WILL RECEIVE AN ADDITIONAL $50 IN CASH!

Now pause for a moment and think seriously about what OMNIVEST is offering you. Let us assume OMNIVEST hired three of your friends and each makes a total of only one sale per week totalling twelve sales a month. This means $600 per month for you. This is in addition to the initial bonus of $50 for each friend we hire and the $100 bonus for his first sale. Just think, three of your friends working for OMNIVEST may mean to you $7,650 *or more* per year!!!

---

* The $50 bonus is payable when your friend has paid, IN FULL, the $10 State exam fee (if he is unlicensed), the $25 Real Estate School materials fee (if he is unlicensed), and the refundable $100 good-faith training deposit, and has completed the one-week Orientation course.

Start contacting your friends *today*. YES, TODAY! Procrastination will not get it done. The money is waiting for you.

8. Consultant equity allowance program

Should you become an OMNIVEST investor yourself, the equity allowance program for Consultants affords you an excellent opportunity to have a substantial share of your property *paid for by the Company* while allowing you to retain full rights to all the profit arising from its eventual resale.

Ownership of investment acreage will also enhance your image in the eyes of your potential client. His logical question is going to be, "if this investment program you're selling is so good, why aren't you in it?" to which the ideal answer is, "Ah, but I *am* in it . . . tell you what . . . I'll show you *my* land when I show you *yours*, how's that?"

For each and every standard sale you make, your own principal balance will be reduced by $100! That means that 100 sales—or two years of diligent, conscientious work—will not only bring you $200,000 in commissions, but will *completely retire* your balance on a $10,000 parcel.

II. THE PREPARATION

A. THE OMNIVEST TRAINING PROGRAM FOR LAND INVESTMENT CONSULTANTS

The OMNIVEST Land Investment Consultant training program—your "Passport to Prosperity"—is the culmination of countless of thousands of hours of dedicated effort by men who are today the giants of the land investment industry.

1. Practice tours of the Antelope Valley

Developing mastery of the touring process is an absolutely indispensable requirement if you're out to achieve great success in our business. You may find an occasional competitor who attempts to short-cut the touring aspect of the land sales business by "mapping" his prospects, but you will also find that his closing ratio is far lower than the consultant who fully understands and utilizes all the benefits that the tour provides. Accordingly, all OMNIVEST Consultant-Trainees are required to participate in a series of practice tours of the Antelope Valley.

Each Consultant is further required to make as many additional "dry runs" of the Antelope Valley as is necessary in order for him or her to develop competence at touring. . . .

Plan your post-Orientation daily schedule wisely. Arrange time for at least *four* practice tours. You'll be glad you did when the commission checks are delivered!

. . . . .

3. Real estate licensing procedure

OMNIVEST is in the land sales business and is subject to all of the laws and regulations of the California Department of Real Estate. Everyone who is involved in any way in the solicitations and negotiations of sales of real estate must have a real estate license.

Contact your Director of Marketing regarding the transfer of your real estate license to OMNIVEST as your licensed broker. Unlicensed personnel must undertake a program of study directed at passing the California real estate license examination. See your DM to enroll in the OMNIVEST-sponsored Real Estate Instruction Program. The tuition is free; you pay only for the materials.

. . . . .

5. Circle of influence—springboard to success

In our own experience and in the entire history of direct-selling, there is one marketing approach that consistently emerges as the *number one success formula* for a salesman.

Here is that winning formula:

Circle of Influence Sales

PLUS

Circle of Influence Referral Sales

EQUALS

A Successful Salesman

Remember when *one sale* yields a list of ten referrals which in turn yields *three* sales, the snowballing effect of working referrals obviously means *wealth* to the sales man who is in the driver's seat!

All you need to get *your* referral-snowball going is to obtain your initial sale. And what's the easiest way to get your first sale? Certainly not from strangers who are notoriously unforgiving if a supposedly professional salesman betrays his lack of experience. The logical place to find your first sale is among the people you already know, your friends and acquaintances. In other words, your circle of influence. At the same time, you will be doing them a very great favor—showing them how to make an outstanding and profitable investment.

6. Telephone follow-up

After your first Circle of Influence letters have been sent out, your Director of Marketing will give you a special dialogue, or script, for telephone follow-up. Carefully and politely worded, this telephone speech is de-

signed to enable you to set appointments to present our investment program to your Circle of Influence prospects.

By this procedure, each of your friends receives a truly valuable education in making money through land investment and you stand the best
chance—inexperienced though you may be—of successfully launching
your new career by obtaining your first sales and your initial referrals.

We would like to remind you, at this point, of *one dominant characteristic* of the entire Circle of Influence Program as employed by OMNIVEST
and outlined in this section:

IT HAS BEEN CONSISTENTLY EFFECTIVE!!

Otherwise, we would not use it.

You are well-advised to have the utmost confidence in it!

7. Prospecting

Occasionally a Consultant will find himself with a day or two in which
he is temporary (sic) prevented from doing anything further within his
Circle of Influence.

Keeping business uppermost in mind, the Consultant starts hitting the
coffee shops, the cocktail lounges, the pool parlors, the bowling alleys,
the retail shops and stores all over town. He strikes up cheerful conversation with gas station attendants, and with the policemen taking their coffee
break at Winchell's, and with the construction workers sitting along the
curb with their lunch pails and thermos bottles, and with a road maintenance crew doing the same thing further down the block. He spots a
trucker whose rig has broken down and offers to help him. From there
he drives to the marina and mingles with the boat folk for two hours. Next
he visits a couple of golf course clubhouses. By now it's dark, so, tired but
happy, he goes home.

And why is he happy? What has he accomplished? What has our enter-
prising and resourceful Consultant gained from nine hours of self-moti-
vated effort? Twelve appointments, that's what! Twelve potential investors,
from whom he will derive four to eight sales initially, plus enough referrals
to keep him going for so long that, because of a subsequent chain reaction, he may never have to prospect again!

But what if he should? What if he does have to resort to cold prospecting from time to time? Remembering what happened the last time he went
out and "hustled," is he likely to consider it a nuisance? An unpleasant
task? Hardly worth the effort? No, he certainly is not.

Is he going to stand around and belly-ache because the Company
doesn't spoon-feed him with leads? Again the answer is no. Not, that is,
if he realizes that 95 out of every 100 John Q's who respond to company
lead promotions are actually nothing more than the spiritually bankrupt
and financially impoverished element of our society looking for free hand-
outs. And not if he realizes that if he did have to chase down leads like that

he would wind up running his fool head off for nothing . . . and burn himself up and out in the process. And not if he realizes that one of the reasons his commission rate is so high is *because* his company doesn't waste its money on worthless, expensive lead programs.

And so, Mr. or Miss Consultant-Trainee, we hope that you now understand a little more about prospecting—how it's done, why it's done and what the two basic kinds are. You have circle of influence prospecting and you have "cold" prospecting. Never turn up your nose at either one, but rather, seize every opportunity to advance your career with *both*. If you will do that, we tell you truly, YOUR SUCCESS IS INEVITABLE!

8. Start your own mail program

Daily contacts. You will find that your friends, clients and merchants whom you patronize can supply you with excellent leads. Ask them for names of people who might be interested in a good investment opportunity, persons to whom you can send an introductory letter.

PEOPLE POCKETS

Here are some groups of prospects and suggested times for seeing them. You may be able to add others as you think of them.

8 to 9	Morning		9 to 11
Garage drivers	Car dealers	Bankers	Barbers
Dentists	Milkmen	Ministers	Implement dlrs.
Corp. executives	Clothing stores	Priests	Garages
Junk dealers	Butchers	Widows	Beauty operators
Retired farmers	_____	Nurses	Morticians
Supermarket mgrs.	_____	Housewives	Railroad workers
Service stn. owners	_____	Liquor stores	_____

11:30 to 12:30

Shoe stores   Construction workers
Dress shops   _____

12:30 to 1:30	Afternoon	1:30 to 3:30
Ideal to see farmers	Take doctors and other	Small grocers
Rural mail carriers	professional men to lunch	Depot agents
Dry cleaners	_____	Bakers
Florists	_____	Butter makers
Lumber yards	_____	_____
Taverns	_____	_____

3:30 to 6:30

Teachers	Factory employees	_____
Painters	Warehousemen	_____
Plumbers	Electrical shops	_____
Carpenters	Plumbing and heating owners	_____
Plasterers	Legal secretaries	_____
Elevator operators	Theater people	_____

B. THE SIX-STEP MARKETING FORMAT

1. Pre-approach

Pre-approach means "preparation"—this is the first step of the official OMNIVEST Six-Step Marketing Format. It is divided into two sections: Materials and Appearance.

Materials.   A list of 25 items including maps, appointment book, forms, tablets, and pens (certain colored pens are used for certain forms or certain purposes).

Appearance.   Your entire appearance should be that of a first-rate professional who positively reeks of success.

Be freshly shaven, hair trimmed—"We recommend styling, because of the superior-groomed look of it, and because it's a more expensive hair treatment and nearly everyone nowadays knows it." Nails clean and trimmed, clothes clean and pressed.

2. Approach

This is a set of guidelines for the Consultant to use when working Company leads.

When Company-generated leads are available, they will be supplied to you only if, in the judgment of your DM . . .

A.   You have done justice to your personal circle-of-influence program;
B.   You have done your best to obtain referral leads from your circle-of-influence investors and have followed up on them properly; and
C.   You are qualified in all respects to handle leads generated at Company expense.

Ordinarily, to develop a lead into a sale, you will see your prospect three separate times—once to set an appointment to come back and give the home presentation, once to keep that appointment, and once to tour your client(s) to the property. In the vast majority of cases, the sale will be consummated immediately after the tour, in your DM's office.

We immediately rule out as being of little value all methods which do not involve direct, face to face conversation with Mr. or Mrs. Prospect. Therefore, when working on a Company lead you make the initial contact at the front door of your prospect's home.

Everyone who becomes a Land Investment Consultant with OMNIVEST has the inherent capability of succeeding, BUT THERE ARE TWO SURE WAYS TO FAIL. In direct sales parlance, they are called "dynamiting" and "machining leads."

To "dynamite" means to lie, misinform, misrepresent, exaggerate, and so forth. These practices are totally unnecessary. Furthermore, the moment the Company hears that you've been dynamiting, your contract will be terminated. OMNIVEST is too large and too reputable to tolerate any unethical behavior.

The other sure way to fail is to "machine" your leads, which means to use the telephone to try to set up appointments with those people. Land investment consultation is too complicated to develop total strangers into a clientele over the telephone. IT IS A PERSONAL, "EYEBALL-TO-EYEBALL" BUSINESS. The easiest way to get a permanent "NO" is on the telephone. . . . Professional investment consultants *do not sell over the telephone.* . . .

Your approach.   Plan your trip to the lead area so that you will arrive on late Monday or Tuesday afternoon, preferably after 3:00 pm. The housewife will normally have completed most of her daily chores by then.

A.   Park your prestige car directly in front of the prospect's door, if possible. . . .
C.   Keep loose and relax as you walk to the door. Walk with an air of dignity, affluence and confidence.
D.   As you approach the door, observe the entire house, landscape, surroundings, apartment house, etc., and identify anything unusual that you might use to compliment your prospect or to open the conversation. This, like the prestige car, is another device or "crutch" which you use as it best benefits you.

Door presentation.   KNOCK ON DOOR OR RING BELL. . . .

Hi, Mrs. Prospect. I'm John Sales from OMNIVEST.

Either you or your husband contacted us and expressed a desire to learn how *YOU* can make money on wise land investments.

DON'T GET INVOLVED IN AN ARGUMENT AS TO WHETHER THEY HAVE OR HAVEN'T REQUESTED INFORMATION. YOU'RE NOT CERTAIN HOW WE GOT THEIR PARTICULAR NAME, BUT YOU HAVE BEEN GIVEN THEIR NAME AS A POTENTIAL CLIENT.

We've prepared maps, brochures, and surveys which explain a little about our land investment program and the tremendous growth which Southern California is now experiencing. I'd like to deliver this information to you.

What time does your husband usually get home? Where does he work? What type of work does he do?

Let's make our appointment for 7:30 on Wednesday then. Would that be okay?

IF SHE SAYS SHE HAS TO CHECK WITH HER HUSBAND: Fine. What is your phone number here so that I can check back with you? If it's more convenient, I'll contact your husband at his office. What is his phone number and extension?

IF SHE IS NEGATIVE TO AN APPOINTMENT: But, you requested that we come by. Aren't you interested in making MONEY?

Many people are getting rich by making sound and sensible land investments. You owe it to yourself and your family to at least find out about it. . . .

Follow-up appointment attempts. . . . Get the husband's place of work, job, office phone and extension, working hours and time that he normally gets home (during the conversation) if possible.

1. Call at the home at an hour when the husband should normally be there. Explain that his wife wasn't aware of his request for information and that you were in the neighborhood, . . . that you stopped by to answer any questions that he might have and that you would be happy . . . to give him all of the facts on his best investment opportunity today.
2. Call him at work using a similar explanation and set up an appointment.
3. Prepare a brief letter to the husband. Address it to his personal attention, preferably to his business address. Say that you dropped by the house but that his wife indicated no interest in making money. Does he share this opinion? If not, you'd like to stop by his home . . . to present the facts on this opportunity for his evaluation. . . .

3. Home presentation

(a) . . . "Well, Mr. and Mrs. Jones, I'm here tonight/today to tell you about a very successful formula for making money. You did say you were interested in making money, right?" . . .

(They'll usually say, "Right. Isn't everybody?")

"Everyone is. That's for sure. All right, before we get too far into the actual science of investing in land—and it does get to be pretty scientific —first let me get some information from you that will show me and the Company I represent how we can make our program do the most for *you.*

"Tell me, how long have you lived in California? . . .

"I see. What type of work do you do, Mr. Jones?" . . .

(Get him to elaborate on his work if the rapport between you needs more building up.)

"Well tell me this, Mr. and Mrs. Jones, have you or any of your relatives or friends ever made money on land investments?" . . .

"Why, at this time, Mr. and Mrs. Jones, are you exploring the possibility of such an investment?" . . .

(Draw them out on this. Make them tell you their dreams, their ambitions, what they're building toward in life.)

(Produce "Let's see what you have earned so far" Chart.)

"Approximately how many years have you been working, Mr. Jones?"
(He says 10 years.)

"And what would you say has been your average monthly income for those 10 years?"

(He says $750.)

(Point to the numbers on the chart—10 years at $750 per month.)

"As you can see, in the past 10 years you've earned $90,000, which is a lot of money to say the least. Tell me, Mr. Jones, are you satisfied with the money you have saved from that $90,000?"

"Now let's look to the future."

"At this time, Mr. Jones, what do you consider to be your most valuable asset?" . . .

(Wait for his answer, then produce MVA chart. Read it out loud.)

"The most valuable asset a man owns is NOT his home, NOT his car, NOT his savings account, NOT his stocks and bonds, but HIS ABILITY TO EARN INCOME, month after month, year after year. We call this 'future earning power.' Let me show you why. In the left-hand column of this chart is an age schedule. Would you point to the age closest to your own?" . . .

(He indicates 36.)

"OK, across the top are monthly incomes. Which one should I circle?" . . .

(To some prospective clients this may seem like too personal a question, but *always* ask it nonetheless . . . and *get an answer.* Just do it casually and naturally. If he objects, don't apologize or back down. All prospects have to be led, and the only way this can happen is if you are strong enough to maintain the initiative. If he reacts negatively to being quizzed about his income, simply assure him, "OMNIVEST is an ethical firm, Mr. Jones. All information given us is held in strictest confidence, and really, there is no way any personal financial consultant can work up a realistic proposal for his client without the client trusting him, whether the consultant is a stockbroker or an insurance man or whatever . . . so how much *do* you earn, Mr. Jones?" . . .)

(He says $1,000.)

"So then prior to your retirement at age 65, you will earn $348,000! (Brief pause.) That's a staggering amount of money, isn't it?" . . .

(b) "OK, Mr. Jones, I'm going to ask you an important question, and I want you to think carefully before you answer me, all right?" . . .

"Since most people like yourself have this enormous earning power, WHY IS IT that 85 people out of 100 reaching age 65 have virtually no cash, or any cushion for their later years?"

(Make him respond.)

"That's right, Mr. Jones. To put it another way, we all know YOU CAN'T MAKE A FORTUNE WORKING FOR WAGES. If a man has to work for a living and he wants to be financially independent some day, that man has some urgent planning to do! Especially if he cares about his family.

"Now there are normally 3 ways to produce a large quantity of money for the future. You can *work* for it, which, in my opinion, can be the hard way . . . and you still might not make it, judging from the statistics. You can hire *other people* to earn the money for you, but that, I'm sure you know, can be difficult too, considering all the businesses that fail. OR . . . you can get *YOUR MONEY* to work for you! . . .

"IF YOU FOUND A PLAN FOR INVESTMENT WHICH, *IN YOUR JUDG-MENT,* WAS ONE OF THE BEST YOU'VE EVER SEEN; THAT OFFERED YOU UNUSUAL OUTSTANDING GROWTH COMMENSURATE WITH YOUR MONTHLY PAYMENT CAPABILITIES, AND AT THE SAME TIME PRO-VIDED SOUND FUTURE SECURITY FOR YOU AND YOUR FAMILY WITHIN 5 TO 8 YEARS—WOULDN'T YOU BE INTERESTED?" . . .

(Remain utterly silent until he answers. If he says, "What was that again?" you repeat the entire question. Say *nothing* until after he has responded. He may hedge or stall or say just about anything to dodge the issue. For example: "It's hard to believe that an investment can be so good . . ." or, "Do you mean to tell *me* that *I* can expect such an outstanding return on my money?" . . . or, "Well, I'm not prepared to commit myself just yet" . . . (Just remember, you can't lead your prospective client if he is leading you. In this case, to maintain control of the conversation, you might say), "Really, Mr. Jones, I haven't asked you to accept or buy anything. Thus far I simply haven't given you sufficient facts that would permit you to make such a decision. The question I am asking, however, is are you interested in such a plan? A plan whereby your investment can multiply many fold! ARE YOU, MR. JONES?" Now just wait quietly. Don't embellish, just wait. When he answers be sure he doesn't place you on the defensive, easily and politely bring the conversation back to your basic objective—and maintain control of the presentation.

Use tact, skill and diplomacy at this critical point. For example, should your prospective client say something like, "There's simply no way I can afford a high monthly payment!" or, "How much of a down payment does it take?" you say, "Mr. Jones, we'll tailor-make a plan to suit you. Give me a ballpark figure that you can comfortably afford to invest every month and we'll go from there . . . For example . . . IF I CAN SHOW JUST SUCH AN INVESTMENT PLAN . . . A PLAN WHICH IN *YOUR* JUDGMENT . . . is one of the best you've ever seen, that offered you unusual, outstanding growth, with maximum future security for you . . . and your family— wouldn't you be interested?" (Once he has answered you in the affirmative, resume your presentation.))

(c) "All right. Now that we know the importance of finding a proper investment for a small portion of your future earnings, let's analyze some different types of investment.

"Let's look at it very objectively. Invest in the stock market and you *could lose* . . . we've all seen ample evidence of *that* happening, true?" . . .

"You can also invest in banks, savings and loans, insurance, government bonds and even mutual funds . . . but the truth is, . . . Under those forms of investment you're lucky if you average out at 5 percent! That means if you invest $1000, at the end of a year you have a big $50! You must also consider *inflation and taxes.* Thanks to inflation, each year that we live our dollars buy less and less. So a 5 percent return on the money we invest *coupled with inflation*—which approaches 5 percent or more a year— either just breaks us even, or may even result in a *net loss!*

(d) "Mr. and Mrs. Jones, we say that SOUTHERN CALIFORNIA *LAND* is one of the soundest investments that can be made today. VERY FEW HAVE EVER BOUGHT GOOD ACREAGE ON THE EDGE OF ANY EXPAND-ING CITY AND LOST MONEY. ESPECIALLY IN THE LOS ANGELES-SAN BERNARDINO METROPOLITAN AREA!! DON'T YOU AGREE?

"Frankly, if you go to a map and draw a 90-mile circle around the Civic Center of Los Angeles, stick a pin in that circle and buy land wherever the pin hits, you've still got the odds in your favor."

"But that would be a helter-skelter way of making an investment, to say the least . . . no matter *how* good the area is. Certainly some parcels of land will go up in value a lot more—and a lot faster—than others . . . *AND THAT'S WHERE OMNIVEST COMES IN!*

"*OUR FORMULA* TELLS YOU WHICH IS WHICH!" . . .

"And therein lies our usefulness to *you,* Mr. and Mrs. Jones. By using the free services of OMNIVEST in the selection of a sound and sensible investment program, you are teaming up with a unique company. We have been educating investors in the ins and outs of making their money work harder for them for over 25 years.

(e) "But this formula only tells you the things you *should* do. What about the things you should *not* do? Wouldn't you agree that knowing what *not* to do is just as important as knowing what *to* do?" . . .

"*The first big DON'T is:* Never become emotional about the acquisition of a piece of land. The land *investor* is different from the fellow who has been so brainwashed by the TV commercials that he can only think in terms of pine trees . . . hunting grounds . . . beautiful lakes and streams . . . mountain trails . . . you know what I mean. The investor likes these things too—but he doesn't get so emotional that he confuses *investment* property with *recreational* property."

"Now let me ask you this: When developers move into a new area, what do they look for; lots or acreage?" . . .

"That's right, acreage! And can you imagine how it feels to have some to sell when they come looking to buy?" . . .

"The *knowledgeable* investor . . . knows that he's got to get in *early*— *ahead* of the development—while the land is still raw. Then, when the developers come along later, he is there waiting for them."

"Raw land is not pretty. Most often it's just rock, soil, gravel and sand. In other words, just plain DIRT. But good predevelopment land—the land where we will build our future cities—is the same dirt that Beverly Hills was before it had water. So when you buy land strictly for profit, forget what it looks like. That doesn't count. Do you see why?" . . .

"Good. *The second big DON'T*—a very common mistake that is easy to make—is seeking the advice of what you might call 'self-styled authorities.' To be very frank with you, Mr. and Mrs. Jones, I'm talking about your relatives, your friends, the people you work with—all good and sincere people. I'm sure. But believe me, only one person in a thousand knows very much about sophisticated land investment."

"Instead, obtain the advice of an expert such as OMNIVEST to help you invest. Deal with facts from governmental agencies, as we do. Acquire your information by investigation and research—just as you are doing now—so you can make a rational evaluation." . . .

"All right, *now we go to the third big DON'T*. The most common thing that people ask me when I first meet them is how much does an acre of land cost . . . and really, the only people who ask this question are the amateurs."

"The only time anyone can supply you with a sensible answer about the price of acreage . . . is if you can tell him the exact location of the land you want to buy, how many acres you want and how you plan to finance the purchase. So don't *you* fall into the 'how-much-an-acre' trap, Mr. and Mrs. Jones. Leave that question for the amateurs. Do you understand what I mean?" . . .

(f) "This will simplify the whole matter for you, Mr. and Mrs. Jones. What's really important—what it all comes down to—is just 3 simple questions . . . and here they are:

> "HOW MUCH MONEY AM I GOING TO INVEST?"
> "HOW MUCH MONEY AM I GOING TO MAKE?"
> "HOW LONG IS IT GOING TO TAKE?"

"Not really very complicated at all, and we'll come back to the 3 Hows in about one minute. But first . . . some people have the notion that to make a good profit in land they need to have *vast holdings*. Well, I'd like to prove to you that it doesn't matter how *much* land you buy."

(Long pause to look around the room . . . stop at the coffee table.)

"Let us assume that I could show you a piece of land the size of this coffee table that you could buy for $100, and I could prove to you that within 5 years you could sell it for $500. In other words, 400 percent profit. I would say *that* is a very good land investment. Would you agree?" . . .

"On the other hand, let us say I could show you where *for the same $100* you could buy *10 acres* of land, but there is one catch. I could *not* tell you that within 5 years you could sell it for any more than you paid for it. I would call that a bad investment, wouldn't you?" . . .

"So, it is not how *much* land you buy that really matters, but rather, how many dollars you invest, how many dollars you make—over and above your investment, naturally—and how much time is required. Isn't that right?" . . .

(g) "Now here is another important reason why land is the best invest-

ment in the world today. Not only does it give you 3, 4 and 5 times as much profit as other recognized forms of investment, but you also have something going for you that *all* sophisticated land investors use to the fullest. Do you know what I'm talking about?" . . .

"*LEVERAGE!* Let me explain how leverage works, very simply. If you go to buy stock on the market, you will have to put up one dollar in cash for a dollar's worth of stock. If that dollar's worth of stock goes up to $1.10, you will have earned 10¢ on $1.00 of cash invested, or 10 percent on your money."

"To buy a dollar's worth of *land,* however, all you need to put up is between *10¢ and 20¢* in cash, not the whole dollar, so if your land goes up in value from $1.00 to $1.10—same as the stock did—you will make the same 10¢ but it will be a profit of *50% to 100%* on your actual *cash* invested of 10 to 20 cents. Do you follow me?" . . .

(h) "Why does it all happen? Why is it possible to make all of this money? Because somebody like myself came along and said you would? Is *that* enough reason to make it happen?" . . .

"No, Mr. and Mrs. Jones, it certainly isn't. The reason why it all happens is the next thing I want to discuss with you. I'm going to give you the OMNIVEST formula for finding a piece of land that will do exactly what we have just talked about. . . .

(i) "Our formula is the result of *isolating* those particular circumstances, Mr. and Mrs. Jones, and now I would like to turn back the clock about twenty years and explain this remarkable profit-guide to you."

(Move to a table if you have not already done so. Take out a 10-point formula chart and a pen or pencil, and hand them to your clients.)

"On that simple-looking sheet of paper is what we have always found to be the very best indicators for making money through land investment. It shows you the 10 most important requirements that determine the right time and place to invest. As you can see, there is a check box opposite each item on the formula to see how it applied to the San Fernando Valley in *1948* and also Orange County in *1953*. You notice there is a blank column on the right . . . *that* is for you to use to evaluate Southern California's *next* major growth area, which we'll be discussing shortly. First, let us look at the San Fernando Valley and Orange County, and as we cover each of those 10 points you simply check the boxes if the test areas measure up to the requirements, OK? Are you ready?" . . .

(j) "Before we do that, Mr. and Mrs. Jones, please let me explain to you why my company takes the time and effort to interest people like you in land as an investment for your future financial security."

"I am sure the thought has crossed your mind: If we know where the future growth areas are, and we own land there which we know will go up in value 3 to 5 times in the next 5 to 8 years, why are we selling it to you? Our reason is pure and simple. We supply you our services for *MONEY* . . . but we derive our profit in a special way."

"We actually participate with you in your investment. We become your partner, in a sense. You are given the opportunity to join the most successful organization of its kind ever developed."

"When you analyze it—the profit-sharing plan—it simply means that when you invest through us, you are the sole owner of the land . . . it belongs to you and you alone . . . you can fence it, dig it, develop it or do anything else that you want with it . . . but the main feature is this: When it is sold, and not before then—only *after* it is sold and your profit is in *your hands*—you give us 10 percent of your profit. Do you follow?" . . .

(k) "OK, Mr. and Mrs. Jones, we've talked about the San Fernando Valley and Orange County. Now let's find the *next* major growth area. Take your 10-point formula there . . . and the first thing we start to look for is flat land."

(Take out relief map.)

1. "This map of Southern California shows us exactly what we're looking for. Here is flat land . . . here are the mountains. Here is the Civic Center of Los Angeles, here is the Civic Center of San Bernardino, and it is from these centers that our population will always push. So far, we have had 3 big pushes. The San Fernando Valley . . . right in here . . . was opened by the Ventura Freeway, which comes straight through the Valley and goes up to Ventura. The second area was opened by the Santa Ana Freeway, which goes straight through Orange County, clear to San Diego. The third area began with the San Bernardino Freeway, which winds up in San Bernardino and has caused the tremendous development of the San Gabriel and Pomona Valleys."

"I want you to look at this map. There are only three major flat land areas left. One is called the San Joaquin Valley, way up here. . . . One is called the Antelope Valley, which is right in here. . . ."

(This is your very first reference to the A.V.!)

". . . and the third one is the Salton Sea area, clear down here. . . . Now I am going to lay my pen on the map and I want you to take a look at the distances of these areas from the Los Angeles Civic Center and the San Bernardino Civic Center. Here is how far it is to the San Joaquin Valley. And here is how far it is to the Salton Sea. And look what we have here . . . a hop, skip and a jump to the Antelope Valley! That, Mr. and Mrs. Jones, is why major land investment firms such as ours—and the *Board of Supervisors of Los Angeles County*—all say:

THE NEXT AREA FOR MASSIVE POPULATION EXPLOSION . . . IS THE ANTELOPE VALLEY!"

"By the way, have you ever been to this area? . . . The first thing we want to know about the Antelope Valley is in which counties is it located. Take a guess. . . ."

(Make them guess. Nine times out of ten they will come up with the wildest answers you ever heard.)

"Well, it may surprise you to know that, first of all, *Los Angeles County* extends northerly into the Antelope Valley . . . right on the other side of this range of hills up heres (sic)."

(Point to the San Gabriel Mountains in the direction of Palmdale.)

"Also in the Antelope Valley are portions of Kern County and San Bernardino County."

2. "Now let's look for water. . . . This blue line here . . . represents the largest single man-made water system in the entire world. It's the Feather River Project, which is virtually completed—and at a cost of over 4 billion dollars."

"Now you HAVE A WATER SUPPLY THAT WILL DO MUCH TO RELIEVE YOUR PRESENT SHORTAGE OF WATER. After that it's up to you."

3. "All right, what about distance from L.A.? Straight as the crow flies . . . 37 miles, or 15 minutes by plane and the Antelope Valley is about the same distance from San Bernardino. Let's look at a map with concentric circles on it."

4. "OK, let's look for freeways, and we'll check the ground mileage too. Starting from the junction of the Golden State and the San Diego Freeways . . . right here . . . (run your finger along the A.V. Freeway) there is a freeway system that is already in operation. The Antelope Valley Freeway is presently completed through Palmdale, Lancaster and Mojave, with the massive interchange joining the Antelope Valley Freeway with the Golden State Freeway presently under construction. Now, the Antelope Valley is just 54 freeway miles from Los Angeles.

5. "What about the road system? As you enter the Antelope Valley from Los Angeles, located on one square city block you will see one of L.A. County's most modern Road Department facilities, with *hundreds of thousands* of dollars worth of equipment *already at work,* paving roads 9 and 15 miles out into the desert."

6. "What about utilities? Southern California Edison has over 100 million dollars invested in the area and is still going strong with expansion. . . .

7. "What about schools? Believe it or not—seemingly in the middle of the desert—there is a *15 million dollar college,* and three miles *farther* into the desert the County has just built a 2.6 million dollar high school! Already existing, you have a total of 38 elementary schools, 7 high schools, the Antelope Valley College, and 3 parochial schools. . . .

8. "What about industry? Right here . . . is a 20-square mile site that is already zoned for industry. *It is the largest single industrial site in the entire world!* Even larger than the Ruhr Valley in Germany. Antelope Valley is the site of numerous industrial plants already, such as: Lockheed's 50 million dollar Tri-Star assembly plant which employs over 5,000 people; Air Force Plant 42 where aircraft testing and maintenance is performed

employs over 3,000; the Federal Aviation Administration Flight Control facility, over 500 employees; . . . Kern County Airport No. 7 which has recently been taken over by the electorate of Mojave. This 2,800-acre facility is destined to become a major freight airport in the not too distant future."

"The nice thing about the Antelope Valley is that it has its own industry. People who live there don't have to travel 50 miles to find work. OK, check off Box #8."

9. "Now, commercial and residential development. The nation's largest retailers—like Sears, Penney's, W. T. Grant, Safeway, Alpha Beta, the banks, the savings and loan companies and so on—they've all seen the handwriting on the wall. Today's annual retail sales for the Valley are well over 100 million dollars. Bank clearings are around 500 million dollars. . . .

"NOW, AS IF THAT WEREN'T ENOUGH, LET'S LOOK AT THE BIGGEST COMMERCIAL ITEM OF ALL. WE'VE COVERED A LOT OF THINGS ALREADY BUT WE HAVEN'T EVEN TOUCHED ON ONE OF THE MOST IMPORTANT AND EXCITING THINGS OF ALL . . . THE WORLD'S LARGEST AIRPORT! THINK OF IT! THE WORLD'S LARGEST AIRPORT! SIX TIMES LARGER THAN L.A. INTERNATIONAL AIRPORT IN INGLEWOOD."

10. *"Now, authoritative population projections.* Today, there are actually about 150,000 people residing in the Antelope Valley."

"The San Bernardino County Planning Department states that the 1970 population of the San Bernardino metropolitan area, or Standard Metropolitan Statistical Area (SMSA) was 1,143,146.

This included portions of Los Angeles and Riverside Counties. The San Bernardino County Planning Department's bulletin of May 8, 1972, contains some very interesting population figures and projections. It shows a total population for San Bernardino County of 682,233 in 1970 increasing to 831,956 in 1980 and 1,064,575 in 1990, with substantial portions of the increase in population occurring in the High Desert regions of the County. It also shows the Barstow region going from a 1950 population of 22,336 to a 1990 projection of 119,217.

"OK, check the last box, Mr. and Mrs. Jones. Now you can see, by using this formula, that the Antelope Valley is truly an area where BILLIONS OF DOLLARS will be spent and made."

11. "Now, does everything I've told you tonight make sense?" . . .

"Fine, then why don't we go up to the Antelope Valley so you can see for yourselves all the developments we've discussed today. How about tomorrow, or would Sunday be better?" . . .

"Good. Then it's confirmed for _____ o'clock on _____."

Make notes. Go directly to your car or any place where there is available light (such as a coffee shop) and record your thoughts and impressions. Use ruled 3 × 5 index cards for this purpose and maintain them in a standard 3 × 5 file box. This is important. Do not rely strictly on memory.

Re-check the tour appointment.

Write down as many of the family names as you can remember, including the dog's!

Make notes on any interesting features of the house, their hobbies and especially *their material and financial goals*. Also their employment!

Note any objections not fully handled so that you can take care of them on the tour.

4. Introduction to touring

There are definite, distinct steps involved in introducing a new client into our investment program. Each one of those steps has its own specific usefulness in enabling you to produce the desired end result—a permanent sale to an informed investor.

The tour, for example, serves to enlighten and educate your prospect—and induce him to invest and maintain his investment—in a way that the home presentation by itself cannot do. The initial contact with a prospective client, his proper indoctrination via the home presentation, and the securing of a tour commitment from him are all important steps in producing a sale. However, it is on the day of the tour that your prospect receives his first glimpse of financial independence through an investment in a *specific* piece of property. Moreover, he gets to verify the ten points of the formula "with his own eyes."

Therefore, consider tour day as "payday." Recognize at the outset that this part of the overall selling process deserves the same kind of preparation and diligence as any other facet of your business operations.

The tour is the official, Company-approved format for showing potential investors the Antelope Valley in its most favorable light and for properly preparing them for the *Close at the office*. Our tour is the product of immeasurable time and effort on the part of successful, professional Land Investment Consultants, contributing researchers and various other authorities. Carefully laid out turn-by-turn, and replete with statistical data, entertaining stories, and strategically worded psychological "implants," the OMNIVEST tour will allow you—with sufficient practice and absolute conformity—to demonstrate your product, entertain your client, and best of all, convert him from a skeptical prospect into a happy, satisfied client-investor. Are you not, after all, marketing the finest investment opportunity available anywhere?

General information regarding the tour:

1. Have many colorful stories memorized for the trip, to maintain control of the conversation and to flavor and romanticize the journey and make it seem shorter.

2. Arrive promptly at the home and remember that your client's "temperature" may be down a bit from the night of the home presentation. . . . Re-establish that rapport, be enthusiastic and don't fall into the trap of "selling land" at the outset. Position your clients in the car the way YOU want them.
3. Always interrupt when you have a point to make, no matter how rude it may seem . . . you may never have an appropriate chance to make that same point again!
4. Plant the idea that your Director of Marketing is sensational . . . you wish they could meet him . . . perhaps on the way home.

THE TOUR*

The first part of the tour—from the San Fernando Valley to Vasquez Rocks—revolves around events and circumstances of the past. By looking into the mirror of the past, your potential investors will find it that much easier to envision the Antelope Valley development of the future.

Remember to call your clients by name as often as you can. (The following dialogue doesn't show this.) A person's own name is just about the sweetest, most tolerable sound in the world to him. By using his name a lot you maintain his attention, you keep his interest up and you also build up rapport and trust. Plus, it keeps you from slipping into the role of "lecturer."

. . . . .

2. *As you go over the hill and descend into the San Fernando Valley:* Have you ever taken a good look at the San Fernando Valley from up here? . . . Take a mental photograph of all this (sweeping gesture) because in a few minutes I'm going to have you visualize the same thing in the Antelope Valley. Now catch the freeways, the city streets, the cars, the hundreds of thousands of homes and buildings . . . take it all in. Got it? . . . Good. Hang onto that picture.

* * * * *

4. *At the Pacific Intertie facility* (on the left): That Pacific Intertie is something else that's vital to our welfare down here . . . so vital, in fact, that 60 million dollars was spent putting it in. The electricity comes all the way from the Columbia River up in Washington and Oregon . . . from the Bonneville Dams, to be exact. This is the Sylmar Station here. It's one of the largest in the country. If you want to know why they put it here instead of closer-in to L.A., it's because there *wasn't room!* That's how desperate the land shortage in L.A. County really is!

---

* The Tour takes up 13 full pages of "script" which the Consultant is expected to memorize verbatim, as well as specific directions for driving the customer to the land site. The following excerpts are typical.

5. *Just before getting on the Antelope Valley Freeway:* About 2 miles that way (point to left) is the Newhall-Saugus area. It's what we call a "pocket" of good, flat land but it's already gone—unless you want to pay $25,000 an acre, that is!

Another term we use a lot is "bedroom community" or "bedroom facility." It means that people live there but have to travel to some other area to go to work every day; they have to commute, in other words.

That's the nice thing about the Antelope Valley . . . it's not a bedroom facility to anyplace; it's already self-contained . . . jobs, schools, whatever you like. It's just a matter of time before it becomes another L.A. Basin. That's kind of a staggering thought, isn't it? . . .

* * * * *

7. *The Three-Investor Story* (verbatim): Y'know, back at your house, and off and on today, we've talked about making money in land investment, right? . . . Well, I'd like for you to pay real close attention now because I'm going to tell you about 3 specific ways of doing it, OK? . . .

First, you have what we call the "one-time" investor. Say he buys a $10,000 parcel of land. It doesn't matter what *size* parcel it is, and it's out in the middle of nowhere, but he holds on to it for 6 years or so, in the hope that the population will move out to him. Suppose the population does just that, and he can sell his property for $30,000. But he decides NOT to sell! The people have moved out to him all right, but he figures if he holds on to the property another 6 years it'll go up in value even more. And let's say it *does!* In the next 6 years it goes up to $60,000. Well, good for him! He's run a $10,000 investment up to $60,000 in 12 years. Maybe that's all he wants . . . $60,000. But not ME!! I may want $5 million!!! I say he made a mistake! Because what actually happened? In his first 6 years he *tripled* his money, but in his *second* 6 years he only *doubled* it, right? . . .

Now, the second way to make money in land is called *subordination.* Assume the same $10,000 invested grows to a value of $30,000 in 6 years the same as before, and the people are really moving out there. Now suppose a developer wants to start building houses on that property. The average developer can't afford to *buy* the land he wants to build on, because he needs all of his borrowing power to get the construction loan. So he goes to the owner of the property and says to him, "Pledge your land to my development, and I will give you 5%, or 10%, or 15% of the revenue from the development, and that sounds real good. He might make 500 or 1,000 dollars a month for 20 years . . . *BUT* . . . he'd be going from land *investment* into *the real estate business!!* He'd have to be concerned with sub-dividing, zoning, taxes, tenants, and on and on. In other words, he's not a passive land *INVESTOR* anymore, he's land *DEVELOPER*, with all the same headaches! Well, OMNIVEST doesn't believe in land *develop-*

ment, because a land *investor* can make the same money as a land *developer*, AND ALL HE HAS TO DO IS *NO WORK AT ALL!!* Do you follow me? . . .

All right, the third way . . . the *best* way . . . is called *PYRAMIDING*. Using the same examples, but pyramiding, our man invests $10,000, waits 6½ years, say, and *SELLS* for $30,000. He invests the $30,000 in more pre-developed land and waits another 6½ years for his money to triple again. He sells this second leg of the pyramid for $90,000; obviously this is a much larger parcel of land. He then takes out his original $10,000 and spends it on anything he wants. Now he is operating entirely on profits. He takes the remaining $80,000 and re-invests it in *more* good, pre-developed land, obtaining an even larger parcel. He lets his money triple again and resells for $250,000 . . . and he's already taken his original investment back in cash!

THAT'S A QUARTER OF A MILLION DOLLARS!!

Can you see that there are large fortunes to be made in pyramiding? . . . And it doesn't work because someone is lucky! We don't believe in luck; we believe in research! . . .

8. *The Pre-Qualify* (verbatim): Everyone says the same thing, _____ _____, but would you believe only about 50% actually do it? . . .

I hope YOU'LL do it, _____, because actually I'm looking for what I call "key clients." I want to build a special group of 75 to 80 investors and just manage their portfolio. . . .

If I show you the way to have $10,000 turn into $40,000 in 7 years, I suspect you'll invest with me the second time around. And I'm more interested in your profits the second time, but *most* of all I'm interested in your profits the *third* time around . . . now we're *really* talking about classic money . . . maybe $500,000!

The only question is, what are you going to spend *your* profits on, _____? . . .

WAIT FOR AN ANSWER

(He may say he wants a big car like yours, or travel, or retirement security, or a legacy for the kids, or a fancy wardrobe for the wife . . . whatever. You may have to prompt them a bit.)

GET THEM TALKING IT OVER—LET THEM TASTE THEIR PROFITS—LET THEM SPEND THE PROFITS RIGHT THERE IN THE CAR

9. *The Qualify—for Monthly Payment* (verbatim): The next question, _____, is what your budget should buy . . . and believe me, it has nothing to do with what we have to sell. We can and do sell everything from 2½ acres to 10,000 acres. When you go to invest in a car, you don't look at the car you really *want* . . . you look at the car you can afford!

In land investment, we don't tailor your budget to the land . . . we tailor the parcel of land to fit your budget! We own all our own land, handle our own financing and there's no credit application or escrow business to go through.

SO WHAT ARE WE REALLY TALKING ABOUT? AFTER YOUR NORMAL EXPENSES—LIKE RENT, FOOD, CAR, AND SO ON—HOW MUCH CAN YOU COMFORTABLY AFFORD TO INVEST EACH MONTH . . . APPROXIMATELY? . . .

(For God's sake, wait for an answer even if it takes 5 minutes! This is the name of the game!! *GET THAT ANSWER!!!* If a person can handle $80 a month, we can handle him. If he says $80, you say, "You mean somewhere between $70 and $90 a month?" Always do this!)

10. *The Qualify—for the Down Payment* (verbatim): HOW MUCH CAN YOU PUT DOWN NOW? . . .

(*Get an answer!* If necessary, remind him of different sources, such as cash savings, stocks, mutual funds, government bonds, loan payments due him, cash value of insurance policies, equity in house, car, boat, etc.)

(If he says, "How much do I need?" you say, "WE can take care of you for 5% down on up to 30% down or more . . . but I want to know what YOU can do, then I'll match that to our inventory.")

(BEFORE YOU PROCEED WITH THE TOUR YOU MUST GET THESE TWO ANSWERS—THE DOWN PAYMENT AND THE MONTHLY PAYMENT!)

(The foregoing should all be accomplished on the freeway before you reach the Valley. It takes about 20 or 30 minutes, so drive slowly and keep talking. When they reach the Valley, they're ready! If they qualify and you have time left before you reach Vista Point, speed up a bit and talk up the pyramid . . . let them "sweat out" whether or not they qualify!)

(WHEN YOU GET TO THE VALLEY, *GET EMOTIONAL! ENTHUSIASM WORKS PURE MAGIC!!* Your client may be stoic and somber as the dickens on the outside, but don't let him fool you. Inside his mind he could be brimming with anticipation! Just keep "turning on" with vitality and enthusiasm, and you'll see miracles happen in him. Don't *push* your enthusiasm on him though; just *exude* it—*radiate* it—and he'll absorb it automatically. And remember, halfway measures come from half-way humans. *Make each tour the command performance of your life!* . . .

11. *As you're pulling off and parking at Vista Point:* There it is, folks! THERE IT IS!!! That's the place where MILLIONS OF DOLLARS are going to be made! In a few years MILLIONS OF PEOPLE are going to be living and working and playing all over this valley! Just feast your eyes on that! Boy, do I love that sight!! I know I told you never to get emotional about land, but I can't help it! No matter how many times I come here, I always get excited when I see this view! I look at it and I see *two* valleys—I see it the way it is *now* and I see it the way it's *going* to be . . . wall-to-wall city. . . . The next San Fernando Valley!! I don't know about you, _____,

but I get a thrill knowing I'm in on the ground floor of all of this! Here, let's stretch our legs and have a better look.

12. *While you're standing at Vista Point:* (Make sweeping arm gestures as often as possible . . . motion creates interest and interest creates motion! Mention and point out the following:)

(a)	Calif. Aqueduct	(g)	Edwards AFB/Space Shuttle
(b)	Palmdale & Lancaster	(h)	Mojave
(c)	Lockheed & Plant 42	(i)	Master road plan
(d)	P.I.A.	(j)	Palmdale-Colton Cut-off
(e)	Lake Los Angeles	(k)	Eight freeways
(f)	Victorville	(l)	Rapid-transit study

13. *Closing:* Following this exciting trip, the Land Consultant is then to drive the client to the particular site for inspection, where he attempts to have him sign several preliminary forms. Once this is accomplished he returns the client to the Los Angeles office of OMNIVEST where a "closer" takes over to have the client sign the actual site purchase documents. This "closer" is usually the Consultant's District Manager, who is better equipped to handle this delicate aspect of the operation.

5. Buyer's remorse

Whenever a person makes a major purchase of any nature, it is natural that he or she have some misgivings a short time after the purchase is consummated. It makes no difference what product or service was purchased. It is a rare human being who can expend a large sum of money and not immediately find some other more important use for the funds. This reassessment, together with the discomfort that goes along with it, is known as "buyer's remorse."

The Consultant should carefully explain to his investor that this most probably will happen, since it happens to all his other investors, and that it is a normal and healthy occurrence. The Consultant should convey this message to the investor during the trip home from the office prior to the arrival at the investor's home. The Consultant need not be afraid to be quite dramatic in portraying the buyer's remorse symptoms, such as tossing and turning through the night, tight feeling in the stomach, etc., because these things do happen. If the investor is forewarned, buyer's remorse will not affect the sale.

SELECTED BIBLIOGRAPHY

Clark, R. G. "Consumer Protection and Real Estate." *Real Estate Today* 9 (October 1976): 50–52.

"Florida Property Market: Crooks, Crocks, and Crocs." *The Economist* 258 (January 31, 1976): 87.

Jones, J. C. "Training Program: The Specifics." *Real Estate Today* 9 (August 1976): 50–54.

Lowe, J. W. "Land Speculation: Does It Have Real Economic Consequences?" *Finance and Development* 12 (September 1975): 3–30.

"New Mexico's War on Land Frauds." *Business Week,* November 17, 1975, pp. 49–50.

Pitman, F. "$40 Million Colorado Land Fraud Alleged." *House and Home* 49 (May 1976): 38.

Reinke, P. G. "Training Programs: The Basics." *Real Estate Today* 9 (August 1976): 46–49.

Seneker, H. "AMREP Accused of $200 Million Swindle of 45,000 Land Buyers." *House and Home* 48 (December 1975): 26.

Sherman, F. "Once More, With Music: A Land-Sale Scandal In—Of All Places—Florida." *House and Home* 49 (July 1975): 20.

"State Crackdown Scares the Developers." *Business Week,* August 11, 1975, p. 22.

"Two Major Land Companies, Horizon and Amrep Corporation, Accused by FTC." *The Wall Street Journal,* December 18, 1975, p. 18.

Verda, D. J. "Marketing Integration for Land Developers." *Journal of Marketing* 40 (October 1976): 105–8.

4 Pharmaceutical (prescription drugs) industry (B): The detailman: Salesman and counselor

I have found that visits by well-briefed detailmen are the most effective means by which physicians and pharmacists can learn of new medicines and pharmaceutical developments. In my experience, most representatives are men of integrity and understanding who, because of the specialized and topical information they bring, can—given half a chance—perform a most useful service for the busy practitioner.[1]

Sir Derrick Dunlop, *A Personal View*

The concept of a well-informed professional, working out of schools of pharmacy or medicine, paid indirectly by the government . . . and visiting with practitioners to inform them about the latest information on safety, relative efficacy, and cost is one which would lead to far more rational prescribing practices. It is, however, the very antithesis of the industry-sponsored drug detailman. The detailman today is selling the chloramphenicol of tomorrow, such as Lincocin and Clindomycin (Upjohn). Years after he has made his sale, the devastating effects of this zealous promotion will continue.[2]

Dr. Sidney M. Wolfe, Testimony before
the Senate Health Subcommittee

The detailman performs a critical role in the success or failure of prescription drugs. He is considered an important source of information by the physician and, at the same time, distrusted as a promoter of drugs whose information can only be biased. The industry regards the detailman as a crucial link in the distribution system and devotes considerable financial resources to the hiring, training, and maintaining of the sales force.

ISSUES FOR ANALYSIS

1. How do different segments of the market—the drug company, the detailman himself, the physician, the pharmacist, the patient, and the

---

[1] Derrick Dunlop, *A Personal View* (Washington, D.C.: Pharmikon, 1973), p. 36.

[2] U.S. Congress, Senate, Committee on Labor and Public Welfare, Subcommittee on Health, *Examination of the Pharmaceutical Industry 1973–74*, May 21, 1974; "Testimony of Dr. Sidney M. Wolfe," part 6, pp. 2632–42.

Food and Drug Administration—view the role of detailmen in the effective distribution and promotion of prescription drugs?

2. To what extent do the background and training given the detailmen by the drug companies prepare them for their dual roles, promoting their employers' drugs and fulfilling the informational function concerning the overuse and misuse of drugs?

3. Given the nature of the rewards and the compensation system for detailmen, can they reasonably be expected to be objective about their drugs and not overpromote them?

4. How well do the pharmaceutical companies in general support their detailmen in promoting drugs in a responsible manner and in not overpromoting them for nonindicated uses?

5. What steps, if any, should be taken by the drug companies, by the physicians, and by the Food and Drug Administration to improve the performance of detailmen in objectively promoting their drugs and providing truthful information about these products?

THE IMPORTANCE OF THE DETAILMAN

The detailman links the drug manufacturer with anyone who may now, or in the future, use or cause the use of his products.

The importance of the detailman in informing the doctor of new drugs, providing information, and persuading him to use these drugs has been suggested by several studies. (See Exhibit 4–1.) A study by T. Caplow and J. J. Raymond in 1954 showed that the detailman was the most important "source of notice" of new drug products, but only a third as important in the adoption of new drugs. Another study by R. Ferber and H. F. Wales in 1958 found the detailman to be the most important first source of drug information and second in importance in convincing physicians to use a drug for the first time. A study by Ben Gaffin and Associates in 1956, although made unreliable by some faults in design, indicated that 68 percent of the physicians mentioned the detailman as the most important source of drug information. A more recent survey prepared for the FDA in 1974 (see Exhibits 4–2, 4–3, and 4–4) indicates that most doctors found detailmen slightly less useful than colleagues; of the total number of doctors surveyed, 37 percent found peer colleagues the most useful, and 25 percent found detailmen most useful. This survey also indicated that of the material issued by the drug company, the detailman's sales material was considered much less useful as a source of drug information than the package insert. Nevertheless, 64 percent of the doctors used material from the detailman a mean of 1.8 times per week.

Many reasons have been given for the influence of the detailman on the doctor. One is convenience: The doctor can get from the detailman exactly the information he needs without reading through large amounts of

EXHIBIT 4–1

A: SOURCES WHICH SERVED AS THE FIRST NOTICE TO DOCTORS OF THE
AVAILABILITY OF NEW DRUGS

Source	Percent of doctors naming as first source		
	Caplow and Raymond	Ferber and Wales	Coleman et al.
Detail men	31%	38%	52%
Medical journals:			
Articles	19	—	—
Advertisements	6	25	9
Direct mail advertisements	16	19	22
Colleagues	14	6	10
Medical meetings	7	4	3
Others	7	8	3
Total	100%	100%	100%
Number of doctors answering	182	328	87

B: SOURCES WHICH LED TO FIRST USE OF A DRUG

Source	Percent of doctors naming source		
	Coleman et al.	Ferber and Wales	Gaffin
Detail men	5%	21%	41%
Medical journals:			
Articles	42	28	15
Advertisements	2	—	—
Direct mail advertisements	14	18	26
Colleagues	28	13	7
Medical meetings	8	4	2
Others	1	16	9
Total	100%	100%	100%
Number of doctors answering	87	328	1,011

C: WHAT IS THE MOST IMPORTANT
SOURCE OF DRUG INFORMATION?

Source	Gaffin
Detail men	68%
Medical meetings	35
Journal advertisements	32
Direct mail advertisements	32
Colleagues	24
Journal articles	26

Sources: T. Caplow and J. J. Raymond, "Factors Influencing the Selection of Pharmaceutical Products," *Journal of Marketing* 19 (1954): 18–23; R. Ferber and H. G. Wales, "The Effectiveness of Pharmaceutical Advertising: A Case Study," *Journal of Marketing* 22 (1958): 395–407; J. S. Coleman, E. Katz, and H. Menzel, *Medical Innovation—A Diffusion Study* (Indianapolis: Bobbs Merrill, 1966), p. 59; B. Gaffin and Associates, *Attitudes of U.S. Physicians Toward the American Pharmaceutical Industry*, Chicago, 1959, p. C–13.

EXHIBIT 4-2

ESTIMATE OF PHYSICIAN UNIVERSE, PERSONAL CONTACTS CONSIDERED MOST USEFUL AS SOURCE OF DRUG INFORMATION

Number and percent of each stratum considering particular personal contact most useful for drug information

Source considered most useful	Total		General practice		Internal medicine		Obstetrics/ gynecology		Pediatrics		General surgery		All other	
	Number	%	Number	%	Number	%	Number	%	Number	%	Number	%	Number	%
Peer colleagues	82,000	37%	8,720	21%	16,850	39%	5,530	39%	5,220	39%	12,490	35%	33,210	47%
Detailmen	55,250	25	18,690	44	6,650	15	4,470	32	2,580	19	9,970	28	12,890	18
Consultants	50,020	23	9,180	22	12,900	30	2,210	16	3,280	25	8,140	23	14,300	20
(Estimated universe)	(218,860)		(42,290)		(43,170)		(14,110)		(13,330)		(35,740)		(70,220)	

Note: Derived from Table 77 of Appendix F; Question No. 2.E.2. "Of the above personal contacts, circle the one you consider to be most useful as a drug information source."

Source: Applied Management Sciences, *Final Report: Survey of Drug Information Needs and Problems Associated with Communications Directed to Practicing Physicians*, prepared for Food and Drug Administration, Bureau of Drugs, Contract No. FDA 72–301, May 8, 1974, p. 3.32.

EXHIBIT 4-3

ESTIMATE OF PHYSICIAN UNIVERSE, DRUG COMPANY MATERIAL CONSIDERED MOST USEFUL AS SOURCE OF DRUG INFORMATION

Number and percent of each stratum considering particular drug company material most useful for drug information

Source considered most useful	Total		General practice		Internal medicine		Obstetrics/ gynecology		Pediatrics		General surgery		All other	
	Number	%	Number	%	Number	%	Number	%	Number	%	Number	%	Number	%
Package inserts	125,900	65%	21,440	57%	27,120	70%	7,760	60%	8,320	71%	19,460	64%	41,800	68%
Material from detailmen	37,090	19	11,480	31			3,370	26						
(Estimated universe)	(192,870)		(37,350)		(38,560)		(12,950)		(11,750)		(30,640)		(61,620)	

Note: Derived from Table 76 of Appendix F; Question No. 2.D.2. "Of the above drug company materials, circle the one that you consider to be most useful as a drug information source."

Source: Applied Management Sciences, *Final Report*, p. 3.27.

EXHIBIT 4-4

ESTIMATE OF PHYSICIAN UNIVERSE'S FREQUENCY OF USE OF DRUG COMPANY MATERIALS

Number and percent of each stratum using source and frequency of use

Source*	Total		General practice		Internal medicine		Obstetrics/ gynecology		Pediatrics		General surgery		All other	
	Number	%	Number	%	Number	%	Number	%	Number	%	Number	%	Number	%
Package inserts:														
Use the source	234,440	83%	44,960	90%	44,990	79%	15,320	86%	14,500	85%	40,250	85%	74,410	81%
Mean occasions of use/wk	2.2		3.1		1.9		2.2		2.3		2.2		2.0	
(Estimated universe = 280,780)														
Journal advertisements:														
Use the source	129,060	50%	26,270	58%	20,800	39%	9,570	57%	6,380	40%	23,210	53%	42,830	50%
Mean occasions of use/wk	1.4		2.0		1.1		1.6		1.1		1.4		1.3	
(Estimated universe = 260,550)														
Materials from detailmen:														
Use the source	169,000	64%	38,650	83%	26,910	50%	13,770	81%	10,110	63%	29,920	68%	49,640	57%
Mean occasions of use/wk	1.8		3.2		1.3		2.3		2.1		1.6		1.4	
(Estimated universe = 192,810)														

Note: Derived from Tables 53–57 of Appendix F; Question No. 2.D.1. "Indicate the number of times in an average week you use each of the following sources of drug information:".

* Estimated base of total physician universe. Estimated base for each reported data cell may be found in the appropriate table in Appendix F from the "Total Answering" data line.

Source: Applied Management Sciences, *Final Report*, p. 3.26.

literature. Detailmen can also act as consultants for doctors, especially in rural areas where experts are not available. In addition, doctors may be influenced to prescribe the detailman's drugs because they are on friendly terms with the detailman. Finally, detailmen as salesmen may use convincing, personalized selling techniques to sell their products.[3]

DEFINITION AND FUNCTIONS OF THE DETAILMAN

The definition of what a detailman is and what functions he performs varies for different sources, from the manufacturer to the physician, from the pharmacist to the detailman himself.

The physician's perspective

The physician sees the detailman as both an important and an unreliable source of information. The importance of the detailman's information to the doctor has been suggested by the preceding exhibits; its unreliability is shown by statements such as that of Dr. William Bean, professor of internal medicine at the University of Texas Medical School, Galveston, Texas:

> Salesmen are interested in sales. If salvation can be gained too, so much the better. Naturally, special products are praised—those of the salesman's firm—often with a memorized monologue delivered with samples and the accompanying folders. The newer drugs get special treatment. The physician, if he is uncertain of what his fellow physicians may be doing, does not want to be left at the post in any new therapeutic race either. So, with the reassurances he gets, the new therapy is launched. The results are variable, but not all according to the spiel.

Doctors especially noted the limitations of the detailman's information regarding new drugs, although it is in this area that doctors rely on the detailman the most. Dr. Harry F. Dowling felt that the information was valuable in regard to the availability and prices of the new drugs, but "not being physicians, they cannot instruct physicians regarding the principles upon which the use of a new drug is based." Some doctors felt that the detailman's information was biased by drug company propaganda, and was but one of his sales tools. Dr. A. Dale Console, a former medical director of E. R. Squibb and Sons, described the detailman's approach as irresponsible "hard sell": "There is a simple maxim I learned from de-

---

[3] Russell R. Miller, "Prescribing Habits of Physicians," *Drug Intelligence and Clinical Pharmacy*, parts 7–8, vol. 8 (February 1974): 84. See also Bennet J. Wasserman, "The Ubiquitous Detailman: An Inquiry into His Functions and Activities and the Laws Relating to Them," *Hofstra Law Review* 1 (1973): 183–213; Harry F. Dowling, *Medicines for Man: The Development, Regulation, and Use of Prescription Drugs* (New York, 1970), pp. 122–135.

tailmen which is known to most if not all in the pharmaceutical industry. 'If you can't convince them, confuse them.' '"[4]

A 1974 survey of physicians' prescribing habits indicated that, in general, physicians balance their feelings that the detailman has important information with their distrust of his selling techniques. The survey found that although detailmen were the most influential source of information for the introduction to a drug, at later stages of the adoption process, particularly at the time when the decision is made to prescribe that drug, the detailman's influence is much less.

Physicians' attitudes toward the detailman are also indicated by their support of the regulations found in the 1974 proposal of the Drug Utilization Improvement Act (S.3441) and the Omnibus Drug Amendments (S.966) which, among other things, provided for federal certification of training programs for detailmen. At the hearings on these proposed acts, John H. Budd, secretary of the board of trustees of the AMA, asserted that the AMA supported an accredited training program for detailmen, but believed these programs should be independent, rather than under federal control.[5]

The manufacturer's perspective

For the manufacturer, the detailman is one of the most important tools for selling the company's products, as is indicated by the amount of money spent on advertising. Current analyses of detailing expenses estimate that the costs are between $600 and $700 million a year, of a total $900 million to $1 billion spent on all drug promotion.[6] Dr. Gerald G. Laubach, president of Pfizer, Inc., called the detailman "the cornerstone of Pfizer's promotional activity in the information area. He is the interface between Pfizer and the physician."

Why is the detailman's role so important to the drug industry? Some manufacturers admit that the importance of detailmen primarily depends on their role as salesmen. Other manufacturers, however, think the detailman transcends this role. They feel that the detailman has a special responsibility to inform, as well as other responsibilities toward the doctor and the community. Detailmen must give accurate, current, and inclusive information about new drugs—their side effects, dangers, and other pertinent data. The manufacturers also assert that the detailman acts as a con-

---

[4] U.S. Congress, Senate, Select Committee on Small Business, Subcommittee on Monopoly, *Competitive Problems in the Drug Industry*, part 18, pp. 10336, 10368; part 24, p. 14172 (January–July, 1975).

[5] U.S. Senate, *Examination of the Pharmaceutical Industry*, part 6 (May 21, 1974), p. 2568.

[6] Milton Silverman and Philip Lee, *Pills, Profits, and Politics* (Los Angeles and Berkeley: University of California Press, 1974), p. 55; Council on Economic Priorities, "In Whose Hands?" *Economic Priorities Report* 4 (August–November 1973): 28.

venient source of information for doctors who may not have the time to obtain this information elsewhere.

According to the manufacturer, the detailman provides many other services. Willaman suggested that these include providing literature and instructional material for patients; forwarding complaints about drugs from physicians to the company; removing unsalable, damaged, or outdated merchandise from pharmacies; and advising wholesale drug personnel about the availability of drugs. Jan Dlouhy, the president of Lederle Laboratories, suggested that in addition to these responsibilities, the detailman may also arrange emergency deliveries of medicines, replace medical stocks lost in disasters, keep the doctor's supplies replenished, and bring the doctor's questions to the manufacturer's medical advisory staff.

The detailman's training

Drug manufacturers assert that in order to carry out these important responsibilities, the detailman is given extensive training. Most of their detailmen are college graduates, usually majors in a medicine-related field, and each undergoes training that includes programs in medical background as well as in the company's products and selling techniques. Merck's training program was described in detail by Henry Gadsden, president of the company. In this program, each person starts with two months of basic training in both medical background and Merck products. For an example of the type of instruction given to detailmen, see Exhibit 4–5.

EXHIBIT 4–5

BALANCED PRESENTATIONS:

Throughout your career as a professional representative, you must constantly evaluate your product discussions to make sure that they are "balanced." This means that you tell both sides of the story; that you always "balance" your presentation by discussing the shortcomings and limitations of a drug—its adverse reactions, contraindications, precautions, etc.—when you discuss its benefits.

The reason for insisting on a balanced presentation is evident. Obviously, no one would deliberately distort facts or make misleading statements when presenting product information to physicians. Inadequate information, however, could lead to distortion and misrepresentation. An unbalanced presentation, one that emphasizes only the benefits of a drug without considering its contraindications, precautions, adverse reactions, and other limitations, would give a false impression.

The pinnacle of balance, therefore, would be a complete recitation of the product circular. However, time rarely permits such a recitation. And it would not be appropriate to recite the circular to a physician who is already well informed about the drug. Balance, therefore, requires you to make a conscientious judgment—a judgment regarding which facts to present in each individual situation and to each individual physician.

The key to balance, therefore, lies in what the physician already knows about the product. If he uses it, he will be familiar with many of the basic facts and you may choose to concentrate on points that will help him to achieve the best re-

EXHIBIT 4–5 *(continued)*

sults. Be sure, however, to include all pertinent facts relating to the points you discuss.

For example, suppose that a physician who regularly prescribes 'Elavil' mentions that he plans to use it in a mentally depressed construction worker. In your discussion you would stress the precautions that apply to the situation. You would remind the doctor that drowsiness may occur and that the patient should be warned about activities requiring alert attention. In this case, however, it would obviously not be as important to remind him that 'Elavil' is not recommended in pregnant women.

On the other hand, suppose the physician has little or no experience with 'Elavil' and merely mentions the construction worker as someone in whom he might try the drug. In this case, you would expand the discussion to include other precautions, side effects, etc., because the doctor needs to have more information about 'Elavil' to use it well. And while he mentioned a specific patient, he may also use it in others and will need to know about the drug's characteristics in all types of patients. If you are not sure how familiar a doctor is with a product, try to "over-inform" him. It is certainly better to cover familiar ground than to omit an important fact that he might not know about.

While no specific rules can be set down for applying balance to all presentations, material is available to help you understand what makes a presentation balanced.

In questions and comments, the Chairman speculated on whether physicians and the public interest would be better served if field representatives would function in a sense as therapeutic advisors to the medical profession—helping them keep informed on all products in all classes of therapy, including all competitive products, instead of limiting their attention to the products their companies make and distribute.

The Merck Sharp & Dohme position on this is clearcut. We recognize that physicians find product comparisons useful, but the medical and scientific data on such comparisons must be valid, and we do not permit our representatives to make comparisons on their own authority. We do not believe our field representatives are or can be equipped to provide a comprehensive informational service on the products of other manufacturers. Moreover, we feel there are actual disadvantages in urging our field representatives to talk with physicians about the relative values and limitations of our products as compared with other products in the same therapeutic class. It is not as though physicians did not have available other sources of comparative drug information. Most physicians, for example, consult the numerous medical journals, postgraduate courses, medical society meetings and symposia, the AMA publication "Drug Evaluations," a variety of medical texts and the Physicians' Desk Reference for this sort of information. It is ironic that concurrent with the criticism that detailmen do not supply balanced information on their own products is the proposition that they should and would provide balanced information on the products of their competitors. Some time ago, field representatives were not so constrained. But it was apparent that under such circumstances they were free to make the very kind of unfair product comparisons which every responsible individual or organization would decry. We now, as a matter of policy, try to handle situations in which our representatives compare our products with those of our competitors in the manner indicated in Section V of "The Responsibilities of an MSD Professional Representative":

PRODUCT COMPARISONS:

Never initiate a discussion that involves a comparison between our products and other drugs unless you receive specific instructions to do so. If the doctor asks a question that leads to a product comparison, keep the following points in mind:

1. Base your discussion only on those items listed under Sources of Information above, and on the current product circulars for drugs produced by other

EXHIBIT 4–5 *(concluded)*

companies. To make sure that a competitive circular is up to date, compare it with the product information in the current PDR and its supplements. If on comparison with PDR, you are not sure that the competitive literature you have is current, don't use it. It is better to make no comparison at all than to mistakenly make an inaccurate comparison.

2. When comparing one of our product circulars with one from another company, present facts only. Do not offer interpretations or draw conclusions. For example, if the "Product X" circular states that special blood tests should be administered to elderly patients taking the drug, you may point that out. Do not, however, go on to say that because our product does not require such tests, it is safer to use in geriatric patients. This requires a medical judgment that you are not qualified to make. The only permissible comparisons involving such a judgment are those presented in the current Sales Bulletins, "Creative Activities," and detail pieces.

3. In comparing one of our products with one from another company, you may use package circulars to discuss indications, contraindications, special instructions about laboratory tests, dosage, availability, and any limitations on therapy (such as statements that a product should be used for short-term therapy only). They are not to be used to compare side effects, because the incidence of these side effects is rarely included in the circulars, so there is no real basis for comparison.

4. A product comparison, like all other types of product discussion, requires balance. Don't present the advantages of our product and the disadvantages of another. Give all the information needed to answer the doctor's questions fairly and accurately.*

---

* Excerpt from "The Responsibilities of an MSD Professional Representative," a document given to Merck representatives during basic training, in a letter from Henry W. Gadsden to Edward M. Kennedy, March 26, 1974, quoted in U.S. Congress, Senate, *Examination of the Pharmaceutical Industry*, part 3, pp. 913–16.

This is followed by two weeks of intensive training for salesmanship. After an evaluation, the salesman is given on-the-job training for six months, after which he returns to headquarters for two weeks of further training, a final examination, and an appraisal. If qualified, he then returns to on-the-job training for 15 to 18 months, at the end of which time he becomes a full representative. He will still receive 45 to 50 hours of instruction a year.[7] Ortho Pharmaceutical adds to a similar training program a voluntary correspondence course that covers anatomy, pharmacology, physiology, medical terminology, and governmental regulations.

According to the manufacturers, this training is reinforced by the evaluation of the detailman's performance on criteria that extend beyond his selling ability. Donald Van Roden, president of Smith, Kline, and French Laboratories, asserted that detailmen are periodically judged by their supervisors on the basis of the "accuracy" as well as "effectiveness" of product knowledge and presentation. To be "accurate," the detailman must remain within the bounds of the "product prescribing information" given to him by the company. Merck's evaluation form for detailmen also indi-

---

[7] U.S. Senate, *Examination of the Pharmaceutical Industry*, p. 987.

cated that they were not judged exclusively on selling ability. The "work performance review" had spaces for evaluating professional conduct, product knowledge, communication skills, work habits, compliance with laws and regulations, and achievement of objectives (see Exhibit 4–6).

EXHIBIT 4–6

Work Performance Review	Professional Representative	Date	D.M.	Region
Name	Terr. #	Age	Years of service	Date last review
			Years on present terr.	Rating last review

1. *Professional Conduct*—The degree to which his behavior is consistent with his responsibilities to the health professions, the public and the Company.
   Measurements
   A. Acceptance by physicians, pharmacists and paramedical personnel.
   B. Ability to see scheduled physicians.
   C. Sense of propriety.
   Comments and Examples:
   • What is the Representative's behavior in the physician's office and *with other contacts throughout the medical community?*
   • *Does he function in a professional manner throughout the business day?*
   • *Are you proud to be with him?*
   • *Do physicians want to see him?*
   • *Is the refusal rate high, low, average?*
   • *Are you "comfortable" when working with this man?*
   • *Is he sensitive to feelings of others?*
   • *Is he well thought of in his community?*

Performance ☐

2. *Product Knowledge*—The degree to which he is fully informed on MSD products.
   Measurements
   A. Performance in Training classes, district meetings, and postgraduate classes.
   B. Grades on product information exams.
   Comments and Examples:
   • *Is the Representative equipped with medical facts to provide physicians with the proper information for prescribing MS&D products?*
   • *Does he know the approved indications, contraindications, side effects, and precautions for the products he is presenting to physicians?*
   • *Does he have enough time set aside for studying product information?*
   • *Does he continually seek to learn?*

Performance ☐

3. *Communication Skills*—The skill with which he presents balanced, complete and accurate product information, adapts his presentations to the needs and interest of each physician.
   Measurements
   A. Use of precise and accurate language.
   B. Ability to listen and observe.

Performance ☐

EXHIBIT 4–6 (continued)

Comments and Examples:
• Is his product knowledge evident in his presentations? If not, what is being done to correct it?
• Does he exhibit confidence commensurate with his knowledge? Skill?
• Does he discuss products with fair balance, both benefits and risks?
• Does the discussion effectively meet the informational needs and time limitations of individual physicians?
• Does the Representative reflect respect and concern for the physician, his patients and MS&D products?
• Is he a presenter or does he really try to make the physician "comfortable" with our product?
• How is his ability in answering questions?
• Does he listen and observe?

4. Position Knowledge—The degree to which he is fully informed on his   Performance
    territory, company policies and procedures applicable to his   ☐
    responsibilities.

    Measurements
    A. Alertness to new physicians in his territory.
    B. Awareness of competitive activities.
    C. Knowledge of each scheduled physician and customer.

    Comments and Examples:
    • Does he know that new physicians are in his territory?
    • Does he know who the new physicians are?
    • Does he know the best time to call on each physician? Does his routing reflect this?
    • Is he calling on physicians at proper intervals?
    • Does he have complete knowledge of hospitals and Government business?
    • Does he know the channel of distribution of welfare prescriptions and the impact welfare prescriptions can have on his territory?
    • Does he have complete knowledge of chain store and wholesale activities in his territory?
    • Does he know the geography and the demography of his territory?

5. Territory Management—The degree to which he effectively plans his   Performance
    work, organizes his territory, utilizes his time and keeps management   ☐
    informed of activities, customer and territory needs as they relate to
    our products.

    Measurements
    A. Evidence of planning.
    B. Existence of records.
    C. Performance compared to call objectives.
    D. Handling of correspondence and administrative duties.
    E. Use of "Reports from the Field."

    Comments and Examples:
    • Does he have an organized plan for each working day; is he planning for the future?
    • Does he follow approved marketing plans?
    • To what extent does he use Creative Activities and Sales Bulletins?
    • Does his routing reflect the territory as it exists today?
    • Is it revised as changes occur?
    • Is he alert to and does he adjust to changes?
    • Are records up-to-date?
    • How effectively is he using all available records and controls for planning? E.G.: R317, Progress Report, Physician Record Book, R-385 Report, Planning Sheets, Territory Information Summary.
    • Does he really analyze his market?

EXHIBIT 4–6 (continued)

- *Does he keep Management informed of changes in Welfare systems and economic conditions that may affect the use of pharmaceuticals in his territory?*
- *Does he keep Management informed?*
- *Are his reports accurate and informational?*

6. *Use of Supportive Material*—The extent to which he effectively utilizes samples, literature and other material to augment his presentations.

   Performance ☐

   Measurements
   A. Plans distribution of samples and literature.
   B. Keeps sample and literature inventories current.

   Comments and Examples:
   - *Does he know the sample needs of each physician in his territory?*
   - *Is his use of samples and literature a part of his total marketing plan?*
   - *Does he use samples as a means to an end or does he consider sample distribution an end in itself?*
   - *Does he submit accurate monthly sample inventories?*
   - *Is he making use of the Postgraduate Program and the Speakers' Program?*

7. *Work Habits*—The degree to which he applies himself to his position: I.e., time and effort.

   Performance ☐

   Measurements
   A. Time spent on the territory.
   B. Number of scheduled calls made.
   C. Time spent preparing for calls and for self-development.
   D. Consistent worker.

   Comments and Examples:
   - *Does he organize his working day, week, month?*
   - *Does a review of physician record book and other planning records show evidence of advance planning and preparation? (SC-224).*
   - *Does he follow the plan he has made; is he flexible enough to follow an alternate plan when necessary?*
   - *Is he a hard and smart worker?*
   - *Does he decide to work hard on the things he likes to do leaving little time for other responsibilities?*

8. *Compliance with Laws and Regulations*—The degree to which he is familiar with and complies with letter and spirit of all laws and regulations which relate to his activities.

   Performance ☐

   Measurements
   A. Periodic review by District Manager.
   B. Observation of performance on territory.
   C. Familiarity with material in his manual on this subject.

   Comments and Examples:
   - *Does he periodically check samples and literature to assure himself that product circulars are current?*
   - *Does he ask for needed information if in doubt about laws and regulations?*
   - *Is his attitude toward the laws and regulations constructive?*
   - *Does he use only approved, current sources of information—Product Circulars, Sales Bulletins, Creative Activities, approved reprints and other materials sent from West Point for this purpose?*
   - *Does he periodically review policy letters which pertain to applicable laws and regulations?*
   - *Is he aware of the necessity for submitting adverse reaction reports when indicated?*

EXHIBIT 4–6 (concluded)

9. Achievement of Objectives—The degree to which he has successfully accomplished all territory and personal objectives. Performance □

Measurements

A. Review of specific objectives set jointly by District Manager and Professional Representative.
B. Comparison of results against annual territory objectives.

Comments and Examples:
• Review performance development goals.
• District Managers should use all available controls and records to measure Representative's progress. For example, (1) R-317, (2) Progress Report, (3) Frequency Report, (4) Representative's Physician Record Book, (5) Territory Information Summary, (6) G.D.R. Data, etc.
• Analyze Region market share data as a guideline for measuring relative progress.

Source: Work Performance Review of Merck and Company, Inc., in U.S. Congress, Senate, Examination of the Pharmaceutical Industry, part 3, pp. 917–921.

The drug company's literature and its view of the detailman

The picture of the detailman presented in the descriptions of the drug manufacturers can be compared to the picture suggested by the materials given to the detailman by the company. This material seems to emphasize the selling aspect of the detailman's job. The weekly newsletters of some companies constantly praise detailmen who have increased their sales or who have helped get a drug on a hospital formulary (the list of drugs a hospital stocks and allows its doctors to prescribe). Other memorandums or bulletins given to detailmen or their supervisors contain tips for selling different products, and for persuading physicians, nurses, and pharmacists of the merits of the product. One tip for selling Bactrim, a Roche product, says:

> Some physicians have been "too busy" to think of patients for Bactrim and write a prescription for them. In that case, let's be considerate of his time. If he will think of the patient's names you can see that a file card or scratch pad note goes into the patient's record.

The same bulletin advises the detailman to maximize his effort to sell on the first call. A similar booklet of information and sales tips for Searle states that at least one in every ten women could use Enovid-E, a birth control pill for women with estrogen deficiency, and asks, "Are you getting your share?"[8] (see Exhibit 4–7).

---

[8] See Pfizer Laboratories Division, Sales Pacer, vol. 17, no. 4 (February 1, 1974); Roche Laboratories, memo from Bob Frisa to Roche Laboratories Field Staff, "Bactrim—A Change in Direction"; Roche Laboratories, "Valium (diazepam): Thrombophlebitis with Diazepam used Intravenously"; Searle Laboratories, "Follow MBO," MBO #4, 1973.

EXHIBIT 4-7

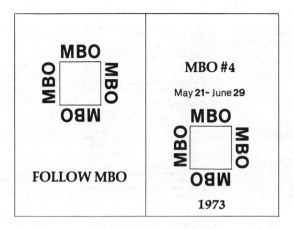

SEARLE FAMILY
OF
BIRTH CONTROL PILLS

A. SALES AIDS
- "It's the Activity that Counts" (#3703)
- "Clinical Management of Side Reactions to Oral Contraceptives" by Paul G. Mc-Donough, M.D. (#3702)
- "Birth Control...with 'the Pill' " booklets
- Compackages,™ trays, request post cards

B. MARKETING BRIEFS
The new Rx leaders are beginning to bunch again and more closely. Searle is closing in on Ortho and Wyeth.

OVULEN® is running at all-time highs, and ENOVID-E® is surging back into favor so briskly that a 15% sales increase in 1973 is certainly possible. DEMULEN® is holding its own but running below profit plan through the 1st quarter.

ENOVID-E® -21 introduction was a success (thanks to your effective salesmanship and a great product); but what is more encouraging is that reorders are also excellent. ENOVID-E-21 is airborne!

C. SALES APPROACH
Whenever a physician sees a young woman who wants birth control pills and whose complexion suggests an excessive endogenous androgen and/or deficient estrogen production, the "clear choice" should be ENOVID-E-21. Tell him so, but be sure he understands why! When he thinks ENOVID-E® everytime he sees acne, hirsutism, enlarged clitoris, etc., as signs of estrogen deficiency he'll prescribe it. And that should be for at least one in every ten young women. Are you getting your share? RP/RP — The Right Pill for the Right Patient!

Birth Control Pills are an ADD for MBO #4, but like the sales aid says, "It's the Activity that Counts"! In this case, your activity!

There is a great temptation to simply drop samples, regardless of what is wanted. Those samples are far too precious to be squandered with the wrong man or without giving the recipient good reasons to select and prescribe them intelligently.

MBO #4 presents the perfect time to concentrate your efforts on that all important nurse.

Remember? You intended to do that when you got "around to it." Well . . . here's A Round To It.

Plan each nurse call as you would an M.D. call. You may do better if you phone in advance to tell her when you expect to be there and book an appointment.

- Do you know her name? Does she know yours?
- Do you know who is the head nurse in a group?
- Do you know the best time to see her so as not to interfere with office routine?
- Do you know her patient responsibilities?
- Does she give the patient pill instructions?
- Does she ever select or advise on brand, pill schedule, package or switch products?
- Does she screen phone calls and handle the majority of pill user complaints?
- Specifically, what complaints does she handle, and how?
- How much influence does she have on the doctor . . . on patients?
- What is her attitude toward "the Pill", the IUD?
- Does she know pill differences and why some formulations are better suited to the hormone profiles of certain women than others?
- Does she correlate monilia complaints with low dose estrogen/progestogen-dominant formulations?

Many of the news bulletins provide information on the results of new research, or information on competing products. However, the detailman is advised not to volunteer this information to the doctor, a practice which indicates that his informational role is subordinate to his selling role. For example, Roche detailmen were told not to initiate a discussion with the doctor about an article on cases of thrombophlebitis occurring with the intravenous use of diazepam (sold by Roche as Valium). If the doctor mentioned the article, detailmen were advised to remind him that no product was without risk, and that any effective drug must be used cautiously.

The drug manufacturers' perception of the detailman can be assessed

EXHIBIT 4–7 (continued)

The sales pieces, "All Steroid Molecules are Not the Same" and "It's the Activity that Counts" should be used to enlighten the nurse, and where appropriate, left with her to take home to study. The greater her patient responsibilities, the greater the reason she should read the Searle Library of Contraceptive Therapy and have copies of each issue for reference.

- Has she read, "Birth Control . . . with the Pill"?

- Is she familiar with the advantages of Sunday starting? The much less expensive refillable Compack®? The Triopack™?

- Has she read and does she know how to acquire quantities from SES of Sensible Sex: Understanding your Vaginal Discharge; Don't Put Off Your Pap Smear; What is a D & C?; Fertile After 40, and Understanding High Blood Pressure?

Time tends to dim the facts of Searle leadership in history. Let's review them:

1. The first (and still best) oral-menstrual therapeutic agent, ENOVID 10 mg., in 1957
2. The first and only non-androgenic oral contraceptive, ENOVID 5 mg., in 1960, with the first pre-packaged pill schedule
3. The first refillable package (for ENOVID-E) in 1965
4. The first patient booklet, "For Your Information" (in 1963), the predecessor to "Planning Your Family" (in 1966), and now "Birth Control with the Pill"
5. The first 1 mg. pill, OVULEN, in 1966
6. The first 21-pill (three weeks on · one week off) schedule for OVULEN-2; in 1967
7. Sunday-starting for women's convenience (1969)
8. Instructional flip charts, film strips and a host of patient booklets to aid them and physicians
9. Complete patient instructions in each package

The others have copied everything we've done . . . if they are doing anything at all.

Following attention to patient history, physical examination and screening to determine whether a woman is really a candidate for using the pill, improper matching is the most common cause of pill dissatisfaction, drop out and complaints of side reaction.

Before a pill is blamed, consider that the formulation selection for that woman may have been poor.

Enlighten the nurse on the importance of proper pill selection. Matching the right pill to the right patient can improve patient acceptance and may avoid or alleviate side reactions.

Source: Searle Laboratories, "Follow MBO," MBO #4, 1973, in U.S. Congress, Senate, Examination of Pharmaceutical Industry, part 3, pp. 1218–27.

further by their position on federal certification for detailmen. The presidents of Pfizer, Ortho Pharmaceutical, and Lederle Laboratories agreed that it was inadvisable for detailmen to be federally licensed. Several reasons were given for this belief. According to these companies, there is no precedent for the licensing of professionals at the federal level; licensing at the state level is more customary. There is no basis for giving a standardized examination to detailmen, since the salesmen for each company will have specialized knowledge of different products and services. Finally, since detailmen are the employees of a company, the company should be responsible for training and supervision. These arguments suggest that drug manufacturers believe the detailman should be more responsible to his company than an independently trained professional would be.

The detailman's perspective

There seems to be a large gap between what the drug manufacturers describe as the role of a detailman and how the detailman sees himself. To a certain extent this is understandable, because individual detailmen will view their activities differently based on training, job experience, and individual personality. However, the reality of the detailman's job will also be greatly influenced by the manner in which his employer defines his job, sets performance standards, and compensates him for services rendered.

Like the drug manufacturer, the detailman sees his job as important, but he is also aware of its ambiguous nature. Bennet Wasserman, a former detailman for Merck, Sharp and Dohme, a division of Merck & Company, felt that the job of detailman is "schizophrenic," because his duty to sell his company's products conflicted with his duty to warn the doctor of possible dangers. A former detailman for Pfizer, Inc., said his feeling that as a well-trained salesman he could help the medical profession was negated by his sense that there were abuses inherent in the selling techniques he used as a detailman. Several former detailmen suggested that the drug company puts them in a situation in which they are torn between two roles. For example, a former detailman for Ortho Pharmaceutical explained that he left his job because "on the one hand I wanted to do exactly what the company wanted and sell my products," while on the other hand he saw many abuses in selling to the medical profession which he could not criticize or try to ameliorate without jeopardizing his job. By emphasizing the selling aspect of the detailman's job, the drug companies, according to former detailmen, forced them to ignore their responsibility to reveal the possible dangers in the use of a drug. Some detailmen resolved this conflict by becoming total salesmen; others looked for different jobs.

THE PRESSURE TO SELL

According to former detailmen, the pressure put on them by the drug companies to sell began almost immediately after training. Wasserman noted that "once the detailman gets into his territory . . . the duty to sell inevitably overshadows the duty to warn." As described by the detailmen, this pressure to sell came from various sources. Some felt that pressure came from the sense of loyalty the detailman felt toward the company and its products. One former detailman suggested that detailmen are convinced by their employers that there is a great need for the employers' product, and that they must spread the word. This mission "can only be achieved by increasing the number of prescriptions to be written for the products being promoted, and that means that the rallying cry is 'sell, sell, sell.' "[9] The pressure to sell also came from monetary incentives. Salary increases and bonuses depended on an evaluation detailmen saw as based primarily on selling skills. They reported considerable pressure to attain their quotas and improve "merit evaluation statistics." Periodic prizes were also awarded for such things as the most deals or special purchase offers sold to pharmacies, or the largest amount of equipment such as diaphragms sold to pharmacists or physicians.

Detailmen also felt pressured by the printed instructions given them. Bulletins contained complete selling strategies, from the use of educational aids to the importance of establishing rapport with the receptionist. The basic aim of drug selling was expressed simply in one bulletin from Roche: "Our primary job on the next call is to keep and expand the usage of those physicians to whom we have sold Bactrim, and to sell the non-users"[10] (see Exhibit 4–8 for typical bulletins).

Gift giving as a selling strategy

Bulletins also instruct detailmen on how to promote products to doctors, pharmacists, and other medical people. Detailmen described the various gifts, gimmicks, and techniques they used to persuade doctors to buy their company's product. Promotional gifts such as pens, memo pads, paperweights, ash trays, desk blotters, or coffee mugs had the name of the company's product clearly printed on them to act as a "reminder" for the physician. Another aspect of this gift giving was offering "bonuses" to doctors who prescribed large amounts of the company's products. This technique was primarily used in the generic drug market, where the doctor must arbitrarily decide which company's generic drug to prescribe.

An order blank and gift catalog for Pfizer showed that if a doctor ordered 1,000 doses of polio immunization, he would win an upright freezer with 5-cubic-foot capacity; if he ordered 500 doses, he would win a Craig rechargeable electronic calculator; and if he ordered 250 doses, he would win a physician bag or a cassette tape recorder. Other gift catalogs offered a dishwasher, a tool chest, a color television, or a stereo system for 1,140 bonus points. These bonus points were gained by prescribing various minimums of drugs. Detailmen were also instructed to give small gifts to receptionists, nurses, or others connected with doctors in order to establish rapport with them and gain their help in persuading the doctor. A former

---

[9] U.S. Senate, *Examination of the Pharmaceutical Industry*, part 3, pp. 721–76; Wasserman, "The Ubiquitous Detailman," p. 183.

[10] Wasserman, "The Ubiquitous Detailman," p. 187; Silverman and Lee, *Pills Profits, and Politics*, p. 63; Roche Laboratories, "Bactrim Phase II: How to Make that Next Bactrim Call," undated, p. 1147.

EXHIBIT 4–8

LABORATORIES DIVISION
PFIZER INC., 236 EAST 42nd STREET, NEW YORK, N.Y. 10017

NEW FOIL-PAK FOR ODD-OUNCE SCRIPTS
VIBRAMYCIN (doxycycline monohydrate)
For Oral Suspension
150 mg./30 ml.

January 22, 1974

Dear Pharmacist:

Pfizer Laboratories is pleased to present Vibramycin for Oral Suspension in Foil-Pak - a new and innovative way to package oral suspension. This new Foil-Pak will enable you to overcome the problem of filling Vibramycin O/S prescriptions that call for odd-ounce sizes — a feature that will be appreciated by your customers. In addition, Foil-Paks require less storage space than the 2-oz. bottles.

At present, our sales force is intensively promoting the Vibramycin Foil-Pak, and we anticipate that you will be receiving many prescriptions for this new item.

Please make note of the following information for future reference:

Sales Code	Description	Price
0704	Vibramycin for Oral Suspension (doxycycline monohydrate) Foil Packet (150 mg./30 ml. x 16)	$15.20

To support your stocking of the Vibramycin Foil-Pak, a 90-day dating period is offered on this shipment. If you have any questions regarding Vibramycin for Oral Suspension in the Foil-Pak, do not hesitate to call your Pfizer Laboratories Representative.

Pay as if dated	April 1, 1974
Billing date	January 30, 1974

Sincerely,

Daniel J. Coakley
Director of Trade Relations
Pfizer Pharmaceuticals

DJC/ti

EXHIBIT 4–8 (*continued*)

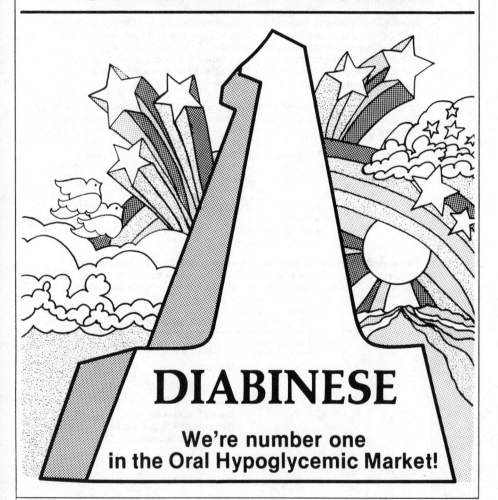

Volume XVII   Number 4   **Pfizer** LABORATORIES DIVISION   February 1, 1974

SALES PACER

DIABINESE

We're number one in the Oral Hypoglycemic Market!

We're number one
in the Oral Hypoglycemic Market!

Based on projected audited Orinase sales for 1973, DIABINESE is now the number 1 selling oral hypoglycemic agent.

Of course, this didn't happen overnight. Long, persistent efforts coupled with selling strategies and programs over a 15-year span have finally brought victory.

Introduced in 1958, Diabinese had to fight a tough battle. Once considered a potent hypoglycemic, to be used only when other agents failed, it had to overcome this limited use to enter the competition.

Now in 1974, we will have to strengthen our position because it won't be easy to continue to increase at the current rate of 21%. Diabinese will be weighted 9% on the 1974 incentive plan and will be counted again in the total segment of this plan.

Diabinese has come a long way — Thanks to you and your hard work!

EXHIBIT 4–8 *(continued)*

TAKE AIM   PFIZER '74

That was the take-off signal for the 1974 Management Planning Seminar.

This Seminar was the culmination of a six-month budget planning process which actually began with the Field Managers. In the early part of June, 1973, teams of Field Managers were assigned and brought to Headquarters to discuss the problems and opportunities of each of our products. These meetings resulted in a frank and complete discussion of each product, the market in which it competes, major obstacles to growth and strengths on which we might capitalize. From these discussions came product strategies, objectives, and ideas for specific programs.

From that focal point, Headquarters Marketing personnel formulated specific programs to support these strategies and readied promotional campaigns. The 1974 Management Planning Seminar was the forum during which the implementation phase began. Now it's up to you to put these programs to work.

Good luck!

FOIL THE COMPETITION WITH THE VIBRAMYCIN FOIL-PAK

The new Vibramycin Foil-Pak is the latest member of the Vibramycin Oral family.

Retailers and wholesalers have now received an automatic shipment of the Foil-Pak. Retailers also received a letter, (enclosed with this issue of Sales Pacer), which described the advantages of the Foil-Pak.

This new dosage form is particularly convenient for the pharmacist to dispense, since the innovative 1-oz. Foil Packets enable him to overcome the frequent problem of filling Vibramycin O/S prescriptions that call for odd-ounce sizes.

This unique packaging, not available with other tetracycline or doxycycline brands, also allows the physician to prescribe the exact number of ounces his patients need and will save work for the pharmacist while reducing the cost to the patient. In addition, Foil-Paks require less shelf space than the 2-oz. bottles and there is no risk of breakage.

A new price list containing all Pfizer Laboratories products will be sent to you shortly. In the meantime, please add the following information to your current price lists:

EXHIBIT 4–8 (continued)

Sales Code	Description	Retail Price	Wholesale Price
0704	Vibramycin for Oral Suspension (doxycycline monohydrate) Foil Packet (150 mg./30 ml. x 16)	$15.20	$14.44

Though it has its own distinctive features, the Foil-Pak also has the usual advantages of all Vibramycin products. These include a pleasant-tasting raspberry flavor for the O/S; the once-a-day dosage (after the first day); and it can be taken with food or milk. In addition, Vibramycin is a broad spectrum antibiotic effective against *Mycoplasma pneumoniae, Klebsiella, Diplococcus Pneumoniae and H. influenza*.

Recently you received an extra supply of Vibramycin Oral Suspension. Utilize these samples and the last page of your POA 1 visual aid to introduce the new Foil-Pak to physicians in your area. Be sure to let all the pharmacists in your territory know you are detailing the Foil-Pak.

Vibramycin O/S, as always, will play a major part in the family of Vibramycin products for 1974.

*   *   *   *   *

ANOTHER RENAL CLAIM PAPER

Enclosed with this week's Sales Pacer is a reprint entitled "The Effect of Doxycycline on Renal Function in Patients with Advanced Renal Insufficiency" from the Scandinavian Journal of Infectious Diseases.

This study by Stenbaek and co-workers supports earlier works claiming that treatment with Vibramycin does not result in, nor does it lead to renal deterioration or accumulation of the drug even in advanced renal failure.

FOR REFERENCE USE ONLY · DO NOT USE IN DETAILING.

SALES PACER   February 1, 1974

Q.C. FILM WINS VIBRAMYCIN HOSPITAL BIDS

The latest film-showing count reveals that the Vibramycin Quality Control film, "The Development of an Antibiotic," was shown in over 100 territories to almost 3,000 physicians and hospital pharmacists. An additional 800 allied hospital personnel have also viewed it.

Many of you were able to schedule showings in several hospitals. For instance, PSR Ivan Saunders of the Columbus District arranged for eight showings to over 100 physicians and hospital pharmacists, as well as 300 others. In each case, he reported high interest from the audiences.

The men of the Great Lakes Region created the most opportunities with the film. ARM Ben Gaines studied the results and reported that the film "has been a significant factor in winning Vibramycin bids in at least two major hospitals in Cincinnati and Indianapolis, while also undermining competitive bidding at several other large hospitals."

Because the film has been so well received, the film-showing contest will be extended through POA 1 and retail pharmacists may now also be included in the audience. 1,000 prize points will again be awarded for each showing to at least ten physicians and/or hospital or retail pharmacists. Quantities of a new card will be sent to you shortly.

Schedule as many showings as possible to physician, hospital and retail pharmacy groups. Use the Patent Visual Aid, the Patent Information Sheet, the Doxycycline Monograph of Professional Information, dosage, file cards and clinical studies to back up the quality control story of Vibramycin. Follow up with an intensive detail to each physician and pharmacist.

EXHIBIT 4–8 *(continued)*

This film can play an extremely important role in maintaining and even increasing Vibramycin sales in both hospital and retail markets. Use it extensively and help make the Vibramycin story a "reel" success story for 1974.

*   *   *   *

VD FILM AVAILABLE

The film, "VD: 'A Plague on Our House' " is now available in the Pfizer Film Library for field force use. Suitable for the general public, this 16 mm. color film has recently been shown around the country by the National Association of Retail Druggists (NARD) as part of a major 1973 VD public awareness program co-sponsored by Pfizer Laboratories.

The film points out that ignorance and fear of social stigma often prevent the afflicted from seeking treatment, although effective treatment is readily available.

As with all Vibramycin films, you can receive "VD: 'A Plague on Our House' " by making the appropriate indication on the Business Reply Card in your Medical Education Catalog. Mail your requests as usual to the Pfizer Film Library.

Sinescope

SINEQUAN BREAKTHROUGH IN OREGON

After two years of intensive effort and carefully planned strategies by DM Al Rose and DHR Paul Hancock, Sinequan is now on the Basic Drug List of the Public Welfare Division in the State of Oregon.

The project to get Sinequan on the Oregon Welfare Formulary was started two years ago. The prospects looked dim. Only two tricyclics were available for Welfare use — Elavil and Tofranil. The problem of getting Sinequan on the Basic Drug List was twofold. The first problem to overcome was to get physicians to prescribe Sinequan. This involved extensive paper work on the part of the physicians. They could prescribe Sinequan but had to fill out lengthy drug exceptions forms. The second problem was to get the Formulary Committee, which included four M.D.s, one Ph.D. in Pharmacology and three pharmacists, to consider the merits of the drug and this was done from physician usage.

This was by no means a one-man operation — it involved the efforts of everyone in the Portland District. Every man tried his best to get physicians to prescribe Sinequan even though paper work for drug exceptions was necessary and cumbersome. The second part of the operation was done by Paul Hancock. His job was to convince the Formulary Committee that Sinequan was a necessary addition to the Basic Drug List. He wrote letters to each member of the Committee outlining the favorable points of Sinequan and documented each point with monographs and clinical studies. He prepared a handsomely bound leatherette portfolio with all the essential materials in it and sent it to each member of the Formulary Committee. Further, he arranged for influential staff and administrative personnel already

EXHIBIT 4–8 *(continued)*

using Sinequan to write to members of the Committee and relate their favorable impressions of Sinequan and recommend its addition to the Welfare List.

At the 1973 meeting of the Drug and Review Committee of the Public Welfare Division, Sinequan was finally approved. After approval, it had to be reviewed by the administrative and budget staff of the Welfare Committee. After a few more incidental hurdles were scaled, Sinequan was officially placed on the Oregon Welfare List and is now available for use in Welfare patients.

It's another plus for Sinequan and extra feathers in the cap of Paul Hancock for his perseverence and ingenuity in selling Sinequan and overcoming all the obstacles in his path to success. Good job, well done Paul!

*   *   *   *   *

BRAINSTORMING WITH THE NEW LEARNING SYSTEM

The backgrounder dealing with the Catecholamine Learning System is enclosed with this issue of Sales Pacer.

This backgrounder will provide you with suggestions for effectively using the film, "Catecholamines and Affective Disorders," and its accompanying monograph. The film features Dr. Shervert Frazier as moderator, with Drs. Joseph Schildkraut, William Bunney and James Maas discussing important areas of their studies with brain catecholamines. All the participants are well recognized for their work in brain chemistry and two of them (Bunney and Schildkraut) were Nobel Prize nominees. The monograph was written by Dr. Schildkraut and will be available during POA 2.

Brainstorm with the greats — study this backgrounder well — and become familiar with the film and the monograph. With these new tools on hand you should have no trouble gaining entry into psychiatrists' offices.

Diabinese®

PHENFORMIN INDUCES ALTERATIONS

Enclosed with this issue of Sales Pacer is an article by Constantine Arvanitakis, et al. entitled "Phenformin-induced alterations of small intestinal function and mitochondrial structure in man," which appeared in the August 1973 issue of the Journal of Laboratory Clinical Medicine.

This preliminary study in normal subjects suggests that phenformin (DBI -Geigy) may depress intestinal absorption rates of glucose, as well as sodium and water. It suggests that "the diminished rates of active intestinal transport is the consequence of mitochondrial injury with phenformin and an important mechanism of action of the drug in man."

FOR REFERENCE USE ONLY - DO NOT USE IN DETAILING

EXHIBIT 4–8 *(continued)*

AGVK's Oral Antibiotics

**Pen A
Pfizerpen G
Pfizerpen VK
Pfizer-E
Tetracyn**

UP TO YOUR EARS IN R.D.P. $ALES

WOW! What a fantastic start! In the first full month of implementation the dynamic Pfizer Labs field force turned in a spectacular 2,230 R.D.P. deals totaling $675,000!

The cumulative $3,000 Super Bonus category has already been surpassed by <u>six</u> retail accounts in the <u>first month</u> . . . and in each case, on a single order. Many other accounts have already made single R.D.P. purchases exceeding $2,000.

Make it a point to see <u>every</u> single retail and wholesale account in your territory with the R.D.P. story and expand your nucleus of loyal buyers of the Oral Commodities line.

SALES PACER   February 1, 1974

1974 HOLIDAY SCHEDULE

Tuesday, January 1   New Year's Day
Monday, February 18   Washington's Birthday
Monday, May 27   Memorial Day
Thursday, July 4   Independence Day
Friday, July 5   Floater
Friday, August 30   Floater
Monday, September 2   Labor Day
Thursday, November 28   Thanksgiving Day
Friday, November 29   Floater
Wednesday, December 25   Christmas

*   *   *   *

NEW MEDICAL PLAN

Enclosed with this issue of Sales Pacer is your new 1974 Group Life and Medical Insurance Plan Booklet.

EXHIBIT 4–8 (*concluded*)

SALES PACER   February 1, 1974

PACKAGE INSERT REVISION

Attached with this week's Sales Pacer is a revised package insert for TETRACYN ORAL, #60-2200-00-2. It differs from prior TETRACYN package inserts in that all oral dosage forms of TETRACYN are combined into this single package insert. Previously, separate package inserts were available for both "TETRACYN 500" and TETRACYN capsules and syrup.

Please remove the old package insert from your Package Insert Reference Manual and replace it with the new package insert enclosed with this issue of Sales Pacer.

Any inventory you may have of TETRACYN ORAL package inserts other than that listed above should be destroyed.

Source: Pfizer Laboratories Division, *Sales Pacer,* Vol. XVII, No. 4, February 1, 1974.

Pfizer detailman described the difficulty of seeing a doctor and said: "His receptionist is often the key to this situation. To win her over we were supplied with several giveaways, including perfume, pens, and scratch pads." The pharmacist might also be won with pens, notebooks, cosmetics, sundries, and personalized gifts.

Other selling methods

Another important promotion method the detailman was instructed to use was supplying doctors and pharmacists with free samples. Detailmen described how hundreds of dollars worth of sample drugs would be given to doctors and pharmacists. The doctors often exchanged these samples with the pharmacist for shaving cream, razor blades, or perfume. The pharmacist would then resell the samples to patients. Many drug companies forbade the selling of samples in this way and would evaluate the detailman on the basis of his "sample utilization"—that is, his providing a doctor only with as many samples as that doctor needed. Detailmen, however, thought they were often pressured into giving samples to doctors and pharmacists by the need to win their good will:

> The pharmacists were well aware that detailmen carried samples and often requested them. This was especially true when the salesman was attempting to fill generic prescriptions with his company's brand. In many cases, ten or more companies were producing the exact same drug and the druggist had his choice as to which one to use.[11]

Detailmen felt that there was another reason to win the favor of the pharmacist: they needed to be able to survey the prescription files. Although this "script survey" may be illegal and is not sanctioned by many drug companies, detailmen often thought it necessary to see which doctors were prescribing which drugs. They explained that since they never knew if they had made a sale when they left the doctor's office, script surveys were the only way they could measure their success. These surveys not only allowed the detailman to see how persuasive he was, but told him where to concentrate his promotional efforts.

In order to make the sales they felt pressured to make, detailmen would often slant their information to make a drug sound more attractive. They would go further than company bulletin advice not to initiate discussions about negative journal articles or competitors' drugs. For example, they might make product comparisons in which the benefits of their products were compared with the disadvantages of the competitor's product. In using journal articles, they underlined positive information about the drug

---

[11] U.S. Senate, *Examination of the Pharmaceutical Industry*, pp. 756, 1015–37. See also Wasserman, "The Ubiquitous Detailman"; Merck Company, Memo to District Managers from Field Meeting Services, "Meeting Plans—November/December Promotional Period" (September 26, 1973).

and ignored negative information. Some detailmen reported that they heard other detailmen giving flatly false information. In general, the detailmen felt that full and accurate information about a drug was rarely given to the doctor.

Former detailmen also described how they would be asked by doctors to advise them on which drugs to use. Physicians would review medical charts and patient records with them and ask for advice on a course of therapy. A detailman described a typical example:

A doctor might say, "I have a tough gram negative pseudomonus; have you heard of this?" I will say, yes, sir, and I will cite a study of a number of patients who were on bradomycin and tell him that had stopped pseudomonus. I know he will go right down to the hospital and put those patients on bradomycin. I know.[12]

Although the former detailmen felt many of their services were useful, they believed that detailing in general had minimal value. When asked whether there were any medical, scientific, or public health benefits from detailing, former detailmen from Merck, Pfizer, Eaton Laboratories, and Ortho answered that there were probably very few. These detailmen also favored legislation prohibiting the use of gifts or free samples to influence drug prescribing.

The pharmacist's perspective

The detailman saw the pharmacist as another potential buyer of his company's drugs. A statement of the American Pharmaceutical Association (APhA) gives some idea about how the detailman, in turn, is regarded by the pharmacist. The APhA supported legislation that would phase out the use of free samples for doctors or pharmacists, substituting instead "starter prescriptions," prescriptions for three to six doses of a drug paid for by the drug industry. Prescription surveys by detailmen were also frowned upon by the APhA, which felt that the surveys violated the privacy of physicians, patients, and pharmacists. On the issue of training detailmen, the APhA favored programs certified by the secretary of HEW. APhA felt this would help curb abusive promotion practices and provide thoroughly trained and competent personnel. APhA recommended that the source of such training should be national pharmacy schools.

The American Society of Hospital Pharmacists (ASHP) agreed that any training of detailmen would benefit from the advice of pharmacists. However, ASHP preferred that detailmen not be required to have certified training programs, since this would mask their role as salesmen. Nevertheless, ASPH agreed with APhA that "the limitations on samples and other free drugs are long overdue."

---

[12] U.S. Senate, Examination of the Pharmaceutical Industry, p. 777.

OVERPROMOTION OF DRUGS

The selling techniques of the detailman have been criticized as over-promoting drugs to the point of harming patients. One incident criticized on these grounds is Parke-Davis' promotion of Chloromycetin (see *Stevens v. Parke-Davis* Case). And claims have been made of overpromotion in other cases. One example is Merck's 1963 campaign to introduce Indocin (the brand name for indomethacin). In this campaign, detailmen were told to tell doctors that "Indocin will work in that whole host of rheumatic crocks and cruds which every general practitioner, internist, and orthopoedic surgeon sees every day in his practice." Detailmen were given other suggestions on promotional practices and urged to increase sales as much as possible. Merck's literature and instructions did not mention that the FDA had approved Indocin for only a few arthritic conditions, that Indocin had caused deaths in children, or that it increased susceptibility to infections. Finally, despite massive promotional efforts claiming that Indocin was a revolutionary step in the treatment of arthritis, later studies showed that the drug was basically an aspirinlike compound.[13]

Charges of overpromotion have also been leveled against drug companies for the selling of antibiotics through detailmen. According to an article in the *Journal of the American Medical Association,* antibiotics were the most prescribed drug in America and were being used in cases where there was no indication that they were appropriate. The report estimated that one out of every two hospitalized Americans who received antibiotics in 1974 was a victim of irrational prescribing. The journal also reported that this overprescribing was causing a rise in adverse drug reactions and the development of virulent strains of bacterial infections resistant to any known antibiotic. Overuse of antibiotics has been partly attributed to the promotion of antibiotics by drug companies.

Some critics claim constant pressure on the detailman to sell more drugs is translated into the overprescribing of drugs by the doctor. A promotional campaign for Bactrim, an antibiotic used for treating urinary infections, suggests the pressure put on detailmen to sell in an already crowded market. In different bulletins, detailmen were urged to have the drug accepted and prescribed by doctors as quickly as possible. Some detailmen were congratulated because they had achieved "the most rapid and complete distribution of any new product in Roche's history." A plan to get Bactrim on hospital formularies was also discussed. Detailmen were told not to discuss a study in *The Medical Letter* which said that Bactrim caused a greater number of severe reactions than ampicillins, cephalexin, or sulfonanimides alone. Another bulletin admitted that Bactrim was iden-

---

[13] Silverman and Lee, *Pills Profits, and Politics,* p. 62; Louis Lasagna, cited in *Medical Tribune,* March 29, 1967.

tical to a drug already on the market, but that doctors should be told to use Bactrim in certain circumstances.[14]

FEDERAL CONTROLS

There is almost no governmental control of the detailman and his activities. Government regulation of drug advertising is based on the 1962 Drug Amendment to the Food, Drug, and Cosmetic Act. Before this amendment, the FTC was responsible for the false advertising of drugs, while the FDA was able to control only labeling.

In 1962, following Senator Estes Kefauver's hearings into the drug industry, an amendment was drafted which in its original form would have extended the FDA's authority over oral and written promotional statements. However, several powerful interest groups, including the AMA, the ABA (American Bar Association), and the PMA (Pharmaceutical Manufacturers Association) lobbied against acceptance of the bill as it stood. The act that was finally passed was similar to the compromise suggested by the PMA. Although the drug amendment no longer contained provisions for any control of oral statements the detailman might make in the promotion of the drug, it did regulate any written promotional materials or literature the detailman showed or left with the physician. Therefore, the government still had no authority to prosecute a drug manufacturer for "misbranding" a product when the detailman exaggerated the advantages of a drug or deemphasized its risks. The manufacturer could be prosecuted only if he had done the same in the drug's labeling or in written advertising.[15]

In 1974, two bills, the Drug Utilization Improvement Act and the Omnibus Drug Amendment, which would have restricted detailing to some extent, were proposed. Although hearings were held on these bills by the Senate subcommittee on health, they were not acted on. In 1976, several new bills that proposed some regulation of the drug industry were introduced. One of these (S.1314) would require the detailman to provide all doctors and pharmacists contacted with an HEW-approved document about the drug. This bill has not yet been acted on.[16]

---

[14] Henry E. Simmons and Paul D. Stolley, "This Is Medical Progress? Trends and Consequences of Antibiotic Use in the United States," *Journal of the American Medical Association* 227 (March 4, 1974): 1023–28; Roche Laboratories, Memo from Bob Frisa; Memo from Walt Maloy to Appalachian Division Members, "Bactrim Launch"; Memo from Howard Rofsky, M.D., to David Harris, "A Review of the Medical Letter"; "Bactrim Phase II: How to Make that NEXT Bactrim Call," undated.

[15] Council on Economic Priorities, "In Whose Hands," p. 6; Wasserman, "The Ubiquitous Detailman," p. 212.

[16] American Enterprise Institute for Public Policy Research, *New Drugs Pending Legislation*, Legislative Analysis No. 13 (Washington, D.C.: August 16, 1976), p. 52.

SELECTED BIBLIOGRAPHY

Council on Economic Priorities. *Economic Priorities Report,* vol. 4, no. 4–5 (August–November 1973).

Funk, Edwin. "Yesterday, Today and Tomorrow in Drug Advertising." *Pharmaceutical Marketing and Media* 2 (March 1967): 13.

Pharmaceutical Manufacturers Association. *Questions and Answers about the U.S. Prescription Drug Industry.* Revised June 1975, 17 pp.

U.S. Congress, Senate, Committee on the Judiciary, Subcommittee on Antitrust and Monopoly. *Administered Prices, Drugs,* June 27, 1961.

Waite, Arthur S. "The Future of Pharmaceutical Drug Promotion." *Medical Marketing and Media* 6 (June 1971): 9.

SECTION C
DISTRIBUTION

5 Acme Markets, Inc., Philadelphia*: Personal liability of a chief executive officer for the failure of subordinates to comply with statutes designed to protect public health

> *The purposes of this legislation (Food and Drug Administration Act, 1938) thus touch phases of the lives and health of people which, in the circumstances of modern industrialism, are largely beyond self-protection. Regard for these purposes should infuse construction of the legislation if it is to be treated as a working instrument of government and not merely as a collection of English words . . . Such legislation dispenses with the conventional requirement for criminal conduct-awareness of some wrongdoing. In the interest of larger good it puts the burden of acting at hazard upon a person otherwise innocent but standing in responsible to a public danger. . . .*
>
> Justice Frankfurter in *United States* v. *Dotterweich*

In June 9, 1975, the United States Supreme Court upheld the conviction of John R. Park, president of Acme Markets, Inc., Philadelphia, for rat contamination found by Food and Drug Administration inspectors in the supermarket chain's Baltimore warehouse. The Court decided that the chief executive of a corporation can be found personally guilty of criminal charges if unsatisfactory conditions anywhere in the company contaminate food or otherwise endanger health or safety.[1]

ISSUES FOR ANALYSIS

The successful and efficient operation of a large corporation hinges on a system of delegated responsibility; top executives must depend on vari-

---

* Robert Katz, University of California, Berkeley, collaborated with the author in the development of this case study.
[1] *United States* v. *John R. Park*, 421 US 658, 44 L Ed 2d 489 95 S. Ct. 1903 (1975).

ous subordinates to perform different functions and carry out separate duties. Given that delegation of responsibility and assignment of tasks is in the nature of things in any organization of reasonable size:

1. Are certain marketing and promotional practices especially suscepti-ble to causing public harm out of proportion to their contribution to the company's growth and profits? What kinds of safeguards can be built within the company organization so that the second-order ef-fects of such practices are carefully evaluated before these marketing practices are implemented?

2. Under what circumstances should a corporate officer be held *person-ally* liable for the acts of subordinates? Should the liability be related to personal knowledge or awareness of criminal wrongdoing on the part of *all* employees in the organization? Should such liability be lim-ited to certain classes of company activities, such as food adulteration, or should it cover all activities?

3. In terms of Acme markets: (a) Can a reasonable case be made that, given the nature of corporate operations, John R. Park did not exer-cise due care and supervision and therefore should be held respon-sible? (b) How is the size of the penalty, a mere $250, likely to become a deterrent for similar actions on the part of other executives in other firms? (c) Should the firm indemnify the executive for any fines paid by the executive?

4. What are the economic, social, and political implications of a broad expansion in the personal liability of corporate officers for the activ-ities of their subordinates? How might it affect the nature and extent of white collar crime?

5. What types of organizational structures and decision-making processes should be developed to maximize the discovery of illegal actions by subordinates without unduly restricting their initiative and discretion-ary decision-making? Should changes be made in a company's reward system to discourage employees from engaging in activities that could be illegal or have the potential of exposing the company and its offi-cers to civil and criminal penalties?

THE FACTS OF THE CASE[2]

Acme Markets, Inc., is a national retail food chain. It has approximately 36,000 employees, 874 retail stores, and 16 warehouses in various parts of

---

[2] The narrative in this case study is primarily derived from the following briefs and court decisions. Rather than cite them repeatedly, each source is identified by a letter and followed by a page number. The sources are as follows: A. *United States* v. *John R. Park,* 499 F 2d 839 (1974). B. *United States* v. *John R. Park,* No. 74-215, Petition for a writ of Certiorari to the United States Court of Appeals for the Fourth Circuit (1974). C. *United States* v. *John R. Park,* No. 74-215, on writ of Certiorari to the United States Court of Ap-peals for the Fourth Circuit, Brief for the United States (1974). D. *United States* v. *John R.*

the United States. Its headquarters and the office of the president are located in Philadelphia, Pennsylvania. Acme's Division 6 was headed by a divisional vice president, Robert W. McCahan, with his office in Towson, Maryland, and consisted of a warehouse complex in Baltimore and approximately 110 retail outlets. The Baltimore warehouse complex was approximately 250,000 square feet, including an older building of three stories with a basement [B–5, see footnote 2].

In November–December 1971, a federal Food and Drug Administration investigator, upon investigation of the basement of the company's Baltimore warehouse, found " 'extensive' evidence of rodent infestation in the form of rat and mouse pellets throughout the entire perimeter area and along the wall." He also found that the doors leading to the basement of the warehouse from the rail siding had openings large enough to permit the entry of rodents. Rodent pellets were found on a number of different boxes stored in the warehouse, on the floor along the walls, on the ledge in the hanging meat room, and beside bales of lime jello. One of the bales had a chewed rodent hole in the product. At a later date the investigator was able to establish that he had seen other insanitary conditions, such as rat and mouse leavings and nesting material in and around food, live and dead rodents in the warehouse, and liquid drain cleaner stored near cooked ham. Extremely overcrowded conditions and accumulated trash were also evident.

Following the inspection, Dr. Norman Kramer, chief of compliance of the FDA's Baltimore office, wrote to Park in January 1972, advising him of the conditions at the Baltimore warehouse. The letter specifically informed Park that the Baltimore warehouse was "actively and extensively inhabited by live rodents" and that these conditions had "obviously existed for a prolonged period of time without any detection, or were completely ignored" [C–5]. Dr. Kramer also sent a copy of the letter to Robert W. McCahan, vice president of the Acme Baltimore division. On February 7, 1972, McCahan, at the direction of Park, responded to Dr. Kramer's letter. His letter claimed that the warehouse and adjacent property had been cleaned, that greater efforts were made to trap rodents, that the building had been inspected and rodent entry points repaired. Hazardous household products had been relocated away from food products, additional cleaning equipment had been purchased, and additional personnel hired to keep the warehouse clean.

In March of 1972, the FDA conducted a second inspection. The inspector noted some improvement in sanitary conditions but still found evidence of infestation. The warehouse still contained rodent nesting mate-

Park, No. 74-215, on writ of Certiorari to the United States Court of Appeals for the Fourth Circuit, Brief for Respondent (1974). E. *United States* v. *John R. Park*, No. 74-215, on writ of Certiorari to the United States Court of Appeals for the Fourth Circuit, Reply Brief for the United States (1974). F. *United States* v. *John R. Park*, on writ of Certiorari to the United States Court of Appeals for the Fourth Circuit, Brief for Respondent in Opposition (1974).

rial, dead rodents, damaged liquid bait traps, poorly fitting exterior doors, and rodent-contaminated food products. The inspection of the warehouse by the FDA in November and December of 1971 occupied twelve days. At its conclusion, the FDA issued a list of observations which described the rodent infestation to the warehouse manager. During the March 1972 investigation, the government recognized that a great effort had been made to clean up the warehouse. Following the second inspection, a second letter was sent by the Food and Drug Administration to Park, with a copy to McCahan. McCahan again responded and stated that close to $70,000 had been expended, including the cost of merchandise destroyed, the cost of new doors, rodent-proofing alterations, automatic sweeping equipment, hiring of additional personnel, and other items. In June 1972 there was a meeting at the Baltimore office of the Food and Drug Administration attended by McCahan and other officers of Acme. Park was not present [D–5, 6].

THE LEGAL PROCEEDINGS

The district court

In March 1973, the United States filed a suit against Acme and Park, charging them with five counts of violations of Section 301(k) of Food and Drug Administration Act, 1938.[3] The first four counts in the indictment related to violations discovered during the November and December 1971 inspection. The fifth count related to the March 1972 inspection. This action was one of two similar prosecutions filed within a year after the release of a report by the comptroller general of the United States recom-

---

[3] Section 301(k) of the Federal Food, Drug and Cosmetic Act of 1938, 52 Stat. 1042, as amended, 21 U.S.C. 331(k) provides: "The following acts and the causing thereof are prohibited: (k) The alterations, mutilation, destruction, obliteration, or removal of the whole or any part of the labeling of, or the doing of any other act with respect to, a food, drug, device or cosmetic, if such act is done while such article is held for sale (whether or not the first sale) after shipment in interstate commerce and results in such article being adulterated or misbranded."

Sections 303 (a) and (b) of the Food, Drug, and Cosmetic Act of 1938, 52 Stat. 1043, as amended, 21 U.S.C. 333 (a) and (b) provide: "(a) Any person who violates a provision of section 331 of this title shall be imprisoned for not more than one year or fined not more than $1,000.00 or both. (b) Notwithstanding the provisions of subsection (a) of this section, if any person commits such a violation after a conviction of him under this section has become final, or commits such a violation with the intent to defraud or mislead, such a person shall be imprisoned for not more than three years or fined not more than $1,000.00 or both."

Section 402 (a) of the Food, Drug and Cosmetic Act of 1938, 52 Stat. 1046, as amended, 21 U.S.C. 342 (a), provides in part: "A food shall be deemed to be adulterated * * * (3) if it consists in whole or in part of any filthy, putrid, or decomposed substance, or if it is otherwise unfit for food; or (4) if it has been prepared, packed, or held under unsanitary conditions whereby it may have become contaminated with filth, or whereby it may have been rendered injurious to health * * *"

mending increased enforcement by the Food and Drug Administration.[4]
Acme pleaded guilty to all five counts in the information. Park pleaded
not guilty and sought to determine the basis upon which the government
alleged liability. The government responded by stating that the evidence
"will simply show that the defendant was a corporate officer who, under
law, bore a relationship to the receipt and storage of food which would
subject him to criminal liability" under the principles set forth in *United
States* v. *Dotterwiech*,[5] a decision of the U.S. Supreme Court issued in 1943
[D–7].

For the prosecution. The government's case was that "Mr. Park was
responsible for seeing that sanitation was taken care of, and he had a system set up that was supposed to do that. This system didn't work three
times. At some point in time, Mr. Park has to be held responsible for the
fact that his system isn't working" [C–9, 10]. The government showed that
Park was aware of the sanitation problems in the Baltimore warehouse,
having received the correspondence from the FDA with copies to McCahan, and McCahan's responses to the FDA's communications. Through
cross-examination of Park, the prosecution showed that with the exception of the divisional vice president, the same corporate officials had responsibility for sanitation in both Baltimore and Philadelphia.

Park conceded that sanitation "is a thing that I am responsible for in the
entire operation of the company," and stated that he had assigned this
phase of the company's operation to "dependable subordinates" [C–8].
Park admitted that since the same problem with regard to sanitation had
occurred twice, once in Philadelphia in 1970 and then again in Baltimore,
it would indicate that the system he had set up for handling sanitation was
not working. He also said that although he would consider McCahan responsible for the failure of the system in Baltimore, ultimately he (Park)
was responsible [C–8, 9]. The government also established that the company's bylaws provided that the chief executive officer shall have "general
and active supervision of the affairs, business, offices and employees of
the company."[6]

---

[4] Comptroller General of the United States, *Dimensions of Insanitary Conditions in the
Food Manufacturing Industry, Report to the Congress*, No. B-164031 (a) (April 18, 1972).
The other case involved Food Fair, Inc., headquarters in Philadelphia, Pennsylvania, and a
Food Fair vice president based in Towson, Maryland. Both were charged with violations of
section 301(k) of the Food and Drug Administration Act, based on the presence of rodents
in Food Fair's Baltimore warehouse. The charges against the individual corporate officer
were subsequently dismissed at the request of the government. Food Fair, Inc. pleaded
guilty. [D–4, 5].

[5] *United States* v. *Dotterweich,* 320 U.S. 277 (1943).

[6] The bylaws provided in pertinent part:
"The Chairman of the board of directors or the president shall be the chief executive
officer of the company as the board of directors may from time to time determine. He
shall subject to the board of directors, have general and active supervision of the affairs,
business, offices and employees of the company. . . .

For the defense. Counsel for Park contended that as the president of a large corporation, he had no choice but to delegate duties to those in whom he had confidence, that he had no reason to suspect his subordinates of failing to ensure compliance with the act, and that, once violations were unearthed, acting through those subordinates he did everything possible to correct them. The basic facts were clearly established and not in dispute. The corporation pleaded guilty to the five counts. The government had no difficulty in establishing the existence of the insanitary conditions. After presentation of the prosecution's case, Park's lawyer moved for a judgment of acquittal, as he did after the close of the presentation of evidence and again after the verdict against Park. Counsel for Park also argued that (1) "Statutes such as the ones the government sought to apply in the Park case were criminal statutes and should be strictly construed," and (2) the fact that John Park was president and chief executive officer of Acme Markets, Inc., "does not itself justify a finding of guilty under Counts I through V of the Information."

The jury found Park guilty on all five counts, and the court sentenced Park to a fine of $50 on each count, for a total of $250. Park appealed.

Decision of the court of appeals for the fourth circuit

Park's major contention on his appeal was that the district court erred in its instructions to the jury. He also contended that the prejudicial evidence of warnings of alleged prior violations of the act was improperly admitted.

The district court's instructions to the jury read, in part, as follows:

> In order to find the Defendent guilty on any count of the Information, you must find beyond a reasonable doubt on each count, that the food that was held was held for sale in the Acme warehouse after shipment in interstate commerce. *Secondly,* that the food involved was held in unsanitary conditions. . . . *Thirdly,* that John R. Park held a position of authority in the operation of the business of Acme Markets, Incorporated. However, you need not concern yourselves with the first two elements of the case. The main issue for your determination is only with the third element, whether *the defendant held a position of authority and responsibility in the business of Acme Markets.* . . . The statute makes individuals, as well as corporations, liable for violations. . . . As I have instructed you in this case, they are, and that the *individual had a responsible relation to the situation, even though he may not have participated personally.* . . . *The issue is, in this case, whether the Defendant, John R. Park, by virtue of his position in the com-*

"He shall from time to time, in his discretion or at the order of the board, report the operations and affairs of the company. He shall also perform such other duties and have such other powers as may be assigned to him from time to time by the board of directors." *United States v. John R. Park,* 421 US 658, 44 L Ed 2d 489, 95 S. Ct. 1903, footnote 7 at 495 (1975).

pany, had a position of authority and responsibility in the situation out of which these charges arose. [Emphasis added] [D–9, 10]

Park's lawyer objected to the instructions on the ground that they were not consistent with this court's decision in *Dotterweich* and did not sufficiently define the standards applicable to Park's responsibility. The District Court judge overruled the argument, saying *"Dotterweich* and subsequent cases had indicated that the definition of the 'responsible relationship' was really a jury question . . . and not even subject to being defined by the Court"* [D–11].

It has long been established as a principle of law that in order for a court to find criminal liability present, there must be an intent and deliberate or aware wrongdoing. Park argued that there was no intent on his part to violate the statute; in addition, there was no overt wrongful action that could be construed as either negligence or inattention to his duties. Thus, to impose a liability upon a person who was "responsible" but was not in direct proximity or actual involvement with the alleged wrongdoing was a departure from the established common law principles of criminal liability.

A divided court of appeals reversed the judgment, the judgment of conviction, and remanded the case for a new trial. The majority held that the charge did not correctly state the law as declared in *United States* v. *Dotterweich.*[7] The Court of Appeals held that *Dotterweich* dispensed with the need to prove "awareness of wrongdoing" by Park but did not dispense

---

[7] In the *Dotterweich* case, the Supreme Court in a five to four decision held that individual corporate officers and employees, as well as corporations, may be convicted for doing or causing the acts prohibited in Section 301 of the Federal Food, Drug and Cosmetic Act of 1938, 21 U.S.C. 331. In that decision, the Court also restated the standard of responsibility for the corporate officers and agents through whom corporations handling food and drugs must act: those standing in a responsible relation to the prohibited acts may be criminally liable for failure to take steps to prevent their occurrence, even though the officers are not aware of wrongdoing.

As *Dotterweich* was presented when it reached the Supreme Court, the primary question was whether "only the corporation was the 'person' subject to prosecution" under the act. Therefore, the Supreme Court's opinion reveals very little about the factual setting in that case. Mr. Dotterweich, president and general manager of Buffalo Pharmacal Company, Inc., was charged with three counts of violation of the FDCA. His company employed only 26 persons, all of whom worked on one floor of the building. Mr. Dotterweich was responsible for "general overseeing" of the company operations; he was the direct supervisor of all employees. The trial transcript establishes that Mr. Dotterweich personally made every executive decision and had direct personal supervisory responsibility over the physical acts which resulted in the interstate shipment of misbranded and adulterated drugs. (These drugs were manufactured by another firm, then repackaged and sold by Buffalo Pharmacal Company.)

The jury in the original trial found Dotterweich individually guilty, but did not find the company guilty. Dotterweich had argued that he was not a "person" within the meaning of the act and that he had not had prior notice of potential liability. The court of appeals reversed the trial court's decision on this basis, because Dotterweich had not been derelict or perpetrated the wrong. But the Supreme Court ruled that Dotterweich could be held liable, thus setting a precedent for criminal responsibility of corporate officials as individuals, rather than any such liability's being limited (as previously) to the corporation as an entity.

with the need to prove that Park was "in some way personally responsible for the act constituting the crime." The court concluded that Park's conviction must be reversed because the instruction "might well have left the jury with the erroneous impression that Park could be found guilty in the absence of 'wrongful action' on his part" [A–841, 842].

Before the Supreme Court

In August 1974, the United States filed a petition with the U.S. Supreme Court asking for a writ of certiorari against the appeals court's decision.[8] In its brief, the government argued that the 1938 act made responsible officials criminally liable for failure to discover and correct insanitary conditions because they have the power and responsibility to prevent such conditions, and have failed to do so. Further, the act "dispenses with the conventional requirement for criminal conduct—awareness of some wrongdoing. In the interest of the larger good it puts the burden of acting at hazard upon a person otherwise innocent but standing in a responsible relation to a public danger" [C–20]. The concept of responsible relation thus served to limit the application of the act to those corporate officials who had the power and responsibility to prevent insanitary conditions. By the same token, it allowed an apparently responsible corporate official to prove—as a matter of defense—that he was without power to affect the prohibited condition [C–23]. The holding of the court of appeals in the Park case would therefore substantially distort this statutory scheme [C–23].

In his brief, Park contended that the appeals court was correct in reversing the district court's decision. In the charge to the jury, the district court twice instructed the jury that the main or only matter for their determination was whether the defendant Park held a position of authority and responsibility at Acme. However, since Park was selected for prosecution because he was president and chief executive officer of Acme, his position had already been established. This portion of the charge was therefore "contrary to the fundamental principle, 'that a judge may not direct a verdict of guilty no matter how conclusive the evidence,' *United Brotherhood of Carpenters* v. *United States*, 330 U.S. 395, 408" [D–13]. Park also contended that the criminal liability of an individual charged under the statute is never a vicarious liability for the conduct of others. The FDA has rarely, if ever, established criminal liability in cases which did not involve facts showing "the personal responsibility" which the court of

---

[8] A writ of certiorari is a writ or order issued by the Supreme Court directing the lower court to send up to the Supreme Court the case from the lower court for review by the Supreme Court. Four justices must agree that a writ should be issued, otherwise the petition will be denied.

appeals required be established on retrial in the present case [D–31, 32; C–25, 26].[9]

Park further argued that no burden is imposed by requiring proof of acts of omission which cause the offenses charged, because the government has always previously required evidence of such acts as a condition to prosecution of corporate officers [D–32], and that evidence of alleged prior crimes should have been excluded at the first trial and admissible at a subsequent trial only if the need for such evidence outweighs prejudicial effect [D–33].

Amicus curiae briefs by trade associations. In view of the importance of the Park case and its potential implications for other companies and industries, a number of trade associations filed *amicus curiae*[10] briefs before the Supreme Court. Those filing briefs were The National Association of Food Chains (NAFC), the Grocery Manufacturers of America, Inc. (GMA), the Synthetic Organic Chemical Manufacturers Association (SOCMA), and The National Canners Association (NCA). There was no brief filed on behalf of the pharmaceutical industry, although it would appear that their stake in the outcome of the case would be quite important. Typical of these briefs were those of NAFC and NCA.

The NAFC brief. The National Association of Food Chains, Inc. (NAFC) submitted its *amicus curiae* brief because of the concern of its members with the matter before the Court. NAFC is a nonprofit trade association whose approximately two hundred members are engaged in the retail distribution of food and grocery products and are therefore subject to the Federal Food, Drug, and Cosmetic Act, 21, U.S.C. 301 et seq. The association is composed of all the larger, most of the medium-sized, and a cross-section of smaller food chains in the United States.

NAFC's brief states that the implications of this case extend beyond the issue of warehouse sanitation and the application of 301(k), 21 U.S.C. 331(k). The decision will have a direct impact on the extent of criminal prosecution for all offenses under the Federal Food, Drug, and Cosmetic Act. As presented to the Court, the issue is whether or not an individual can be held criminally liable for a corporate violation of this act where there is no evidence of his or her participation in the alleged violation. If a corporate officer or other employee has diligently undertaken to establish and implement a comprehensive compliance program, neither the

---

[9] *United States* v. *H. B. Gregory Co.,* 502 F 2d 700, petition for a writ of Certiorari pending, No. 74-142; *United States* v. *Shapiro,* 491 F 2d 335–337 (C.A. 6); *Lelles* v. *United States,* 241 F 2d 21, certiorari denied, 353 U.S. 974; *United States* v. *Cassaro, Inc.,* 443 F 2d 600 (C.A. 7); *United States* v. *Parfait Power Puff Co.,* 163 F 2d 1008 (C.A. 7); certiorari denied, 332 U.S. 851; *United States* v. *Diamond State Poultry Co.,* 125 F. Supp. 617 (D. Del.).

[10] An *amicus curiae* brief is one filed by a friend of the court, generally a party who has no direct involvement in the case but who has an interest in and would be affected by the decision of the court.

statute nor prior cases require that he or she be convicted of a criminal offense. Effective compliance with the act will best be obtained by requiring a high standard of effort, as evidenced in part by NAFC's warehouse sanitation guidelines.

The decision of the court of appeals provides that an individual's criminal liability under 303 of the Federal Food, Drug, and Cosmetic Act, 21 U.S.C. 333, must be based on his or her own acts or omissions which contribute to a violation. NAFC's members strongly urge that this standard be affirmed, both because it correctly interprets applicable law, and because it establishes a workable rule for compliance with the act.

The NCA brief.   The National Canners Association is a nonprofit trade association of approximately six hundred members who have canning operations in forty-four states and the territories. Members of the association pack 80 to 90 percent of the entire national production of canned fruits, vegetables, juices, specialties, meat, and fish. Many aspects of its members' operations are subject to the requirements of the Federal Food, Drug, and Cosmetic Act, as amended, 21 U.S.C. 301–392 [1970].

The NCA brief states that since *Dotterweich*, the country's economy has evolved to a point where most of the goods covered by the act are produced and distributed by corporations having chains of management command that necessarily function by delegation. Many members of the association have scores of packing plants and warehouses located throughout the nation and employing tens of thousands of employees. The management of these companies must necessarily function by delegating operational authority to subordinates, in large part because of the physical separation between management, usually located at a corporate headquarters, and the various processing operations, which must be located close to where different crops are grown.

Another factor which has lead to an increased need for delegation of operational authority, particularly with respect to compliance with the act, has been the increasingly complex technical requirements imposed by the Food and Drug Administration under the act since *Dotterweich*, which now fill six volumes of the Code of Federal Regulations. These regulations are now so complex that they are literally unintelligible except to an expert. One need merely examine, as an example, the regulations applicable to "Thermally Processed Low-Acid Food Packaged in Hermetically Sealed Containers [21 C.F.R. Part 90 (1974); 21 C.F.R. Part 128b (1974)], to comprehend that only a specially trained individual can be expected to understand and implement those requirements. Indeed, the regulations specifically provide that the processing be conducted:

> . . . under the operating supervision of a person who has attended a school approved by the Commissioner for giving instruction in retort operations, processing systems operations, aseptic processing and packaging systems operations, and container closure inspections, and has been identified by that school as having satisfactorily completed the prescribed course of instruction. (21 C.F.R. 128b. 10)

Since no company president can be expected to develop the requisite expertise in each of the fields needed to interpret and implement compliance with the bulk of the FDA's present regulations, he or she must rely on technically trained subordinates. It is against this background that trial courts today must consider and charge juries as to under what circumstances it is consistent with the intent of Congress and the purposes of the act to impose absolute criminal sanctions, in the absence of knowledge or intent, on chief executive officers and other management personnel for corporate violations because of the failure of a remote subordinate to conform to one of the massively detailed and technically complex regulations the FDA routinely promulgates today.[11]

In the cases since *Dotterweich* in which individual defendants have denied having a "responsible share" in the transaction, the trial and appellate courts have generally justified a conviction with little more than a citation to or quotation from the rhetoric in *Dotterweich*. In those cases it is clear that the individual defendants were intimately involved in and usually present on a day-to-day basis at the site of the operations giving rise to the violations. This case clearly demonstrates that the approach is no longer adequate, in view of the changes in the regulated industries and the requirements under the act since *Dotterweich*. Some defined direction to lower courts is needed because of the difficulties inherent in applying a standard enunciated in a case involving a one-man operation with 26 employees to the realities of today's disparate mass production.[12]

The Supreme Court decision.   In a 6 to 3 decision, the Supreme Court reversed the decision of the court of appeals and held that (1) criminal liability under the Federal Food, Drug, and Cosmetic Act does not turn on awareness of some wrongdoing or conscious fraud, and the act permits conviction of responsible corporate officials who have the power to prevent or correct violation; (2) viewed as a whole, the jury instruction was adequate; and (3) the evidence that the president had previously been advised of insanitary conditions at the Philadelphia warehouse was admissible since it served to rebut the official's defense that he had justifiably relied upon subordinates to handle sanitation matters. The main elements of the Court's decision are as follows:[13]

1.   The Court agreed with the prosecution's reading and interpretation

---

[11] Criminal prosecution of individuals under the act is a frequent occurrence. A recent study of the agency's enforcement activities reveals that in 1973 approximately 90 criminal cases were forwarded to United States attorneys for prosecution and in most, consistent with the FDA's policy, at least one responsible individual was charged. The United States attorneys and the Department of Justice declined to prosecute only a very small percentage of these cases. See Daniel F. O'Keefe, Jr., and Marc H. Shapiro, "Personal Criminal Liability under the Federal Food, Drug, and Cosmetic Act: The Dotterweich Doctrine," *Food, Drug, Cosmetic Law Journal* 30 (1975): 5.

[12] O'Keefe and Shapiro, "Personal Criminal Liability Under the Federal Food, Drug, and Cosmetic Act: The Dotterweich Doctrine," p. 24.

[13] *United States* v. *John R. Park*, 421 U.S. 658, 44 L Ed 2d 489, 95 S. Ct. 1903 (1975), 489–490.

of the Supreme Court's earlier decision in *United States* v. *Dotterweich*. Central to the Court's conclusion (in the Dotterweich case) "that individuals other than proprietors are subject to the criminal provisions of the Act" was the reality that "the only way in which a corporation can act is through the individuals who act on its behalf." The Court also noted that corporate officers had been subject to criminal liability under the Federal Food and Drugs Act of 1906, and it observed that a contrary result under the 1938 legislation would be incompatible with the expressed intent of Congress to "enlarge and stiffen the penal net" and to discourage a view of the act's criminal penalties as a "license fee for the conduct of an illegitimate business." The Court recognized that, because the act dispenses with the need to prove "consciousness of wrongdoing," it may result in hardship even as applied to those who share "responsibility in the business process resulting in" a violation. It regarded as "too treacherous" an attempt to define or even to indicate by way of illustration the class of employees which stands in such a "responsible relation." The question of responsibility depended on the evidence produced at the trial and its submission to the jury under appropriate guidance. The Court added that in such matters the good sense of prosecutors, the wise guidance of trial judges, and the ultimate judgment of juries must be trusted.

2.   The Court stated that the rule of subjecting corporate employees with responsible positions to the criminal provisions of the act was not formulated in a vacuum. Cases under the Federal Food and Drugs Act of 1906 reflected the view both that knowledge or intent were not required to be proved in prosecutions under its criminal provisions, and that responsible corporate agents could be subjected to the liability thereby imposed. Moreover, the principle had been recognized that a corporate agent through whose act, default, or omission the corporation committed a crime was himself guilty individually of that crime. The principle had been applied whether or not the crime required "consciousness of wrongdoing," and it had been applied not only to those corporate agents who themselves committed the criminal act, but also to those who by virtue of their managerial positions or other similar relation to the actor could be deemed responsible for its commission.

3.   The Court observed that the act imposed not only a positive duty to seek out and remedy violations when they occurred, but also, and primarily, a duty to implement measures to ensure that violations do not occur. The requirements of foresight and vigilance imposed on responsible corporate agents are demanding and perhaps onerous, but they are no more stringent than the public has a right to expect of those who voluntarily assume positions of authority in business enterprises whose services and products affect its health and well-being. Although the act did not make criminal liability turn on "awareness of some wrongdoing" or "conscious fraud," the duty imposed by Congress on responsible corporate agents was one that required the highest standard of foresight and vigilance. But the act does not require the impossible:

The theory upon which responsible corporate agents are held criminally accountable for "causing" violations of the Act permits a claim that a defendant was "powerless" to prevent or correct the violation to "be raised defensively at a trial on the merits" [*United States* v. *Wiesenfeld Warehouse Co.,* 376 US 86, 91 (1964)]. If such a claim is made, the defendant has the burden of coming forward with evidence, but this does not alter the Government's ultimate burden of proving beyond a reasonable doubt the defendant's guilt, including his power, in light of the duty imposed by the Act, to prevent or correct the prohibited condition. Congress has seen fit to enforce the accountability of responsible corporate agents dealing with products which may affect the health of consumers by penal sanctions cast in rigorous terms, and the obligation of the courts is to give them effect so long as they do not violate the Constitution.[14]

SELECTED BIBLIOGRAPHY

Comptroller General of the United States. "Dimensions of Unsanitary Conditions in the Food Manufacturing Industry." Report to Congress, No. B-164031, April 18, 1972. Washington, D.C.: Government Printing Office, 1972.

"Developments in The Law—The Federal Food, Drug, and Cosmetic Act." *Harvard Law Review* 67 (1954): 632.

Drucker, Peter. *Management: Tasks, Responsibilities, Practices.* New York: Harper & Row, 1974.

"Executive Liability Faces Its Biggest Test." *Business Week,* February 24, 1975, p. 102.

Galbraith, Jay. *Designing Complex Organizations.* Lexington, Mass.: Addison-Wesley, 1973.

Greenwood, Ronald G. *Managerial Decentralization: A Study of The General Electric Philosophy.* Lexington, Mass.: Heath, 1974.

Grocery Manufacturers of America, Inc. *Guidelines for Product Recall.* Washington, D.C., 1974.

Hagan, John T. *A Management Role for Quality Control.* New York: American Management Association, 1968.

Iseman, Robert H. "The Criminal Responsibility of Corporate Officials for Pollution of the Environment." *Albany Law Review* 37 (1972): 61.

"The Law Closes In on Managers." *Business Week,* May 10, 1976, p. 110.

National Association of Food Chains. *Voluntary Industry Sanitation Guidelines for Food Distribution Centers and Warehouses.* Washington, D.C., 1974.

O'Keefe, Daniel F., and Shapiro, Marc H. "Personal Criminal Liability under the Federal Food, Drug, and Cosmetic Act: The Dotterweich Doctrine." *Food, Drug, Cosmetic Law Journal* 30 (January 1975): 5.

"The Rising Cost of Corporate Guilt." *Business Week,* November 8, 1976, p. 36.

Tullock, Gordon. *The Politics of Bureaucracy.* Washington, D.C.: Public Affairs, 1965.

Wasserstrom, Richard A. "Strict Liability in the Criminal Law." *Stanford Law Review* 12 (1960): 731.

---

[14] *United States* v. *John R. Park,* 421 U.S. 658, 670 (1975), 673.

6 Mobil Oil Company and its franchised dealers: Big corporation, small entrepreneur, and consumer interest and convenience

Big oil isn't out to get the independent gasoline dealers out of a sense of malice or anything like that. It's just good business. . . . they don't renew leases. They say they're eliminating uneconomic stations. But why should the uneconomic stations always be independents?

Martin Lobel, lawyer and former executive
assistant to Senator William Proxmire

In February 1974, Mr. Lawrence Ancker, the owner of North Avenue Service Center, a Mobil gas outlet, joined twenty other Mobil dealers in a class action suit to prevent the company from canceling their leases. Mr. Ancker had been notified by Mobil in October 1973 that the lease would not be renewed.

THE INDEPENDENT DEALER'S POSITION

Mr. Ancker's case against the company can be summarized as follows:

In April 1972 Mr. Ancker entered into an agreement with Mobil Oil to lease Mobil-owned land, a building on that land, and the use of Mobil trademarks and advertising in order to operate a gas station and affiliated service facilities in Norwalk, Connecticut. The lease was to run one year and was subject to renewal every year. Ancker contended that with an investment of money, time, and effort, he built his station into a high-volume dealership (over 500,000 gallons a year). He regards himself as the Lord & Taylor's of Norwalk's gas stations.[1] His lease was renewed for a second year. However, in October 1973 he received a letter from Mobil simply saying that his lease was being canceled and that it was inadvisable to renew it. "That's all. No cause. No nothing."[2] Mobil offered him a job

---

[1] "Service Stations Battle Mobil Oil in Connecticut," *The New York Times,* March 19, 1974, p. 47. See also "Dealer Claims Mobil Oil Forces Him to Clear Out," *The Hour* (a Norwalk, Connecticut, daily newspaper), February 28, 1974, p. 1.

[2] "Service Stations Battle Mobil Oil," *The New York Times,* March 19, 1974, p. 47.

with the company to run the same station as contract manager. Ancker maintained that Mobil was following a similar policy in Connecticut and New Jersey and had canceled the leases of a majority of their dealers who were operating gas stations with high sales volumes.

> Under this plan, Mobil will *own* the gasoline that the station will sell, *fix* the price at which it will be sold and reap the profit therefrom. The contract manager selected will be an *employee* of Mobil. He will be paid a weekly salary, and as additional income will keep the profit he makes on the sale of tires, batteries, accessories and repairs.[3]

Ancker contended that Mobil's move was directed at controlling the movement and disposal of gas and its pricing at every point from the oil well to the gas pump and would result in "a monopolistic bonanza" for the oil companies. The independent retailer would be the loser but the public would be the real victim, "as it would be at the mercy of the major oil companies, which would control prices."[4] Ancker further maintained that although he would be making essentially the same amount of money under the new arrangement, he could not go along with it because he wanted to retain his "independent status and continue to serve the community on that basis."[5]

MOBIL OIL COMPANY'S POSITION

Mobil contended that the company's action was in response to the Franchise Act amendments enacted in 1973. (As of February 1974, Mobil had canceled 14 of its 200 franchises in Connecticut and had sent notices of cancellation to another 90 dealers.) This act prohibits an oil supplier from failing to renew a service station lease except for "good cause," but the act does not define the phrase "good cause." In a communication to the author, J. William Dalgetty, a Mobil Oil regional attorney, stated:

> The 1973 Connecticut Franchise Act had the effect of giving a dealer, who had invested approximately $10,000 in inventory and equipment, the same long term property rights in a service station as an oil company supplier that had invested $300,000.
> . . . the supplier/landlords did not know under what conditions they would be able to discontinue doing business with a service station dealer once they entered into a lease arrangement.
> . . . this legislation is basically anti-consumer because it denies an oil company landlord the flexibility to discontinue doing business with those dealers that operate a dirty service station, and engage in price gouging and other practices not in the best interests of the consuming public.[6]

---

[3] Letter dated February 20, 1974, from Lawrence Ancker to Fred Ferretti, staff reporter of *The New York Times*.

[4] "Dealer Claims," *The Hour*, February 28, 1974, p. 1.

[5] Ibid.

[6] Letter to the author dated October 21, 1974.

The company further stated that this law removed nearly all control the company then had over such an investment "even to the extent of preventing us from choosing not to continue doing business with a dealer after a lease or a supply contract has expired."[7] The company was left with "no alternative but to work out a new relationship with dealers in Connecticut."[8] The dealers so chosen were invariably high-volume, high-value stations.

The company's response implied that it was simply taking defensive measures, confined to Connecticut, to protect its long-term interests as well as those of the consuming public. However, a perusal of news reports and a flurry of private and government civil and criminal lawsuits indicated, at least on the surface, that Mobil's activities were not confined to Connecticut. Nor was it alone in its efforts to increase the number of company-owned stations. It seemed that most of the major oil companies were taking advantage of the fuel shortage and endeavoring to squeeze out the independent operators by denying them adequate fuel supplies and other practices aimed at making these dealers' operations unprofitable (see Appendix).

THE STATE OF CONNECTICUT STEPS IN

The Connecticut State Assembly responded to the complaints of many dealers by introducing a new bill—5096—which would amend the 1973 Franchise Act and make a material alteration of a franchise an unfair trade practice. The bill also provided for compulsory arbitration in case of contract disputes between dealer and company. The bill had the support of an overwhelming majority of the state's independent gasoline station operators (those opposing it felt it did not afford them enough protection), the state's Department of Consumer Protection, and Connecticut Governor Thomas J. Meskill.

The hearings[9] were held before the General Law Committee of the Connecticut State Assembly. The only organized group objecting to the bill was the petroleum industry, which instead supported bill 328 (discussed later in this case). The arguments for and against the bill throw a great deal of light on the practices of the oil industry as seen by the industry and the independent dealers. Equally important, they tell us something about the rhetoric employed by various parties.

Arguments against Bill 5096

The representative from Mobil Oil made the following arguments:
1. Bill 5096 suffers from the same defects as the 1973 amendment to

---

[7] "Service Stations Battle Mobil Oil," *The New York Times,* March 19, 1974, p. 51.

[8] Ibid.

[9] Transcripts of hearings before the General Law Committee on bills 5096 and 328 dated March 19, 1974, pp. 256–84; April 1, 1974, pp. 114–20; April 23, 1974, pp. 1280–1336; May 3, 1974, pp. 2462–63.

the Franchise Act: there is no definition of "good cause." What would constitute good cause? An oil company's wish to sell a service station when a lease has expired? The company's desire to convert the property to another use? If poor appearance constitutes good cause, who would determine the standards of poor appearance?

2. The purpose of this bill is to give franchisees more security when dealing with their franchisors. However, the bill will actually have the opposite effect. By not being able to make any materially different changes in the terms or conditions of the agreement, the franchisor might simply have to change its way of doing business. The term "materially different change" is too vague and only adds to the uncertainties already present in the 1973 Franchise Act.

3. The bill would make an unfair trade practice out of the termination, nonrenewal, or modification of a franchise. The Unfair and Deceptive Trade Practices Act passed last year is a consumer protection act. Franchisees, including service station dealers and various restaurant and hotel/motel operators, are not consumers but businessmen, and as such should be regulated by laws affecting trade and commerce.

4. Compulsory arbitration is not a good solution. The courts are better equipped to resolve such disputes and thus should be used.

These arguments were supplemented by those of the Shell Oil Company: (1) The provisions of bill 5096 were discriminatory, confiscatory, and vindictive and therefore undesirable and unnecessary. (2) A group of dealers misled the committee. Good dealers don't need the protection of this bill—it is only the "unprofessional, inept, inefficient" dealer who needs it in order to remain in business. (3) The rights of dealers and suppliers must be balanced so that the interests of gasoline consumers can be protected.

Arguments for Bill 5096

The Department of Consumer Protection presented the following arguments in support of the bill:

1. The State of Connecticut had the power to enact legislation involving a contract which in turn involved a trademark.

2. The so-called ambiguity about the definition of "good cause" was a red herring on the part of the oil companies to direct attention from the main issue of protecting the rightful and legitimate interests of gas station operators.

3. "Good cause" is a positive declaratory statement of conduct and accepted as such in a great number of other states—for example, Iowa, Nebraska, Florida, and New Jersey. There are many similar phrases in existing state and federal statutes: "undue influence," "unfaithfulness," "unfair use," "unreasonable rate," "unfair competition," "unjust discrimination," and the like have been left undefined. They have been constantly

interpreted by reasonable people operating in good faith throughout our history and at all levels of our judicial system.

4. Why a company would or would not renew a franchise is a question not of semantics but of motives.

5. Mobil was not concerned with the provisions of the Franchise Act or bill 5096. Its concern lay with the acquisition of high-volume, high-value stations as part of the company's long-range plans. For example, on February 5, 1974, a Mobil representative testified before the district court in Hartford that the company made an analysis of all 175 Mobil stations in Connecticut and discovered that some 40 percent of them were grossing over 500,000 gallons a year. He further testified that Mobil's policy was that any station doing business of over 500,000 gallons a year would be taken over by Mobil and run by a Mobil employee. The company would renew any license of an operator making less.

6. Nothing in the bill will interfere with the free enterprise system. The oil companies want to choose for themselves how "free" it should be.

A number of retail gas station operators and representatives of retail gas station dealers testified in support of the bill. It appeared that Mobil was not particularly concerned about the welfare of the gas-consuming public. There were recorded instances when the company congratulated a station operator for doing an excellent job in running his station and building volume sales. This was then followed by a terse letter indicating that the lease would be canceled or that the terms of the lease would be radically changed. Other operators testified that their leases were canceled because of "poor performance." They contended that the company used this as an excuse. The real bone of contention was that the dealers had refused to carry Mobil's other items—products they thought were overpriced and noncompetitive. (It should be noted that forcing dealers to carry these items is against the law.) The company representative denied pursuing such practices.

BILL 328—PUBLIC ACT NO. 74–292

Despite all the testimony supporting bill 5096, it was not reported out for action by the assembly. Instead, the committee reported out bill 328, amended according to the suggestions of the Mobil representative. It was signed by the governor and became effective as Public Act No. 74–292 on May 10, 1974. The main provisions of this act are as follows:

SUMMARY: The bill defines "good cause" for cancellation, termination or failure to renew a franchise, requires six months notice of failure to renew because of change of use of the property used in the franchise, removes a requirement that notice of termination, cancellation or non-renewal be filed with the Department of Consumer Protection, and requires franchise renewals to be for a term of three years.

CONTENT AND OPERATION: *Good Cause.* Good cause includes, but is not limited to, failure to comply substantially with any material and reasonable obligation of the franchise agreement. Good cause also includes conversion of the property involved in the franchise to a different use by the franchisor, sale or lease of the property, and failure of the property owner (other than the parties themselves) to renew the lease. If the property is sold or leased to a subsidiary or affiliate of the franchisor, however, it would not be able to be used in the same business as the franchise agreement. *Notice of Intent Not to Renew.* Written notice of intent not to renew because of a different use of the property is required to be given to the franchisor six months prior to the expiration of the franchise agreement. Notice of cancellation or nonrenewal no longer has to be filed with the Department of Consumer Protection. *Term of Franchise.* Franchise renewals are required to be for a term of three years.

Mobil's reaction

With the passage of the new bill, Mobil began offering for lease those stations it had earlier converted from franchise to salary operations. Larry Ancker, who had operated his station for six months without any contract, also received a new lease and is now operating his station at the same location.

Notwithstanding, Mobil's views about such laws remain unchanged. J. William Dalgetty, the company attorney who took an active part in the Connecticut assembly hearings and also offered amendments that were incorporated into the law, stated in a communication to the author:

> . . . we are still philosophically opposed to any law that restricts a landlord's right not to renew a lease agreement after it has expired. . . . we believe that this type of legislation unconstitutionally transfers long term property rights from a land owner, who has invested substantial sums of money to acquire the property, to a lessee dealer who has put up little or no capital that he can't otherwise get back out of his business.[10]

APPENDIX: RELATIONSHIP BETWEEN MAJOR OIL COMPANIES AND THEIR FRANCHISED DEALERS

It appears that the problems of Mobil dealers in Connecticut were not isolated cases spawned by the Connecticut Franchise Act. During the energy crisis, there were nationwide complaints that major oil companies were trying to use the gasoline scarcity as a means of eliminating competition at the retail distribution level.

---

[10] Letter dated October 21, 1974.

The retail distribution of gasoline is carried out by three types of operators. First, there are company-owned and operated stations selling branded gasoline and other products known as TAB (tires, accessories, and batteries) supplied by the company. The second type of station is operated by independent dealers who have franchises to sell the branded gas at a certain location. These are the franchised dealers. Quite often the property and equipment are owned by the company, which then leases them to an independent operator who works on commission. He is free to raise or lower prices even in competition with the company-owned stations selling the same brand, in response to market conditions. The third type is another independent dealer who sells private brand (nonmajor) gasoline and competes primarily on the basis of price. These operators buy gasoline either from independent refiners or wholesalers who, in their turn, may have bought their supplies from major oil companies trying to unload surplus inventories.

One issue arising out of the energy crisis of the winter of 1974 concerns the marketing practices of the major oil companies. Although consumers were noticeably upset by the rapidly rising price of gasoline and long lines at the pumps, dealers were voicing their displeasure over aspects of their relationships with the big oil companies. There were allegations that the major companies were engaged in an ambitious campaign to drive the independent dealers out of business.

There were widespread complaints of gas station closings. However, evidence indicates that most of the closings were concentrated in small, independent stations selling private brands or off-brand gasoline, and in franchised dealers.

During the peak years of 1969–70, there were 222,000 gasoline stations. As the fuel crisis of 1973–74 worsened, the number dropped to 216,000. The drop is even larger than the 6,000 indicates, however, because as many small stations closed, they were replaced by fewer but larger stations. In Los Angeles County alone, the world's largest single gasoline market, there were 7,076 service stations before the crisis. Six thousand twenty-eight sold major brand names and 1,048 were independents. After the crisis had peaked, 704 big brand stations and 270 independents closed. While independents and franchised dealers were dwindling in number, company-owned outlets were becoming more numerous. Before 1973, Shell owned only 174 of the 9,500 stations selling Shell gasoline. But then in 1973 it opened 163 more—an almost 100 percent increase in just one year.[1]

Complaints reverberated throughout the ranks of the independent dealers. They accused the oil companies of using the oil crisis to squeeze the independents out while setting up their own company-owned and oper-

---

[1] Fred Ferretti, "Gasoline Stations Threaten to Close in Protest to U.S.—Squeeze on Independents," *The New York Times*, February 16, 1974, p. 1.

ated stations. Other complaints included that of independents having to stock their stations with company-owned TAB upon threat of loss of lease. Mobil Oil and Union Oil were charged in suits on this point. The independents selling nonmajor gasoline exhibited higher failure rates than did the other independents. By 1973 these independents constituted approximately one-sixth of the stations in the United States, but accounted for roughly one-fourth of all the gasoline sold. Nearly 12 percent were forced to close during the oil crisis, compared with only 9 percent of the major brand name stations.[2] To these dealers, the gasoline shortage in the winter of 1974 was contrived by the major oil companies as a way of forcing the unbranded independents out of business. With a shortage, of course, the major companies would not be able to provide excess gasoline to the independents. Thus, the stations would be forced out of business. Presently, the independents' share of the retail market has shrunk from its high of 25 percent to half that, and it will get even smaller, some sources say.[3]

The reaction of the oil companies to these complaints was to insist, first of all, that the oil shortage was indeed real and that they had allocated fuel as equitably as possible. As to not renewing leases, they said they were changing their marketing practices and the station closings were a tightening up process. "We were overbuilt," says one executive; "what we're doing is eliminating uneconomic stations."[4]

In September 1974, *The New York Times* published the remarks of Z. D. Bonner, president of Gulf Oil Company, U.S. In his remarks, Mr. Bonner said that the major oil companies shared the frustration felt by the American public because of the previous winter's gasoline shortage. He indicated that although charges of a created shortage had been shown to be without basis, there had been a persistent trend to lay all the blame on the major oil companies. Mr. Bonner stated that punitive measures instituted by federal authorities had occurred and would continue to occur. If regulatory agencies would refrain from exerting any influence on the operations of American business, in particular the oil companies, the free enterprise system would work as advertised. Mr. Bonner seemed to imply that the gasoline shortage was not contrived by the oil companies, but instead resulted from the activities of federal regulatory agencies. He called for business to enter into a stewardship for the free enterprise system, so as to educate the public concerning the functioning of the market economy and the need to deregulate industry. Nowhere in his remarks was there any attention paid to claims by the various dealers that the major companies were attempting to make the industry noncompetitive. Instead, the tone of Mr. Bonner's remarks seemed to be that, if left alone,

---

[2] Ibid.
[3] Ibid.
[4] Ibid.

American business (the oil industry) would operate efficiently and in the best interests of the consumer.[5]

Some legal action has been taken by various sources to remedy the situation. The situation of the independent dealer spawned a hearing in Salt Lake City in March 1973 before the consumer subcommittee of the U.S. Senate commerce committee. The hearings contained testimony from several local and independent dealers. One of those was a lessee of two Texaco stations. At one time this individual had been a district sales representative for Texaco. He testified that during the time he worked for Texaco, there was a 30 to 40 percent annual dealer turnover rate. After two years, only five of his original dealer accounts were still maintained. He indicated that the reason for the turnover could be explained by the company's marketing practices: "It is a common occurrence for a major oil company dealer to find himself competing with some gasoline marketing by his own company at prices from 4 to 10 cents below the price at which he is asked to sell."[6]

The various other individuals who testified at the hearings presented stories similar to this one. It was suggested that although the issue of dealer-company relationships had appeared to surface in Utah, there was reason to expect that a nationwide trend was developing.[7] In March 1974, a grand jury was empaneled at the request of the New York State attorney general's office to investigate alleged criminal activities in New York by the petroleum industry. One of the resulting indictments charged Mobil Oil with "restraint of trade and competition" between May 1972 and April 24, 1974, in four New York City counties. The specific charges stated:

> . . . certain agents and employes of Mobil attempted, by means of threats, to coerce certain Mobil dealers to purchase automobile tires, batteries and accessories solely from Mobil. [This was done] even though the prices charged by Mobil for such articles were higher than the prices for which such articles could be purchased elsewhere, and even though said dealers had no legal obligation to purchase [them from Mobil].[8]

In September 1974, seven oil companies—Mobil, Exxon, Shell, Gulf, Sunoco, Amoco, and Texaco—were indicted and charged with "criminally acting together to restrain competition in the sale of gasoline" in New

---

[5] Z. D. Bonner, "How Industry Can Regain Public's Trust—Point of View," *The New York Times*, September 1, 1974, sec. 3, p. 10.

[6] Statement of Gary Anderson before the Consumer Subcommittee of the Senate Commerce Committee, March 17, 1973.

[7] Statement of Charles Binsted, president of the National Congress of Petroleum Retailers, before the Consumer Subcommittee of the Senate Commerce Committee, March 17, 1973.

[8] "Mobil Oil Is Arraigned, Pleads Innocent to Forcing Dealers to Buy Its Products," *The Wall Street Journal*, July 2, 1974, p. 4.

York City.[9] Another indictment accused Exxon, Mobil, and Gulf of entering into an agreement in order to thwart open bidding for the gasoline sold to governmental agencies throughout New York State.[10] In October the same grand jury suggested but did not formally charge that more than a year before the 1973–74 Arab oil embargo, the major American oil companies conspired to create a fuel shortage so that prices could be driven up and independent dealers forced out of business. Because the oil companies created the shortage in 1972, the United States became vulnerable to the Arab oil embargo later on.[11]

In other actions against the oil industry, a state suit was filed in California against Union Oil for trying to force the operators of a service station to stop selling other firms' products.[12] A $200 million suit was filed against Mobil Oil by a former California service station operator who charged that his lease had been illegally terminated because he sought to buy his TAB supplies from a source other than Mobil.[13] A provisional consent order was arrived at between the Federal Trade Commission and Phillips Petroleum in order to free 1,400 of Philips' 26,000 retail outlets from practices the FTC deemed anticompetitive. These included allowing the outlets to purchase TAB supplies from non-Phillips sources, easing restrictions on purchasing gasoline from other suppliers, and renewing leases for at least five years in most cases and giving dealers the right to arbitrate disputes about lease cancellations. James T. Halverson, director of FTC's Bureau of Competition, hopes that the consent order will serve as a model for other oil companies in their dealings with their retail outlets.[14]

SELECTED BIBLIOGRAPHY

Allvine, Fred C., and James M. Patterson. *Competition Ltd.: The Marketing of Gasoline*. Bloomington: Indiana University Press, 1975.

Allvine, Fred C., and James M. Patterson. *Highway Robbery: An Analysis of the Gasoline Crisis*. Bloomington: Indiana University Press, 1975.

American Motor Inns, Inc. v. Holiday Inns, Inc., 365 F. Supp. 1073 (D.N.J. 1973).

Comanor, William S. "Vertical Territorial Restrictions and Customer Restrictions: *White Motor* and Its Aftermath." *Harvard Law Review* 81 (1968): 1419.

Grether, E. T. *Marketing and Public Policy*. Englewood Cliffs, N.J.: Prentice-Hall, 1966.

---

[9] "Oil Companies Are Indicted Here in Gasoline Sales," *The New York Times*, September 1974, p. 1.

[10] "Seven Major Oil Concerns Plead Innocent to Antitrust Charges in New York City," *The Wall Street Journal*, September 6, 1974, p. 8.

[11] "Jury Hints Big Oil Plot by U.S. Firms," *San Francisco Chronicle*, October 8, 1974, p. 8.

[12] "Antitrust Suit Against Oil Firm," *San Francisco Chronicle*, December 25, 1974, p. 14.

[13] William Moore, "Ousted Gas Dealer Is Suing Mobil Oil," *San Francisco Chronicle*, January 8, 1975, p. 2.

[14] "Phillips Petroleum to Free 1,400 Dealers from Curbs FTC Calls Anticompetitive," *The Wall Street Journal*, September 18, 1974, p. 5.

GTE Sylvania, Inc. v. *Continental R.V., Inc., et al.* No. 71-1705 (9th Cir., May 9, 1974).

Hunt, Shelby. "Socio-Economic Consequences of Franchise System of Distribution," in *Contractual Marketing Systems,* ed. Donald L. Thompson. Lexington, Mass.: Heath Lexington Books, 1971.

Kitson, Peter W. "Trademark Franchising and Antitrust Sanctions: The Need for a Limited Rule of Reason." *Boston University Law Review* 52 (1973): 463.

LaFortune v. *Ebie,* 26 Cal. App. 3d 72, 102 Cal. Rptr. 588 (1972).

McGuire, E. Patrick. *Franchised Distribution.* New York: The Conference Board, 1971.

Moyer, Reed. "Competitive Impact of the Emerging Energy Company." *California Management Review* 16 (summer 1974): 4.

Posner, Richard A. "Exclusionary Practices and the Antitrust Laws." *University of Chicago Law Review* 41 (1947): 506.

Preston, Lee E. "Restrictive Distribution Arrangements: Economic Analysis and Public Policy Standards." *Law and Contemporary Problems* 30 (summer 1965): 506.

Sealy Mattress Company of Southern California v. *Sealy, Inc.,* 346 F. Supp. 353 (N.C. Ill. 1972).

Thompson, Donald N. *Franchise Operations and Antitrust.* Lexington, Mass.: Heath Lexington Books, 1971.

Timberg, Sigmund. "Territorial Restrictions on Franchisees: Post-Schwinn Developments." *Antitrust Law Bulletin* 19 (1974): 205.

United States v. *Topco Associates, Inc.,* 319 F. Supp. 1031 (1970).

United States v. *Topco Associates, Inc.,* 405 U.S. 596 (1972).

U.S. Congress, Senate, Judiciary Subcommittee on Antitrust and Monopoly. *Hearings on Exclusive Territorial Allocation Legislation.* 92nd Cong., 1972.

SECTION D: PRODUCT
WARRANTIES:
MANUFACTURER'S
LIABILITY FOR
PRODUCT-RELATED
CONSUMER INJURY

7

Stevens v. Parke, Davis & Company, and A. J. Beland, M.D.*

Product abuse due to overpromotion, implied warranty and the manufacturer's liability. Ethical and societal implications

The record of chloramphenicol production, promotion and prescribing is one compounded in part from complacency, laziness, stupidity, carelessness, deceit, and greed. It likewise poses questions that must be answered by physicians. Why did all the efforts of the AMA, the National Research Council, the FDA, and even the courts fail for almost two decades, and why did the promotional strategy of the drug company succeed?

Dr. Harry Dowling, expert in the field of infectious diseases.[1]

---

* The author is grateful to Mr. Robert L. Charbonneau of the law firm of Harney, Ford, Charbonneau & Bambic, Los Angeles, California, attorneys for the plaintiffs, for generously providing material which assisted in the preparation of this case study. The attorneys for defendant Dr. A. J. Beland—Ball, Hunt, Hart, Brown, and Baerwitz of Long Beach, California—also furnished relevant material and their assistance is appreciated. Parke, Davis & Company supplied some supporting material useful to the study.

[1] Dr. Dowling is professor emeritus of medicine at the University of Illinois and former chairman of the AMA Council on Drugs.

On March 14, 1973, the California Supreme Court upheld a jury verdict of $400,000 against Parke, Davis & Company and Dr. A. J. Beland. This was one of the largest such awards in similar cases in the United States, and it was made because of the wrongful death of Mrs. Phyllis Stevens. Her death was the result of using Chloromycetin,[2] a brand name antibiotic manufactured by Parke, Davis & Company and prescribed for Mrs. Stevens by Dr. A. J. Beland, her physician. The Supreme Court held that Parke, Davis & Company was guilty of so overpromoting the drug as to induce physicians to prescribe it more widely than should be warranted in terms of sound medical practice (and also to minimize, if not ignore, the dangerous side effects arising from the use of such drugs).[3]

ISSUES FOR ANALYSIS

This case raises some important issues relating to the practice of medicine in the United States, the nature of the pharmaceutical industry, and the role of various regulatory bodies in providing adequate safeguards. A careful analysis of the circumstances surrounding the case, the facts as determined by the courts, and the decisions of the courts can help us understand the nature and magnitude of the conflicts that arise between the individual and the corporation, between a corporation's desire to increase its profits and society's expectations for a high level of ethical standards of performance, especially where an individual's health and safety are at stake. The case may also be used to study the effectiveness of various control mechanisms—the marketplace, self-regulation, and regulatory agencies—in safeguarding the public interest.

---

[2] Chloromycetin is the trade name for chloramphenicol. It is a wide-spectrum antibiotic, an antibiotic that kills or stops the growth of a great number of different disease-causing organisms.

[3] The narrative in this case study is primarily derived from the following legal briefs and court decisions. Rather than cite them repeatedly, each source is identified by a letter and followed by a page number. The letters are as follows: A. *Stevens et al. v. Parke, Davis & Co. et al.*, Ca. 2d App. Dist. 2 Civil 38475. Opening Brief of Appellants (Stevens), June 1971. B. *Stevens et al. v. Parke, Davis & Co. et al.*, Ca. 2d App. Dist. 2 Civil 38475. Opening Brief of Appellants (Parke-Davis), September 1971. C. *Stevens et al. v. Parke, Davis & Co. et al.*, Ca. 2d App. Dist. 2 Civil 38475. Opening Brief of Appellants (Parke-Davis), September 1971. D. *Stevens et al. v. Parke, Davis & Co. et al.*, Ca. 2d App. Dist. 2 Civil 38475. Reply Brief of Respondent (Beland), December 1971. E. *Stevens et al. v. Parke, Davis & Co. et al.*, Ca. 2d App. Dist. 2 Civil 38475. Closing Brief of Appellants (Stevens), January 1972. F. *Stevens et al. v. Parke, Davis & Co. et al.*, Ca. 2d App. Dist. 2 Civil 38475. Brief of Respondents (Stevens), January 1972. G. *Stevens et al. v. Parke, Davis & Co. et al.*, Ca. 2d App. Dist. 2 Civil 38475. Reply Brief of Appellants (Parke-Davis), March 1972. H. *Stevens et al. v. Parke, Davis & Co. et al.*, Ca. 2d App. Dist. 2 Civil 38475. Court of Appeal Decision, March 1972. I. *Stevens et al. v. Parke, Davis & Co. et al.*, Ca. 2d App. Dist. 2 Civil 38475. Petition for Rehearing (Stevens), April 1972. J. *Stevens et al. v. Parke, Davis & Co. et al.*, Ca. 2d App. Dist. 2 Civil 38475. Answer to Petition for Rehearing (Beland), April 1972. K. *Stevens et al. v. Parke, Davis & Co. et al.*, 9 Cal. 3d 51 (1973). Petition for Hearing in Supreme Court (Beland), May 1972. L. *Stevens et al. v. Parke, Davis & Co. et al.*, 9 Cal. 3d 51 (1973). Answer to Petition for Hearing in Supreme Court (Beland), May 1972. M. *Stevens et al. v. Parke, Davis & Co. et al.*, 9 Cal. 3d 51 (1973). Supreme Court Decision, March 1973.

The questions related to Parke-Davis' liability go beyond the legal considerations in the California Supreme Court decision. Although we are not questioning the court's decision, we must analyze what behavior should be expected of a company beyond that compelled by strict governmental regulations and existing market constraints, and in terms of controlling the behavior of persons over which it may have only partial control or no control at all. For example:

1. Was Parke, Davis negligent in preparing or using the material that described the drug in 1964? Did the company, by its actions, "water down" the warning label?
2. Did Parke, Davis promote or contribute to the overprescription and overuse of Chloromycetin for unindicated purposes?
3. To what extent can a company actually control the activities of its detailmen in their communications with physicians? Remember, the personal and career goals of a salesman are only partly in congruence with those of the company.
4. How can a company be made accountable for the activities of independent intermediaries such as the physician, the hospital, and the pharmacist? These intermediaries are professional individuals and organizations and have legally and socially recognized independence in their operational spheres. Such accountability may require total control on the part of the manufacturer over all elements of the distribution channel leading to the final consumer. Even if such a control were possible, is it socially desirable? What are its implications?
5. How should a company develop its marketing strategy, in a heavily regulated environment, to protect itself from situations in which it may be held responsible for the activities of others?

In addition, some technical questions have a bearing on management decision-making and long-range planning. For example:

1. It is not clear whether the California Supreme Court made its decision solely on procedural grounds, substantive facts and applications of laws thereto, or both. It would be interesting to speculate what the court would have done had the trial court judge specified the grounds on which he was rejecting the jury's decision. The importance of this case as a precedence for future cases and also as a determining variable for management policy depends heavily on this interpretation.

2. Stevens' attorneys cited three specific causes for action against Parke, Davis: negligence, breach of warranty, and strict liability. An analysis of the evidence and the court's decision seems to indicate that negligence and breach of warranty, as legally defined, would not be the probable causes and that the decision against Parke, Davis rested primarily on the application of strict liability. However, strict liability as a legal concept is of more recent origins and is constantly evolving. Since legal cases take a long time before their final disposition, it is quite likely that a case may be decided based on the concept of strict liability as it existed at the time

of the incident but not as it was by the time the court made the decision. An analysis of legal definitions and their implications for negligence, breach of warranty, and strict liability would be helpful in understanding the implications of this case for management policy.

We should also realize that a corporation does not act in a vacuum. Its practices are largely determined and constrained by the nature of the marketing practices employed by the industry as a whole, as well as the economic and sociopolitical environment in the country. Thus, an understanding of the industry is important for an evaluation of the activities of a particular company. This information is presented in a subsequent case entitled "The Pharmaceutical Industry: Marketing Policies in the Promotion, Distribution, and Sale of Ethical Drugs."

THE CIRCUMSTANCES

The facts or events of the case are simple and straightforward and were not contested in the courts by the defendants. What *is* in dispute are the causes that led to the occurrence of the events. Most important is the question of the responsibility of the various parties (the patient, the doctor, and the manufacturer) in causing these events to take place and how the consequences or costs of such acts should be borne or apportioned by various parties. Of equal importance are two related questions: (1) Could this tragic event have been avoided if one or more parties had exercised prudent and reasonable care in performing their relative roles, and (2) what might be done to minimize, if not avoid, similar occurrences in the future? In other words, to what extent is this an isolated incident caused by the failure on the part of one or more parties to behave prudently, and to what extent could the incident be attributed to the structure and the process of interaction between the patient, the doctor, and the drug manufacturer, and the environment in which this triad of interactions takes place.

On Christmas Day, 1965, Phyllis Stevens died of pneumonia as a result of aplastic anemia—the failure of the bone marrow to produce enough white blood cells to ward off infection—caused by the administration of Chloromycetin.[4] At the time of her death she was 38 years old.

Phyllis Stevens was born in 1925. When she was 20, she developed a chronic lung condition called bronchiectasis. However, this did not prevent her from entering into any normal activities, and in 1948 she married and subsequently had three children. Testimony at the trial by the plaintiffs and the deceased's doctor established that Mrs. Stevens had been leading a normal and fairly active life as a housewife and mother. She was proficient in cooking and camping and enjoyed partaking in them. She had hoped to enjoy even more recreational activities with her family after

---

[4] Aplastic anemia is the depression or destruction of the bone marrow caused by a drug or chemical or radiation damage.

her surgery. The family spent two weeks each year camping in national parks. In addition, they spent weekends and holidays at Big Bear Lake, where they owned a cabin. Mrs. Stevens also found time to return to college, where she completed the courses required for a teaching credential and in fact taught for five days prior to entering the hospital. In sum, despite her lung condition Phyllis Stevens enjoyed a full, rich life.

On May 25, 1964, she visited Dr. Arthur J. Beland to see if he could recommend some treatment for her bronchiectasis that would make it easier for her to teach. Dr. Beland described her as "being a well-developed, well-nourished, intelligent lady who does not appear acutely or chronically ill" [E–3]. He did recognize a lung abnormality which, upon X ray examination, was diagnosed as bilateral bronchiectasis, the same condition Mrs. Stevens had had for 18 years. Dr. Beland recommended surgery, which he subsequently performed on September 1, 1964. (Surgery had also been recommended 18 years previously.) Due to complications resulting from the operation, he prescribed Chloromycetin shortly thereafter. The drug was given to her six times between September and November 20, 1964. She was also operated on twice more—October 23, 1964 and February 18, 1965—for further removal of portions of the afflicted lung. Her condition failed to improve, and in June 1965 Dr. Nathaniel Kurnick, a hematologist, was brought in on the case. Dr. Kurnick's tests showed that Mrs. Stevens was suffering from bone marrow failure—that is, aplastic anemia. Her bone marrow was unable to produce enough red cells, white cells, and platelets, the three components of blood. Her body lacking the ability to produce white cells in sufficient numbers to ward off infection, Mrs. Stevens consequently died on December 25, 1965.

THE CASE AGAINST BELAND AND PARKE, DAVIS

The case for the wrongful death of Mrs. Phyllis Stevens was filed by and on behalf of her three children, Janet Stevens, Suzanne Stevens, and Kennon Stevens, all minors, and her husband, John Stevens, in Los Angeles Superior Court.

Based on the plaintiffs' briefs and the testimony of various witnesses during the trial, the plaintiffs' case can be summarized as follows:

1. Dr. A. J. Beland (hereinafter referred to as Dr. Beland) was accused of malpractice and was called negligent in prescribing and administering the drug Chloromycetin, which has known dangerous side effects. A less dangerous antibiotic could have been used just as effectively.

2. Parke, Davis & Company (hereinafter referred to as Parke, Davis) was charged with negligence in failing to sufficiently warn the medical profession of the dangers of the drug and in so overpromoting it as to negate the effect of the written warnings that were available to the prescribing physician. Such negligence in this case was the proximate cause of the death of Phyllis Stevens. The plaintiffs cited three specific causes of

action against Parke, Davis: negligence, breach of warranty, and strict liability [C-3].

During the trial, Dr. Beland testified to the fact that he was indeed aware of the dangerous side effects of repeated and/or prolonged use of Chloromycetin; of the drug's being the most dangerous antibiotic available; of Parke, Davis's warnings with respect to its use and of the information contained in the 1964 PDR (Physician's Desk Reference)[5] concerning its dangers; of the risks attending its use and the recommendation for adequate blood studies; and of the drug's association with aplastic anemia. He also testified that in prescribing drugs he did not rely on drug company detailmen or magazine advertising and had no recollection of talking to Parke, Davis detailmen or their leaving literature for him to read [C-7, 8].

The plaintiffs contended that, Beland's testimony notwithstanding, he could not help but be influenced by the promotional bombardment directed by Parke, Davis at the medical profession and aimed at negating the effect of "warnings" concerning the use of this drug. Thus, the plaintiffs maintained that Dr. Beland's testimony should be ignored as it related to Parke, Davis and that the company should be held liable as charged.

The history of chloramphenicol

To understand the allegations made against Parke, Davis, it is necessary to review the history of the development of chloramphenicol.[6] Chloramphenicol was discovered in 1946 and put on the market three years later under the trade name of Chloromycetin after it was tested by Parke, Davis. It was found to be an extremely effective wide-spectrum antibiotic. However, by 1952 there were so many reports about its possible association with the development of blood disorders (also known as blood dyscrasias), including aplastic anemia, that the Food and Drug Administration, in conjunction with the National Research Council, began an investigation. Until the investigation was completed, the FDA stopped further certification of the sale of the drug. This research resulted in a "recommendation" [C-5, 6] to Parke, Davis to include the following warning on each label

---

[5] The *Physician's Desk Reference* is a reference book used by doctors to obtain information on various drugs. It is published yearly. The information contained therein is supplied by the drug manufacturers on a voluntary basis.

[6] The history of chloramphenicol and the studies relating it to aplastic anemia, including the numbers and types of articles published, is well documented in U.S. Congress, Senate, Subcommittee on Monopoly of the Select Committee on Small Business, *Competitive Problems in the Drug Industry: Present Status of Competition in the Pharmaceutical Industry*, part 6 (90th Cong., 1st and 2nd sess., November 1967 and February 1968). Part 5 (90th Cong., 1st and 2nd sess., December 1967 and January 1968); and part 11 (91st Cong., 1st sess., February and March 1969) are also cited in this study. All citations from this source are hereinafter referred to in the text as *Hearings, Competitive Problems in the Drug Industry*, followed by part and page number. For a more favorable discussion on the use of Chloromycetin and arguments against further restrictions on its usage, see Marvin Henry Edwards, "Chloromycetin: Special Report," *Private Practice* 3 (March 1971): 42–56.

of the drug: "Warning—Blood dyscrasias may be associated with inter-mittent or prolonged use. It is essential that adequate blood studies be made" [M–4]. The drug continued to receive scrutiny and widespread comment as a result of its association with aplastic anemia. Literally hun-dreds of articles concerning the possible development of aplastic anemia after treatment with Chloromycetin appeared in medical journals.

In 1961, the Senate Kefauver hearings on the drug industry[7] resulted in the FDA's requirement that Parke, Davis strengthen the warning on the label. Beginning in that year, the warning label read as follows:

> Warning—Serious and even fatal blood dyscrasias (aplastic anemia, hypo-plastic anemia, thrombocytopenia, granulocytopenia) are known to occur after the administration of chloramphenicol. Blood dyscrasias have occurred after short term and with prolonged therapy with this drug. Bearing in mind the possibility that such reactions may occur, chloramphenicol should be used only for serious infections caused by organisms that are susceptible to its antibacterial effects. Chloramphenicol should not be used when other less potentially dangerous agents will be effective, or in the treatment of trivial infections such as colds, influenza, viral infections of the throat, or as a prophylactic agent.
>
> Precautions: It is essential that adequate blood studies be made during treatment with the drug. While blood studies may detect early peripheral blood changes, such as leukopenia or granulocytopenia, before they be-come irreversible, such studies cannot be relied upon to detect bone mar-row depression prior to development of aplastic anemia. [C–6, 7]

The plaintiffs pointed out that Parke, Davis did not take adequate steps to bring this warning to the attention of the medical profession. In fact, it took a Senate investigatory hearing to even get Parke, Davis to include a truthful warning about the drug. Between the time of the FDA's 1952 recommendation and its 1961 order, Parke, Davis avoided the issue. In the 1952 *Physician's Desk Reference* (PDR), there was no warning about the link between Chloromycetin and blood disorders. In 1953 a warning was included, but it did not state that the blood disorders could be fatal. The same was true of the 1955 entry, which read:

> Chloromycetin is a potent therapeutic agent; and because certain blood dyscrasias have been associated with its administration, it should not be used indiscriminately nor for minor infections. Furthermore, as with certain other drugs, adequate blood studies should be made when the patient re-quires prolonged or intermittent therapy. [F–10]

---

[7] Senator Kefauver headed the following two investigations into the drug industry: U.S. Congress, Senate, Subcommittee on Antitrust and Monopoly of the Committee of the Ju-diciary, *Drug Industry Antitrust Act Hearings,* 7 parts (87th Cong., 1st sess., 1961); and U.S. Congress, Senate, Subcommittee on Antitrust and Monopoly of the Committee of the Judiciary, *Administered Prices in the Drug Industry,* 29 parts (85th, 86th, and 87th Cong., 1957–61).

Even after the 1961 order, Parke, Davis was not disseminating the information. The 1962 entry read:

> Chloromycetin. Chloramphenicol. Parke, Davis & Co. Product Information Section. Detailed information on Chloromycetin, including dosage, administration, contraindications and precautions, may be obtained by consulting the package circular or by contacting your local Parke, Davis representative or the Office of Medical Correspondence, Parke, Davis & Co., Detroit 32, Michigan. [F–10, 11]

When called upon to testify, Mr. Bradshaw, chief attorney for Parke, Davis, said no warning information was included because the company concluded that it would have been an "unwarranted expense" to have it printed in the book. The same reason was given for its exclusion in the 1963 book as well. The warning was finally included in the 1964 edition, but only because of criticism aimed at Parke, Davis by physicians who wanted the warning included.

Advertising and promotion

Soon after the FDA directive in 1952, Parke, Davis took steps to minimize the effect of the warning labels on potential sales. The testimony at the trial brought out the following evidence:

In 1952 the president of Parke, Davis issued a press release to all its representatives which stated that "Chloromycetin has been officially cleared by the Federal Drug Administration and the National Research Council with *no restrictions* on the number or the range of diseases for which Chloromycetin may be administered" [F–5]. In a letter dated November 20, 1952, the medical director of Parke, Davis wrote to all the company's representatives attesting to the fact that

> Chloromycetin is "well tolerated" and in the hands of the physician is an extremely valuable therapeutic agent. Some physicians are of the opinion that Chloromycetin has been taken off the market or its use restricted. Some physicians have formed the impression that this antibiotic has been associated with the development of blood depression in large numbers of patients, and will be amazed when we point out the facts. Tell the Chloromycetin story to every physician in your territory in the shortest possible time. If the situation is understood, physicians will readily use this valuable therapeutic agent when indicated. [F–6]
>
> Additional plans are under study and in preparation in behalf of Chloromycetin products, which will support your detailing efforts in a substantial way, such as a major Chloromycetin hospital display program, a Chloromycetin issue of Therapeutic Notes, literature, Chloromycetin products brochure blotters, special promotion pieces, samples, and standard packages, new Chloromycetin product forms, general advertising, direct mail advertising, laity promotion of an institutional character, plans for pharmaceutical meetings, and plans for medical meetings. [F–8]

In another document, "Suggested Details for the Benefit of Salesmen in Promoting This Drug," sales representatives were told that

> Intensive investigation by the Food and Drug Administration carried on with the assistance of a special committee of eminent specialists appointed by the National Research Council resulted in unqualified sanction of the continued use of Chloromycetin for all conditions in which it had previously been used. [F–7]

Sales representatives' visits to doctors urging them to prescribe the drug were frequent and took place constantly from 1956 on. Although literature left with the doctors apparently did contain warnings about the possible side effects of Chloromycetin, the representatives themselves never voiced any warnings. Giveaway calendars, rulers, and other materials were used in the promotion campaign as well as full-page ads in medical journals. None of these contained any mention of the possibility of harmful side effects. Doctors were thus bombarded with personal visits and promotional material. Medical journal ads also added to a distorted view of the drug.

The trial testimony showed that not a single piece of promotional material or instructions received by the field representatives from the home office contained any mention of a warning as to the drug's side effects. Nor were the representatives ever asked or reminded to mention to the physicians, on their sales calls, the dangerous side effects of Chloromycetin.

The only other warning issued by Parke, Davis, in addition to the one contained on the label, was a mass-produced "Dear Doctor" letter cautioning physicians about the dangers associated with the use of Chloromycetin. When asked why the full-page advertisements for Chloromycetin in medical journals did not contain any warning language, the attorney for the defendants replied that those ads were in the nature of reminders and therefore did not contain any warning of side effects.

Parke, Davis was clearly concerned about the effect of its promotional material on the case. In 1968, Donald Swanson, a regional sales manager for Parke-Davis whose territory was the Los Angeles/Long Beach area, received a letter from Walter Griffith, the Director of Promotion, stating that all materials concerning the promotion of Chloromycetin should be destroyed. This was done. Parke, Davis's attorney also testified that all of the promotional material relating to Chloromycetin during the 1960s was destroyed by Parke, Davis and thus was not available. The only evidence produced at the trial by Parke, Davis to support its contention of additional warnings were a "Dear Doctor" letter dated 1962 and a products information brochure.

The response by Dr. Beland and Parke, Davis

Dr. Beland admitted that he was fully aware of the dangerous side effects associated with the use of Chloromycetin but nevertheless maintained that he was not negligent in his prescription and administration of the drug to Mrs. Stevens. He filed a motion for nonsuit.

Parke, Davis made the following points in its defense:

1.   As a matter of law, the company was not guilty of negligence either in the distribution of the product or in the failure adequately to warn of its dangers. Also, there was no evidence that any act on the part of Parke, Davis caused injury to Mrs. Stevens. Exclusion of any warnings from the advertisements and other promotional material was perfectly legal. The FDA directive stipulated that a warning must be included only in advertising material that stated specific recommendations as to proper use and dosage.

2.   Hundreds of articles relating the link between aplastic anemia and Chloromycetin appeared in medical journals. Parke, Davis wrote letters to doctors about the link. The medical profession further learned about it "through teaching, symposiums, lectures and the general methods by which the medical profession self-instructs itself" [F–6], and the warning label, used from 1961 on, was extremely explicit.

3.   Dr. Beland was fully aware of the dangers of the drug and admitted that "in prescribing drugs he did not rely on drug company detailmen or magazine advertising, and has no recollection of talking to Parke, Davis detailmen" [F–8].

4.   All ten doctors who testified at the trial both for the plaintiffs and for the defendants, agreed on the following points: Mrs. Stevens' death was caused by aplastic anemia resulting from the administration of Chloromycetin; the association between aplastic anemia and Chloromycetin was well known to the medical profession in and before 1964; and the 1964 warning label printed an adequate picture of the inherent dangers. Dr. Phillip Sturgeon, one of the plaintiff's witnesses, stated (with no disagreement expressed by either side) that by 1964 sufficient information had been disseminated so that doctors should have known that Chloromycetin could cause fatal aplastic anemia and that it should not have been used unless it was the only drug effective in a certain situation. (Chloromycetin is extremely effective in treating Rocky Mountain spotted fever, typhus, and typhoid.) There were other drugs available by that time that would have been as effective in treating various infections.

The superior court order

After a three-week trial, the jury returned a verdict in favor of the plaintiffs and awarded them $400,000 in damages. However, Superior Court Judge Shea ordered the amount reduced to $64,673.42 ($60,000 in general damages and $4,673.42 in special damages), stating that the verdict "is not sustained by the evidence, and that it is based upon prejudice and passion on the part of the jury" [A–2]. He therefore ordered a new trial to be granted on the issue of damages unless the plaintiffs would accept the reduced amount. He also denied the motion for a new trial on the issue of liability and the motion for judgment notwithstanding the verdict [A–1, 2].

The plaintiffs did not agree to accept reduced damages and instead chose to appeal the case. Defendants Beland and Parke, Davis also chose to appeal for reasons that will be shown in the succeeding pages.

THE APPEAL

Plaintiffs' arguments in their appeal

1.　Judge Shea's order for a new trial was invalid because it did not contain the specific written reasons required for such an order by the Code of Civil Procedure, Section 657 (as amended in 1965 and 1967).[8]

2.　Plaintiffs contended that Judge Shea was "guilty of a gross abuse of discretion in attempting to grant a new trial on the issue of damages or in the alternative reducing a verdict of $400,000 to $60,000 in general damages." Such an attempt to reduce the verdict by 85 percent, said plaintiffs, is "virtually unprecedented" [A–11]. In one of the first cases ever sat before the California Supreme Court, the situation presented was quite similar to that of *Stevens* v. *Parke, Davis,* in which the trial judge ordered the jury award vastly reduced. In its decision, the Supreme Court stated that a judge

> ought never to set aside a verdict for such a cause, unless, beyond doubt, the verdict be unjust and oppressive, obtained through some undue advantage, mistake or in violation of law, as upon questions so peculiarly pertaining to the powers and investigation of the jury, it ought to be presumed that the verdict of the jury is correct.[9] [A–12]

3.　The right of trial by jury in civil cases as well as in criminal cases is secured by the Bill of Rights. The Seventh Amendment of the United States Constitution states: "The right of trial by jury shall be preserved, and no fact tried by a jury, shall be otherwise re-examined in any court of the United States, than according to the rules of the common law." Article I, section 7 of the California Constitution provides that the "Right of trial by jury shall be secured to all and remain inviolate." Based on these provisions, plaintiffs declared that any attempt on the part of the trial judge to disturb the jury's findings would be in violation of these rights.

4.　The trial judge made the following statement at the time of the proceedings on the hearing regarding the motion for a new trial:

---

[8] Section 657 was dealt with at length and interpreted by the Supreme Court in *Mercer* v. *Perez,* 68 Cal. 2d 104, and *Scala* v. *Jerry Witt and Sons,* 3 Cal. 3d 359. (See A–5–11 for a detailed discussion.) In both cases the court reversed orders granting new trials because of the violation of section 657.

[9] *Payne* v. *Pacific Mail Steamship Co.,* 1 Cal. 33.

Actually, had I been making a finding on this thing in my own judgment, it would have been in the neighborhood of $25,000. . . . All I can say is, gentlemen, I have not been able to find any case that would sustain a verdict anywhere near approaching this, and that is why I have taken the tactic that I have. [A–14, 15]

The trial judge's instructions to the jury stated that, according to a mortality table, the life expectancy of a female person aged 40 years is 37.5 additional years. Thus the verdict for general damages in the amount of $400,000 averaged $100,000 per plaintiff. Over the life expectancy of the deceased, the award amounted to approximately $2,600 per year per plaintiff [A–17]. The plaintiffs argued that there was no legal, factual, or reasonable basis for holding that each of the plaintiffs would not be entitled to $200 per month for the losses sustained due to the death of Mrs. Stevens:

[She] died in the prime of her life and during the prime of her husband's life and during the adolescent and maturing years of her children. Each of the plaintiffs suffered a profound loss and the translation thereof into monetary damages totaling $400,000 makes much more sense than the unfounded conclusion of the trial court that damages should have been in some far lesser sum (whether the same be $60,000 or $25,000). [A–18]

Arguments made by Dr. Beland and Parke, Davis in their appeal against Judge Shea's order

Defendant Dr. Beland appealed from the judgment against him but filed no brief in support of his appeal. Also, he contested plaintiffs' appeal from the order granting a new trial on the issue of damages. Defendant Parke, Davis appealed on the following grounds:

1. The jury's verdict for damages was indeed excessive, and plaintiffs' appeal for a new trial on the issue of damages should be denied.

2. The court committed reversible error when ruling on evidence and when instructing the jury as well as allowing misconduct by plaintiffs' counsel.

3. Parke, Davis was not negligent, and therefore the company should have been granted a directed verdict or judgment, notwithstanding the verdict on all issues; that is, the trial court judge should have directed the jury to bring in a verdict of not guilty [A–1, 2].

4. In case the appellate court were to disagree with the company on this subject, a new trial on all issues should be granted.

In support of its appeal, Parke, Davis made the following arguments:

1. Parke, Davis was not negligent in preparing or using the warning label that accompanied the drug in 1964. The warning labels clearly spelled out that aplastic anemia had been associated with the use of chloramphenicol and that chloramphenicol should not be used when other less

potentially dangerous agents would be effective. The essence of the plaintiffs' case against Dr. Beland was that, considering the nature of the decedent's illness, he should have used other drugs. This again was precisely the point covered in the warning label.

2. Dr. Beland was aware of the warning label. Dr. Beland's testimony left no doubt in anyone's mind that he was aware of the dangers inherent in the drug. He was 100 percent aware of it and had been in 1964 when he prescribed it. Plaintiffs' counsel contended time and again, in arguments, that it was Parke, Davis's duty to disseminate the information on the warning label. Parke, Davis contended that it had met its duty by placing the warning label in the package inserts and by the distribution of "Dear Doctor" letters. It also argued that the issue of the method of dissemination of the warning label was meant to mislead the jury so that plaintiffs' counsel could assert that Parke, Davis should have done something else they did not do. The law was clear. If the doctor was aware of the information, it made no difference how he acquired it [C–17].

3. The warning label to Dr. Beland was not watered down. Parke, Davis asserted that plaintiffs' counsel was allowed to introduce into testimony events of alleged overpromotion and watering down by Parke, Davis by assuring the court he would connect this evidence with Dr. Beland's prescription of Chloromycetin in 1964 in order to come within the statement in *Love v. Wolf* [(1964) 226 C.A. 2d 378]: "If the overpromotion can reasonably be said to have induced the doctor to disregard the warnings. . . ." Then, under certain circumstances, the drug company would be liable along with the prescribing doctor. Note, however, that in *Love v. Wolf,* Dr. Wolf testified that he had been influenced by Parke, Davis's promotion of Chloromycetin. In 1958, the year he prescribed it for Mrs. Love (who subsequently contracted aplastic anemia), the warning label was not specific enough to have led him to choose another drug. Dr. Beland, on the other hand, specifically testified to no causal link between the drug promotion and his prescription of it. Dr. Beland's testimony in this connection was uncontradicted and should have supported defendant Parke, Davis's motion for a directed verdict.

Assuming that plaintiffs were correct in finding that Parke, Davis was guilty of a "breach of duty" in overpromoting the drug, that breach must be the proximate cause of the injury.[10] Although Dr. Beland stated he was not influenced by alleged overpromotion, plaintiffs' counsel argued that maybe that wasn't true. In denying defendant's nonsuit, Judge Shea stated:

---

[10] In *Spencer v. Beatty Safway Scaffold Co.* (1956) 141 Cal. App. 2d 875, the court said: "The plaintiff in a tort action must establish the presence of every fact essential to his cause, especially that the negligence complained of was the proximate cause of the injury and not a mere speculation." See also *McKellar v. Pendergast* (1945) 68 Cal. App. 2d 485; *Reese v. Smith* (1937) 9 Cal. 2d 324; *Puckhaber v. Southern Pac. Co.* (1901) 132 Cal. 363, 366. [C–24]

It is a question of the measure of conjecture and speculation, and this lies in the use of the word, inferences to be deduced from the testimony. The rule is that we do not allow speculation and conjecture, but what else is an inference predicated on? Is there evidence here from which an inference may be drawn that this was what happened? [C–26, 27]

Parke, Davis believed that the trial court misunderstood the permissible inferences that may be drawn from evidence. While permissive, logical inferences may be drawn, speculative possibilities did not really constitute a true inference. In any event, the inference must fail when it was confronted with clear, explicit testimony [C–27].

Parke, Davis contended that the evidence on record clearly demonstrated that Dr. Beland prescribed the drug Chloromycetin with full knowledge of the side effects suffered by plaintiffs' decedent. In this situation, the intervening acts of Dr. Beland superseded any possible negligence on the part of Parke, Davis and insulated Parke, Davis from liability. California courts have consistently held that a warning given to an intermediate third party or his discovery of the danger relieves the original supplier from liability.[11]

4. Parke, Davis also contended that plaintiffs' counsel prevented defendant from receiving a fair trial by making inflammatory statements and playing on the emotions of the jury, and was therefore guilty of gross misconduct.

The Court of Appeals decision

The court of appeals decision was filed on March 21, 1972. Justice Roth reversed the judgment against Parke, Davis with directions to the trial court to enter judgment in favor of Parke, Davis. The court did not dismiss the lawsuit against Dr. Beland, but granted an order to him for a new trial.

Judge Roth said that the trial court's decision to lower damages "was an appropriate exercise of its discretion" and that it was "based in part on the vague showing in respect of decedent's earning power and primarily on passion and prejudice equating with the desire of the jury to punish and resulting in a verdict far in excess of what would have been reasonable and just. . . ." [H–4] Judge Roth also said that Section 657 had not been violated.

THE SUPREME COURT DECISION

The attorneys for the Stevens family appealed to the California Supreme Court, the highest state court, from an order granting the defendants a

---

[11] The brief quotes decisions to substantiate this: *Youtz v. Thompson Tire Co.* (1941) 46 Cal. App. 2d 672; *Boeing Airplane Co. v. Brown* (1961) 291 F.2d 310, 318–319; *Stultz v. Benson Lumber Co.* (1936) 6 Cal. 2d 688, 693; *McLaughlin v. Mine Safety Appliances Co.* (N.Y. 1962) 181 N.E. 2d 430, etc.

new trial on the issue of damages. Defendant Parke, Davis appealed from the judgment entered on the verdict in favor of the plaintiffs and against Parke, Davis, and from the order denying its motion for judgment notwithstanding the verdict.[12]

Supreme Court Justice Raymond L. Sullivan's decision, filed on March 14, 1973, affirmed the verdict of the jury that granted the plaintiffs $400,000 in damages. In rendering a decision in favor of the plaintiffs, Judge Sullivan concluded that all the arguments made by Parke, Davis were without merit and therefore its appeals were denied.

The Supreme Court's rationale

It is not necessary to review the briefs submitted to the Supreme Court by the various parties, as they cover essentially the same ground and use logic similar to that applied in their briefs to the court of appeal. Instead I will summarize the reasons and their logic employed by the court in rendering its decision.

The court agreed with the plaintiffs' contention that the order for a new trial should be reversed "because it fails to contain an adequate specification of reasons in compliance with Code of Civil Procedure section 657" [M–9].[13]

The court stated that although it had not laid down any hard and fast rule as to the content of such a specification, it had emphasized on several occasions[14] that, if the ground relied upon was insufficiency of evidence, the trial judge's specification of reasons "must briefly identify the portion of the record which convinces the judge 'that the court or jury clearly should have reached a different verdict or decision' " [M–10].

The objective of specificity in section 657 was to encourage careful deliberation by the trial court before ruling on the new trial motion and to make a sufficiently precise record to permit meaningful appellate review (*Mercer v. Perez*, 68 Cal. 2d 104, at pp. 112–116). Furthermore, a specification that merely recited the court's view of evidence as to whether "the defendant was not negligent or the plaintiff was negligent" was of little if any assistance to the appellate or to the reviewing court [M–12].

The court also held that the same rules which apply to a specification of reasons in respect to the ground of insufficiency of the evidence should apply to a specification of reasons in respect to the ground of excessive or inadequate damages. Indeed, to state that the damages awarded by the jury were excessive is simply one way of saying that the evidence does not

---

[12] Dr. Beland also took an appeal from the judgment but later abandoned it.

[13] Section 657 provides in relevant part as follows: "When a new trial is granted, on all or part of the issues, the court shall specify the ground or grounds upon which it is granted *and the court's reason or reasons* [original italics] for granting the new trial upon each ground stated" [M–9, 10].

[14] *Mercer v. Perez* (1968) 68 Cal. 2d 104; *Miller v. Los Angeles County Flood Control District* (1973) 8 Cal. 3d 689; *Scale v. Jerry Witt & Sons* (1970) 3 Cal. 3d 359.

justify the amount of the award.[15] The same statutory test applied in determining whether a new trial should be granted either on the ground of excessive or inadequate damages, or on the ground of insufficiency of the evidence.[16]

The court stated that the trial judge's order for a new trial made no pretense of specifying reasons upon which the judge based his decision to grant the defendants' motions. The statement that the verdict was excessive, that it was not sustained by the evidence, was a statement of ultimate fact that did not go beyond a statement of the ground for the court's decision. It did not indicate the ways in which the evidence dictated a less sizable verdict, and failed even to hint at any portion of the record that would tend to support the judge's ruling. The mere statement that the amount of the verdict was "based upon prejudice and passion on the part of the jury" was not a "reason" that provided an insight into the record [M–14].

The new trial order in this case was based solely on the ground of excessive damages. Since no reasons were specified, the conditions under section 657 were not met. The order granting a new trial could not be sustained on this ground. Therefore, the judgment would be automatically reinstated as to both defendants [M–16].

Noting that Dr. Beland abandoned his appeal from the judgment, Justice Sullivan stated that the judgment would thus automatically be final.

The Supreme Court's opinion of defendant Parke, Davis's appeal

The court rejected Parke, Davis's contention that (1) the record showed that as a matter of law Parke, Davis was not negligent; and (2) that the court committed reversible error in respect to rulings on the evidence, rulings as to the alleged misconduct of plaintiffs' counsel, and instructions to the jury [M–17]. In rejecting Parke, Davis's contention of not being legally negligent, the court provides us with an excellent statement as to the circumstances under, and the extent to which, a producer is liable for the harmful effects of its products:

> One who supplies a product directly or through a third person "for another to use is subject to liability to those whom the supplier should expect to use the [product] with the consent of the other . . . for physical harm

---

[15] *Doolin v. Omnibus Cable Co.* (1899) 125 Cal. 141, 144; 5 Witkin, Cal. Procedure (2d ed. 1971), p. 3618.

[16] Section 657 states in relevant part: "A new trial shall not be granted upon the ground of insufficiency of the evidence to justify the verdict or other decision, nor upon the ground of excessive or inadequate damages, unless after weighing the evidence the court is convinced from the entire record, including reasonable inferences therefrom, that the court of jury clearly should have reached a different verdict or decision" [M–12, 13].

caused by the use of the [product] in the manner for which and by a person for whose use it is supplied, if the supplier . . . knows or has reason to know that the [product] is or is likely to be dangerous for the use for which it is supplied, and . . . has no reason to believe that those for whose use the [product] is supplied will realize its dangerous condition, and . . . fails to exercise reasonable care to inform them of its dangerous condition or of facts which make it likely to be dangerous" [M–19, 20].[17]

It is established that in the case of medical prescriptions, where adequate warning of potential dangers of a drug has been given to doctors, there is no duty by the drug manufacturer to insure that the warning reaches the doctor's patient for whom the drug is prescribed. The courts have nevertheless held that mere compliance with regulations or directives as to warnings, such as those issued by the United States Food and Drug Administration in this case, may not be sufficient to immunize the manufacturer or supplier of the drug from liability. The warnings required by such agencies may be minimal in nature, and when the manufacturer or supplier has reason to know of greater dangers not included in the warning, its duty to warn may not be fulfilled. What is more to the point, these warnings can be considered to be eroded or even nullified by an "over-promotion of the drug through a vigorous sales program which may have the effect of persuading the prescribing doctor to disregard the warnings given."[18]

It is ironic that the two earlier court decisions most cited by all the parties (*Love v. Wolf* and *Incollingo v. Ewing*) and those on which this case also drew involved Chloromycetin and Parke, Davis, and in both cases the verdict went against Parke, Davis. A careful reading of these decisions leads one to wonder why Parke, Davis did not change its marketing practices for promoting and distributing Chloromycetin or, failing that, why the company did not try to settle the case out of court instead of fighting it all the way to the state Supreme Court. The answer may perhaps lie in two sets of interrelated factors. One, industry practices for the promotion and distribution of drugs are so well entrenched that it is extremely difficult, if not impossible, for one company to go against them for all or one of its products. Two, the profit margins and potential for promoting and selling ethical drugs in the present manner are so high that companies are willing to risk lawsuits and often absorb hearing costs of adverse judgments rather than tamper with a tried and proved success formula. However, these suppositions need further substantiation through a rigorous

[17] Rest. 2d Torts, § 388; see also *Love v. Wolf* (1964) 226 Cal. App. 2d 378, 395; *Tingley v. E. F. Houghton & Co.* (1947) 30 Cal. 2d 97, 102; *Gall v. Union Ice Company* (1951) 108 Cal. App. 2d 303, 209–310; *Yarrow v. Sterling Drug Co.* (D.C. S. Dak. 1967) 263 F. Supp. 159, 162, affd. in *Sterling Drug Inc. v. Yarrow* (8th Cir. 1969) 408 F. 2d 978, 993; *Sterling Drug Inc. v. Cornish* (8th Cir. 1967) 370 F. 2d 82, 84–85.

[18] *Love v. Wolf*, 266 Cal. App. 2d, 226, 395–396; *Yarrow v. Sterling Drug Co.*, 263 F. Supp. at pp. 162–163; *Incollingo v. Ewing*, (Pa. 1971) 282 A.2d 206, 220.

analysis of the drug industry before their causative extent can be established.

In the first case, Love v. Wolf [(1964), 226 Cal. App. 2d 378], the plaintiff sued her physician, Dr. Wolf, and Parke, Davis & Company for damages for personal injuries after she had developed aplastic anemia following the administration of Chloromycetin. The court rejected as without merit Parke, Davis's contention that the trial court should be directed to enter a judgment for Parke, Davis, because, so it was argued, the record showed as a matter of law that the defendant was liable neither for breach of warranty nor for negligence. After taking note of the numerous warnings distributed by Parke, Davis, the court nevertheless stated: "[W]e must accept the evidence leading to justifiable inferences that Parke, Davis, believing otherwise, had watered down its regulations-required warnings and had caused its detail men to promote a wider use of the drug by physicians than proper medical practice justified" [M–21, 22].[19]

In Incollingo v. Ewing [(Pa. 1971) 282 A.2d 206], the Supreme Court of Pennsylvania refused to reverse a judgment against Parke, Davis for damages arising from plaintiff's death as a result of the administration of Chloromycetin. Parke, Davis's evidence of warning was similar to that introduced in the present case. The court held:

> We think that whether or not the warnings on the cartons, labels and literature of Parke, Davis in use in the relevant years were adequate, and whether or not the printed words of warning were in effect cancelled out and rendered meaningless in the light of the sales effort made by the detail men, were questions properly for the jury. . . . [I]f detail men are an effective means of selling a product and explaining its nature, a jury could find that they also afforded an effective medium of conveying a warning. [M–22, 23]

In reviewing the evidence within the framework of the principles alluded to in these two cases, the California judges stated they were satisfied that the jury could draw a reasonable inference that Parke, Davis negligently failed to provide an adequate warning as to the dangers of Chloromycetin by so "watering down" its warnings and so overpromoting the drug that members of the medical profession, including Dr. Beland, were caused to prescribe it when it was not justified. The California Supreme Court also rejected Parke, Davis's contention that, even if it did overpromote the drug, it was exonerated from any liability because the testimony in the case clearly established Dr. Beland's negligence, thus making him, as a matter of law, an intervening cause in Mrs. Stevens's death (see Magee v. Wyeth Laboratories, 214 Cal. App. 2d, at pp. 251–352).

The court based its dismissal of Parke, Davis's argument on two grounds. One, it was the province of the jury to resolve the conflicts in the evidence and to pass on the weight to be given the evidence. Citing various legal

---

[19] On retrial, Parke, Davis was again found liable and judgment against it was affirmed on appeal. Love v. Wolf (1967) 249 Cal. App.2d 822.

authorities, the court stated that it was within the province of the trier of fact to accept one part of the testimony of a witness and reject another part even though the latter contradicts the part accepted [M–26]. The court concluded there was adequate circumstantial evidence on the record to support a reasonable inference by the jury that Dr. Beland was induced to prescribe the drug for Mrs. Stevens because of Parke, Davis's overpromotion. Like many others of the profession, he had been exposed to the promotional tactics employed by Parke, Davis. It was reasonable to assume that the company's heavy advertising and promotion efforts for the drug consciously or subconsciously influenced him.

The court's second argument had to do with the definition of the "legal" responsibility of a producer. The court stated that even if the jury were to accept Dr. Beland's testimony that he was cognizant of the dangers of the drug, *nevertheless his negligence was not, as a matter of law, an intervening cause which exonerated Parke, Davis* [M–28]. According to the court:

> It is well settled that "an actor may be liable if his negligence is a substantial factor in causing an injury, and he is not relieved of liability because of the intervening act of a third person if such act was *reasonably foreseeable* at the time of his negligent conduct. [Citations.] Moreover, 'If the likelihood that a third person may act in a particular manner is the hazard or one of the hazards which makes the actor negligent, such an act whether innocent, negligent, intentionally tortious or criminal does not prevent the actor from being liable for harm caused thereby.' " [*Vesely* v. *Sager* (1971) 5 Cal. 3d 153, 163–164, quoting Rest. 2d Torts, § 449; italics added.] Thus, if it was reasonably foreseeable that physicians, despite awareness of the dangers of Chloromycetin, would be consciously or subconsciously induced to prescribe the drug when it was not warranted, Parke, Davis cannot be relieved of liability because of the intervening act of Dr. Beland in prescribing the drug while cognizant of its dangers. If there is room for reasonable men to differ as to whether the intervening act was reasonably foreseeable, then the question is properly left to the jury. [*McEvoy* v. *American Pool Corp.* (1948) 32 Cal. 2d 295; Rest. 2d Torts, § 453, com. a.]
>
> We are satisfied from a review of the evidence set forth in detail, *supra*, that the jury could reasonably find that Dr. Beland's negligent prescription of Chloromycetin for Mrs. Stevens was a foreseeable consequence of the extensive advertising and promotional campaign planned and carried out by the manufacturer. The record reveals in abundant detail that Parke, Davis made every effort, employing both direct and subliminal advertising, to allay the fears of the medical profession which were raised by knowledge of the drug's dangers. It cannot be said, therefore, that Dr. Beland's prescription of the drug despite his awareness of its dangers was anything other than the foreseeable consequence—indeed, the desired result—of Parke, Davis' overpromotion; this intervening act was "one of the hazards which makes [Parke, Davis] negligent." [*Vesely* v. *Sager, supra,* 3 Cal. 3d at p. 163.]

Having rejected Parke, Davis's substantive arguments against the jury's verdict, the court also dismissed as without merit the company's contentions that (1) the trial court erred in denying its motion for a judgment notwithstanding the verdict, and (2) there were flagrant examples of misconduct of plaintiffs' counsel to compel a new trial. The court's decision was thus stated: "The order granting a new trial is reversed. The order denying defendants' motion for judgment notwithstanding the verdict is affirmed. The judgment is affirmed" [M–37].

EPILOGUE

In a communication to the author dated January 27, 1975, concerning the Stevens case, a spokesman from Parke, Davis stated:[20]

> Parke, Davis does not agree that the promotion or marketing of any of its products, including Chloromycetin, has ever been improper. The promotion of prescription drugs is so regulated, as to what can be written, that it precludes any thought of over-promoting.
>
> The Food and Drug Administration first issued regulations in December 1960, later revised in October 1968, covering promotion literature. These regulations required that in detailing a product to a physician, the brochure given to the physician contain the full disclosure of the product, or a package insert be left with the doctor.
>
> There have been changes, approved by the Food and Drug Administration, in the labeling of chloramphenicol since 1965, when the Stevens litigation had its origin. However, these changes were not the result of the lawsuit. All labeling, promotion and advertising is reviewed with the FDA prior to its release.
>
> Parke, Davis' promotion and distribution of ethical drugs through physician detailing and pharmacy contact has remained much the same. . . . Parke, Davis does not feel that its prescription drugs have been over-promoted, nor has it made any changes in its marketing of these products as a result of the Stevens lawsuit.

SELECTED BIBLIOGRAPHY

Ball, Robert. "The Secret Life of Hoffman-LaRoche." *Fortune* 84 (August 1971): 130.

Bartenstein, Fred, Jr. "Images of the Drug Industry: The Industry View." In *The Economics of Drug Innovation*, ed. Joseph D. Cooper. Washington, D.C., 1970.

Boyd, Eldon M. "The Equivalence of Drug Brands." *Rx Bulletin* 2 (July–August 1971): 101.

Buchan, J. W. "America's Health: Fallacies, Beliefs, Practices." *FDA Consumer* 6 (October 1972): 4.

CBS Reports. "Prescription: Take With Caution." CBS Television Network, January 10, 1975.

---

[20] Letter from M. Thorn Kuhl, Public Affairs Division, Parke, Davis & Company, Detroit, Michigan, dated January 27, 1975.

Cooper, Michael H. *Prices and Profits in the Pharmaceutical Industry.* Oxford, N.Y.: Pergamon Press, 1966.

Dowling, Harry F. *Medicines for Man.* New York: Knopf, 1970.

"Drug Substitution: How to Turn Order into Chaos." *Journal of the American Medical Association* 217 (August 9, 1971): 817.

Edwards, Marvin H. "Chloromycetin: Special Report." *Private Practice* 3 (March 1971): 3.

Firestone, John M. *Trends in Prescription Drug Prices.* Washington, D.C.: American Enterprise Institute for Public Policy Research, 1970.

Flesh, George. "Pharmaceutical Advertising." *New Physician* 20 (March 1971): 137.

Funk, Edwin. "Yesterday, Today and Tomorrow in Drug Advertising." *Pharmaceutical Marketing and Media* 2 (March 1967): 13.

Garai, Pierre R. "Advertising and Promotion of Drugs." In *Drugs in Our Society,* ed. Paul Talalay. Baltimore: Johns Hopkins Press, 1964.

Harris, Richard. *The Real Voice.* New York: Macmillan, 1964.

Harris, Richard. *A Sacred Trust.* Baltimore: Penguin Books, 1969.

Hoge, James F. "Legislative History of Home Remedies." *Annals of the New York Academy of Sciences* 120 (1965): 833.

Incollingo v. *Ewing* (Pa. 1971) 282 A. 2d 206.

"In Whose Hands?" *Economic Priorities Report* 4 (August–November 1973): 4–5.

Jick, Hershel; Miettenin, Olli S.; Shapiro, Samuel; Lewis, George P.; Siskind, Victor; and Slone, Dennis. "Comprehensive Drug Surveillance." *Journal of the American Medical Association* 213 (August 31, 1970): 1455.

Kiefer, David M. "Risk and Reward in Ethical Drugs." *Chemical and Engineering News* 46 (January 29, 1968): 22.

Love v. *Wolf* (1964) 226 Cal. App. 2d 378.

Magee v. *Wyeth Laboratories,* 214 Cal. App. 2d.

Maronde, Robert F.; Seibert, Stanley; Katzoff, Jack; and Silverman, Milton. "Prescription Data Processing: Its Role in the Control of Drug Abuse." *California Medicine* 117 (September 1972): 22.

May, Charles D."Selling Drugs by 'Educating' Physicians." *Journal of Medical Education* 36 (January 1961): 15.

McEvoy v. *American Pool Corp.* (1948) 32 Cal. 2d 295.

Mercer v. *Perez* (1968) 68 Cal. 2d 104.

Mintz, Morton. "Drug Ad Exports Pose a Problem." *Washington Post,* May 21, 1968.

Mintz, Morton. "The Pill: Press and Public at the Experts' Mercy." *Columbia Journalism Review* 7 (winter 1968–69): 4.

Modell, Walter. "Editorial: Requiem for the FDA." *Clinical Pharmacology and Therapeutics* 11 (January–February 1970): 1.

Myers, Maven J. "Distribution Aspects in the Potential Misuse of O-T-C Preparations." *American Journal of Pharmacy* 142 (January–February 1970): 29.

Norwood, G. Joseph, and Smith, Mickey C. "Market Mortality of New Products in the Pharmaceutical Industry." *Journal of the American Pharmaceutical Industry,* N.S.11 (1971): 592.

Opinion Research Corporation. *Physicians' Attitudes Toward Drug Compendia. A National Survey Sponsored by Pharmaceutical Manufacturers Association.* Princeton, N.J., 1968.

Oppenheimer, Robert. "Ethics Is Alive and Well in Medical Ad-Land." *Pharmaceutical Marketing and Media* 3 (April 1968): 9.

Pearson, Michael. *The Million-Dollar Bugs.* New York: Putnam, 1969.

Pharmaceutical Manufacturers Association. *The Medications Physicians Prescribe: Who Shall Determine the Source?* Washington, D.C., 1972.

Sesser, Stanford. "Peddling Dangerous Drugs Abroad: Special Dispensation." *New Republic* 164 (March 6, 1971): 17.

Silverman, Milton. *Magic in a Bottle.* 2nd ed. New York: Macmillan, 1948.

Silverman, Milton, and Lee, Philip R. *Pills, Profits, and Politics.* Berkeley and Los Angeles: University of California Press, 1974.

Sterling Drug Inc. v. *Yarrow* (8th Cir. 1969) 408 F.2d 978.

Stolley, Paul D., and Goddard, James L. "Prescription Drug Insurance for the Elderly under Medicare." *American Journal of Public Health* 61 (March 1971): 574.

Teeling-Smith, George. "The British Drug Scene." In *The Economics of Drug Innovation,* ed. Joseph D. Cooper. Washington, D.C.: American University, Center for the Study of Private Enterprise, 1970.

U.S. Congress, Senate, Subcommittee on Antitrust and Monopoly of the Committee on the Judiciary. *Physician Ownership in Pharmacies and Drug Companies,* 88th Congress, 2d Session, August 1965.

U.S. Congress, Senate, Subcommittee on Health of the Committee on Labor and Public Welfare. *Examination of the Pharmaceutical Industry, 1973–74.* Parts 1–6, 93rd Cong., 1st and 2nd sess., December 1973, February, March, and May 1974.

U.S. Congress, Senate, Subcommittee on Monopoly of the Select Committee on Small Business. *Advertising of Proprietary Medicines: Effect of Promotion and Advertising of Over-the-Counter Drugs on Competition, Small Business, and the Health and Welfare of the Public.* Part 3, 92nd Cong., 2nd sess., December 1972.

U.S. Congress, Senate, Subcommittee on Monopoly of the Select Committee on Small Business. *Competitive Problems in the Drug Industry: Present Status of Competition in the Pharmaceutical Industry.* Parts 5, 6, and 11, 91st Cong., 1st and 2nd sess., 92nd Cong., 1st sess., 1967, 1968, 1969.

Vesely v. *Sager* (1971) 5 Cal. 3d 153.

Vogt, Donald D., and Billups, Norman F. "The Merger Movement in the American Pharmaceutical Complex." *Journal of the American Pharmaceutical Association,* N.S.11 (November 1971): 588.

Waite, Arthur S. "The Future of Pharmaceutical Drug Promotion." *Medical Marketing and Media* 6 (June 1971): 9.

Wasserman, Bennett. "The Ubiquitous Detailman." *Hofstra Law Review* 1:183–213, Spring, 1973.

Yarrow v. *Sterling Drug Co.* (D.C. S.Dak. 1967) 263 F.Supp. 159.

Youtz v. *Thompson Tire Co.* (1941), 46 Cal. App. 2d 672.

Zalaznick, Sheldon. "Bitter Pills for the Drugmakers." *Fortune* 77 (July 1968): 82.

8 The Commodore Corporation and the mobile home industry*

Uses and abuses of warranties as a marketing device in the sale of mobile homes

*Few things strengthen like
the shedding of illusions*
Eric Sevareid

Warranties have been an integral part of selling a product, especially big-ticket items, in the market. To consumers, it is an assurance of quality. They feel secure in the belief that should anything go wrong because of faulty materials or manufacturing defects, the manufacturer stands ready to correct it. This is especially important because manufacturing-related defects may not be apparent at the time of purchase, may appear after a product has been in use for some time, and may cost the unprotected consumer an exorbitant amount to correct.

Manufacturers on their part recognize and accept their responsibility for correcting product defects that are not the consumer's fault. At the same time, a clear and specific warranty protects manufacturers from unwarranted and exaggerated claims by users.

The last few decades have seen a dramatic change in the nature and use of warranties. With the increased technological complexity built into products, quality control and inspection at the manufacturer's level has become increasingly expensive. At the same time, product failures have increased, as has the cost of failure-related injuries. To protect themselves, manufacturers have more and more resorted to warranties couched in legal language that in fact severely limits the maker's responsibility. The courts and legislatures have been moving in the other direction, and through specific legal mandates and more contemporary interpretation

---

* The author is grateful to Eric Rubin, attorney with the Federal Trade Commission, Washington, D.C., for his assistance in the development of this case study.

of common law doctrines, as well as of the existing laws, have been expanding the scope of a manufacturer's liability under such concepts as "implied warranty" and strict liability.

ISSUES FOR ANALYSIS

The case of the Commodore Corporation highlights some of the problems related to the uses and abuses of warranties, the rights and obligations of consumers and manufacturers, and the relative effectiveness of various corrective measures, such as market competition, self-regulation, judicial remedies, and regulatory mechanisms. In particular, it focuses attention on these issues:

1. How effective is the market mechanism in providing alternative choices to consumers for buying better warranty protection? As we shall see in this case, warranty defaults and abuses were not confined to a minority of small or weak manufacturers, but were common practice in the industry, even for the largest companies.
2. Is there anything special about certain types of products or industries where warranty abuses are likely to be widespread? More specifically, what are the characteristics of the mobile home industry that caused its dominant members to indulge in warranty abuses? Do other industries have similar characteristics?
3. To the extent that warranties are a marketing tool management can employ to promote sales and brand loyalty, how effective is this tool likely to be as a part of total marketing mix, if warranties become uniform and management loses a large part of its discretionary decision-making power to differentiate its warranties from those of its competitors?
4. Given the nature of the product, to what extent should we expect the buyer to assume responsibility for purchasing a product carefully? Or under what circumstances and to what extent should *caveat emptor* still apply?
5. In terms of marketing management, how should management improve and manage its warranty program to keep it an effective marketing tool?
6. In terms of consumer protection, the questions to be raised are these: (a) Under what circumstances can the industry be depended upon to regulate itself? (b) How effective is the FTC procedure, outlined in the case, likely to be in providing adequate consumer protection? The extensive and detailed procedures for compliance also have counterparts in compliance costs at the manufacturer's end and enforcement costs at the FTC's end. Are these costs justified in terms of benefits? Could the FTC have asked for different (and less cumbersome and expensive) criteria for effectuating similar performance? (c) How effective are judicial remedies such as lawsuits by consumers to seek relief

from manufacturers, especially because of the high cost of litigation, court delays, and the recent curbs on class action suits imposed by the U.S. Supreme Court?[1] (d) What other measures can be developed to achieve the desired ends—that is, prevent warranty abuses—while at the same time keeping freedom of the market, for sellers and buyers, to the maximum extent possible?

THE BACKGROUND

On August 17, 1974, the Federal Trade Commission (FTC) entered into a consent order with The Commodore Corporation, a manufacturer of mobile homes located in Omaha, Nebraska. Under the agreement, the company agreed to cease and desist from making fraudulent claims in its warranties to the retail purchasers of the company's mobile homes,[2] and to take immediate and effective steps to fulfill its obligations under the said warranties.[3] At the same time, similar consent orders were entered into between the FTC and three other manufacturers of mobile homes: Skyline Corporation, Redman Industries, and Fleetwood Enterprises. In entering into the agreements, none of the companies admitted to any wrongdoing alleged in the FTC complaint, nor did they admit to a violation of any law.

The mobile home industry[4]

The mobile home industry has undergone meteoric growth over the last decade and constitutes a key factor in the effort to reduce the nation's

---

[1] Philip G. Schrag, *Counsel for the Deceived: Case Studies in Consumer Fraud* (New York: Pantheon, 1972); Babette Barton, "Forms and Forums of Consumer Relief: Redress or Rape," paper presented at a symposium on new perspectives in consumerism, sponsored by the National Affiliation of Concerned Business Students (Chicago, November 1974); "Importance of Being Adequate: Due Process Requirements in Class Actions under Federal Rule 23," *University of Pennsylvania Law Review* 173 (May 1975): 1271–61; Benett, E. J., "*Eisen v. Carlisle and Jacquelin* (94 Sup. Ct. 2140) Supreme Court Calls for Revamping Class Action Strategy," *Wisconsin Law Review* (1974), 801–32.

[2] For the purposes of this complaint, a mobile home is defined as "a movable or portable dwelling over 32 feet in body length and over 8 feet in width, constructed to be towed on its own chassis and designed so as to be installed with or without a permanent foundation for human occupancy as a residence, which may include one or more components which can be retracted for towing purposes and subsequently expanded for additional capacity, or two or more units separably towable but designed to be joined into one integral unit. 'Mobile home' as used herein includes the mobile home structure, including the plumbing, heating, and electrical systems." United States of America Before Federal Trade Commission in the matter of *The Commodore Corporation, complaint, docket No. 742-3202* (hereinafter referred to as the *Complaint*), p. 1.

[3] United States of America Before Federal Trade Commission, *In the Matter of the Commodore Corporation: Agreement Containing Consent Order to Cease and Desist, File No. 742-3202* (Hereinafter referred to as the *Agreement*).

[4] The description in this section is based on the material in United States of America Before Federal Trade Commission, *Commodore Corporation, File No. 742-3202; Fleetwood Enterprises Inc., File No. 742-3200; Redman Industries, Inc., File No. 742-3199; Skyline Corporation, File No. 742-3201: Analysis of Provisionally Accepted Consent Orders* (hereinafter referred to as the *Analysis of Consent Orders*), pp. 6–9.

housing shortage. In 1960, 103,700 mobile homes were shipped to retail outlets. By 1972, this figure reached 626,000 homes, for retail sales of $4.1 billion. It is anticipated that due to the generally troubled economy, 1974 production will decline to 410,000 homes for sales of approximately $3 billion. These figures are particularly meaningful when contrasted with the fact that in 1972, total production of single-family dwelling units, excluding mobile homes, was only about 1.5 million units. Mobile homes therefore now account for a substantial percentage of all new housing starts. These figures take on added significance in light of the fact that mobile homes represent a majority of the sales of new low and moderately priced housing. They make up approximately 95 percent of all new single-family dwellings selling for under $15,000 and 60 percent of such dwellings costing $25,000 or less. Over 6 percent of all rural housing now consists of mobile homes.[5] Given the fact that mobile homes constitute the major source of inexpensive housing, it is not surprising to find that 1970 census figures showed that 21.1 percent of mobile home owners had annual family incomes of under $4,000 and 41.8 percent had incomes of under $6,000.

The mobile homes sold today are significantly different from the "gypsy trailer" of the 1940s. They can best be viewed as relocatable houses, since they are most often placed on a prepared foundation with their wheels and axles either removed or raised so that they are not functional. Most of the homes are not removed again during their useful lives. The average price of a new mobile home is approximately $7,500.

Approximately 46 percent of all mobile homes sold are 12 feet wide and 60 feet long, although many states have now authorized shipment of "fourteen-wides." As a result, "fourteen-wides" now account for 30 percent of the industry's production. More spacious "double-wides," which are composed of two 12 X 50 foot (or longer) sections, have become increasingly popular and now represent approximately 22 percent of the mobile home market nationally.[6] Double-wides range in price up to $20,000. Most mobile homes have two or more bedrooms, a large central living area, a kitchen, and often a separate dining or family room.

The Mobile Home Manufacturers Association (MHMA) estimates that there are approximately 330 manufacturers of mobile homes throughout the country. However, production is concentrated in the top 25 companies, which manufactured approximately 61 percent of the homes produced in 1973.[7] The majority of the remaining companies are very small. The four respondents are all dominant companies in the industry, and three of the four are among the industry's top five. In 1973 sales they were ranked as follows:

[5] 1970 Census of Housing, HC(1) A-1, Table 5.

[6] Jenkins Mobile Industry Newsletter, September 1974, vol. 4, no. 11.

[7] Jenkins Mobile Industry Newsletter, July 1974, vol. 4, no. 9.

Skyline Corporation	(1)	52,000 homes
Redman Industries	(2)	41,478 homes
Fleetwood Enterprises	(4)	28,600 homes
Commodore Corporation	(7)	12,120 homes

The respondents in 1973 together shared approximately 22 percent of the mobile home market.

In general, mobile homes are sold to independent dealers, usually referred to by the manufacturers as "authorized dealers," who then resell the homes to the public. The manufacturer-dealer relationship is usually oral, with no precise contractual delineation of mutual obligations or any firm commitment as to the duration of the relationship made by either party. These relationships are therefore highly unstable, and the rate of dissolution is high.

The complaint

The FTC complaint charged the Commodore Corporation and other respondents with committing "false, deceptive, and unfair acts and practices in violation of section 5 of the Federal Trade Commission Act in connection with the manufacture and sale of mobile homes."[8]

The investigation was initiated in late 1972. At that time, Commodore was engaged in the design, manufacture, promotion, and sale of mobile homes. Incorporated in Delaware in 1968, Commodore had its head office at 8712 Dodge Road in Omaha, Nebraska. With eleven manufacturing facilities scattered in nine states, it distributed and sold homes in forty-nine states. In 1972, Commodore produced 15,685 mobile homes and ranked sixth in the industry in production volume.[9] Commodore had since suffered heavy financial losses and, at the time this consent order was signed, had entered into a proceeding in bankruptcy under Chapter XI of the Federal Bankruptcy Act in the U.S. District Court for the District of Nebraska. Commodore, like other major producers of mobile homes, places primary reliance on authorized dealers for the sale of its homes to the public.

Warranty. In the course of selling their mobile homes, Commodore and other respondents[10] made the following warranties to the retail purchaser.[11] These warranties were made both orally and in writing, and directly or indirectly through their authorized dealers or the sales representatives of these authorized dealers.

1. Each *written* warranty disseminated by the companies in all states

---

[8] *Analysis of Consent Orders,* p. 9.

[9] Ibid., p. 4.

[10] Except where specifically stated, the four manufacturers will be referred to as "the companies" or "the manufacturers."

[11] *Complaint,* pp. 1–9.

except California represented either directly or by implication that the companies would correct, for the original purchaser and any subsequent owner, all defects in workmanship or materials in the new mobile homes during the first twelve months from the time of the first purchase, with certain specified exceptions of components enumerated therein, including but not limited to appliances.

The warranty also stated that the manufacturer's obligation would be limited to repairing or replacing defective parts which are returned to one of its factories and which the company "shall determine to have been defective." In California, because of the state laws, the company was to correct similar defects *at the site of the mobile home.*

The written warranty disseminated in all states except California further disclaimed "all other warranty rights which are imposed by force of law, including but not limited to the implied warranties of merchantability and fitness for a particular purpose, and represents directly or by implication that the aforesaid warranty sets forth the full extent of respondents' warranty obligations."

2. Despite these provisions, it was the companies' uniformly applied warranty policy that the aforesaid service and repair of defects covered by the written warranty will be provided at the mobile home site and that the return of the home, or the defective parts, with transportation charges prepaid was not a condition for the performance of such service.

Failure to fulfill warranty obligations. The complaint charged that the companies engaged in practices that had the effect of denying the retail purchasers of mobile homes full service and repair of defects within a reasonable time. Typical of such acts and practices were these:

1. It was nowhere stated that it would be the "authorized dealers" who would have sole and complete responsibility, at least in the first instance, to perform repair and service under the warranty without reimbursement by the companies.
2. The companies failed to scrutinize, regulate, and continuously evaluate the activities of authorized dealers and their agents to ensure that those dealers in fact had the necessary facilities for carrying out repairs and did in fact provide the services stipulated under the warranty to the purchasers of mobile homes within a reasonable time.
3. The warranty stated or implied that the purchasers' rights under the warranty were *only* those expressly stated in the warranty, and that no other claims of implied-in-law warranty would be accepted, when in fact, under the applicable laws of several states, such exclusions, disclaimers, or limitations are unenforceable.
4. The companies failed to establish and maintain an effective and regular mechanism for the prompt and fair resolution of mobile home consumer complaints stipulated under the warranty.

Thus, Commodore and other manufacturers were disseminating a warranty that (a) failed fully and completely to inform purchasers as to the actual protection offered by the companies, and (b) failed to establish or maintain an effective or adequate system to ensure that all defects covered by the aforesaid warranty would be fully corrected or repaired within a reasonable time.

These acts and practices were considered in violation of Section 5 of the Federal Trade Commission Act. It was contended that were these facts known to consumers, they (a) would be likely to affect the decision to purchase one of the manufacturers' mobile homes, and (b) would enable retail purchasers to understand the true nature and extent of their warranty rights and to secure the performance of warranty services.

The consent orders

The salient features of the consent orders signed by Commodore and the three other mobile home manufacturers were as follows:

1. Dissemination of information of the consent order to retail purchasers. Commodore and other manufacturers will, within 90 days of the effective date of this order, make a written inquiry of all known retail purchasers[12] of mobile homes manufactured by the companies during the period July 1, 1972, to June 30, 1974. The inquiries are to be made on specific forms with accompanying letters and self-addressed postage-paid return envelopes (Appendixes A, B).

2. Undertaking repairs. The companies will undertake, directly or indirectly, to repair or service within a reasonable time *at the site of the home* all defects and malfunctions in mobile homes due to manufacturing defects.

The reasonable time was defined as repair of no less than fifty mobile homes per month per manufacturing plant, or at least 10 percent of the mobile homes sold at retail covered under this consent order. *(a)* Beginning within 120 days of the effective date of the consent order, in the case of a dispute arising between the authorized dealers and their assigned agents or third parties as to the liability of carrying out repairs under warranty, the companies shall be responsible for carrying out the repairs, expeditiously in the normal course of business, regardless of whether the dispute is resolved at the time the repairs are carried out. *(b)* In case the repairs required are of a nature that affects the safety of a mobile home or renders it substantially uninhabitable, the repairs shall commence as soon

---

[12] Retail purchasers do not include local, state, or federal governments or their agencies, cases under litigation, foreign buyers, those who bought homes on "as is" basis, and certain other minor classes of buyers such as those who do not communicate with the manufacturers or their dealers within 60 days after the manufacturer's inquiry has been mailed to them.

as possible but in no event later than three business days following receipt of notice of such defects by the companies. *(c)* In case of other repairs under the warranty, the companies shall respond to notice of the need for repairs within 7 business days, and complete repairs within a reasonable time not to exceed 30 days following receipt of notice for repairs.

3. Inspection. *(a)* Beginning within 120 days of the effective date of this order, the companies shall inspect at the home site, directly or through authorized dealers or other third parties, each mobile home prior to or at the time of delivery, and ascertain that the said home is being delivered free of all ascertainable defects and is properly set up, except for deficiencies which do not affect the home's safety or habitability, which shall be noted in the owner-dealer final delivery checklist (Appendix C) and which shall then be remedied in accordance with 2(b) and 2(c) above. *(b)* Beginning within 120 days of the effective date of this order, the companies shall *re-inspect,* directly or through their dealers or other third parties, each mobile home within 45 and 90 days after possession has been taken by the retail purchaser to determine the existence of and to correct any defects covered by the warranty. *(c)* Results of such inspections required under 3(a) and 3(b) will be documented in reports that shall be signed by the companies' dealers and, if possible, by retail purchasers. The reporting documents may be in the formats provided in Appendixes C and D. *(d)* The companies shall send a questionnaire (Appendix E or equivalent) to all persons other than "as is" purchasers who after the effective date of this order purchase the companies' mobile homes at retail. The inquiries made will relate to the complaints, if any, that the retail purchaser has about the setup or functioning of the mobile home that were covered under the warranty, and whether or not those complaints have been satisfactorily resolved.

4. Clear warranty. The manufacturers were prohibited from disseminating, directly or indirectly, any express or implied warranty to the retail purchasers of mobile homes unless it covers, but is not limited to, the following standards of performance: The identity and address of the warrantor; the nature and extent of the warranty offered; the remedies available to the purchaser under such warranty; the manner in which the manufacturer intends to provide for performance of warranty obligations; the requirements a purchaser must fulfill as a condition for securing performance under the warranty; and a uniform procedure a retail purchaser can follow for a systematic review and disposition of complaints arising out of warranty disputes.

The manufacturers shall establish and maintain a regular and effective system of authorized dealers or other agents to ensure that every purchaser of their mobile homes will receive full performance under the warranty.

All repairs arising out of warranty conditions shall be performed at the site of the mobile home.

5. Restraints. The companies involved henceforth will not sell homes without an express or implied warranty—that is, on an "as is" basis, or with any limitations or disclaimers of liability assumed by the companies under the warranty, unless it is determined in the opinion of legal counsel that such "as is" sales are enforceable under governing state law. Even so, the manufacturer will give the prospective purchaser a notice in clear and unambiguous language that contains, at a minimum, the following information:

NOTICE

The manufacturer of this mobile home sells it "as is" and refuses to assume any responsibility for defects. The purchaser of this mobile home must accept it with all defects and take the entire risk, under contract law, as to its condition.

6. Authorized dealers. The consent order set stringent standards manufacturers must follow to ensure (1) that their authorized dealers have the necessary capabilities to perform all services under the warranty, where such a responsibility is delegated to them by the manufacturers, and (2) that their authorized dealers in fact do carry out their obligations under the warranty fairly and expeditiously. The duties and responsibilities of the dealers in regard to retail purchases were to be the same as those of the manufacturers themselves under the consent order.

The consent order stipulates that authorized dealers must demonstrate the necessary capability of fulfilling their obligations to the retail purchasers of the companies' mobile homes within 180 days of the effective date of the signing of this order, failing which the companies shall not accept any further orders from such dealers until they have executed agreements to abide by the conditions of dealership as outlined in the consent order.

7. Organizational requirements. The direct administration of the respondents' warranty service program at the corporate level and the responsibility for supervising and ensuring implementation of the warranty service program shall, beginning within 120 days of the effective date of the order, be vested only in those corporate officials who have no direct responsibilities on a day-to-day basis for the sale of respondents' mobile homes. Furthermore, these executives will be required to make periodic reports, at least on a monthly basis, to their superiors, as to the current costs of the warranty service; the incidence and nature of frequently recurring defects; measures undertaken by the respondent to remedy these defects; and an analysis of the manner in which manufacturers, employees, dealers, and other third parties are performing warranty and setup responsibilities.

Within 120 days of the effective date of this order, respondents shall establish a uniform procedure for the systematic receipt, analysis, and fair disposition of all complaints and disputes arising between retail purchasers of respondents' mobile homes and respondents, their authorized dealers, and third parties. These procedures shall incorporate but not necessarily be limited to (a) a prompt evaluation and response of all complaints within a period of 5 business days after receipt of a complaint; (b) the designation of a single department within the corporate organization to handle all warranty-related complaints; (c) the development of an effective mechanism for the fair and impartial resolution of all warranty-related disputes by executives not responsible for sales on a day-to-day basis; (d) the keeping of accurate and complete records pertaining to all warranty-related complaints and their disposition; and (e) a periodic review and evaluation of the effectiveness of such procedures and correction of such procedures where necessary.

   8. Reporting requirements: Commodore.[13] (a) Commodore shall forthwith distribute a copy of the consent order to each of its operating divisions or manufacturing plants engaged in the manufacture, sale, and distribution of mobile homes. (b) The company shall notify the FTC at least 30 days prior to any proposed change in the company corporate structure such as dissolution assignment, or sale resulting in the emergence of a successor corporation, or any other change in the corporation that may affect compliance obligations arising out of this order. (c) At intervals of 9, 18, and 24 months following the execution of this order, Commodore shall file written reports with the FTC setting forth in detail the manner and form in which the company has complied with the order. (d) Within 9 months following the execution of this order, Commodore shall provide the FTC with a report outlining the manner in which the dealers and retail purchasers were contacted, their reaction to these contacts, and the subsequent actions taken by Commodore. Furthermore, Commodore must maintain records for two years indicating the nature of its compliance with the above-mentioned requirement and must produce this data for the FTC's inspection. (e) Commodore shall submit to the FTC for its review copies of any proposed substantial revisions in its various questionnaires and the warranty documents described in the consent order at least 60 days prior to the proposed effective date of any such revisions. Such submissions will be required for the three years following the effective date of this order. (f) Since Commodore had filed for bankruptcy at the time the consent order was proposed, the order provided that notwithstanding its provisions, retail purchasers of mobile homes will have at least 180 days to file claims under the bankruptcy proceedings as a matter of law. Furthermore, Commodore shall give each retail purchaser written notice of the right to file such a claim in said Chapter XI proceedings. The form and content of such notice shall be subject to the prior approval of the FTC.

---

[13] Slightly modified reporting requirements were applied to Commodore because the company had filed for bankruptcy proceedings under Chapter XI of the Federal Bankruptcy Act.

APPENDIX A: LETTER TO PURCHASERS

(Date)

Dear Mr. and Mrs. _____:

In _____ of _____ you took occupancy of a _____ mobile home produced by _____ in _____. This home was purchased from _____ in _____.

Our homes are warranted for one year to be free from defects in material and workmanship. Any repairs required by this warranty should have been performed in full by the dealer who sold you your home or, if this is not possible, by the factory which manufactured it.

Through the attached questionnaire, we are seeking to determine your experience with regard to service so that we may be sure you have received full performance of warranty obligations. If you have not received such full performance your response to the following questions will enable us to provide you with the warranty service to which you are entitled.

Please respond to the following questions and return this letter to _____ in the enclosed postage-paid envelope.

(1) (a) Have you experienced problems with your mobile home that you feel are covered by our warranty described above? (check one) _____ yes _____ no

(1) (b) If the answer to (1) (a) is yes, please tell us when the problems occurred and *describe* them: _____
_____
_____

(2) If you have experienced problems that you feel are covered by our warranty, please advise us of *whom* you contacted and *when* the contact was made: _____
_____
_____

(3) (a) If you contacted someone regarding a warranty problem was the problem corrected? (check one): _____ yes _____ no

(3) (b) If the answer to (3) (a) was yes, please indicate *how long* it took to correct the problem, and *who* performed it: _____
_____

(3) (c) If the answer to (3) (a) was no, does the problem still exist? (check one): _____ yes _____ no

(3) (d) If the answer to (3) (c) was yes, please describe the current condition of the problem and any attempts at correction you have made: _____
_____
_____

(4) (a) If warranty service was amended, were you satisfied with:

APPENDIX A (*continued*)

(1)   the promptness of repairs (check one) _____ yes _____ no

(2)   the quality and completeness of repairs (check one) _____ yes _____ no

(4) (*b*) If your answer to (4) (*a*) (2) was no, does the problem which was the subject of warranty service still exist? (check one) _____ yes _____ no

(4) (*c*) If your answer to (4) (*b*) was yes, please explain and describe the current condition of the problem and any attempts at correction you have made: _____

_____

(5) (*a*) Who performed the setup or installation of your mobile home?

_____
(name)

_____
(relationship, trailer park operator, independent contractor, etc.)

_____
(location)

(5) (*b*) Has there been any doubt or dispute as to whether a problem you have experienced with your mobile home was a problem covered by your warranty or due to improper setup or installation? (check one) _____ yes _____ no

(5) (*c*) If the answer to (5) (*b*) was yes, does the problem still exist? (check one) _____ yes _____ no

(5) (*d*) If the answer to (5) (*c*) was yes, please describe the current condition of the problem and any attempts you have made to get the problem corrected:

_____

_____

(5) (*e*) Are you satisfied with the manner in which your mobile home was set up or installed? (check one) _____ yes _____ no

(6) Please advise us of any suggestions you might have that will enable us to increase the quality, utility, and value that we strive to build into our homes: _____

_____

_____

Note: Below is your name and address as they appear in our records. If there is need for a correction, please make it in the space provided. Also we ask that you supply us with your telephone number in the space provided, as it will facilitate our reaching you to discuss any problems with our product or service that you have pointed out:

(Name of customer)   _____

(Street address)   _____

(City, State, Zip)   _____

(Telephone number, including area code):   (_____) _____ – _____

We thank you for responding to the questions set forth above. Please return this letter to us in the enclosed postage-paid envelope.

Sincerely,

APPENDIX B: LETTER TO DEALERS REQUESTING NAMES AND ADDRESSES OF PAST PURCHASERS

Dear _____:

    Pursuant to an agreement with the *Federal Trade Commissioner,* Commodore Corporation is securing from the present and the former dealers all names and addresses of retail purchasers of its mobile homes built between July 1, 1972, and June 30, 1974, identified with Serial Numbers _____ through _____. Dealer submission of these names and addresses is necessary since warranty registration cards fail to provide the information for a substantial number of homes.

    Please fill in the names and addresses of the retail purchasers of these units and serial numbers of the homes and return this letter in the postage-paid envelope provided before _____, 1974, as called for by the above agreement.

Signed _____
Plant General Manager

Serial Numbers	*Names and Addresses*
_____	_____
	_____
	_____
_____	_____
	_____
	_____
_____	_____
	_____
	_____

APPENDIX C: OWNER-DEALER FINAL DELIVERY CHECKLIST

Manufacturer:

_____

_____

_____

Dealer:

_____

_____

_____

Owner:

_____
(Name)

_____
(Address)   (Phone No.)

_____
(City)   (State)   (Zip)

Date of Retail Delivery _____

Model   _____

Unit Serial No.   _____

Tire Identifications _____

If the home was not set up by the dealer, indicate the name and location of the party performing this service: _____

The above dealer acknowledges that he has completed the following procedures and checks and that he has inspected the home with the owner and except as set forth herein, all items listed below have been found to be a satisfactory condition.

Mobile Home Supports, Tie Downs or Connection of Modules:

_____ All pierings and supports have been installed in accordance with instructions contained in the Installation Manual.

_____ The mobile home floor has been properly leveled.

_____ In the case of double-wide units and expandable units, the components have been properly aligned, all molding and carpet has been applied, and all exterior siding, caps and flashing has been installed in accordance with the instruction contained in the Owner's Manual.

_____ All anchors and tie downs required by local conditions and regulations have been installed.

Systems Checks:

_____ Before connection to the utility secure, the unit's fuel piping system was pressure tested with all appliance valves closed. Such test consisted of pressurizing the entire system for not less than 10 minutes, at not less than five ounces (5 oz) nor more than 10 ounces (10 oz) pressure with no pressure loss.

_____ After connection to utility secure, all appliances fueled by L.P., natural gas, or oil have been checked out to determine that they operate properly and have the proper orifice.

_____ Where there is a fuel-fired furnace for heating: a check had been made to determine that all ducts are connected, unobstructed and distribute heat properly.

After connection to the electrical source, the following were checked for proper operation (indicate or N/A, not applicable):

_____ all interior lights	_____ dishwasher
_____ all light switches	_____ clothes dryer
_____ all fans	_____ electric dryer
_____ furnace thermostat	_____ refrigerator

APPENDIX C (*continued*)

_____ heat registers   _____ garbage disposal
_____ all receptacles   _____ electric water heater
_____ circuit breakers   _____ (other) _____
_____ range and/or oven

After connection to the water supply and drain sources, all air has been bled from the water system, the water heater has been turned on and the following checks have been made:

_____ Where there is an air conditioner, the system has been checked for proper operation including thermostat control and assuring that all ducts are connected, unobstructed and distribute cooling properly.

_____ All hot and cold water lines are connected to the proper fixtures.

_____ No water leaks are evident in any exposed joints, connections, fittings or fixtures.

_____ All faucets are functioning properly and no leaks are evident.

_____ All sinks, basins, tubs, shower pans and toilets have been filled with water and flushed several times and no leaks are evident in their drain lines.

Exterior:

_____ All exterior doors close properly.

_____ All windows operate properly.

_____ All exterior screens and/or storm windows fit properly.

_____ The roof seams and all windows and doors have been caulked or weatherproofed.

_____ The exterior siding and trim including rodent proofing has been inspected and is acceptable.

Interior:

The following components have been inspected:

_____ ceiling   _____ interior doors
_____ paneling   _____ cabinet doors
_____ molding   _____ drawers
_____ carpet and floor covering   _____ furniture and cabinets
_____ curtains and drapes   _____ plumbing fixtures
_____ lamps and light fixtures

Manuals, Warranties, Instructions, Etc.:

The following items have been delivered to the owner by the dealer or performed by the dealer:

_____ Warranty covering this mobile home.

_____ Owner's Manual for this mobile home.

_____ Setup instructions for this mobile home.

_____ Separate operational and service manuals, and warranties covering the water heater, furnace, refrigerator, range and oven, and, if applicable, the dishwasher, garbage disposal, washer and dryer.

_____ All required keys.

_____ The retail customer has been instructed in the proper use of all the appliances in the unit.

Dealer/Customer comments and/or minor deficiencies outstanding _____
_____
_____
_____
_____

APPENDIX C (concluded)

Our company requires its dealers to perform this Delivery Checkout and a subsequent reinspection between 45 and 90 days after the initial occupancy. The owner should not sign this statement until all of the items indicated above have either been performed or explained to his satisfaction.

The dealer is not authorized to give the owner possession of the mobile home unless the above indicated inspections have been performed and all deficiencies which affect the home's safety or habitability have been corrected.

Uncorrected deficiencies should be noted in the space above and will be corrected by your dealer as soon as possible.

Your reinspection should be performed before _____.

I acknowledge that the above has been reviewed with me.

Signed: _____   Date: _____
(Retail Customer)

Signed: _____   Date: _____
(Dealer's Representative)

APPENDIX D: REINSPECTION REPORT

Manufacturer: _____   Dealer: _____

_____

_____

Owner: _____

(Name)

(Address)   (Phone No.)

(City)   (State)   (Zip)

Date of Original Delivery _____

Date of Reinspection _____

Model _____

Unit Serial No. _____

If the home was not set up by the dealer, indicate the name and location of the party performing this service: _____

Each mobile home manufactured by a subsidiary of _____ will be reinspected by the selling dealer between 45 and 90 days after the home was first occupied by the retail customer. This report, documenting this reinspection, will

be filed with the: _____.

The following items have been completed:

(1) All supporting piers have been retightened or reshimmed and checked and the home has been rechecked to determine that the floor is leveled properly.

(2) All roof seams and roof jacks have been coated with roof seal and all windows have been inspected and recaulked, if required.

The following items were checked and repaired or adjusted as required (please note None if appropriate):

Doors and Windows:

Action Required	Action Taken

Plumbing System:

Action Required	Action Taken

Heating and Air Conditioning Systems:

Action Required	Action Taken

Electrical System:

Action Required	Action Taken

APPENDIX D *(continued)*

Appliances:

      Action Required   Action Taken

_____   _____

_____   _____

Dealer/Customer Comments: _____

_____

_____

_____

Our company requires its dealers to perform this reinspection. The owner should not sign the statement until all the items indicated above have either been performed or explained to his satisfaction.

I acknowledge receipt of a copy of this Reinspection Report and agree with the information in it.

_____   _____

(Signature of Owner)   (Date)

_____   _____

(Signature of Dealer's Representative)   (Date)

APPENDIX E: QUESTIONNAIRE TO PURCHASERS

(Date)

Dear Homeowner:

For more than _____ years Commodore Corporation and its subsidiaries have man-ufactured quality, low cost mobile homes. Our records indicate that in _____ of _____ you purchased a Commodore-produced mobile home, Serial No. _____.

Your home is warranted to be free from defects in material and workmanship for one year from the date of original purchase. If a defect comes to your attention during this time period, the dealer who sold you the home should be contacted. In most cases, he will be able to correct the problem. If the dealer is unable to make the correction, he is required to notify the manufacturer who will then assist in resolving the matter.

In order for us to determine if you have been satisfied with your home, we request that you respond to the following questions (if you need more space please attach a sepa-rate page):

(1) Have you experienced any problems with your home that you feel are covered by our warranty or arise from the improper setup or installation of your home?
(2) If so, whom did you notify of these defects or setup problems (if any) and when did notification occur?
(3) Were these problems satisfactorily resolved?
(4) Do you have any suggestions that would be useful to us in improving our product for future customers?

It would be greatly appreciated if you would respond to the above questions and re-turn this letter in the enclosed postage-paid envelope.

We thank you in advance for your help in this matter.

Sincerely,

Director of Product Integrity

SELECTED BIBLIOGRAPHY

Barton, Babette. "Forms and Forums of Consumer Relief: Redress or Rape." Paper presented at a symposium on new perspectives in consumerism, sponsored by National Affiliation of Concerned Business Students. Chicago, November 1974.

Benett, E. J. "*Eisen v. Carlisle and Jacquelin* (94 Sup. Ct. 2140) Supreme Court Calls for Revamping Class Action Strategy." *Wisconsin Law Review* (1974), pp. 801–32.

Benningson, Lawrence A., and Benningson, Arnold I. "Product Liability: Manufacturers Beware!" *Harvard Business Review* (May–June 1974), pp. 122–32.

Bucklin, Louis P. "The Uniform Grading System for Tires: Its Effect upon Consumers and Industry Competition." *The Antitrust Bulletin* 19 (winter 1974): 783–99.

Cochran, Brian D. "Emerging Products Liability under Section 2-318 of the Uniform Commercial Code: A Survey." *Business Lawyer* 29 (April 1974): 925–45.

Condon, W. J. "Product Liability—1974." *Food, Drug, Cosmetic Law Journal* 30 (May 1975): 267–75.

Dam, K. W. "Class Action Notice: Who Needs It?" *Supreme Court Review* (1974), pp. 97–126.

Dam, K. W. "Class Actions: Efficiency, Compensation, Deterrence, and Conflict of Interest." *Journal of Legal Studies* 4 (January 1975): 47–73.

Eovaldi, Thomas L., and Gestrin, Joan E. "Justice for Consumers: The Mechanism for Redress." *Northwestern University Law Review* 66 (July–August 1971): 281–325.

"Extrajudicial Consumer Pressure: An Effective Impediment to Unethical Business Practices." *Duke Law Journal* (October 1969), p. 1011.

Federal Trade Commission. *Report on Automobile Warranties.* Washington, D.C., February 1970, pp. 1–70.

Gray, Irwin. *Product Liability: A Management Response.* New York: Amacom, 1975.

Henderson, James A., Jr. "Judicial Review of Manufacturer's Conscious Design Choices: The Limits of Adjudication." *Columbia Law Review* 73 (December 1973): 1531–78.

Horan, D. J. "Class Actions—Current Developments." *Trial Lawyer's Guide* 18 (winter 1975): 430–42.

Kendell, C. L., and Russ, Frederick A. "Warranty and Complaint Policies: An Opportunity for Marketing Management." *Journal of Marketing* 39 (April 1975): 36–43.

Magnuson-Mass Warranty-Federal Trade Commission Improvement Act. Public Law 93-637, 93rd Cong., S.356. January 4, 1975.

Moss, John E. "Buyers Still Get the Short End of Warranties." *Business and Society Review* 13 (spring 1975): 80–82.

"New Law Sets Warranty Rules, Widens FTC Rulemaking Power." *Industry Week* 184 (January 13, 1975): 18.

Patrick, J. V., Jr. "Securities Class Action for Damages Comes of Age (1966–74)." *Business Lawyer* 29 (March 1974, special issue): 159–66.

Phillips, Jerry J., and Noel, Dix W. *Product Liability*. West Publishing, 1974.

Posner, Richard A. "Antitrust Policy and the Consumer Movement." *Antitrust Bulletin* (summer 1970), pp. 361–66.

Posner, Richard A. "National Monopoly and Its Regulation." *Stanford Law Review* 21 (February 1969): 548–643.

"Product Liability Storm Warnings." *Industry Week* 183 (October 21, 1974): 37.

Roadoes, David L. "Product Liability: Tougher Ground Rules." *Harvard Business Review* 47 (July–August 1969): 144–52.

Schrag, Philip G. *Counsel for the Deceived: Case Studies in Consumer Fraud*. New York: Pantheon, 1972.

Schrag, Philip G. "On Her Majesty's Secret Service: Protecting the Consumer in New York City." *The Yale Law Journal* 80 (July 1971): 1529.

Shapo, M. L. "Representational Theory of Consumer Protection: Doctrine, Function, and Legal Liability for Product Disappointment." *Virginia Law Review* 60 (November 1974): 279.

Sorensen, H. C. "Product Liability: The Consumers Revolt." *Best's Review Property/Liability Insurance Edition* 75 (September 1975): 38.

"Special Products Liability Issue." *Hofstra Law Review* 2 (summer 1974): 356.

"Symposium on Product Liability." *Marquette Law Review* 57 (1974): 623–89.

U.S. Congress, House. *Consumer Product Warranty and Federal Trade Commission Improvements Act*. Conference Report No. 93-1606, 93rd Cong., 2nd Sess., December 1974.

U.S. Congress, House. *Consumer Product Warranty and Federal Trade Commission Improvements Act*. Report Together with Separate and Individual Views, Report No. 93-1107, 93rd Cong., 2nd Sess., June 13, 1974.

Ursin, E. "Strict Liability for Defective Business Premises—One Step Beyond Rowland and Greenman." *UCLA Law Review* 22 (April 1975): 820–46.

Wollman, J. "Warranties: Pushing Retailers to Rethink Merchandising Approaches." *Merchandising Week* 107 (March 3, 1975): 1.

9 Trouble lights: Hazardous nature of a new product—manufacturer's responsibility for product recall; the role of the U.S. Product Safety Commission

The only wisdom we can hope to acquire
is the wisdom of humility.

T. S. Eliot

On July 26, 1974, the U.S. Consumer Product Safety Commission (CPSC) issued a press release warning consumers that some 200,000 "trouble lights" or "mechanic's lights" sold in the past year posed an imminent danger of serious or fatal electric shock. The release stated:

Consumers should immediately cease use of the product, taking extreme care not to touch any metal parts when disconnecting the light from the electrical outlet.

The light was manufactured by A. K. Electric Corporation, Brooklyn, New York. It has been distributed by several firms and sold by stores across the country, including Woolco Department Stores, Zayre, Korvettes, Food Fair, and J. J. Newberry.

The trouble light retails for about $1.50.

The potentially dangerous "trouble light" bears no brand name, label, or other distinguishing marks. Its appearance is similar to many other mechanics' lights. Consumers who are uncertain whether they own a potentially hazardous light should immediately discontinue use of the product and check with the store where it was purchased to identify the manufacturer.

The product consists of either a 5-, 10-, or 20-foot flexible cord with a male plug at one end and a light socket assembly at the opposite end. The light bulb is enclosed by a metal case and hinged wire guard with a hook at the top. The socket assembly contains an on-off switch together with a double female receptacle subassembly. The insulating cover for the socket assembly serves as a handle for the unit and is made of exceptionally soft, flexible plastic [Exhibit 9–1].

EXHIBIT 9–1

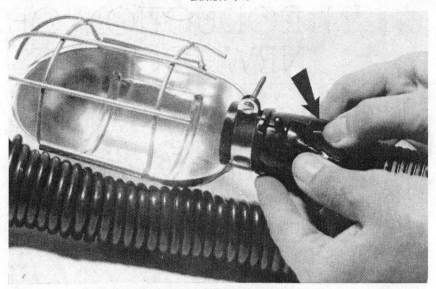

Metal conductor in the female receptacle

If the handle is grasped in a normal manner, the user's hand or fingers may, because of the soft, flexible plastic cover, contact the metal of the receptacles, creating a serious potential for electric shock.

This warning is being issued because it is the view of the Commission that the "trouble light" in question is imminently hazardous and presents an imminent and unreasonable risk of death or severe personal injury to the public.

This was the first CPSC action in its sixteen-month life under Section 12 of the Consumer Product Safety Act, 1972, which deals with an imminent hazard related to the use of a consumer product and the responsibility of the manufacturer, and all distributors of that product, to comply with CPSC's requirements for reporting such hazards to the commission, consumers, and arranging for the product recall (Appendix A).

ISSUES FOR ANALYSIS

The case demonstrates the complexity of the problems that confront manufacturers, distributors and retailers, and government agencies in preventing the distribution and sale of a hazardous consumer product, and when it does occur, in warning all consumers about the danger of using such a product and arranging a product recall. In particular:

1. It appears from the case that the manufacturer did little pretesting of the product for potential safety hazards. This may have been partly

due to the manufacturer's poor financial condition. How can the introduction of similar products be minimized?

2. The CPSC press release indicated an "imminent hazard" and gave the impression of extreme urgency. Yet as events show, there was a significant elapsed time between notification of the hazard to CPSC and its press release. How can such time delays be minimized?

3. CPSC asked the manufacturer, distributors, and retailers of the product to undertake an immediate nationwide paid advertising program to warn consumers about the trouble light. The requirement, if enforced, would have put the company out of business.[1] (a) In requiring A. K. Electric Corporation and distributors and retailers to undertake a prohibitively expensive advertising program, was CPSC simply doing what it had to do, or was the agency attempting to cover its own bureaucratic delays? (b) CPSC also required a standard of measuring information effectiveness—that is, the number of units returned. How realistic was this measure? What other measures are possible and relevant? (c) Should CPSC be required to consider the financial ability of the manufacturer, distributors, and retailers before determining the desirability and feasibility of a communication program to warn consumers?

4. What does the case demonstrate about CPSC's expertise in monitoring potential consumer hazards and developing an effective communication system?

5. Is there a need for CPSC to perform such a function? Can it be better performed through other conventional means—namely, adequate industry testing and safety standards, product liability insurance, and individual and class action damage suits?

6. How can CPSC and manufacturers better cooperate to prevent the sale of unsafe products to consumers and speed up consumer warning and recall when safety hazards are discovered?

THE EVENTS

The problem first came to light in October 1973, when a Florida man was electrocuted while using an A-K light in his attic. It was not until May 29, 1974, that the CPSC's Bureau of Information and Education received a call on the hotline about the death in Florida, and it took two weeks for a record of the call to reach another office in the same building (the Bureau of Epidemiology). Another three weeks passed until the Atlanta office completed its investigation on July 8, and another week and a half went by until the Bureau of Engineering Sciences received a sample of the product

---

[1] Ray Elden Hiebert, "Communications on Trial: Massive Advertising vs. Public Relations," *Public Relations Journal,* December 1974, pp. 16–19.
This article is reproduced in Appendix B.

from Atlanta. One week later, the commission declared the trouble light imminently hazardous and began procedures for a nationwide recall. The process had taken two months from the time of the phone call. The existence of a unit called the Office of Product Defect Identification, which is supposed to identify and handle grossly dangerous products quickly, had made no appreciable difference in speeding up the bureaucratic pace.[2]

CPSC staff procedures have since been changed to prevent similar delays in the future. But as one CPSC critic maintains:

> . . . the Bethesda headquarters [of CPSC staff] today is bulkier and more Balkanized than ever, and not everyone is so sure that an A-K Electric can't happen again. The staff's fumbling in that case was not so much a mistake as the inevitable outcome of asking an organization to do something it isn't set up to do. For the most part CPSC headquarters has neither the capability nor the desire to be a quick, modest, surefooted stimulator of private-sector activity. It is geared instead to supplant such activity by playing the imperial role of chief safety engineer for all U.S. Consumer products.[3]

In addition to the long delay in moving on a product that is literally a death trap, this particular incident also generated a controversy over what constitutes the "public notice" manufacturers and distributors are required

---

[2] Paul Weaver, "The Hazards of Trying to Make Consumer Products Safer," *Fortune*, July 1975, pp. 134–35. The problem of excessive delay was also commented upon in a report on the CPSC activities prepared by the House Appropriations Committee. The report states: "One Area Office Director stated that excessive delays by the 15(b) Group were eroding his credibility with the U.S. Customs in his area. A potentially hazardous shipment of 17 cartons of 'trouble lights' was discovered and held by the U.S. Customs. Samples were collected and shipped to Washington. The 15(b) Group was notified by teletype that the U.S. Customs was holding a 'bad product.' The first response from the 15(b) Group came a month later at which time the Area Office Director was advised that the same 'might' be substantially hazardous although it would be necessary for further examinations of the sample by the engineering bureau. This Area Director stated that the CPSC's inability to move decisively and competently makes it less credible to other Government agencies such as U.S. Customs."

CPSC responds: "To put this situation into perspective one must understand that the total universe of *trouble lights* that we were required to review was national in scope. This situation involving an evaluation of the 17 cartons of trouble lights, samples of which were submitted from one of the Area Offices to OPDI was delayed primarily because of the burden on the Bureau of Engineering Sciences at that particular time in analyzing many samples of trouble lights submitted as part of the imminent hazard program involving the A. K. Electric Corporation. OPDI received over 100 such samples and the case involving the 17 cartons of trouble lights was not considered to be of the level of risk that would warrant immediate attention. This information was provided verbally to the Area Office involved, whereas a final written report on the subject was not forthcoming for approximately two (2) weeks. In attempting to analyze and compare all the different samples of trouble lights received by Engineering Sciences and OPDI, the particular trouble lights in question did not raise immediate dangers and therefore other investigations into trouble lights were given higher priority." *Commentary Upon "A Report to the Committee on Appropriations U.S. House of Representatives on A General Review of the Operation of the Consumer Product Safety Commission" by Survey and Investigation Staff (March 1975).* Commentary prepared by U.S. Consumer Product Safety Commission, Washington, D.C., April 1975, p. 79.

[3] Weaver, "Hazards," p. 135.

by the CPSC to give in such cases. The commission itself issued press releases describing the product and the hazard on July 26, 1974, and in August devoted *Fact Sheet* No. 60 to the same hazard. On July 31, CPSC members met with manufacturer's representatives, wholesalers, and retailers who handled the product, which sold for between $1.50 and $2 and carried no label or other identification. About 200,000 had been distributed nationwide, but no one really knew how many had been sold, to whom, and where. The CPSC demanded recall from customers, removal from shelves, and destruction of all items.

It also presented a plan for public notice based on paid prime-time TV advertising for three consecutive nights on all networks and three 200-line ads in newspapers that account for 85 percent of all circulation. The content of the ads must have commission approval and be ready within seven working days and the overall plan itself must be completed *within 24 hours,* or the trouble light people would be taken to court. Although no one questioned the necessity of reaching the public with a warning, the trouble light group, which included a manufacturer in poor financial straits and such retail chains as Woolworth's and Penney's, was appalled not only at the cost of such a campaign ($366,000 by CPSC estimate; $500,000 by ad agency estimate), but also at what it implied for the future in terms of the commission being able to dictate to business (Appendix B).

At this stage, Woolworth, one of the companies involved, decided to get its public relations counsel, Carl Byoir & Associates, involved. It put together an alternate plan to warn the public by means of a public relations campaign—a press conference to be called by the chairman of the CPSC, with television newsclips and a radio tape for distribution to 500 TV stations and 750 radio stations; a press kit for newspapers; an admat for insertion in local newspapers; point-of-sale posters; contact with special groups such as the American Retail Federation; and special materials for specific media designed to reach those most likely to have purchased such a product (Appendix B). (The events surrounding the development of alternate plans, their relative merits, and a criticism of CPSC were detailed in an article by Ray Eldon Hiebert in the *Public Relations Journal,* December 1974. This article and a response by Ron Aaron Eisenberg, public affairs director, Consumer Product Safety Commission, are reproduced as Appendixes B and C.)

This plan was presented to the commission on August 1, but was rejected by the CPSC because, in the view of Ron Eisenberg, a campaign based on free coverage left dissemination of the information to chance—a news editor might or might not consider it worthwhile. The only way to guarantee that the message would be adequate and contain the right information was through paid advertising. The CPSC then sued in federal district court to compel the manufacturer, distributors, and retailers to carry out the commission's plan. The parties were ordered to negotiate and return on August 19, but the defendants were unwilling to wait until then to begin warning the public. They went ahead with the public relations campaign (commission chairman Simpson agreed to hold a press conference), collected some evidence of its success in terms of numbers of stations carrying the story, and returned to court. The CPSC, however, was still not satisfied that effective notice had been given, and a new court date was set for August 29.

At this hearing before Judge George L. Hart, Jr., the defendants contended that "adequate public notice had been achieved by the public relations effort," and presented evidence to show that news stories had been used by 374 TV stations, 506 radio stations, and 738 newspapers all over the country. They based their claim of success on these assumptions: (1) that mere transmission of information had not been the objective, but rather effective reception; (2) that a tailor-made news approach was superior to straight advertising because as a valid news story, the trouble light would receive better and faster attention; (3) that the public relations approach was more effective because it involved many participants in transmitting the message. In the opinion of Ray Hiebert:

> This grass-roots approach helped get the message targeted to the specific audience far more effectively than national prime-time advertising. . . . By the time John Chancellor of NBC and Harry Reasoner of ABC used the story on evening shows, their personal involvement gave the piece a wallop that advertising could never have achieved. [Appendix B]

Defendants' counsel held that "the major issue was not news media techniques versus advertising, but rather voluntary communications efforts versus compulsory advertising. The public relations plan did include advertising where it would serve most effectively" (Appendix B).

Although the CPSC continued to maintain that the only way of proving the industry approach effective was to show that the campaign had resulted in a majority of the trouble lights being returned, Judge Hart thought this irrelevant to the major issue, which was to "get the message out." It was the danger that was important, not the way it was communicated. He did, however, agree that the commission could have ten weeks to gather data on returns, and he pressed for one more effort to inform the public through a plan to be agreed upon by both sides. When the court met after lunch, the plan presented was for the judge himself to ask the news media to cover another press conference—an unprecedented step. Judge Hart agreed, and the story was given wide play over the Labor Day weekend (Appendix B).

After the newsbreak there were no reported electrocutions because of the trouble light. The recall program resulted in a return of 6,300 trouble lights out of 86,000 subsequent to the court order. CPSC court costs were estimated at $200,000.[4] The CPSC does not appear to have been satisfied

---

[4] Official Transcript of Proceedings Before the Consumer Product Safety Commission on Imminent and Substantial Product Hazards, Washington, D.C., October 3, 1974, pp. 101–2.

with the general applicability of the approach taken in the trouble light case by Judge Hart. In a meeting of CPSC, industry, and news media representatives, Ron Eisenberg suggested that the participants might want to discuss a plan proposed in an editorial in *Advertising Age* to deal with similar situations in the future. He emphasized that neither he nor the CPSC had taken any position on the plan; nor was it being endorsed in any manner. He suggested that the preparation of a proposed communication plan on any one subject should be left to the expert hired for the event—whether an expert from the CPSC or the public relations counsel for the manufacturer or some other party involved in the case. However, in order that this plan might have authority behind it, it should then be submitted for review by a panel representing various communication skills —public relations, television news, newspapers, and so on. This panel would then certify that it was a workable plan, and that would be the extent of the panel's involvement.

In a later communication on March 3, 1977, a CPSC spokesperson emphasized to the author that Mr. Eisenberg's comments were purely personal. The commission could not and would not delegate its legal authority to any outside agency or individual. Moreover, situations like that with the trouble lights have not since occurred and are not likely to occur, given the new procedures instituted by the commission. The actual work would continue to be done by professionals in each case, according to the facts of the situation. All that was called for in this plan was the creation of a mechanism patterned on the National Advertising Review Board. There would be a governing body with representation from the various skill areas, and this governing body would then provide panels—a mirror image of itself—so that each panel would have all the skills available. After the review panel's recommendations, any disagreement would be brought before a judge who would have been given a plan supported by an unbiased group of experts. The judge would then be on firm ground when making a decision.[5]

According to Ray Hiebert, who was a consultant to the public relations firm in this case, the results have real importance for two reasons. One, they show that industry need not accept a decision by a government body when it does not like it; it can present and carry out an equally acceptable alternative, a tactic far more effective than just resisting. Two, a precedent had now been set so that, in the future, the CPSC would not treat advertising as the best or only solution for other safety alerts and would not be able to compel business to use this method (Appendix B).

The latter point was also made quite strongly by Eisenberg at a special meeting to discuss the problem of public notice held by the CPSC with media and industry representatives in Washington on October 3, 1974. He emphasized that the commission's goal was also reaching the right people with the right message, and that the CPSC in no way regarded advertising

---

[5] Ibid., pp. 113–15.

as the best or only solution in every case. It was the alternative proposed in the case of the trouble light because of certain factors peculiar to the product: it was distributed nationwide; it bore no identifying marks to distinguish it from other similar products; its low retail price made returns unlikely; the sales pattern could not be pinpointed in detail, so that it would be almost impossible to find out to whom the product had been sold and where. In Eisenberg's words, "the Commission was concerned that, in this particular case, given the fact pattern associated with the 'Trouble Light,' and the imminently hazardous nature of the product, there was a need for direct control over the message warning consumers, as well as assurances that the message would at least have an opportunity to reach people."[6]

APPENDIX A: CONSUMER PRODUCT SAFETY ACT, 1972 (TEXT OF SECTIONS 12 AND 15)

Sec. 12.   (a)   The Commission may file in a United States district court an action (1) against an imminently hazardous consumer product for seizure of such product under subsection (b) (2), or (2) against any person who is a manufacturer, distributor, or retailer of such product, or (3) against both. Such an action may be filed notwithstanding the existence of a consumer product safety rule applicable to such product, or the pendency of any administrative or judicial proceedings under any other provision of this Act. As used in this section, and hereinafter in this Act, the term "imminently hazardous consumer product" means a consumer product which presents imminent and unreasonable risk of death, serious illness, or severe personal injury.

(b) (1)   The district court in which such action is filed shall have jurisdiction to declare such product an imminently hazardous consumer product, and [in the case of an action under subsection (a) (2)] to grant (as ancillary to such declaration or in lieu thereof) such temporary or permanent relief as may be necessary to protect the public from such risk. Such relief may include a mandatory order requiring the notification of such risk to purchasers of such product known to the defendant, public notice, the recall, the repair or the replacement of, or refund for, such product.

(b) (2)   In the case of an action under subsection (a) (1), the consumer product may be proceeded against by process of libel for the seizure and condemnation of such product in any United States district court within the jurisdiction of which such consumer product is found. Proceedings

---

[6] Official Transcript, pp. 11, 13.

and cases instituted under the authority of the preceding sentence shall conform as nearly as possible to proceedings in rem in admiralty.

(c)   Where appropriate, concurrently with the filing of such action or as soon thereafter as may be practicable, the Commission shall initiate a proceeding to promulgate a consumer product safety rule applicable to the consumer product with respect to which such action is filed.

(d) (1)   Prior to commencing an action under subsection (a), the Commission may consult the Product Safety Advisory Council (established under section 28) with respect to its determination to commence such action, and request the Council's recommendations as to the type of temporary or permanent relief which may be necessary to protect the public.

(d) (2)   The Council shall submit its recommendations to the Commission within one week of such request.

(d) (3)   Subject to paragraph (2), the Council may conduct such hearing or offer such opportunity for the presentation of views as it may consider necessary or appropriate.

(e) (1)   An action under subsection (a) (2) of this section may be brought in the United States district court for the District of Columbia or in any judicial district in which any of the defendants is found, is an inhabitant or transacts business; and process in such an action may be served on a defendant in any other district in which such defendant resides or may be found. Subpoenas requiring attendance of witnesses in such an action may run into any other district. In determining the judicial district in which an action may be brought under this section in instances in which such action may be brought in more than one judicial district, the Commission shall take into account the convenience of the parties.

(e) (2)   Whenever proceedings under this section involving substantially similar consumer products are pending in courts in two or more judicial districts, they shall be consolidated for trial by order of any such court upon application reasonably made by any party in interest, upon notice to all other parties in interest.

(f)   Notwithstanding any other provision of law, in any action under this section, the Commission may direct attorneys employed by it to appear and represent it.

Notification and repair, replacement, or refund

Sec. 15.   (a)   For purposes of this section, the term "substantial product hazard" means—

(1)   a failure to comply with an applicable consumer product safety rule which creates a substantial risk of injury to the public, or

(2)   a product defect which (because of the pattern or defect, the number of defective products distributed in commerce, the severity of the risk, or otherwise) creates a substantial risk of injury to the public.

(b) Every manufacturer of a consumer product distributed in commerce, and every distributor and retailer of such product, who obtains information which reasonably supports the conclusion that such product—

(1) fails to comply with an applicable consumer product safety rule; or

(2) contains a defect which could create a substantial product hazard described in subsection (a) (2),

shall immediately inform the Commission of such failure to comply or of such defect, unless such manufacturer, distributor, or retailer has actual knowledge that the Commission has been adequately informed of such defect or failure to comply.

(c) If the Commission determines (after affording interested persons, including consumers and consumer organizations, an opportunity for a hearing in accordance with subsection (f) of this section) that a product distributed in commerce presents a substantial product hazard and that notification is required in order to adequately protect the public from such substantial product hazard, the Commission may order the manufacturer or any distributor or retailer of the product to take any one or more of the following actions:

(1) To give public notice of the defect or failure to comply.

(2) To mail notice to each person who is a manufacturer, distributor, or retailer of such product.

(3) To mail notice to every person to whom the person required to give notice knows such product was delivered or sold.

Any such order shall specify the form and content of any notice required to be given under such order.

(d) If the Commission determines (after affording interested parties, including consumers and consumer organizations, an opportunity for a hearing in accordance with subsection (f)) that a product distributed in commerce presents a substantial product hazard and that action under this subsection is in the public interest, it may order the manufacturer or any distributor or retailer of such product to take whichever of the following actions the person to whom the order is directed elects:

(1) To bring such product into conformity with the requirements of the applicable consumer product safety rule or to repair the defect in such product.

(2) To replace such product with a like or equivalent product which complies with the applicable consumer product safety rule or which does not contain the defect.

(3) To refund the purchase price of such product (less a reasonable allowance for use, if such product has been in the possession of a consumer for one year or more (A) at the time of public

notice under subsection (c), or (B) at the time the consumer receives actual notice of the defect or noncompliance, whichever first occurs).

An order under this subsection may also require the person to whom it applies to submit a plan, satisfactory to the Commission, for taking action under whichever of the preceding paragraphs of this subsection under which such person has elected to act. The Commission shall specify in the order the persons to whom refunds must be made if the person to whom the order is directed elects to take the action described in paragraph (3). If an order under this subsection is directed to more than one person, the Commission shall specify which person has the election under this subsection.

(e) (1)   No charge shall be made to any person (other than a manufacturer, distributor, or retailer) who avails himself of any remedy provided under an order issued under subsection (d), and the person subject to the order shall reimburse each person (other than a manufacturer, distributor, or retailer) who is entitled to such a remedy for any reasonable and foreseeable expenses incurred by such person in availing himself of such remedy.

(e) (2)   An order issued under subsection (c) or (d) with respect to a product may require any person who is a manufacturer, distributor, or retailer of such product for such other person's expenses in connection with carrying out the order, if the Commission determines such reimbursement to be in the public interest.

(f)   An order under subsection (c) or (d) may be issued only after an opportunity for a hearing in accordance with section 554 of title 5, United States Code, except that, if the Commission determines that any person who wishes to participate in such hearing is a part of a class of participants who share an identity of interest, the Commission may limit such person's participation in such hearing to participation through a single representative designated by such class (or by the Commission if such class fails to designate such a representative).

APPENDIX B: COMMUNICATIONS ON TRIAL— MASSIVE ADVERTISING VS. PUBLIC RELATIONS*

On October 24, 1973, a retired Air Force captain was electrocuted in an attic in Orlando, Florida. He had been using a mechanic's light, called a "trouble light," purchased a few days earlier. His death set in motion a

---

* By Ray Eldon Hiebert. Reprinted from *Public Relations Journal*, December 1974, pp. 16–19.

unique case which could have long-range implications for public relations and communications in the increasing confrontation between government, consumers, and business. This is a real case of "Consumerism."

Seven months later, on May 29, 1974, the widow's attorney asked the Federal Consumer Product Safety Commission to investigate the "trouble light" as a possible faulty product. It took the Commission nearly two months to complete its examination and say the product was unsafe. July 26, the Commission issued a press release saying the "trouble light" posed an imminent danger of serious or fatal electric shock because the handle's soft, flexible plastic permitted contact with electricity-bearing metal in the handle. It was the first "imminent hazard" declared by CPSC in its 16-month life.

July 31, the Commission met with representatives of the "trouble light" manufacturer, plus wholesalers, and retailers who handled it. The Commission demanded product recall from customers, shelf removal and destruction of all units. But how could effective public notice of the imminent hazard of the "trouble light" be given?

The Commission had its own plan. CPSC Public Affairs Director Ron Eisenberg told the hearing the only effective warnings could come from paid prime-time TV 30-second spots on each network for three consecutive nights, plus three inserts of 200-line ads in newspapers accounting for 85% of all circulation. "Trouble light" reps were told ad approaches must have Commission clearance, they must complete them within seven working days, and they had 24 hours to adopt a plan or be taken to court.

A staggering blow

The "trouble light" people were staggered. Figuring conservatively, the campaign could cost from $366,000 (Commission's estimate) to over $500,000 (ad agency estimates). The product itself had sold for only one to two dollars; about 200,000 were on the market; and the Commission had only vague notions of the number sold. A. K. Electric Company, the manufacturer, was in serious financial straits and would be wiped out by the Commission plan. Wholesalers and retailers, including Action Industries, Woolworth, Penney's, the Association of General Merchandise Chains, and others, were deeply concerned, not only by the immediate Commission order, but by the precedent, and the long-range consequences it posed. They had 24 hours to reply.

One defendant in the case, Woolworth, decided to get its public relations counsel involved. After that evening Carl Byoir & Associates officials met with the "trouble light" people and were told the whole story. An alternate plan was drafted to warn the public of the "trouble light" hazard. What they came up with was a classic public relations campaign. Here is what they suggested:

The plan

The chairman of the Commission should call a press conference for the Washington press corps to demonstrate the hazards of the "trouble light."

Television coverage would be supplemented by a commercial TV newsfilm crew paid to cover the press conference, and the film special newsclip would be sent to 500 TV stations.

A one-minute radio tape of the press conference would be sent to 750 stations in the 50 major population areas.

A press kit would be prepared for newspapers, with an in-depth release, and captioned photos of the "trouble light."

An admat would be prepared which could be inserted in local newspapers by local merchants who had sold the product.

Posters would be prepared for the sales counters in stores that had sold the "trouble light."

Special groups, such as the American Retail Federation, with its scores of member associations at the state and local level, and consumer groups at the federal, state, and local levels would be contacted to encourage dissemination of the information.

Specialized materials would be prepared and sent to specific media to shoot the target reader who might have purchased a "trouble light." This included consumer reports, handicraft magazines, automotive publications, and similar trade journals.

Advertising versus public relations

Thus, the Commission plan and the public relations plan were opposed solutions to the problem of achieving adequate public notice. Confrontation was classic; massive communication versus selective communication; advertising versus public relations; hard sell versus news. The arguments have been posed hundreds of times in dozens of board rooms. But in the case of "trouble light," the arguments could be brought into the open and, even though both positions could not get an equal test, an impartial court could given an objective reading.

The next day, August 1, the public relations plan was presented to the Commission. Eisenberg did not wait long to turn it down. He said a public relations campaign, based on free coverage, left public notification to the whim of news editors already preoccupied with impeachment and Watergate, and he felt the only way to get the notice out was to have complete control of the message, which advertising alone guaranteed.

The Commission then instituted a suit in the Federal District Court to compel manufacturer, distributors, and retailers to implement its public notification program. The court ordered the parties to negotiate and return August 19.

Defendants acted

In the meantime, however, the defendants wanted to show their good faith. They had never quarreled with the danger of the product. They wanted to get it off the market to avoid as much further trouble as possible, and to get the message out in the most effective way. Could the public wait until August 19 to be told of the danger?

The defendants decided to proceed with the public relations program. They sent a telegram to Richard O. Simpson, chairman of the Consumer Product Safety Commission, requesting that, in the interest of consumers, he proceed with the proposed press conference. Simpson agreed.

The conference was held Tuesday, August 6, and media turnout was successful. Early returns indicated the story was widely used by radio, television, and newspapers. Other groups participated in spreading the message, as well. The American Retail Federation distributed more than 500 press kits, with a covering letter from the president. The Association of General Merchandise Chains worked directly with its membership, and Action Industries with its retailer customers. Stores put up posters, and some placed ads in their local media. But when the defendants returned to the Commission for the August 15 hearings, they were told the Commission was not yet convinced that adequate notice had been given. This finally led to full scale confrontation before the Federal District Court, District of Columbia, on August 29.

Face to face

Public Relations counsel worked with legal counsel to Action Industries in preparing for the court proceeding. Together they developed a case that adequate public notice had been achieved by the public relations effort. The public relations counsel, which had been working nearly around the clock to arrange the press conference and get out newsclips, press kits, and tapes, now had to get back the results . . . clips, return cards, and any other evidence of communication. They sought outside advice from experts on the validity of their approach and consolidated their viewpoint to present to Judge George L. Hart, Jr., of the United States District Court.

As they struggled to pull their case together, the basic assumptions on which they had operated were clarified and validated.

First, they had proceeded on the basis that mere transmission of information had not been the objective, but rather effective reception, and the impact of that information on recipients. They avoided arguments on the costs of advertising, and on safety, even though frightening implications could be drawn from establishing a precedent for recurring requests for massive advertising of similar hazards among the thousands of products moving through the marketplace.

Second, they concluded a tailor-made news approach was superior to straight advertising, for a variety of reasons. The "trouble light" was a valid news story of genuine public concern. As such, it probably got more actual time in broadcast media and more real space in print media than it would have received in the Commission's ad plan. In addition, the time and space obtained probably commanded more attention and achieved more impact than paid advertisements. It was obvious news, had more credibility than advertising, and also, a news story featuring the chairman of a government safety commission had authority and stature. Finally, it was clear that news presentations got the message out much faster than an ad campaign.

Total communications approach

Third, they concluded it was the total approach to communication that had been important in the public relations campaign, rather than the single-channel ad campaign approach. This total concept involved many media and a repetition of the message over a period of time. Perhaps the most important part of this total effect, they concluded, was the involvement of hundreds—perhaps thousands—of participants in transmitting the message.

The Commission's plan, through an ad campaign, would have directly involved only a few people at an ad agency. The public relations plan involved media "gatekeepers," association executives, store managers, and salespeople at the counter for real person-to-person contact.

This grass-roots approach helped get the message targeted to the specific audience far more effectively than national prime-time advertising, it was concluded. The involvement of those sending out the message reinforced the impact. By the time John Chancellor of NBC and Harry Reasoner of ABC used the story on evening shows, their personal involvement gave the piece a wallop that advertising could never have achieved.

Public relations counsel concluded the major issue was not news media techniques versus advertising, but rather voluntary communications efforts versus compulsory advertising. The public relations plan did include advertising where it would serve most effectively. Some retailers used local ads where they felt it was important.

Here come de judge!

This was the case taken to Judge Hart's court on August 29. Public relations counsel laid out the evidence to show that news stories had been used by 374 television stations, 506 radio stations, and 738 newspapers across the nation. A large map of the United States used colored dots to show which media had carried the story in each region. The map was dramatic defense testimony.

The Commission was adamant. It would agree only that the industry approach could be proved effective if defendants could show that a majority of "trouble lights" had been returned by purchasers. Judge Hart found this notion ridiculous, telling the court that the average consumer would not take the time to return a $1 or $2 item. But he did agree to give the Commission ten weeks to see what data could be obtained on returns.

The important thing, Judge Hart told the court, was to get the message out. He said he felt the publications plan had "pretty well saturated" the market, "that defendants have made a tremendous effort to try to solve this situation and alleviate the danger." The Judge said it was the danger that he was interested in, not the method of communicating. But he would like to see one more effort to tell the people, if plaintiff and defendants could get together and agree on a plan. The session was adjourned for lunch. Both parties were to return with a plan.

The involved parties had lunch in the cafeteria of the District Court Building. There was agreement that, with the court's help, an effort could be launched that would certainly spread the message, once more, in a most dramatic way. If Judge Hart would take the unprecedented step of asking the major network news chiefs to cover one more press conference on the subject, the news media would respond. Besides, the next day would be the start of a news-short Labor Day weekend, and the Watergate and Presidential resignation were now history.

The judge acts

When the court reconvened and the plan was presented, Judge Hart agreed. He offered then and there to dictate a statement for the press: ". . . of all the dangerous instrumentalities I have ever considered, whether on or off the bench . . . this probably appeals to the court as being the most dangerous." As soon as the proceeding was adjourned, he went to his chambers to call the network news chiefs.

The story hit precisely as public relations counsel had predicted. It was a slow Friday, Saturday, and Sunday, and the "trouble light," with the unprecedented plug from a District Court Judge, got on all the networks, both TV and radio, and into most major newspapers. It is still being written up.

Some very real lessons have emerged from the "trouble light" case for public relations and government relations people. First of all, it showed that when private organizations don't like a decision by a government body, they need not take it lying down if they have a viable and effective alternative and can demonstrate the expertise and will to carry it out. Public relations counsel felt strongly that blind resistance was insufficient in a case like this where the public was faced with a genuine danger. It was the industry's voluntary and constructive communications action that impressed Judge Hart enough to warrant his decision to reject compulsion.

Sets a precedent

The "trouble light" case also set a precedent for future product safety alerts. It is doubtful the CPSC will again automatically resort to massive advertising as its sole answer to such problems; it now knows there are other effective ways to communicate. This was again emphasized at a special hearing of media representatives on October 3.

Public relations counsel has also suggested that a communications advisory committee might be set up by CPSC to offer advice on these matters. Another suggestion is a cooperative CPSC-industry approach, with two lines of attack. First, the Commission could make a much more vigorous, major effort to obtain wide national news coverage of its original announcement of a grave product hazard. And second, industry could communicate this to customers through the same channels used to market the item—whether this involved direct mail, point-of-sale posters, newspaper ads, radio or TV commercials, or any other medium.

For those interested in the study of effective communication, the "trouble light" incident offered a unique opportunity to observe different methods of achieving one end—adequate public notice. We will be studying the case for many months to come.

APPENDIX C

U.S. CONSUMER PRODUCT SAFETY COMMISSION
WASHINGTON, D.C. 20207

January 14, 1975

Dear Leo:

I read with interest Ray Hiebert's account of the "Trouble Light" case in the December 1974 issue of the *Journal* and am sorry to say I was rather disappointed in several respects.

1. In all fairness, I would have assumed that the author or the editors would have noted that Dr. Hiebert served as a paid consultant for Carl Byoir and Associates in this case. And while I certainly do not believe that that necessarily would have undermined Dr. Hiebert's objectivity, I believe it would have placed some of his comments in better perspective for the reader.

2. At no time did the Commission view the case as a classic "confrontation" between advertising and public relations. Rather, we sought then and will seek in every situation in which public notice is needed, adequate and effective vehicles of communication which will assist us in providing a meaningful warning to consumers who may have in their possession imminently hazardous products.

3. Contrary to Dr. Hiebert's statement that the media turnout at the August 6 news demonstration "was successful," none of the broadcast networks nor the wire services covered the event and an analysis of coverage as reported to the Commission revealed very serious gaps in terms of national play.

4. The implication that the Commission sought ONLY a campaign of paid warnings is false and misleading. Certainly we outlined a series of paid warnings which we felt were necessary, but this was coupled with the supplementary public relations activities one traditionally utilizes in similar situations.

5. We applauded then and applaud now industry's voluntary efforts to warn consumers of the dangers associated with the trouble light in question, but I believe it would be a mistake to consider the case precedential.

6. To imply that the Commission "automatically" resorted to "massive advertising as its sole answer" to public warnings cuts below the belt and I believe Dr. Hiebert knows better.

Finally, we continue to welcome and encourage comments and suggestions on the very difficult and complicated communication problems with which we're dealing—how do we provide effective warnings to consumers who may have potentially hazardous products in their possession?

And, even more importantly, when will manufacturers, distributors and retailers implement voluntary programs to eliminate as far as possible the "trouble light" situations in the first place?

Sincerely,
(original signed by Ron Aaron Eisenberg)

Ron Aaron Eisenberg, Director
Public Affairs

Mr. Leo Northart, Editor
Public Relations Journal
Public Relations Society of America
845 Third Avenue
New York, New York 10022

RAEisenberg:cps:1–14–75

SELECTED BIBLIOGRAPHY

Allen, James B. "Let's You and Him Fight." *Nation's Business,* February 1973, pp. 38–39.

Benningson, Arnold I. "Product Liability—Producers and Manufacturers Beware." *Research Management,* March 1975, pp. 16–19.

Busch, Paul. "A Review and Critical Evaluation of the Consumer Product Safety Commission: Marketing Management Implications." *Journal of Marketing* 40 (October 1976): 41–49.

"Consumer Notes: Huge Recall of Wire Sought by U.S. Unit." *The New York Times,* August 20, 1975, p. 30.

"The Consumer Product Safety Act: A Federal Commitment to Product Safety." *St. John's Law Review* 48 (1973): 126–58.

"Consumers: Living Dangerously." *Newsweek,* January 28, 1974, p. 66.

"The CPSC Is Not a Benevolent Agency." *Management Review,* December 1974, pp. 41–43.

"Dictating Product Safety." *Business Week,* May 18, 1974, pp. 56–62.

Gould, Wendy Lee. "The Consumer Product Safety Act: Bold New Approaches to Regulatory Theory." *Loyola University Law Journal* 5 (summer 1974): 447–69.

Gray, Robert T. "Washington's New Little Giant." *Nation's Business,* September 1973, p. 21.

Hiebert, Ray Eldon. "Communications on Trial: Massive Advertising vs. Public Relations." *Public Relations Journal,* December 1974, pp. 16–19.

"Hold on to Your Hats." Editorial, *The Wall Street Journal,* August 31, 1973, p. 14.

Hussey, Edward O. "Developing and Marketing a Safe Product." *Research Management,* March 1975, pp. 20–22.

Kelman, Steven. "Regulation by the Numbers—the Consumer Product Safety Commission." *Public Interest,* summer 1974, pp. 83–102.

Kushner, Lawrence. "Consumer Product Safety Commission: What It Is and What It's Doing." *Research Management,* March 1975, pp. 12–15.

McLaughlin, Robert. "Consumer Safety and the Botched Trouble Light Recall." *New Engineer,* September 1975, p. 20.

Matschulat, James O. "Making America Safe for Consumers." *Management Review,* August 1974, pp. 9–14.

Meehan, James F., and Sullivan, Mark L. "The Consumer Product Safety Act." *Practical Lawyer* 19 (October 1973): 13–26.

"More Muscle in the Fight Against Unsafe Products." *U.S. News and World Report,* March 11, 1974, pp. 49–50.

"A Mower Safety Code with a Sharper Edge." *Business Week,* August 11, 1975, pp. 17–18.

Official Transcript of Proceedings before the Consumer Product Safety Commission on Imminent and Substantial Product Hazards. Washington, D.C., October 3, 1974, 157 pp.

Patton, James R., Jr., and Butler, E. Bruce. "The Consumer Product Safety Act—Its Impact on Manufacturers and on the Relationship between Seller and Consumer." *Business Lawyer,* April 1973, pp. 725–40.

"Richard O. Simpson Has Singular Ideas about Independence." *The Wall Street Journal,* March 13, 1974, pp. 1, 14.

Rosen, Gerald R. "We're Going for Companies' Throats." *Dun's Review,* January 1974, p. 39.

Savage, John. "We Test a '75 Spec Safety Bike." *Mechanix Illustrated,* February 1975, p. 32.

"Shirt Maker's First Ad Effort: Warnings Urged by CPSC." *Advertising Age,* April 14, 1975, p. 62.

Simpson, Richard O., and Eisenberg, Ron Aaron. "The Consumer Product Safety Commission: An Open Agency." Statement. Washington, D.C.

Snyder, James D. "Washington's Product Safety Crew is Loaded with Clout." *Sales Management,* October 15, 1973, p. 38.

Transcript of remarks of Hon. Richard O. Simpson, chairman, Consumer Product Safety Commission, before the Federal Bar Association General Counsel's Committee. Washington, D.C., November 13, 1974.

U.S. Consumer Product Safety Commission. *Commentary Upon "A Report to the Committee on Appropriations U.S. House of Representatives on A General Review of the Operation of the Consumer Product Safety Commission,"* by the Surveys and Investigations Staff (March 1975). Washington, D.C., April 1975.

U.S. Consumer Product Safety Commission. *Justification of Appropriation Estimates for the Committee on Appropriations Fiscal Year 1976.* Washington, D.C.

"Washington's New Little Giant." *Nation's Business,* September 1973, pp. 21–24.

Weaver, Paul H. "The Hazards of Trying to Make Consumer Products Safer." *Fortune,* July 1975, p. 133.

Weidenbaum, Murray L. "Higher Costs of Consumer Products." In *Government-Mandated Price Increases: A Neglected Aspect of Inflation.* Domestic Study 28. Washington, D.C.: American Enterprise Institute for Public Policy Research, February 1975, pp. 31–41.

Williams, John J. "A Positive Approach Program for Product Safety." *Research Management,* March 1975, pp. 23–25.

"The Wisdom of the CPSC." Editorial, *The Wall Street Journal,* January 31, 1974, p. 12.

PART II

GOVERNMENT REGULATION OF CORPORATE MARKETING STRATEGIES

10 General Electric Company and Matsushita Electric Corporation of America

FTC's ad substantiation program— advertising of color television sets

*He that wrestles with us, strengthens
our nerves and sharpens our skill.
Our antagonist is our helper.*

Edmund Burke

In June 1971, the Federal Trade Commission announced a set of rules requiring advertisers to submit to the commission data and information substantiating any claims made in their advertising (Exhibit 10–1).[1] The ad substantiation program was the latest step in the revitalized commission's activities to protect the consumer from deceptive and misleading advertising.

EXHIBIT 10–1

UNITED STATES OF AMERICA, FEDERAL TRADE COMMISSION

SPECIAL REPORTS RELATING TO ADVERTISING CLAIMS REQUIREMENT FOR SUBMISSION AND DISCLOSURE THEREOF BY THE COMMISSION.

Notice is hereby given that the FTC has approved, adopted and entered on record the following resolution:

Resolution Requiring Submission of Special Reports Relating to Advertising Claims and Disclosure Thereof by the Commission

Production of Documentation

The claims made in advertising consumer products often lead the consuming public to believe that such claims are substantiated by adequate and well-controlled scientific tests, studies, and other fully documented proof.

---

[1] 36 Fed. Reg. 12058 (June 24, 1971) *amended* 36 Fed. Reg. 14680 (August 7, 1971)

EXHIBIT 10–1 (continued)

If the public and the Commission knew that such substantiation actually exists and the adequacy of substantiation, they would be aided in evaluating competing claims for products and in distinguishing between the seller who is advertising truthfully and one who is unfairly treating both customers and competitors by representing, directly or by implication, that it has proof when in fact there is none or the proof is inadequate.

Considering the importance of these questions to consumers and businessmen, the Commission, in fulfilling its statutory obligation under Section 5 of the Federal Trade Commission Act (15 USC 45) with respect to false and deceptive advertising and unfair methods of competition, resolves that advertisers shall be required on demand by the competition to submit, with respect to any advertisement, such tests, studies, or other data (including testimonials or endorsements) as they had in their possession prior to the time claims, statements, or representations were made in the advertisement regarding the safety, performance, efficacy, quality, or comparative price of the product advertised.

The claims, statements, or representations subject to the above requirement will be identified in order to file special reports which will be issued to such advertisers as may be selected from time to time by the Commission. If the advertiser has no data to substantiate these claims before they were made, he shall notify the Commission of this fact before the return date of the order to file special reports. The Commission will compel the production of said tests, studies, or other data (including testimonies and endorsements) in the exercise of the power vested in it by Sections 6, 9, and 10 of the FTC Act and with the aid of any and all powers conferred upon it by law and any and all compulsory processes available to it.

Publications of Documentation Submitted

Except for trade secrets, customer lists, or other financial information which may be privileged or confidential persuant to Sec. 6(f) of the FTC Act, the material obtained by the Commission pursuant to this resolution will be made available to the public under such terms and conditions as the Commission may from time to time determine. In addition, the Commission may release summaries, reports, indices, or other such publications which will inform the public about material delivered or not delivered to it hereunder.

In deciding to make this material available to the public, and to publish summary reports, the Commission is persuaded by the following policy considerations:

1. Public disclosure can assist consumers in making a rational choice among competing claims which purport to be based on objective evidence and in evaluating the weight to be accorded such claims.
2. The public's need for this information is not being met voluntarily by most advertisers.
3. Public disclosure can enhance competition by encouraging competitors to challenge advertising claims which have no basis in fact.
4. The knowledge that documentation or the lack thereof will be made public will encourage advertisers to have on hand adequate substantiation before claims are made.
5. The Commission has limited resources for detecting claims which are not substantiated by adequate proof. By making documentation submitted in response to this resolution available to the public, the Commission can be alerted by consumers, businessmen, and public interest groups to possible violations of Sec. 5 of the FTC Act.

BACKGROUND

Following its establishment in 1914 during the Progressive Reform era, the FTC embarked on a regulatory career to implement its basic mandate of policing the predatory practices of big business toward the consumer. Section 5 of the FTC act states: "Unfair or deceptive acts or practices in or affecting commerce are hereby declared unlawful."[2] After an initial period of successful activity, however, the commission settled into an easy relationship with the business it was supposed to regulate and then gently stagnated in a pattern that has become all too familiar in the life cycle of regulatory agencies.

This phase persisted until 1968, when a group of young lawyers under the direction of Ralph Nader began an investigation of the commission and its record of performance. The report published in 1969[3] charged the FTC with gross failure in discharging its regulatory responsibilities. The newly installed Nixon administration asked the president of the American Bar Association to investigate the charges and recommend proposals for reform. The ABA report concurred with most of the charges made in the Nader study and concluded that the FTC should be abolished if its "several serious and pervasive deficiencies" in leadership, staff, policies, and performance were not corrected.[4] This report resulted in a major reform effort when the chairman of the ABA study committee, Miles Kirkpatrick, was appointed by President Nixon as the new chairman of the FTC in January 1970. A shakeup in the agency's operations followed.[5]

It is against this background of a revitalized FTC that we must review the new regulatory thrust in the 1970s. One of the more significant of these developments concerns the advertising substantiation efforts undertaken by the FTC. Holding that deceptive advertising was "unfair" to consumers, and acting under the authority of the FTC act, which allows it to make rules and regulations to enforce its mandate,[6] the commission brought legal proceedings against a number of firms which were considered to have been engaged in deceptive advertising. These included Standard Oil of California because of its claims regarding Chevron gasolines with "F 310"; ITT-Continental Baking Company, whose Wonder Bread "builds strong bodies eight different ways"; Coca-Cola's "nutritious" Hi-C fruit drink; and the Charles Pfizer, Inc., drug company claims about the

---

[2] 15 U.S.C. Section 45.

[3] Edward Cox, Robert Fellmeth, and John Schultz, *The Nader Report on the Federal Trade Commission* (New York: Richard W. Baron, 1969).

[4] *Report of the ABA Commission to Study the Federal Trade Commission* (Chicago: American Bar Association, September 15, 1969), p. 3.

[5] For an interesting analysis of this, see Robert E. Freer, Jr., "The Federal Trade Commission: A Study in Survival," *Business Lawyer* 26 (July 1971): 1505–26.

[6] See "The FTC Ad Substantiation Program" (Notes), *Georgetown Law Journal* 61 (1973): 1432, n. 44.

soothing effects of its "Unburn Sunburn Treatment Preparation."[7] In all cases, the FTC asked the firms to cease and desist with such advertising claims unless they could be substantiated. The firms were invited to submit tests, studies, and other such data as available.

The *Pfizer* case became the legal benchmark, and in it the commission ruled that the consumer was entitled to rely on the manufacturer to have a "reasonable basis" for any performance claims made; lack of such a reasonable basis was an unfair trade practice and hence a violation of the FTC act.[8] Because of the random nature of its complaints against these companies—which aroused considerable criticism in the business community—the FTC sought to standardize its ad substantiation program with a set of requirements applicable to all advertisers.[9]

The program has been the subject of intense criticism from industry sources because of the cost burdens it imposes. It has also been criticized by various congressional sources for its ad hoc nature, poor implementation, and the large gap between promise and fulfillment.[10] However, the program has not lacked supporters. Undeterred by the controversy, the commission has moved ahead in widening the scope of the program, improving its enforcement, and enlisting the cooperation and support of various consumer and public interest groups. They were to act as watchdogs to ensure the companies do not resort to deceptive and misleading advertising and, when found to be in violation of FTC regulations, abide by the agreed-upon corrective measures. FTC commissioners and other administrators have since given congressional testimony and made public statements outlining the extent of these revisions and their potential impact. Selected parts of a statement by FTC chairman Calvin J. Collier, out-

---

[7] Freer, "Federal Trade Commission," pp. 1517–18; Pfizer, Inc., 3 Trade Reg. Rep. ¶ 20,056 at 22,030 (FTC, July 11, 1972); ITT-Continental Baking Co., 3 Trade Reg. Rep. ¶ 19,681 at 21,727, 21,728 (FTC, July 2, 1971); Coca-Cola, Inc., 3 Trade Reg. Rep. ¶ 19,351 at 21,484 (FTC, September 29, 1970); Standard Oil Co. of California, 3 Trade Reg. Rep. ¶ 19,352 at 19,428 (FTC, 1970).

[8] "FTC Ad Substantiation Program," pp. 1429–32; Pfizer, Inc., 3 Trade Reg. Rep. ¶ 20,056, at 22,030 (FTC, July 11, 1972).

[9] "This Way to the Egress," editorial, *The Wall Street Journal,* August 28, 1972, p. 6. "FTC: Advertising Substantiation Requirements," 36 Federal Register 12058 (1971).

[10] The only congressional appraisal of the ad substantiation program on record, which was also quite critical, was carried out by the GAO in 1972. The GAO report is entitled *Advertisement Substantiation Program, B-174702, Federal Trade Commission, Report to the Consumer Subcommittee, Committee on Commerce, U.S. Senate, by the Comptroller General of the United States Government Accounting Office (GAO) (1972),* pp 25–26. See also Statement of Miles Kirkpatrick, chairman, Federal Trade Commission, before the U.S. Senate Committee on Commerce, *Hearings on S. 1461, Advertising 1972,* 92nd Congress, 2d Session, Serial 92-70 (1972), pp. 23–24; A. H. Travers, "Foreword," *Kansas Law Review* 17 (1969): 551, 556–57; Tracy Weston, "Deceptive Advertising and the Federal Trade Commission: Decline of Caveat Emptor," *Federal Bar Journal* 24 (1964): 548, 561; Richard Posner, *Regulation of Advertising by the FTC* (Washington, D.C.: American Enterprise Institute for Policy Research, 1973); Francesco Nicosia, *Advertising Management and Society: A Business Point of View* (New York: McGraw Hill, 1974); and S. Prakash Sethi, *Advocacy Advertising and Large Corporations* (Lexington, Mass.: Heath, 1977).

lining the FTC's proposed actions, before the House Committee on Government Operations (1976) appear in Appendix A.[11] Excerpts from a letter addressed to the author dated July 14, 1976, from Richard B. Herzog, assistant director for national advertising, Federal Trade Commission, are presented in Appendix B.

THE COLOR TELEVISION CASE

On August 17, 1975, the FTC issued complaints against Matsushita Electric Corporation of America and General Electric Company alleging these two firms had "misrepresented in advertising the service required by their color television sets" (Exhibit 10–2). These complaints arose out of the

EXHIBIT 10–2

FEDERAL TRADE COMMISSION, WASHINGTON, D.C. 20580

News Release, August 17, 1975

FTC ISSUES COMPLAINTS AGAINST
TWO COLOR TV MANUFACTURERS

The Federal Trade Commission has issued complaints alleging that Matsushita Electric Corp. of America and General Electric Co. have misrepresented in advertising the service required by their color television sets.

The complaint against Matsushita, 1 Panasonic Way, Secaucus, N.J., challenges the advertising statement: "In fact, the National Electronics Association rated the Quatre-color CT 701 as the easiest to service of all color televisions they tested in plant through June 1973."

This statement is misleading, the complaint alleges, because:

- The tests conducted by NEA did not, in fact, establish that the Panasonic set was the easiest, least time consuming, or least expensive to service of all color television sets tested.
- A broad sample of major or well-known brands of color television sets was not tested.

The complaint against General Electric Co., 3135 Easton Turnpike, Fairfield, Conn., alleges that contrary to representations made in advertisements:

- GE did not have a reasonable basis for claiming that its color television sets purchased or in use in 1973 required less service in that year than Zenith or RCA color television sets.
- Independent surveys did not show that GE color television sets bought in 1973 (1) required less service during the initial period of ownership or (2)

---

[11] Statement of Calvin J. Collier, chairman, Federal Trade Commission, before the Subcommittee on Commerce, Consumer and Monetary Affairs of the Committee on Government Operations, House of Representatives, June 1976. See also Richard B. Herzog, "The Policy Planning Protocol for Deceptive and Unsubstantiated Claims: A Management and Legal Perspective," remarks before the 1976 Institute of Advanced Advertising Studies, American Association of Advertising Agencies, New York Council, Tarrytown Conference Center, Tarrytown, New York, June 24–27, 1976.

EXHIBIT 10–2 (*continued*)

would require less service than all other U.S. brands of color television sets bought in 1973.

• During the time GE continued to disseminate advertisements which referred to the independent survey results, it had evidence which contradicted the 1973 survey evidence expressly referred to and relied upon in the ads.

• Upon consumer request, GE did not forward the true and complete details regarding data obtained from the surveys of recent color television set buyers in 1973.

The proposed orders would prohibit the misrepresentation of test or survey results for Matsushita's video and audio equipment and major home appliances and for products manufactured or marketed by General Electric's Home Entertainment Division (except lamps) or Major Appliance Division.

Commissioner Thompson voted against issuing these complaints.
Respondents have 30 days within which to file answers to the complaints.

Note: The FTC issues a complaint when it has "reason to believe" that the law has been violated and that a proceeding is in the public interest. Such action simply marks the beginning of a formal proceeding in which the allegations will be ruled upon after a public hearing.

---

commission's ad substantiation "round" with the color television manufacturing industry, in which it reviewed the advertising claims made by GTE-Sylvania, Philco-Ford, RCA, and Zenith in addition to Matsushita and GE. Each manufacturer was advised to submit data substantiating specific claims made in certain ads chosen by the FTC (from its continual monitoring of all major media in the United States. From the responses, which were lengthy—GE submitted 956 pages of data, Matsushita, 1,002 pages— the FTC determined that the other four manufacturers were making "reasonably" substantiable claims, while GE and Matsushita were not.

After extensive pretrial proceedings, the FTC and the two companies agreed on consent decrees (Matsushita, December 28, 1976; General Electric, January 31, 1977) by which the firms terminated their alleged unsubstantiable advertising, while not specifically admitting to any wrongdoing or violation of the law. In neither case did the FTC require the firms to run "counter" or "corrective" ads, a highly controversial FTC program in which violators must inform consumers of their previous deceptions in "confessional" ads.[12]

---

[12] See, "Back on the Warpath Against Deceptive Ads," *Business Week*, April 19, 1976, p. 148. See also D. A. Anderson and J. Winer, "Corrective Advertising: The FTC's New Formula for Effective Relief," *Texas Law Review* 50 (1972): 312; Tom A. Collins, "Counter Advertising in the Broadcast Media: Bringing the Administrative Process to Bear upon a Theoretical Imperative," *William and Mary Law Review* 15 (1974): 799; Ira Mark Ellman, "And Now a Word Against Our Sponsor: Extending the FTC's Fairness Doctrine to Advertising,"

ISSUES FOR ANALYSIS

The nature of deceptive and misleading advertising through regulatory mechanisms carries with it a variety of knotty problems of definition, proof, and enforcement. These problems are so difficult that they make the matter of public good, although extremely simple on the surface, hard to prove and measure. In addition, the nature and extent of regulation has to be carefully and precisely defined so as not to abridge the advertiser's right of free speech, protected under the First Amendment. The questions to be analyzed are these:

1. Underlying the need for a governmentally instituted ad substantiation program are the assumptions that both the market mechanism and self-regulation by industry are insufficient to protect the consumer and deter the advertiser from making misleading and deceptive claims. What is the basis of these assumptions and to what extent are they tenable?[13]

2. The need for regulating advertising or commercial speech is in conflict with the broad constitutional constraints against regulating pure speech. Historically the Supreme Court has held that commercial speech can be regulated and pure speech cannot. The Court has not been consistent in defining commercial speech. Furthermore, recent Court decisions have tended to narrow the limits of what could be considered commercial speech and, therefore, restricted speech. What

---

California Law Review 60 (1972): 1416; Keith H. Hunt, "Effects of Corrective Advertising," *Journal of Advertising Research* 13 (October 1973): 15–24; Paul D. Scanlon, "The FTC, The FCC, and the 'Counter Ad' controversy: An Invitation to Let's You and Him Fight?" *Antitrust Law and Economic Review* 43 (fall 1971): 43; Weston, "Deceptive Advertising and the Federal Trade Commission"; William L. Wilkie, "Research on Counter and Corrective Advertising," paper presented at the Advertising and Public Interest Conference, American Marketing Association, Washington, D.C., May 9–11, 1973; William L. Wilkie, "Consumer Research and Corrective Advertising: A New Approach," working paper, Marketing Science Institute, Cambridge, Mass., October 1973; Robert F. Dyer and Philip G. Kuehl, "The 'Corrective Advertising' Remedy of the FTC: An Experimental Evaluation," *Journal of Marketing,* January 1974, pp. 48–54; Robert E. Wilkes and James B. Wilcox, "Recent FTC Actions: Implications for the Advertising Strategist," *Journal of Marketing,* January 1974, pp. 55–61.

[13] Posner, *Regulation of Advertising by the FTC;* Howard H. Bell, "Self-Regulation by the Advertising Industry," in *The Unstable Ground: Corporate Social Policy in a Dynamic Society,* ed. S. Prakash Sethi (Santa Barbara, Calif.: Wiley/Hamilton, 1974), pp. 474–82; Channing H. Lushbough, "Advertising: Consumer Information and Consumer Deception," in *The Unstable Ground,* pp. 483–86; Guenther Baumgart, "Industrywide Cooperation for Consumer Affairs," in *The Unstable Ground,* pp. 498–508; *Guidelines on Advertising Substantiation,* Report of the Sub-Council on Advertising and Promotion of the National Business Council for Consumer Affairs (Washington, D.C., U.S. Government Printing Office, #0300-00365, September 1972); Ralph Winter, *Consumer Advocate versus the Consumer* (Washington, D.C.: American Enterprise Institute, 1972); Nicosia, *Advertising Management and Society;* Thomas J. Krattenmaker, "The Federal Trade Commission and Consumer Protection: An Institutional Overview," in *Protecting Consumer Interests: Private Initiative and Public Response,* ed. Robert N. Katz (Cambridge, Mass.: Ballinger, 1976), pp. 105–30.

are the social and political implications of further broadening or narrowing the area of commercial speech?[14]

3. Assuming that an ad substantiation program is indeed needed and desirable, how effective are current FTC procedures in achieving the desired results? In particular: (a) How can one define misleading and deceptive advertising? (b) What is the extent of information usage of the type demanded by the commission, by the consumer? Since all information costs money, which the consumer ultimately must pay, how should the costs and benefits of such information be balanced? (c) To what extent should buyers be expected to assume responsibility for their actions in the marketplace? (d) Has there been any change in buyer behavior, as reflected in market shares, as a result of the FTC actions against different companies and the resultant publicity?[15] (e) Given the prevailing criticism of the FTC's ad substantiation program, how effective are the revisions planned by the commission? What additional measures can be suggested to improve the effectiveness of the program?

The Federal Trade Commission had expected that the ad substantiation program would (1) act as a deterrent to potential violators; (2) enable consumer and public interest groups to actively monitor the data on the public record and encourage them to alert the commission to any discrepancies between the ad claims and the substantiating documentation; and (3) strengthen competition in the market-

---

[14] For a discussion of free speech and commercial speech, various constitutional arguments for and against making distinction between pure speech and commercial speech, and relevant Supreme Court decisions, see Sethi, *Advocacy Advertising and Large Corporations;* "Developments in the Law, Deceptive Advertising," *Harvard Law Review;* Thomas I. Emerson, *Toward a General Theory of the First Amendment* (New York: Vintage Books, 1966); William J. Brennan, "The Supreme Court and the Meiklejohn Interpretation of the First Amendment," *Harvard Law Review* 79 (1965): 1; "Community, Privacy, Defamation, and the First Amendment: The Implications of *Time, Inc.* v. *Hill,*" *Columbia Law Review* 67 (1967): 926; "Notes: Freedom of Expression in a Commercial Context," *Harvard Law Review* 78 (1965): 1191; Martin H. Redish, "The First Amendment in the Marketplace: Commercial Speech and the Value of Free Expression," *George Washington Law Review* 39 (1970): 429; "Corporate Freedom of Speech," *Suffolk University Law Review* 7 (1973): 1117; *Bigelow* v. *Virginia,* 95 S.Ct. 2222 (1975); *Bread* v. *Alexandria,* 341 U.S. 622 (1951); *Valentine* v. *Chrestensen,* 316 U.S. 52 (1942); *Virginia State Board of Pharmacy* v. *Virginia Citizens Consumer Council, Inc.,* 74-845, 44 *U.S. Law Week,* 4686 (May 25, 1976).

[15] Sethi, *Advocacy Advertising and Large Corporations;* "The FTC Ad Substantiation Program" (Notes), (1973); GAO Report on *Advertisement Substantiation Program* (1972); *U.S. Senate Committee on Commerce, Hearings on S. 1461, Advertising 1972;* Posner, *Regulation of Advertising by the FTC;* Nicosia, *Advertising Management and Society;* Winter, *Consumer Advocate versus the Consumer;* Herzog, "The Policy Planning Protocol for Deceptive and Unsubstantiated Claims"; George S. Day, "Assessing the Effects of Information Disclosure Requirements," *Journal of Marketing,* April 1976, pp. 42–52; William H. Cunningham and Isabella C. M. Cunningham, "Consumer Protection: More Information or More Regulation?" *Journal of Marketing,* April 1976, pp. 63–68; David M. Gardner, "Deception in Advertising: A Conceptual Approach," *Journal of Marketing,* January 1975, pp. 40–46.

place by encouraging companies to challenge one another's ads on the basis of substantiation filed with the commission.[16]

The program, however, has not worked out as anticipated. Miles Kirkpatrick, then chairman of the Federal Trade Commission, stated in Senate hearings that few members of the public used the opportunities offered them to study these materials; where an effort was made, it was generally found that the supporting documents were too lengthy and too complicated to be understood by ordinary people. Nor did competitors come forward to challenge one another on the discrepancies in their respective ad claims. The only hopeful prediction made by Kirkpatrick was that in view of the commission's substantiation program, advertisers were likely to be more careful about making performance claims in their ads.[17] The FTC has since made efforts to streamline the program and improve its overall effectiveness.[18]

4. How effective are judicial remedies such as lawsuits by consumers seeking relief from manufacturers, especially because of the high cost of litigation, court delays, and the recent curbs on class action suits imposed by the U.S. Supreme Court?[19]

5. In terms of the color television industry, are there any special characteristics of the industry in which allegedly unsubstantiable claims are made in advertising? That is, do such industries tend toward oligopoly, with only a few competitors? In terms of this particular case, what are the characteristics of the color television industry? How might these characteristics affect the advertising programs of the industries' products and services?

6. Given the nature of the product in this case, to what extent can the buyer be expected to assume responsibility for weighing technical specifications and then making a careful and informed product choice? Is this product too technical, and thus worthy of governmental advertising restrictions, or do some elements of *caveat emptor* still merit inclusion in the buying decision?

---

[16] Statement of Miles Kirkpatrick, chairman, Federal Trade Commission, before the *U.S. Senate Committee on Commerce, Hearings on S.1461, Advertising 1972,* 92nd Congress, 2d Session, Serial 92-70 (1972), pp. 23–24.

[17] Ibid., 23–25; see also *Advocacy Advertising and Large Corporations;* "The FTC Ad Substantiation Program," p. 1440; Harrison Wellford, "How Ralph Nader, Tricia Nixon, the ABA, and Jamie Whitten Helped Turn the FTC Around," *Washington Monthly,* October 1972, pp. 5, 10.

[18] See statements of Collier and Herzog, and Appendixes A and B.

[19] Philip G. Schrag, *Counsel for the Deceived: Case Studies in Consumer Fraud* (New York: Pantheon, 1972); Babette Barton, "Forms and Forums of Consumer Relief: Redress or Rape," in Katz, *Protecting the Consumer Interest;* "Importance of Being Adequate: Due Process Requirements in Class Actions Under Federal Rule 23," *University of Pennsylvania Law Review* 173 (May 1975): 1271; E. J. Benet, "*Eisen* v. *Carlisle and Jacquelin* (94 Sup. Ct. 2140) Supreme Court Calls for Revamping Class Action Strategy," *Wisconsin Law Review,* 1974, pp. 801–32.

7. In terms of marketing management, how should management improve and manage its advertising program to keep it an effective marketing tool? Advertising is a major element in the marketing mix that managers utilize to achieve their sales goals, for it not only allows them to inform the consumer of product information, but also allows the manager to establish product differentiation over competing brands. How might the FTC's ad substantiation program change this marketing basic tool? What effect would this be likely to have on advertising management practices—any, or are there other means to communicate one's message in the marketplace?

8. How effective is the FTC procedure outlined in the case likely to be in providing adequate consumer protection? The extensive and detailed procedures for compliance also have counterparts in compliance costs at the manufacturer's end and enforcement costs at the FTC end. Are these costs justified in terms of benefits? Could the FTC have asked for different (and less cumbersome and expensive) criteria for achieving similar performance?

THE COMPLAINTS AGAINST GE AND MATSUSHITA

The complaint against GE[20]

The FTC complaint against GE alleged that certain advertisements (Appendix C), as well as others not specifically referred to, had represented directly or by implication that General Electric color television sets purchased or in use in 1973 required less service in that year than did Zenith or RCA models. However, at the time of such representations, the respondent (GE) did not possess and rely upon a reasonable basis for making its claims, and therefore the representations set forth in the ads constituted a deceptive or unfair act or practice under FTC regulations.

Moreover, these same advertisements represented directly or through implication that independent surveys of persons who had bought a color television set in 1973 showed that GE color sets bought in that year both did and would require less service during the initial period of ownership than all other American brands sold in 1973. The FTC alleged that these surveys made no such representation, and therefore constituted a violation of the law.

The FTC also maintained that GE continued to disseminate the aforementioned advertisements—representing that 1973 survey evidence of service levels of GE color television sets is a reason to purchase such sets

---

[20] United States of America before the Federal Trade Commission, *In the Matter of General Electric Company*, Docket No. 9049, July 29, 1975 (The FTC did not file complaints against GTE-Sylvania, Philco-Ford, RCA, or Zenith, the other firms asked to submit ad substantiation data to the agency.)

in 1974–75—when GE knew of and had available to it evidence from substantially identical sources that contradicted or was inconsistent with the 1973 survey data. This, the FTC alleged, demonstrated that GE neither possessed nor relied upon a "reasonable basis" for making ad claims, and was thus guilty of an unfair practice. Finally, through the use of these advertisements, the FTC said, GE represented directly or by implication that it would upon request forward the true and complete details regarding the comparative service information obtained from surveys of recent color television set buyers conducted in 1973. In truth and in fact, however, the FTC alleged that upon request GE did not and does not forward the survey data, and that its claim to do so was therefore misleading and deceptive.

In summarizing the allegations against GE, the FTC said that:

> The use by the respondent of the aforesaid false, misleading, deceptive or unfair statements, representations and practices has had, and now has, the capacity and tendency to mislead members of the consuming public into the erroneous and mistaken belief that said statements and representations were and are true and into the purchase of substantial quantities of respondent's products by reason of said erroneous and mistaken belief.[21]

Furthermore,

> The aforesaid acts and practices of respondent, as herein alleged, were and are all to the prejudice and injury of the public and of respondent's competitors and constituted and now constitute unfair and deceptive acts and practices and unfair methods of competition, in or affecting commerce, in violation of Section 5 of the Federal Trade Commission Act.[22]

The commission's consent order to GE stipulated that any future advertising the firm employed must in no way misrepresent the facts regarding its products, and that any such advertising claims must be substantiable by evidence. If GE adds any new features to existing products, or if it introduces new models, it may make claims regarding dependability and reliability. But it must immediately undertake tests or surveys to validate such claims, and it must discontinue any claims not supported by the evidence.

The complaint against Matsushita[23]

The FTC complaint against Matsushita, the manufacturer of the Panasonic line of color televisions, alleged that an advertisement disseminated by the firm was false, misleading, and deceptive (see Appendix D). The offending ad contained this statement:

---

[21] Ibid., p. 4.

[22] Ibid., p. 5.

[23] United States of America before the Federal Trade Commission, *In the Matter of Matsushita Electric Corporation of America*, Docket No. 9048, July 29, 1975.

In fact, the National Electronics Association rated the Quatrecolor CT-701 as the easiest to service of all color televisions they tested in plant through June 1973.

   1.   The test(s) conducted by the National Electronics Association ("NEA") in plant through June 1973 established that the Panasonic Quatrecolor CT-701 was the easiest to service of all color televisions tested.

   2.   The test(s) conducted by NEA in plant through June 1973 established that the Panasonic Quatrecolor CT-701 was the least expensive or least time-consuming to service of all color televisions tested.

   3.   A broad sample of major or well-known brands of color television sets was tested in plant by NEA through June 1973.[24]

The FTC alleged that none of these representations or implications was true (based on the FTC interpretation of the NEA test results). The agency therefore asked that Matsushita discontinue the questioned ads. Furthermore, Matsushita should refrain from any future advertising misrepresentations of "in any manner, directly or by implication, the purpose, content, validity, reliability, results, or conclusions of any test, survey, evaluation, report, study, research, demonstration, or analysis."[25]

THE CONSENT DECREES

Following lengthy discussions between the FTC staffs and representatives of Matsushita and GE, the two firms agreed to consent orders not to engage in any future misrepresentations in advertisements making claims that could not be substantiated.[26] It should be noted that a consent agreement does not constitute an admission by the respondent firm that the law has been violated or that any of the facts as alleged in the complaint by the commission are true. The consent agreements came nearly a year and a half after the filing of the complaints by the FTC, and nearly three years after the FTC first undertook its color television investigations.

The salient features of the consent agreement with Matsushita are as follows:

1.   Matsushita was prohibited from referring in advertising to any test as evidence that one of its products is superior to any other product unless the following conditions were met:
   a.   the test must have been appropriately designed and conducted for measuring the characteristic referred to in the ad;
   b.   the results of the test must establish the superiority of respondent's product for that characteristic;

---

[24] Ibid., p. 2.

[25] Ibid., p. 6.

[26] United States of America before the Federal Trade Commission, *In the Matter of Matsushita Electric Corporation of America*, Docket No. 9048, Agreement containing Consent Order to Cease and Desist, December 28, 1976. United States of America before the Federal Trade Commission, *In the Matter of General Electric Company*, Docket No. 9049, Agreement containing Consent Order to Cease and Desist, January 31, 1977.

   c. the results of the test must establish a degree of superiority which is significant to consumers in making purchase decisions; and

   d. the test must have included a broad sample of the major or well-known competing brands of the product; or, if only a small sample was tested, the ad must identify by name the products which were tested.

This provision applied to all video and audio equipment (e.g., televisions, stereos, radios, tape recorders), all major home appliances (e.g., microwave ovens), and all bicycles advertised by respondent, excluding those products which are not advertised to consumers for personal, family, or household use (e.g., videotape recorders advertised for business use). [Emphasis added]

2. Matsushita was prohibited from advertising that one of its television receivers is *easier* to service than any other receiver if respondent knew or had reason to know that its receiver was more *costly* or more *time-consuming* to service than the products to which it is being compared.

3. Matsushita was prohibited from making misrepresentations about any test or any survey, evaluation, report, study, research or analysis regarding television receivers.

4. Matsushita was required to distribute a copy of the order to each of its operating divisions.

5. Matsushita was required to report to the Commission within sixty days after the order became effective how it was complying with the order. Additional compliance reports were to be made annually for three years.

6. Matsushita was required to notify the Commission at least thirty days prior to any anticipated change in its corporate structure which would affect its obligations under the order.

The salient features of the consent agreement with General Electric were as follows:

1. The consent order covered not only the advertising claims pertaining to both color and monochrome sets *but was extended to other GE products, namely, clothes washers, clothes dryers, ranges, dishwashers, trash compactors, refrigerators, freezers, room air conditioners, stereophonic consoles and non-portable stereophonic sound systems and components.* [Emphasis added]

2. GE was prohibited from the citation of any "evidence" as support for advertising claims unless certain conditions were met. Evidence was defined to mean tests, experiments, demonstrations, studies or surveys, and the requirements on the use of evidence vary with the type of claim that the evidence was used to support, show, or prove.

If the claim concerned any fact or feature about a covered product, then the cited evidence must in fact support or prove the stated claim.

If GE claimed that cited evidence supported or proved that a covered product was superior to any competing product, then the cited evidence must support or prove that superiority. Also, GE must either (a) disclose in what way or by how much the product was superior, or (b) it must have a reasonable basis for believing that the superiority would be discernible to or of benefit to consumers.

If the claim referred to different models or to competing products, then the cited evidence must support or prove the claim with respect to each model or product referred to in the advertisement.

If evidence was cited to support a "less service" claim, then the evidence must in fact support or prove that claim, and GE must disclose the exact nature of its product's superior service performance unless the cited evidence showed that the product required *both* less costly service and less frequent service than its competitors.

If the evidence was cited to support or prove a greater dependability or reliability claim, then the cited evidence must support or prove that claim and the respondent must disclose in what way its product was more dependable or more reliable.

3. GE was prohibited from using any "evidence" to support, show, or prove any of the claims covered in (2) above when it knew of any valid, reliable, or substantially identical evidence which was inconsistent with the cited evidence unless a qualified expert stated in an affidavit that the inconsistent evidence could be disregarded and gave reasons.

4. GE was prohibited from representing that the details of any evidence would be forwarded upon request unless it furnished a full, fair and accurate summary of all the details of such evidence as to all products referred to in the advertisement.

5. In case GE made "comparative" claims with regard to any service, dependability or reliability—whether or not such a claim cited evidence in support—the company must possess a reasonable basis consisting of competent and reliable studies, surveys, or scientific or engineering tests. However, for a reasonable period following the introduction of a new product feature or model, GE could make comparative service claims based on literature or generally recognized scientific principles while it was awaiting the results of the studies, surveys, or tests required. If these studies, surveys, or tests did not provide a reasonable basis for the comparative claims, GE must cease making them. GE must also possess a reasonable basis for any noncomparative service-related claim.

A NOTE ON THE COLOR TELEVISION INDUSTRY IN THE UNITED STATES

The FTC complaints against General Electric and Matsushita were filed during a turbulent period for the color TV industry. Although the sales of color television sets to dealers rose fairly steadily from 5,012,000 in 1966 to a record high of 9,660,000 sets in 1973, the industry experienced a severe downturn in the recessionary period beginning in 1974. Sales fell to 6,651,000 sets in 1975, and an estimated 7,500,000 sets in 1976 (see Exhibit 10–3).

EXHIBIT 10–3

FACTORY SALES OF TELEVISION RECEIVERS BY TYPES
(000)

A: MONOCHROME TELEVISION RECEIVERS, 1956–1975*

Year	Table and portable	Table and portable (% of total)	Console	Console (% of total)	Combinations	Combinations (% of total)	Total	Total (%)	Number with UHF	Number with UHF (% of total)
1956	4,700	63.9%	2,563	34.9%	88	1.2%	7,351	100.0%	1,027	14.0%
1957	3,859	60.4	2,359	36.9	170	2.7	6,388	100.0	773	12.1
1958	2,823	55.9	2,088	41.3	140	2.8	5,051	100.0	435	8.6
1959	3,580	57.0	2,523	40.2	175	2.8	6,278	100.0	450	7.2
1960	3,277	57.4	2,220	38.9	210	3.7	5,707	100.0	436	7.6
1961	3,793	61.6	2,131	34.6	231	3.8	6,155	100.0	386	6.3
1962	4,316	65.8	1,954	29.8	288	4.4	6,558	100.0	596	9.1
1963	4,781	68.1	1,925	27.4	313	4.5	7,019	100.0	1,030	14.7
1964	6,150	76.6	1,661	20.7	217	2.7	8,028	100.0	5,451	67.9
1965	6,912	82.2	1,382	16.4	115	1.4	8,409	100.0	8,409	100.0
1966	6,078	84.5	1,061	14.8	50	.7	7,189	100.0	7,189	100.0
1967	4,633	87.6	631	11.9	26	.5	5,290	100.0	5,290	100.0
1968	5,169	89.5	584	10.1	25	.4	5,778	100.0	5,778	100.0
1969	4,716	90.9	457	8.8	18	.3	5,191	100.0	5,191	100.0
1970	4,322	91.9	382	8.1			4,704	100.0	4,704	100.0
1971	4,542	91.9	399	8.1			4,941	100.0	4,941	100.0
1972	5,235	95.0	277	5.0			5,512	100.0	5,512	100.0
1973†	6,991	96.5	251	3.5			7,242	100.0	7,242	100.0
1974	6,168	97.6	150	2.4			6,318	100.0	6,318	100.0
1975	4,880	98.5	75	1.5			4,955	100.0	4,955	100.0

EXHIBIT 10-3 (continued)

B: COLOR TELEVISION RECEIVERS, 1966–1975*

Year	Table and portable	Table and portable (% of total)	Console	Console (% of total)	Combinations	Combinations (% of total)	Total	Total (%)
1966	901	18.0%	3,725	74.3%	386	7.7%	5,012	100.0%
1967	1,751	31.5	3,440	61.8	372	6.7	5,563	100.0
1968	2,449	41.0	3,274	54.8	249	4.2	5,972	100.0
1969	2,608	45.4	2,940	51.2	196	3.4	5,744	100.0
1970	2,462	52.1	2,135	45.1	132	2.8	4,729	100.0
1971	3,533	56.5	2,607	41.7	116	1.8	6,256	100.0
1972	4,671	59.7	3,073	39.3	81	1.0	7,825	100.0
1973†	6,346	65.7	3,252	33.7	62	.6	9,660	100.0
1974	5,411	67.5	2,571	32.1	34	.4	8,016	100.0
1975	4,496	67.6	2,126	32.0	29	.4	6,651	100.0

C: TOTAL TELEVISION RECEIVERS, 1966–1975*

Year	Table and portable	Table and portable (% of total)	Console	Console (% of total)	Combinations	Combinations (% of total)	Total	Total (%)
1966	6,979	57.2%	4,786	39.2%	436	3.6%	12,201	100.0%
1967	6,384	58.8	4,071	37.5	398	3.7	10,853	100.0
1968	7,618	64.8	3,858	32.8	274	2.4	11,750	100.0
1969	7,324	67.0	3,397	31.1	214	1.9	10,935	100.0
1970	6,784	71.9	2,649	28.1			9,433	100.0
1971	8,075	72.1	3,122	27.9			11,197	100.0
1972	9,906	74.3	3,431	25.7			13,337	100.0
1973†	13,337	78.9	3,565	21.1			16,902	100.0
1974	1,579	80.8	2,755	19.2			14,334	100.0
1975	9,376	80.8	2,230	19.2			11,606	100.0

* Prior to 1973, data reflect factory sales of domestic label which includes products produced or purchased by U.S. manufacturers for sale with their brand name, and excludes those products imported directly by distributors or dealers for resale.

† 1973–75 data reflect factory sales by U.S. manufacturers plus those products imported directly by distributors or dealers for resale.

Source: Electronic Industries Association, *1976 Electronic Market Data Book* (Washington, D.C., 1976), p. 13.

Along with the negative effect of recession on the U.S. color television market, the 1974–76 period saw a steep rise of imports of color televisions, primarily from Japan, into the U.S. market. From 1965, when no color receivers were being imported, imports rose to make up more than 30 percent of total U.S. imports in the first six months of 1976. This was a 133.3 percent increase over 1975 imports (see Exhibit 10–4). Although in the early 1970s the market share rank-order would have been RCA, Zenith, and Magnavox, with GE, Sylvania, and Motorola all competing for fourth slot, by 1976 the following order prevailed:[27]

Manufacturers	Percent
Japanese manufacturers	35
Zenith	25
RCA	20
Sears (Warwick Electronics)	10
Other U.S. manufacturers (GE, Sylvania)	10
Total	100

As a result of the Japanese imports, the number of U.S. firms producing color television sets has declined from twenty in the 1960s to seven. In the last three years, five television companies have been forced into mergers or acquisitions. For example, in 1974 Motorola sold its TV business to Matsushita; Ford Motor Company sold the Philco brand name and television inventories to GTE Sylvania; and Warwick is in the process of being sold to Sanyo of Japan. Zenith and RCA have complained of inadequate profitability in 1978. Admiral is going out of business. In addition, some observers estimate that more than 60,000 jobs in color TV plants have been lost in the United States since 1971.

Some American electronics companies believe that the Japanese have gained their top spot in the market through unfair competition. George Konkol, head of the consumer electronics business of General Telephone and Electronic Corporation's GTE Sylvania, said: "We see a conspiracy." Another proponent of the conspiracy theory, John J. Nevins, chairman and president of Zenith Radio Corporation, asserted that the Japanese government rebates commodity taxes on every TV receiver a Japanese Company exports to the United States, a tax benefit ranging from 15 to 20 percent of the value. This rebate allows Japanese manufacturers to undercut U.S. manufacturers, who in the last five years made before-tax profits averaging only 7.7 percent of sales. According to Nevins, the Japanese have conspired to maintain high prices in Japan and to sell at low prices in the United States until the American market is weakened enough to permit

---

[27] N. R. Kleinfield, "Troubled Picture: U.S. Color TV Makers Say Japanese Conspire to Take Over Industry," *The Wall Street Journal*, December 16, 1976, p. 1.

EXHIBIT 10–4

SUMMARY OF 1976 U.S. IMPORTS OF CONSUMER ELECTRONIC PRODUCTS

Selected products	4th quarter (units only)			Year to date (units only)		
	1976	1975	Percent change	1976	1975	Percent change
Television						
Color	890,475	448,743	+ 98.4	2,833,738	1,214,664	+133.3
Monochrome	1,249,810	799,497	+ 56.3	4,327,022	2,974,622	+ 45.5
Total	2,140,285	1,248,240	+ 71.5	7,160,760	4,189,286	+ 70.9
Radio						
Home	10,402,980	8,801,978	+ 18.2	35,394,252	27,944,986	+ 26.7
Auto	1,356,475	1,316,184	+ 3.1	5,969,904	3,996,058	+ 49.4
Total	11,759,455	10,118,162	+ 16.2	41,364,156	31,941,044	+ 29.5
Phonograph						
Phonograph only	131,846	112,040	+ 17.7	363,020	238,004	+ 52.5
Phono-combination	731,631	344,324	+112.5	2,092,178	1,061,201	+ 97.2
Total	863,477	456,364	+ 89.2	2,455,198	1,299,205	+ 89.0
Record players, record changers, turntables	2,283,266	1,720,329	+ 32.7	8,119,459	4,703,874	+ 72.6
Tape recorder/player only						
Audio	4,062,675	2,568,038	+ 58.2	12,663,933	7,653,249	+ 65.5
Video (color & monochrome)	23,572	10,046	+134.6	69,869	39,829	+ 75.4
Total	4,086,247	2,578,084	+ 58.5	12,733,802	7,693,078	+ 65.5
Tape players only						
Audio (home type)	1,187,807	940,730	+ 26.3	4,142,899	3,100,490	+ 33.6
Audio (auto type)	2,802,550	1,422,329	+ 97.0	9,136,100	4,903,472	+ 86.3
Video (color & monochrome)	70,396	25,696	+174.0	220,969	121,682	+ 81.6
Total	4,060,753	2,388,755	+ 70.0	13,499,968	8,125,644	+ 66.1

Source: Electronic Industries Association, "EIA Marketing Services Department Reports Fourth Quarter and Total 1976 Import/Export Figures," News Release, February 22, 1977.

Japanese domination. Zenith's 1970 complaint about this matter to the U.S. Treasury Department, which asked for countervailing U.S. duties on Japanese imports, was denied in 1976. In April 1977, Zenith's position was unanimously upheld by a three-judge panel in the U.S. Customs Court. The decision was reversed, however, in a 3-to-2 decision by the Court of Customs and Patent Appeals. In June 1978, the matter was finally resolved when the U.S. Supreme Court unanimously rejected Zenith's arguments.[28]

APPENDIX A: POLICY PLANNING PROTOCOL, DECEPTIVE AND UNSUBSTANTIATED CLAIMS*

These questions are not cumulative. The answers to less than all of them may indicate the need for action. Moreover, answers to certain of these questions will frequently not be available at all, or may not be available except at considerable cost and delay. Answers to these questions therefore should not be required where obtaining the answers would be unduly burdensome or speculative, or where the answers to other of the questions indicate that the action proposed is a particularly good one, or, of course, where the answers could be obtained only by compulsory process and the action which the Commission is being asked to take is to authorize such process.

A. Consumer interpretations of the claim

1. List the main interpretations that consumers may place on the claim recommended for challenge, including those that might render the claim true/substantiated as well as those that might render the claim false/unsubstantiated.

2. Indicate which of these interpretations would be alleged to be implications of the claim for purposes of substantiation or litigation. For each interpretation so indicated, state the reasons, if any, for believing that the claim so interpreted would be false/unsubstantiated.

B. Scale of the deception or lack of substantiation

3. What is known about the relative proportions of consumers adhering to each of the interpretations listed above in response to question 1?

---

[28] John J. Nevin "Can U.S. Business Survive Our Japanese Trade Policy?" 56 *Harvard Business Review* No. 5, September–October 1978, pp. 170–71.

* This material appears as attachment D in the "Statement of Calvin J. Collier, chairman, Federal Trade Commission," before the Subcommittee on Commerce, Consumer and Monetary Affairs of the Committee on Government Operations, House of Representatives, June 24, 1976.

4.   What was the approximate advertising budget for the claim during the past year or during any other period of time that would reflect the number of consumers actually exposed to the claim? Is there more direct information on the number of consumers exposed to the claim?

C. Materiality

5.   If consumers do interpret the claim in the ways that would be alleged to be implications, what reasons are there for supposing that these interpretations would influence purchase decisions?

6.   During the past year, approximately how many consumers purchased the product* about which the claim was made?

7.   Approximately what price did they pay?

8.   Estimate, if possible, the proportion of consumers who would have purchased the product only at some price lower than they did pay, if at all, were they informed that the interpretations identified in response to Question 2 were false.

9.   Estimate, if possible, what the advertised product would be worth to the consumers identified by Question 8 if they knew that the product did not have the positive (or unique) attributes suggested by the claim. If the claim can cause consumers to disregard some negative attribute, such as a risk to health and safety, to their possible physical or economic injury, so specify. If so, estimate, if possible, the annual number of such injuries attributable to the claim.

D. Adequacy of corrective market forces

10.   If the product to which the claim relates is a low-ticket item, can consumers ordinarily determine prior to purchase whether the claim, as interpreted, is true; or invest a small amount in purchase and then by experience with the product determine whether or not the claim is true? Does the claim relate to a credence quality, that is, a quality of the product that consumers ordinarily cannot evaluate during normal use of the product without acquiring costly information from some source other than their own evaluative faculties?

11.   Is the product to which the claim relates one that a consumer would typically purchase frequently? Have product sales increased or decreased substantially since the claim was made?

12.   Are there sources of information about the subject matter of the claim in addition to the claim itself? If so, are they likely to be recalled by consumers when they purchase or use the product? Are they likely to be used by consumers who are not aggressive, effective shoppers? If not, why not?

---

* Throughout, "product" refers to the particular brand advertised.

E. Effect on the flow of truthful information

13. Will the standard of truth/substantiation that would be applied to the claim under the recommendation to initiate proceedings make it extremely difficult as a practical matter to make the type of claim? Is this result reasonable?

14. What are the consequences to consumers of an erroneous determination by the Commission that the claim is false/unsubstantiated? What are the consequences to consumers of an erroneous determination by the Commission that the claim is true/substantiated?

F. Deterrence

15. Is there a possibility of getting significant relief with broad product or claim coverage? What relief is possible? Why would it be significant?

16. Do the facts of the matter recommended present an opportunity to elaborate a rule of law that would be applicable to claims or advertisers other than those that would be directly challenged by the recommended action? If so, describe this rule of law as you would wish the advertising community to understand it. If this rule of law would be a significant precedent, explain why.

17. Does the claim violate a Guide or is it inconsistent with relevant principles embodied in a Guide?

18. Is the fact of a violation so evident to other industry members that, if we do not act, our credibility and deterrence might be adversely affected?

19. Is there any aspect of the advertisement—e.g., the nature of the advertiser, the product, the theme, the volume of the advertising, the memorableness of the ad, the blatancy of the violation—which indicates that an enforcement action would have substantial impact on the advertising community?

20. What, if anything, do we know about the role advertising plays (as against other promotional techniques and other sources of information) in the decision to purchase the product?

21. What is the aggregate dollar volume spent on advertising by the advertiser to be joined in the recommended action?

22. What is the aggregate volume of sales of the advertised product and of products of the same type?

G. Law enforcement efficiency

23. Has another agency taken action or does another agency have expertise with respect to the claim or its subject matter? Are there reasons why the Commission should defer? What is the position of this other agency? If coordination is planned, what form would it take?

24. How difficult would it be to litigate a case challenging the claim? Would the theory of the proceeding recommended place the Commission

in a position of resolving issues that are better left to other modes of resolution, for instance, debate among scientists? If so, explain. Is there a substantial possibility of whole or partial summary judgment?

25.   Can the problem seen in the ad be handled by way of a rule? Are the violations widespread? Should they be handled by way of a rule?

H. Additional considerations

26.   What is the ratio of the advertiser's advertising expense to sales revenues? How, if at all, is this ratio relevant to the public interest in proceeding as recommended?

27.   Does the claim specially affect a vulnerable group?

28.   Does the advertising use deception or unfairness to offend important values or to exploit legitimate concerns of a substantial segment of the population, whether or not there is direct injury to person or pocketbook, e.g., minority hiring or environmental protection?

29.   Are there additional considerations not elicited by previous questions that would affect the public interest in proceeding?

APPENDIX B

Excerpts from a letter from Richard B. Herzog, assistant director for national advertising, Federal Trade Commission, Washington, D.C., and addressed to Professor S. Prakash Sethi. This letter was in response to the addressee's queries as to the current status of the ad substantiation program, and also to the addressee's criticism of the said program.

FEDERAL TRADE COMMISSION

Washington, D.C. 20580

Bureau of   July 14, 1976
Consumer Protection

Professor Prakash Sethi
University of California
School of Business Administration
350 Barrows Hall
Berkeley, California 94720

Dear Professor Sethi:

Late in 1973, the staff proposed and the Commission approved a complete and substantial revision of the ad substantiation program. There were many facets to this revision. In particular, there was an increased focus on the suitability of actually instituting law enforcement action should the questioned claims be unsubstantiated. Moreover, outside experts are now being used in choosing the subjects of request, in the actual development of the technical questions to be directed to the advertiser, and in the evaluation of the materials proffered by the advertiser to substantiate the claim. This use of outside experts has been made possible by a substantial increase in the amount of contract funds available to the Commission for this program since the period about which you are apparently writing.

(The contracts to which I am referring are those available for preliminary evaluation to determine whether it appears that the claim is unsubstantiated. If that is the preliminary evaluation, then a full case on the merits is prepared, and for that undertaking there are still additional contract funds to be used in the actual litigation.)

Because outside experts have been used, and because the staff itself has greatly increased its own ability in these matters, the questions directed to the advertiser in the ad substantiation orders have become very much more focused and sophisticated than they previously were. As a result, the fruitfulness of the requests has been greatly enhanced. Of the approximately 200 separate ad substantiation orders issued between 1971 and 1973, 18, or about 10 percent, resulted in cases. In contrast, the 30 ad substantiation orders issued since January 1974 have already resulted in nine cases, a rate of 30 percent, or three times that in the pre-1974 period. Moreover, since a number of the more recently requested substantiation materials are now under analysis, both the number of cases and the percentage of cases per request may actually turn out to be greater. And because of the greater focus in the selection of subjects for ad substantiation, each and every request is now evaluated by outside experts.

In short, any observations that "the program . . . has bogged down in the masses of data furnished the Commission by the corporation that have far out stripped the Commission's ability to evaluate them both in terms of manpower resources and technical competence" does not accurately reflect the Commission's current ad substantiation activities. . . .

In point of fact, . . . the Commission undertakes a general monitoring and law enforcement effort with respect to advertising, and many other advertisers as part of this effort have been asked to substantiate claims as part of nonpublic investigations commenced with respect to individual advertisers. These, too, are part of the ad substantiation program, involving as they do the enforcement of the Commission's *Pfizer* requirement that an advertiser, at the time of first dissemination of the claim, possess and rely upon a reasonable basis for it. As these requests are individual, however, they do not amount to a so-called "round" in which a number of current claims and advertising involving the same product or technique are simultaneously the subject of a request for substantiation.

You also assert as an aspect of the inadequacy of the program that there is "an enormous time gap between the time of the initial request and final action. By the time an action is taken, the ad campaign in question may already been discontinued. . . ."

I believe that this kind of criticism reflects a fundamental misunderstanding of the law enforcement purpose of the Commission. The argument that there is no longer public interest in prosecuting a matter once an ad has stopped is an argument typically made by industry—the so-called "discontinuance" defense. The Commission routinely rejects this defense for reasons going to the fundamental nature of Section 5 of the Federal Trade Commission Act.

The stopping of the particular ad that gave rise to the violation is neither the only purpose nor, in most instances, the primary purpose of a law enforcement action under that section. What the Commission is "empowered and directed" to do by that section is "to prevent" deceptive and unfair acts or practices in commerce. Section 5(a) (6). As the Commission recently emphasized, "[T]he purpose is prevention, and the violation only a triggering device. . . ." *Rubbermaid Incorporated,* Slip Op. n. 13 (Docket 8939). A copy of this opinion is enclosed.

Because the purpose is prevention, the time has long since passed when anyone can argue that an order must be confined to the very acts or practices that constituted the violation. To the contrary, the Commission in an order can prevent all those acts or practices that are reasonably related to the acts or practices that gave rise to the violation. Violations frequently give rise to cease and desist orders that cover a broad range of products and claims by the offending company. It is in the coverage of the order that the public benefits of national advertising cases are ordinarily to be found. I am enclosing a speech that I gave a year ago on this subject of the scope of the order in national advertising cases. In it you will see the considerations that support very broad orders in such cases. In fact, we have been obtaining such orders both in litigated matters and consent decrees. (See, e.g., Chrysler Corporation, Dkt. 8995; Crown Central Corporation, Dkt. 8851; General Electric Corporation, Dkt. 9049 [Consent order removed from adjudication and pending before Commission for tentative approval].)

Thus, the length of time between the advertising that is questioned and the issuance of a cease and desist order is not the measure of the efficacy of the Commission's law enforcement, within, of course, reasonable limits. The central concern is the scope of the order—with respect to the products covered and the claims covered—that results from the enforcement proceeding. Criticism that ignores these fundamental, central purposes of the Federal Trade Commission Act, is to my mind, seriously inadequate. . . .

I should add generally that the overall efficiency of our law enforcement programs, and the public benefits derived from a given commitment of resources, can only be enhanced by our adoption late in 1975 of a policy planning protocol to guide in the disposition of our law enforcement resources with respect to deceptive and unsubstantiated claims [Appendix A]. . . . I am sure that you will agree that the questions contained in the protocol can induce a very comprehensive examination of the costs and benefits to be gained by a given Commission action.

Although I am not quite sure what you mean . . . when you say that the "unintended effect of the ad substantiation program has been an over-emphasis on whether a given ad would pass the 'legal' test and not whether its claims are any more sound than before," I do believe that my point about the scope of the order bears upon that statement. Presumably, whether the program has future effects in deterring unsubstantiated claims by the advertiser who receives an ad substantiation request depends in part upon the nature of the order that can result from an enforcement proceeding. It should be clear that our enforcement proceedings can, indeed, result in orders covering a very broad range of claims and imposing substantiation requirements of varying degrees of specificity, and which are enforceable by substantial penalties. Moreover, I would argue that the sophistication of the ad substantiation request itself can cause an advertiser to consider more carefully his duties under *Pfizer,* even if the particular request does not result in a case against that advertiser.

. . . You assert that "the need for elaborate documentation and the procedural delays with their associated costs in money and time may lead advertisers to resort to inane claims, thereby removing even more information content from the ad messages." I am not sure whose "procedural delays" you are referring to here. As we do not preclear ads, and as substantiation is not submitted prior to the running of the ad, I take it you are referring to procedures internal to the advertiser.

In any event, we constantly monitor all network broadcast advertising, and a broad range of print advertising in numerous publications. It is our observation, based on that monitoring, that the phenomenon that you predict simply has not come to pass. Our impressions may, of ocurse, differ, but it is our impression that, if anything, the informational content of ads has been increasing within the last few years. I believe that general observations from time to time in trade publications support this view. (See, e.g., *Ad Age*, July 5, 1976, p. 25.)

Moreover, the criticism that you make is not a criticism of the ad substantiation program but of the legal requirement that an advertiser possess and rely upon a reasonable basis for his claim when he first disseminates the claim. I see no argument . . . as to why that is an unwise or unreasonable requirement to impose on an advertiser. In its opinion in which it first announced this interpretation of the statutory prohibitions on deception and unfairness, the Commission discussed at length the policies that support such a legal requirement. These include considerations both of economic efficiency and of competition. (See *Pfizer, Inc.* 81 FTC 56, 61–63 [1972].) I do not see how the requirement of substantiation can be criticized without coming to grips . . . with these fundamental considerations.

If your criticism has to do with the rigor with which adequate substantiation is defined, that criticism could of course be made even if the standard were truth, i.e., the inescapable, core requirement under Section 5. For even under that standard, "truth" can be defined with varying degrees of statistical and other kinds of rigor.

In any event, we are quite aware of the question of the effects of our action on the flow of truthful information in the marketplace. Subsection E of the policy planning protocol is specifically designed to get at that issue. . . .

. . . You offer some general observations about "reasons for the lack of effectiveness" of a program such as ad substantiation: "clear-cut cases of misrepresentation or deception in advertising are identifiable, and few reputable corporations with nationally advertised brands are likely to resort to such practices intentionally where millions of dollars in sales and earnings are at stake and where the reputation of a given brand has been built over time."

. . . Whether the deception was intentional or not is essentially irrelevant under Section 5. That section is concerned with the actual marketplace impact of acts or practices. In the context of advertising, that concern is with the meanings to consumers, whether or not intended.

More generally, your observation appears to reflect a view that big corporations simply do not do anything deceptive or unfair because, among other things, they value their reputations too highly. I believe that there may be a fundamental logical fallacy in that kind of analysis, in that it proceeds from the *relative* incentives of major corporations to deceive to a conclusion that the *absolute* level of deception by them is so infrequent as not to be worthy of attention. In any event, the facts are otherwise. Actual experience tells us that some of the major instances of deception in recent years have involved major corporations with national advertised brands, including both durables and low priced packaged goods.

You [also state that]: "The problem lies in the major gray area where persuasion is subtle and the benefits alleged are essentially psychological. How on earth can the FTC prove whether a product would or would not 'make you feel good' or that over 60 percent of the users contacted were 'happy' with the products?"

I believe that you have set up a false dichotomy between blatant falsehoods on the one hand and, on the other, what is essentially puffery. There is, however, a broad middle range of claims in which the claim may be implied, and the violation is not simple or black and white, but, nevertheless, has occurred. That is, in fact, precisely the area in which we have been encountering the most problems in the ad substantiation program and in our enforcement efforts over the last few years. It simply is not accurate to say that problems in advertising consist of claims that are incapable of being assessed for their truth. Performance claims for automobiles or television sets, or denture cleansers, or OTC drug products, or hearing aids, are all matters in which we have been actively involved and which are clearly not of the "make you feel good" variety.

Finally, you ask whether the FTC would not be better advised to concentrate on "policing the extreme abuses" and leaving "the market and the consumer to ferret out the incompetent. . . ."

It is, of course, not our task to ferret out the incompetent. We are concerned, rather, with those who deceive or engage in unfair practices. In any event, the policy planning protocol to which I have earlier made reference is precisely designed to ask just this question, and, in fact, includes an express section on the question whether the market will punish the deception.

I must reiterate, however, that the dichotomy you pose here is a specious one. There is no inherent relationship between the extremity of the abuse and the capacity of the market to punish the deception. Indeed, to the extent that there is such a relationship, it is likely that the more extreme abuses are precisely those that the marketplace will punish so that the sense of your question, i.e., that we should concentrate on extreme abuses and let the market punish other kinds of abuse, is internally inconsistent. With respect to abuses that are not extreme, again, the market may or may not punish a particular deception. That is a judgment that must turn on the particular product attribute being advertised, and the claims being made—points which are elaborated in the policy planning protocol. . . .

Your reference to extreme abuses does, however, call to mind one further observation that bears on the Commission's fundamental role. When the Congress created the Commission, it denied its orders retroactive effect, limiting them to the control of future conduct, precisely because it wanted to provide the Commission with very broad *definitional* powers under Section 5 as to what it is that is deceptive or unfair. A very great Judge, Learned Hand, stated almost 40 years ago that the duty of the Commission "in part at any rate, is to discover and make explicit those unexpressed standards of fair dealing which the conscience of the community may progressively develop." *FTC* v. *Standard Education Society,* 86 F.2d 692, 696 (2d Cir. 1936), rev'd on other grounds, 302 U.S. 112 (1937). Obviously, if we were to concentrate only on extreme abuses, we would be abandoning that crucial role, i.e., to advance a bit the standards of the marketplace, and to enhance the opportunities for the scrupulous competitor.

I trust that this letter, and the accompanying enclosures, will be helpful to you. . . .

Sincerely yours,

Richard B. Herzog
Assistant Director for
National Advertising

APPENDIX C: EXTRACTS FROM *COMPLAINT,* UNITED STATES OF AMERICA, BEFORE THE FEDERAL TRADE COMMISSION, *IN THE MATTER OF GENERAL ELECTRIC COMPANY,* DOCKET NO. 9049, JULY 29, 1975

PARAGRAPH FOUR:* In the course and conduct of its said business, respondent General Electric Company has disseminated or caused the dis-

---

* Paragraph numbers correspond to those in the FTC complaint.

semination of, certain advertisements concerning the said products by the United States mails and by various means in or affecting commerce as "commerce" is defined in the Federal Trade Commission Act, for the purpose of inducing and which were likely to induce, directly or indirectly, the purchase of said products, and has disseminated and caused the dissemination of advertisements concerning said products by various means for the purpose of inducing and which is likely to induce, directly, or indirectly, the purchase of said products in or affecting commerce, as "commerce" is defined in the Federal Trade Commission Act.

PARAGRAPH FIVE: Typical of the representations and statements contained in said advertisements, disseminated as aforesaid, but not all inclusive thereof, are the following print advertisements which have been reproduced, attached to this complaint [Exhibits C–1 and C–2], and made a part hereof.

PARAGRAPH SIX: Through the dissemination of these advertisements and others similar thereto not specifically set out herein, respondent has represented directly or by implication that General Electric color television sets purchased or in use in 1973 required less service in that year than Zenith or RCA color television sets.

PARAGRAPH SEVEN: At the time of said representation, respondent did not possess and rely upon a reasonable basis for making such representation.

Therefore, the representation set forth in Paragraph Six was, and is, a deceptive or unfair act or practice.

PARAGRAPH EIGHT: Through the use of these advertisements and others similar thereto not specifically set out herein, respondent had represented directly or by implication that independent surveys of persons who had bought a color television set in 1973 show that General Electric color television sets bought in that year required less service during the initial period of ownership than all other U.S. brands of color television sets bought in 1973.

PARAGRAPH NINE: In truth and in fact, independent surveys of persons who had bought a color television set in 1973 did not and do not show that General Electric color television sets bought in that year required less service during the initial period of ownership than all other U.S. brands of color television sets bought in 1973.

Therefore, the representation referred to in Paragraph Eight was and is false, misleading and deceptive.

PARAGRAPH TWELVE: Respondent continued to disseminate the aforementioned advertisements, representing that 1973 survey evidence of service levels of General Electric color television sets is a reason to purchase such sets in 1974/75, when respondent knew of and had available to it subsequently acquired evidence of a substantially identical type and quality which contradicted or was inconsistent with the 1973 survey evidence expressly relied upon.

PARAGRAPH THIRTEEN: Therefore, at the time of the representation

EXHIBIT C–1

WHICH COLOR TV REQUIRED LESS SERVICE IN 1973?

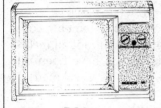 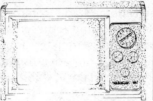 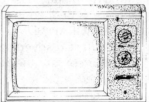

RCA   **GENERAL ELECTRIC**   **ZENITH**

In 1973, independent surveys* of recent color TV buyers showed that General Electric color required less service than any other U.S. brand. Not merely an opinion poll, this was a survey of actual TV owners. People like you, who expect the most in reliable TV performance for their money.

To get the kind of picture you expect for your money, go into a store and compare pictures. Ours against any other set.

The best way we know to buy color TV is to compare performance.

To help you compare, get GE's booklet, "How to Buy Color TV in Plain English." For the store nearest you, where you can pick it up free, call this special toll-free number anytime. 800-243-6000. Dial as you normally dial long distance. (In Connecticut, call 1-800-882-6500.)

PERFORMANCE TELEVISION

GENERAL ELECTRIC

*Details available on request

TV Receiver Products Dept., Portsmouth, Va.

Source: U.S. News & World Report, *October 7, 1974.*

EXHIBIT C–2

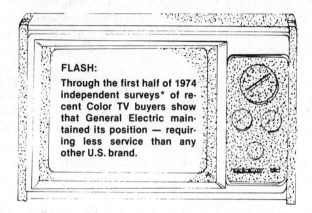

referred to in Paragraph Twelve respondent did not possess and rely upon a reasonable basis for making such representation, and the representation set forth in Paragraph Twelve was, and is, an unfair act or practice.

PARAGRAPH FOURTEEN: Furthermore, through its continued dissemination of the aforementioned advertisements, respondent represented, directly or by implication, that it neither knew of nor possessed evidence which contradicted or was inconsistent with the 1973 survey evidence expressly relied upon.

PARAGRAPH FIFTEEN: In truth and in fact, during the time respondent continued to disseminate the aforementioned advertisements, it did know of and possess evidence of an identical type and quality which contradicted or was inconsistent with the 1973 survey evidence expressly relied upon.

Therefore, the representation referred to in Paragraph Fourteen was false, misleading and deceptive.

PARAGRAPH SIXTEEN: Through the use of these advertisements and others similar thereto not specifically set out herein, it was represented directly or by implication that respondent would upon request forward the true and complete details regarding the comparative service information obtained from surveys of recent color television set buyers conducted in 1973.

PARAGRAPH SEVENTEEN: In truth and in fact, upon request respondent did not and does not forward the true and complete details regarding the comparative service information obtained from the surveys of recent color television set buyers conducted in 1973.

Therefore, the representation referred to in Paragraph Sixteen was false, misleading and deceptive.

PARAGRAPH EIGHTEEN: The use by the respondent of the aforesaid false, misleading, deceptive or unfair statements, representations and practices has had, and now has, the capacity and tendency to mislead members of the consuming public into the erroneous and mistaken belief that said statements and representations were and are true and into the purchase of substantial quantities of respondent's products by reason of said erroneous and mistaken belief.

PARAGRAPH NINETEEN: The aforesaid acts and practices of respondent, as herein alleged, were and are all to the prejudice and injury of the public and of respondent's competitors and constituted and now constitute, unfair and deceptive acts and practices and unfair methods of competition, in or affecting commerce, in violation of Section 5 of the Federal Trade Commission Act.

WHEREFORE, THE PREMISES CONSIDERED, the Federal Trade Commission on this 29th day of July, A.D. 1975, issues its complaint against said respondent.

APPENDIX D: MATSUSHITA ELECTRIC CORPORATION OF AMERICA, DOCKET NO. 9048, JULY 29, 1975

PARAGRAPH FOUR:* In the course and conduct of its business, respondent has disseminated and caused the dissemination of advertisements concerning the aforementioned products, including color television receivers, in or affecting commerce by means of advertisements printed in magazines and newspapers distributed by the mail and across state lines and transmitted by television stations located in various states of the United States and in the District of Columbia, having sufficient power to carry such broadcasts across state lines, for the purpose of inducing and which were likely to induce, directly or indirectly, the purchase of said products, including color television receivers.

PARAGRAPH FIVE: Among the advertisements disseminated or caused to be disseminated by respondent is the advertisement attached [Exhibit D–1], which includes the following statements and representations:

"In fact, the National Electronics Association rated the Quatrecolor CT-701 as the easiest to service of all color televisions they tested in plant through June 1973."

PARAGRAPH SIX: Through the aforesaid advertisement, respondent has represented directly or by implication that:

1. The test(s) conducted by the National Electronics Association ("NEA") in plant through June 1973 established that the Panasonic Quatrecolor CT-701 was the easiest to service of all color televisions tested.

2. The test(s) conducted by NEA in plant through June 1973 established that the Panasonic Quatrecolor CT-701 was the least expensive or least time-consuming to service of all color televisions tested.

3. A broad sample of major or well-known brands of color television sets was tested in plant by NEA through June 1973.

PARAGRAPH SEVEN: In truth and in fact:

1. The test(s) conducted by NEA did not, in fact, establish that the Panasonic Quatrecolor CT-701 was the easiest to service of all color televisions tested in plant by NEA through June 1973.

2. The test(s) conducted by NEA did not, in fact, establish that the Panasonic Quatrecolor CT-701 was the least expensive or least time-consuming to service of all color televisions tested in plant by NEA through June 1973.

3. A broad sample of major or well-known brands of color television sets was not tested in plant by NEA through June 1973.

---

* Paragraph numbers correspond to those in the FTC complaint.

EXHIBIT D-1

Therefore, the statements and representations contained in [Exhibit D–1], as set forth in PARAGRAPHS FIVE and SIX, were and are false, misleading and deceptive.

PARAGRAPH EIGHT: The use by the respondent of the aforesaid false, misleading and deceptive statements, representations and practices has had, and now has, the capacity and tendency to mislead members of the purchasing public into the erroneous mistaken belief that said statements and representations were and are true and into the purchase of substantial quantities of respondent's products by reason of said erroneous and mistaken belief.

PARAGRAPH NINE: The aforesaid acts and practices of respondent, as herein alleged, were and are all to the prejudice and injury of the public and of respondent's competitors and constituted and now constitute unfair and deceptive acts and practices and unfair methods of competition in or affecting commerce in violation of Section 5 of the Federal Trade Commission Act.

WHEREFORE, THE PREMISES CONSIDERED, the Federal Trade Commission on this 22nd day of July, A.D. 1975, issues its complaint against said respondent.

SELECTED BIBLIOGRAPHY

"FTC: Advertising Substantiation Requirements." 36 *Federal Register 12,058* (1972), pp. 23–24.

Garfield, Harry A. III. "Consumerism: A Law Enforcer's View." Speech before the Store Principals Meeting of Frederick Atkins, Inc., The Homestead, Hot Springs, Virginia, May 3, 1971.

"Importance of Being Adequate: Due Process Requirement in Class Actions Under Federal Rule 23." *University of Pennsylvania Law Review* 173 (May 1975): 1271.

Jones, Mary Gardiner. "Our Need for New Corporate Decision-Making Models." Address before the Second Annual Social Indicators Conference of the American Marketing Association, Washington, D.C., February 23, 1973.

Kirkpatrick, Miles. "Statement," U.S. Senate, Committee on Commerce, *Hearings on S.1461, Advertising 1972* (Washington, D.C.: U.S. Government Printing Office, 1972), pp. 23–24.

Markham, Jesse W. "Advertising: An Analysis of the Policy Issues." In *Business Problems of the Seventies,* ed. Jules Backman. New York: NY Press, 1973.

Preston, Ivan L. "A Comment on 'Defining Misleading Advertising' and 'Deception in Advertising.'" *Journal of Marketing* 40 (July 1976): 54–60.

Travers, A. H. "Foreword." *Kansas Law Review* 17 (1969): 551–57.

United States of America before the Federal Trade Commission. *Petition to the Federal Trade Commission (1) For rules to extend the advertising substantiation campaign to all advertising (2) To request substantiation for certain commercial advertisement by certain advertisers (3) And to Commence generally an advertisement substantiation campaign in the oil, utility and electric appliance industries in regard to environmental or energy-related claims in commercial advertisements.* Washington, D.C.: Media Access Project, January 9, 1974.

U.S. Congress, House, Committee on Appropriations, Subcommittee on Agriculture—Environmental and Consumer Protection. *Agriculture—Environmental and Consumer Protection Appropriations for 1973.* Washington, D.C.: U.S. Government Printing Office, 1972.

U.S. Congress, House, Committee on Government Operations, Subcommittee on Commerce, Consumer and Monetary Affairs. *Statement of Calvin J. Collier.* Washington, D.C.: U.S. Government Printing Office, June 24, 1976.

PART III

SOCIAL PRESSURE FOR CHANGES IN CORPORATE MARKETING AND PROMOTION PRACTICES

11 Proposition 9—The Clean Environment Act of 1972*: Selling of an idea— in the public interest

All of us get our thoughts entangled in metaphors, and act fatally on the strength of them.

George Elliot, *Middle March*

On June 6, 1972, the California voters rejected Proposition 9, The Clean Environment Act of 1972, by a margin of almost 2 to 1. The proposition had received widespread local and national publicity as a fight between David and Goliath, between big business and little people, between vested interests backed by powerful political and financial resources and citizen groups spontaneously created to fight for a cause they believed in against heavy odds. It was an excellent example of the interplay between various interest groups—business, the social activists, the conservationists—all clamoring to protect the public interest. It was the first major test of the strength and political savvy of a nonprofit, politically activist group called People's Lobby, the prime mover behind the initiative. The group opposing the passage of the initiative was also appropriately named Californians Against the Pollution Initiative (CAPI).

Note: Unless otherwise specifically stated, all direct quotations attributed to various spokespeople are from personal interviews and written communications with the author.

* Reprinted from S. Prakash Sethi, *Advocacy Advertising and Large Corporations: Social Conflict, Big Business Image, the News Media, and Public Policy* (Lexington, Mass.: D. C. Heath and Co., copyright © 1977).

PAID MASS COMMUNICATION IN PUBLIC POLICIES AND POLITICAL PROGRAMS

Apart from the interests of the various parties involved and the legitimacy of their cause, the case provides an excellent study in the art of public persuasion in a pluralistic society and in the process of public policy formulation by the citizenry at large when publicly elected officials have been unable or unwilling to enact programs and legislation in a given direction. The fascination of the case and its major importance as an analytical tool lies in the fact that it is an attempt to sell an idea or a promise.

In the case of products and services, the seller offers a tangible product and fulfillment of certain needs and desires the buyer wants satisfied. The tangible nature of the product or service provides a link between the seller and the buyer, thereby making the job of communication simpler and more straightforward. The political campaign offers a higher level of complexity; it is selling a promise of performance in the future. But even here the public can relate to the candidate, and if he or she has previously run for a public office, evaluate promises and appeals in terms of past performance.

The selling of a mere idea is a still higher level of abstraction and presents a more difficult and complex problem in persuasion. In most cases, the recipient of the message is only vaguely aware of a need for what the communicator of the idea is selling and is not sure whether he wants it, to what extent, in what form, and at what cost. The promise of delivery is almost always in the future, and the rewards are generally esthetic or intangible in nature—clean air, better quality of life, preservation of life. The rewards are also likely to be in the nature of public goods. Thus, the communicatee may not enjoy any special privileges as a result of buying (voting for) this service. Nor is that person deprived of the enjoyment of the public goods thus created if he or she declines to vote for community purchase of such services.

Although the promised benefits lie in the uncertain future, the costs in terms of taxes, high prices, and restrictions on personal consumption and life styles may be immediate and real. Furthermore, although the benefits may be shared equally by all members of a community, the costs may fall disproportionately on various buyers, depending on income, home ownership, or some other similar criterion. The promisers of rewards are generally unknown groups with no prior track record who purport to act in the public interest; the groups that oppose the sale of these ideas also present themselves as acting in the interest of the communicatee. These groups have an apparent vested interest in seeing that the idea does not succeed. Thus, although their credibility may be suspect, the projected costs to the communicatee appear more realistic and therefore frightening.

ISSUES FOR ANALYSIS

Use of mass media and paid communication to sell a particular political program to the public raises important questions of public policy that range from political propaganda and brainwashing to the right of an individual or a group to state a position publicly and to persuade others to join with them. On a broader level:

1. Along what dimensions can we measure the effectiveness of advocacy-type advertising campaigns by large corporations and industry groups? What are some of the short- and long-run criteria by which business should measure effectiveness?

2. The large-scale use of paid communication in a political campaign by industry has been criticized as "campaign buying." But other kinds of groups, such as volunteers, have resources not ordinarily available to industry. Should a limit be set on the total amount of spending, both in cash and in kind, permitted for a particular political campaign? Should there be restrictions on individual components of campaign spending to provide a balance of resources between opposing groups? What are some of the legal and sociopolitical implications of imposing these restrictions?

3. Should companies and industry groups be allowed to consider the costs of mass media campaigns normal expenses of doing business and therefore tax deductible? In this case, the expenses will be passed on to the consumer in the form of higher prices to the extent that competitive conditions in the market will allow it, or higher rates in the case of utilities. If these advertisements are regarded as essentially political in nature, shouldn't the stockholders pay for them?

4. If the purpose of those communication programs is to educate and inform the public, should there be some mechanism to ensure accuracy and truthfulness? Commercial communications are currently subject to the substantiation requirements of the Federal Trade Commission, while drug advertising is controlled by the Federal Food and Drug Administration. If advocacy advertisements by businesses are considered normal business responses, should they be subject to "truth-in-advertising" laws and the companies obliged to substantiate the claims made in them before the Federal Trade Commission, or before some other forum?

5. If the industry advertisements are considered wholly or partly political in nature, is there a need to provide for a right of reply? Can such a right be guaranteed without at the same time abridging the free speech rights of the corporation involved? Although the fairness doctrine in broadcasting has so far been applied in only one case (cigarette advertising), this has had the effect of barring all advocacy or even slightly controversial advertising from the broadcast media. Is there

a need for some protection for the opposing view and its exposure before the public? What are the existing channels of such exposure, and are they adequate?

6. What other measures are possible to enable various groups to state their viewpoints publicly on a controversial social issue, increase the quality of information available to the public, and thereby contribute to the improvement of public decision-making?

With respect to the campaigns of CAPI and the People's Lobby for Proposition 9, the pertinent questions for analysis are these:

1. How useful and desirable is the initiative process? What are the strengths and weakness of Proposition 9 as it was drawn? What are the major distinctions in the objectives and strategies pursued by the opposing groups?

2. What are the relative weights placed by CAPI on the various elements of the communication mix?

3. What are the major themes pursued in the two campaigns? To what extent are they related to the problems faced by the society at large? In terms of tactics, how did the two groups exploit each other's weaknesses in pursuing their objectives during the campaign?

4. To what extent do the advertisements present a balanced and objective picture of differing viewpoints? How do they contribute to the quality of information and the public debate on this specific issue? How have the complex issues been presented? Does the attempt at simplifying end in misleading rather than educating the public?

5. What were the main factors that led to the defeat of the People's Lobby? How well have the lessons learned in the fight for Proposition 9 been applied in similar campaigns since 1972? In 1974 People's Lobby was successful in the passage of a political reform initiative in California. The 1976 election year witnessed the biggest crop of public-initiated referendums in various states, with mixed results.[1]

THE INITIATIVE

The initiative is a device that empowers the people of California to directly initiate laws. It is identical to laws enacted by the legislature, with one exception: "An initiative statute may not be amended, except by another initiative statute or by a statute passed by the legislature and ap-

---

[1] See for example: "Nuclear Plant Critics Fighting for Passage of Safety and Liability Curbs in Six States," *The Wall Street Journal*, October 7, p. 36; "Those Nuclear Initiatives," *The Wall Street Journal*, November 2, 1976, p. 16; "Voters Approve Expanding Use of Nuclear Units," *The Wall Street Journal*, November 4, 1976, p. 4; "Coastal Acquisition—Yes on 2," *Los Angeles Times*, November 1, 1976, part 2, p. 6; Lynd McCormack, "An Anti-Goal: Bottle Up the Non-Returnables," *Los Angeles Times*, November 2, 1976; "Farm Labor Initiative: No on 14," *Los Angeles Times*, October 29, 1976, p. 6; William Endicott, "Farm Labor, Dog Racing Issues Lose," *Los Angeles Times*, November 3, 1976, p. 1.

proved by the people, unless the original initiative statute provides to the contrary.[2]

In November 1970, an initiative petition sponsored by the People's Lobby was filed with the California attorney general and the secretary of state. In May 1971, the secretary of state certified that the clean environment initiative would appear on the June 6, 1972, election ballot; People's Lobby had obtained the required number of signatures. The official ballot summary read as follows:

> Primary Election, June 6, 1972. Proposition 9, Environment Initiative. Specifies permissible composition and quality of gasoline and other fuels for internal combustion engines. Authorizes shutting down of businesses and factories violating air pollution standards. Imposes restrictions on leasing and extraction of oil and gas from tidelands or submerged lands, or onshore areas within one mile of mean high tide line. Prohibits construction of atomic powered electric generating plants for five years. Establishes restrictions on manufacture, sale, and use of pesticides. Prohibits enforcement officials from having conflicting interests. Provides for relief by injunction and mandate to prevent violations. Imposes penal action and civil penalties.[3]

Proposition 9 contained 23 sections aimed at rewriting a good portion of the California pollution control laws. The affected issue areas were these:

1. Air pollution—stationary and vehicular sources (Sections 3, 4, 5, 6, 8, and Sections 2 and 11)
2. Energy development—oil drilling and nuclear facility construction (Sections 12, 13, 16, and 17)
3. Pesticides—chlorinated hydrocarbons (Section 18)
4. Government procedure—public information access, conflict of interest, class actions, repeal, and amendment (Sections 7, 9, 10, 14, 15, 19, 20, 21, 22, and 23).

PEOPLE'S LOBBY, INC.

The chief architects of Proposition 9 were the husband and wife team of the late Edwin Koupal and Joyce Koupal, and the nonprofit organization they launched in 1969 and called People's Lobby, Inc. A nonprofit organization, People's Lobby operates from a headquarters it owns near Los Angeles. It functions with a mostly volunteer staff that varies in size, but according to Joyce Koupal averages around fifty members. Only four employees are salaried. The size of the organization in terms of number

---

[2] Portfolio of documents prepared by People's Lobby, 1971.

[3] "Initiative Measure to be Submitted Directly to the Electors," as reprinted in Kahl Associates, *Policy Analysis of the California Pollution Initiative* (Washington, D.C., February 1972), p. 411.

of members is not easily discernible. Assemblyman Brown asserts "they have almost no members"; and Leo McCarthy, also an assemblyman from San Francisco, claims People's Lobby is "a paper membership, the whole thing is run by four or five people."[4] Mrs. Koupal, however, explains that the claimed membership of 20,000 stems from the fact that 20,000 people have donated money to the Lobby. The mailing list was prepared from financial statements filed with the secretary of state. By running initiatives and educating people concerning its side of the controversy, People's Lobby claims to provide voters with opposing information concerning an issue. In Joyce Koupal's opinion,

> If people have all the facts and they want to vote something in, that's fine. . . . People get a one-sided view of the facts. They are stampeded into making decisions which are probably not in their best interest and they don't even know it. And so what we have been trying to do is equalize what is happening.

Launching the initiative

The Koupals, with the aid of volunteer attorney Roger Jon Diamond and other interested persons, drafted the Clean Environment Act, as it was called by its proponents. It was originally named the Pollution Initiative by the California attorney general, and was referred to as the Environment Initiative on the official ballot.[5]

To qualify the initiative for the ballot, 325,000 valid signatures were required. People's Lobby volunteers were able to obtain 339,000 signatures —220,000 in Los Angeles County and 180,000 in the twenty-seven other counties. The next step was to translate voter's addresses into precinct numbers, a cumbersome and time-consuming task, so that they could be checked by a county registrar.

Financing the campaign

People's Lobby did not have any major contributors and therefore resorted to innovative ways of generating small donations whose cost of collection was minimal. One of these was by using bicycle riders in a campaign called "Bike for Life." Using its then only paid employee, People's Lobby went throughout the state getting people—usually schoolchildren —to ride a bicycle over a 30- to 40-mile route. The riders would obtain their own sponsors.[6] The program raised $174,032 in the 1972 fiscal year.

---

[4] Jerry Carrol, "People's Lobby—A Thorn for Politicians," *San Francisco Chronicle*, April 7, 1975, p. 9.

[5] *People's Lobby* v. *Reinecke*, Los Angeles Superior Court, Decision No. WEC 25264, 1972.

[6] Richard R. Leger, "Sweeping 'Clean Environment' Referendum in California Looks Too Close to Call Now," *The Wall Street Journal*, June 1, 1972, p. 25.

The entire initiative campaign was largely supported through small individual contributions, with the exception of two large contributions of $1,000 each from actor Paul Newman and Congressman Fortney H. Stark (D., California). A significant amount of support also came through membership dues—$10 for adults and $2 for students. The total resources available to run the campaign eventually amounted to $233,421.05, of which $82,348, or 35 percent, was donated in amounts of $25 or less.

In contrast, opponents of the initiative received a total of $586 in contributions of less than $25. The campaign expenditures of People's Lobby in supporting Proposition 9 amounted to approximately 12.56 percent of the $1,483,971 spent by the opposition. Although the difference in spending is substantial, it does not convey the whole story. People's Lobby was able to get the necessary signatures for the initiative petition by using volunteers. In the actual campaign, People's Lobby used ingenious methods to garner as much free publicity as possible and thereby reduce the need for cash. Thus, People's Lobby's campaign activities were greater than its expenditures would indicate.

The campaign strategy

The People's Lobby campaign strategy had three main components:

1. To secure the support of influential opinion leaders, especially among such established conservation and environmental groups as the Sierra Club; of congressmen and legislators; of the League of Women Voters; and of activist groups and students.
2. To develop an effective means of refuting the charges of the opposition—Californians Against the Pollution Initiative, large corporations and industry groups, and individual opinion leaders.
3. To create public awareness and understanding of the position of People's Lobby and generate support for Proposition 9 through mass media campaigns.

People's Lobby realized from the start that it must have broad-based community support in order to succeed. (To achieve this end, the initiative was drafted in terms that would encompass the concerns of all environmental and conservation groups. This also opened the initiative to the charge of being vague and of requiring much legislation.) People's Lobby was able to put together a group of attorneys, businesspeople, associated student unions, educators, environmental organizations and individuals, labor organizations, physicians, and politicians. Unfortunately, this was not enough. Inadequate support was particularly critical in the case of People's Lobby because of its lack of financial resources and the need for volunteers. Among the environmental organizations, the reputable and well-established Sierra Club chose to remain neutral.

Another major element in the drive for community support was door-to-door canvassing with volunteers and holding small-group discussions and seminars. The proponents of the initiative also made use of their supporters whenever they could. For example, the "Voter's Argument for the Clean Environment Act," as it appeared in the official argument on the ballot, was signed by William M. Bennett, member of the California State Board of Equalization and an attorney; Congressman Fortney H. Stark; and Hifinio Romo, United Rubber Workers Union 131, AFL-CIO. Inside the cover of this reprint of both official arguments and rebuttals was a copy of the letter from the United Rubber, Cork, Linoleum, and Plastic Workers of America, signed by Mr. Romo, the union treasurer.[7]

People's Lobby felt that one of the ways to undermine the credibility of its opponents and also bring to public attention "the inaccuracies and falsehoods on which their campaign was based" was to expose the underlying motives of those who sought to defeat Proposition 9. When asked whether these tactics did not amount to a smear campaign and a strategy of coercion, the late Mr. Koupal replied:

> I will use any of the political tools available to me as long as I don't break the law. Too many times we find the people who call themselves environmentalists, civil rightists, etc., idealistically say "we are not going to do the same thing our opposition does." "Even if we lose, we know we lose with the highest morals." Well, I don't agree with that at all. It is your idea and your law, and if you feel honest enough to have written it in the first place to bring it to the voters, then you should use all tools available to you that the political machine of the day will afford you.

Sympathizers assisted People's Lobby by anonymously providing evidence that was embarrassing and potentially incriminating to the opposition. One of the more important pieces of this type, and the one People's Lobby tried to publicize the most, was the Miller Memorandum (Exhibit 11–1). This memorandum, dated June 4, 1971, was addressed to Mr. Otto

EXHIBIT 11–1

June 4, 1971

People's Lobby Initiative

Mr. O. N. Miller
18th Floor
Building

As you requested, this memorandum outlines the most urgent questions that must be faced in connection with the so-called "clean environment" initiative, which the People's Lobby has qualified for the primary election in June, 1972. A copy of CMA's summary of the proposal is attached.

---

[7] People's Lobby, *Pro and Con* (1971), p. 2.

EXHIBIT 11–1 *(continued)*

Selection of "Front" Organization

From discussions with people who are more or less my counterparts in other oil, gas and electric companies, I have learned that some companies are proposing that the California Chamber of Commerce should be the "front" to organize and manage the campaign against this measure. There are also some indications that the staff of the California Manufacturers Association might like to be the focal point of the campaign.

While the support of both of these organizations will be valuable, the choice of either to front the campaign would, in my judgment, be a serious mistake. Both are much too identified in the public mind with business interests, and either would evoke a certain amount of unnecessary negative public reaction.

I believe it would be far better to organize a citizens committee with a very broad base, including well-known conservationists, Democrats, labor leaders, and minority group leaders. I am confident that this can be done if skillful campaign managers are employed to do it.

The Role of Governor Reagan

I have also learned that there is a fair amount of sentiment within the business community to ask Governor Reagan to spearhead the organization of a campaign effort against the measure. I think that too would be a mistake. The people behind this measure are the same ones who circulated petitions to recall Governor Reagan some time back, and they would delight in having him as a target. I think too, that Governor Reagan would be no great asset with respect to the 18, 19 and 20 year-olds who may be voting by June, 1972. Certainly, the Governor's support, along with that of responsible Democrats, should be sought in due course, but I do not think he should be asked to take the lead.

Selection of Campaign Managers

Both Spencer, Roberts and Whitaker & Baxter have let it be known that they would like to be chosen to manage the campaign against this measure. As I have told you before, I think these are the two best campaign organizations in California, and I strongly urge that one or both of them be retained. I believe this step not only is important in winning the campaign, but also in avoiding the extraneous difficulties that often result when less experienced people manage a campaign.

As between these two firms, my recommendation for this particular job would be Whitaker & Baxter. I think the record is clear that Whitaker & Baxter has more experience and more success in running campaigns on measures than has Spencer, Roberts. I believe Whitaker & Baxter also has broader and better contacts with Democrats, labor leaders, agriculture, conservationists, and other elements of the community who have perhaps as great, if less direct, a stake in this measure as the energy companies. Spencer, Roberts is almost entirely Republican oriented and has specialized in elections of candidates rather than ballot issues.

Urgency

While I think it is important that the citizens most directly concerned choose a campaign manager who can start organizing a citizens committee at an early date, I believe it is even more urgent to head-off the efforts I mentioned above to put the Chamber of Commerce and the Governor into positions of leadership in organizing the campaign. If you agree, you might wish to make your views known to Mr. Burnham Enersen and others before leaving the city for any extended period.

James L. Wanvig [initialed]

Enc.
cc: Messrs. James E. O'Brien
George T. Ballou

N. Miller, chairman of the board, Standard Oil of California, San Francisco (SOCAL) by his lobbyist, Mr. James L. Wanvig.[8] In this memo, Mr. Wanvig recommends that SOCAL urgently take steps to launch a counterattack against "the so-called 'Clean Evironment Initiative.'" The memo enclosed a copy of a "Preliminary Plan Against the People's Lobby Initiative" (see the section on the opponents), prepared by Whitaker & Baxter, a San Francisco-based public relations firm, and recommended that this firm be retained to organize and conduct the campaign against Proposition 9. The original memo, a copy of which was reproduced by People's Lobby, contains handwritten notes by Mr. Miller indicating his agreement with all the points made by Mr. Wanvig.

In another case, People's Lobby obtained copies of letters written by executives of Gulf Energy and Environmental Systems to employees and supervisors of the corporation. The letters pointed out the sections of the initiative that directly affected Gulf operations and urged a No vote. One letter spelled out the following requirement:

> Any employee who is invited or who volunteers to make a speech, prepare an abstract, or present a paper before any group or organization; prepare an article for any publication; or be interviewed by any publication editor or reporter must obtain in advance of any commitment the approval of the appropriate division vice president, division director, or other officer to whom he is accountable.[9]

People's Lobby also publicly attacked prominent members of the Californians Against the Pollution Initiative for selling out to big money. The following exchange between the author and Mr. and Mrs. Koupal explains their rationale for such tactics:

Sethi: It seems to me that by attacking the integrity of various prominent citizens and also exaggerating the environmental dangers if the initiative is not enacted into law, you were using the same smear and scare tactics you accused the opposition of.

Edwin Koupal: I do not like the words "smear tactics." Whitaker & Baxter filled their citizens committee with people who had some ax to grind or something they had to protect. They put up Dr. Emil Mrak (Chancellor emeritus, University of California, Davis) as a great white father. They have the power to give money and grants to professors who then go out and bastardize the grant system and their Ph.D.s. Another element is the financial involvement of these people in the industry itself. How can a professor like Emil Mrak stand up in front of the students and teach them about pesticides when he has a financial interest in the selling of pesticides and it makes him a fortune?

[8] "Memorandum dated June 4, 1971, from James L. Wanvig to O. N. Miller," reprinted in People's Lobby, *Proposition 9, The Political Reform Act—A Fact for California, A Proposal for America* (Los Angeles, July 1974), pp. 58–59. (Hereinafter referred to as *The Political Reform Act.*)

[9] Gulf Energy and Environmental Systems letters in the California State Archives.

When you take Tom Lantos (another CAPI supporter), who has actually taken state funds, and expose him to the public, that is not a smear campaign, that is truth and fact and something that should be made public knowledge.

Joyce Koupal: We did not use scare tactics in our advertising either. It was CAPI that ran ads saying since we are trying to get rid of the DDT that kills mosquitoes, we must therefore love mosquitoes, that we are a religious cult that worships the mosquito and I am the head religious leader. . . .

Whitaker & Baxter's strategies for running national campaigns have not changed over the years. They emphasize the development of opinion leaders, finding them, keeping in touch with them, and convincing them with one-to-one communication, and burying them in tons of material. . . .

The buying of every kind of news media and "types of personalities" that we all have is hit from every angle; you may be a husband, a father, a hunter, a businessman, etc. Ads are bought and articles run favoring W&B's perspective in every special-interest newspaper, magazine, and newsletter. You get hit with the short, hard message everywhere you look, and from every aspect of your personality. Over and over—you are buried in the message—and it works.

The media campaign

Of the total campaign expenditures of $186,511 for Proposition 9, People's Lobby spent 25 percent on radio air time and recording expenditures, 13 percent on magazines and newspapers, 15 percent on printing and other media, and less than 3 percent on television and videotape. The remaining funds were allocated to postage and shipping (4.5 percent) and miscellaneous expenditures (39.5 percent). Lack of financing did not affect the professional quality of the ad message or the production of commercials. People's Lobby was able to attract professional people who donated their time and resources to produce first-rate magazine and newspaper advertisements and radio and television commercials.

The largest part of the media campaign was devoted to airing 60-second and 30-second radio commercials concentrated between May 23 and June 5, 1972 (the last two weeks of the campaign period). In all, a total of 2,567 spots were used, with about 50 percent going to the Los Angeles area and the remaining distributed in the rest of California. In addition, newspaper ads of varying sizes were used at the rate of one insertion per newspaper in twenty local and regional newspapers and magazines. A considerable amount of People's Lobby resources was devoted to a direct mail campaign in an effort to reach potential contributors and voters. TV advertising was almost nonexistent: three commercials were produced and occasionally aired. According to Bernice F. Livingston of Diener/Hauser/Greenthal, a Los Angeles-based advertising agency:

We developed a careful plan to buy time in order to achieve maximum audience reach and frequency. However, unpredictability of finances made the plan implementation quite difficult. Despite these handicaps, we were able to reach most of our targeted audience by concentrating on the densely populated areas and also putting most of our resources in radio during the final weeks of the campaign.

Exhibit 11–2 gives the text of some specimen radio commercials used

EXHIBIT 11–2

TEXT OF PEOPLE'S LOBBY RADIO COMMERCIALS

No. 1. What happens if something goes wrong with a nuclear power plant? (Sound effect: very long sustained blast)

An accident could cause Hiroshima-like destruction. The Atomic Energy Commission found out last year that the fail-safe devices on nuclear power plants don't necessarily work. . . . Proposition Nine calls for a little sanity in terms of nuclear power plants. . . . Let's check into them a little more before we start stringing them the length and breadth of earthquake-prone California. . . .

Vote Yes on Proposition Nine . . . The Clean Environment Act . . . You'll be voting for better health, more jobs, a stronger economy . . . and a safe place to live. . . .

Vote Yes on Proposition Nine. . . .

No. 2. Why should you vote *Yes* on Proposition Nine?

It seems that the little guy always pays the way for big industry. . . .

Right now we've got economic controls . . . wages are controlled. . . . But prices are rising . . . and industrial profits get bigger every day . . . they make the money . . . you pay the taxes. . . . Industry makes a mess . . . *your* tax money pays to clean it up. . . .

It's time to tell the big guys that you're tired of paying for their profits . . . tell them you're tired of living in a filthy environment that they've created. . . .

Tell them that you're voting for your health . . . and the health of your children . . . tell them by voting *Yes* on Proposition Nine . . . the Clean Environment Act.

No. 3. My uncle is dying of emphysema and the oil companies are telling me that I need lead in my gasoline. . . .

I'm not buying that . . . and I'm not buying their lead. . . .

I'm voting *Yes* on Proposition Nine . . . that's the Clean Environment Act.

Vote *Yes* on Proposition Nine . . . The Clean Environment Act.

No. 4. You've probably been hearing a lot about how much money it'll cost to clean up pollution . . . and it's always tax money they're talking about . . . your money and my money. . . .

EXHIBIT 11–2 *(continued)*

Proposition Nine changes all that. . . . It requires the industries that create pollution to pay for cleaning it up. . . .

Let's put the responsibility back where it belongs. . . . They made the mess . . . they should clean it up. . . .

Vote *yes* on Proposition Nine . . . The Clean Environment Act. . . . Vote *yes* for a better place to live. . . .

No. 5.   Yes we all drive cars . . . Yes we all need fuel to run the cars . . . but no we don't have to ruin our cities and countrysides by polluting ourselves beyond salvation. . . . Concerned citizens created Proposition Nine . . . The Clean Environment Act . . . concerned citizens *must* vote yes on Proposition Nine on June 6th. . . .

You won't lose your car . . . You won't lose your job . . . You may save your life. . . . Clean days shouldn't be a once in a while special treat . . . Clean days *can be* an everyday. . . . You owe it to the birds and trees and the fish *and* yourself to vote *Yes* June 6th on Proposition Nine.

by People's Lobby. The commercials contain multimessages generally of the negative type—namely, warning of health hazards, big business manipulation of government and people, and what pollution can do to the quality of life for present and future generations if the measures proposed in Proposition 9 are not enacted.

The newspaper and magazine ads are reproduced in Exhibits 11–3 to 11–7. Some of the advertisements have long messages. Exhibit 11–5 provides a long list of people who have endorsed Proposition 9. Against this list, the ad carries a big headline and four categories of people who are against the proposition. The names mentioned are oil companies, power companies, big industrial polluters, and the chemical industry. The nonendorsers occupy less than 5 percent of the ad space. Television commercials are presented in Exhibits 11–8 and 11–9. Exhibit 11–8 is a 5-minute commercial that discusses substantive issues involved in Proposition 9.

It was noted earlier that People's Lobby mailed hundreds of thousands of copies of the Miller memorandum. In addition, the Lobby published an economic analysis of the effects of the passage of the Clean Environment Act initiative and distributed it among concerned citizens. Entitled "Economics of a Clean Environment,"[10] the document detailed the losses to property, agriculture, and human health due to pollution; the costs of cleaning the environment through controlling emissions; the savings made in agriculture, fuel, motor vehicle operations, and better health with a cleaner environment; and additional jobs that would be created through increased activity in pollution control areas.

---

[10] People's Lobby, *Economics of a Clean Environment* (Los Angeles: People's Lobby Press, 1971).

EXHIBIT 11–3

YES
ON 9

The Clean
Environment
Act

EXHIBIT 11–4

IT'S TIME FOR THE PEOPLE TO ACT

Some Facts About Proposition 9

It's time for us to let the special interests know that we the people are running California. California belongs to us and we will not allow them to despoil and pollute her any longer. The legislature has known for more than a year and a half that Proposition 9 was going to be on the ballot June 6, 1972, but in all that time they have not been able to enact one pollution control measure, let alone one which might be better than Proposition 9. The special interests do not want to clean up. We the people must act. We must vote for Proposition 9, the Clean Environment Act.

TOGETHER WE CAN BUILD A STRONGER ECONOMY

We can make California the center of a whole new industry—the pollution control industry. Many economists think pollution control will be a bigger industry in the next thirty years than aerospace has been in the past thirty years. When we pass Proposition 9, we will create a market for pollution control devices. This means more jobs. As we build such equipment, the rest of the nation will demand that their air and water be cleaned up too, and California will become the supplier to the nation and ultimately the world. California led the way in demanding auto emission controls. Now we will lead the way in demanding a truly healthy and clean environment.

WE CAN'T BE FOOLED AGAIN

We won't accept the old either/or argument—"either you and your children breathe dirty air, or you will lose your job." It's far cheaper to clean up a dirty smokestack or filthy sewer than it is to move a whole factory to another location. (Another location which doesn't want their pollution anyway and where they would have to build the same pollution control devices we are demanding here.) However, the cheapest thing of all is to scare us, to keep us from writing and enforcing anti-pollution laws, then the special interests, the polluters, don't have to do anything at all. We have to pay the costs of their pollution—in health care costs, mentally retarded children, property damage and lowered property values. It's time for the polluters to pay the costs—the costs of cleaning up their own filth.

LET'S ANSWER SOME OF THEIR ARGUMENTS WITH SOME FACTS

POWER FAILURES

We are more likely to have power failures if Proposition 9 does NOT pass than if it does succeed. Our power companies have tried to rush us into nuclear fission power plant construction before all the dangers and problems have been adequately solved. Most people do not want a nuclear power plant built near them, and the delays in construction of these plants have been and will continue to be very great.

When Proposition 9 passes, the power companies will be forced to consider other sources of power, at least for the next five years. Some immediate expansion of present fossil fuel (oil and gas) plants is possible and can be accomplished much more quickly to take care of our immediate needs. Proposition 9 assures that these fossil fuel plants will be clean and not pollute the atmosphere. In the Los Angeles basin today, where anti-pollution laws are tougher, electrical plants contribute 1.1 percent to our pollution problem.

In the long run, better, cheaper, safer, and completely clean power supplies can be developed. Geothermal power (power created by using the steam from beneath the earth's surface), is already being used in some parts of California, Italy, Japan and Israel. The largest geothermal fields in the world are beneath California, and Proposition 9 with its five year moratorium on the construction of nuclear fission power plants will encourage their development.

Other possibilities include the use of fuel cells like the ones which powered the men on the moon. Solar power, magnetohydrodynamic generators (MHD), nuclear fusion power, and even using power of the wind or the tides are being suggested by scientists who are concerned about pollution.

In the past thirty years, 84 percent of our research into energy sources has gone into nuclear fission energy, while truly clean sources have been neglected. Proposition 9 will help to bring a rethinking of our energy goals, research and sources.

NUCLEAR POWER

Nuclear fission power is Not Clean. Radiation pollution is a serious problem. Last November a nuclear power plant in Minnesota poured 50,000 gallons of radioactive wastes into the Mississippi River just above the water intakes for Minneapolis-St. Paul. Before these intakes could be closed, some of the cities' water supply was contaminated, to say nothing of the River itself. Accidents have occurred at many nuclear facilities, but so far only the lives of workers in these plants have been sacrificed. Since nothing which involves people is infallible, how soon before an entire city or region of the country is contaminated with radiation?

According to the Atomic Energy Commission, the safety devices on nuclear power plants have not been properly tested. When one type of fail-safe device was tested last year, it failed. The result was that out of a total of eight nuclear power plants now in operation, three were asked to shut down until they modified their safety equipment while the other five were asked to operate at 30 to 40 percent of total capacity. Thus nuclear fission power is not even a reliable source of electricity, since new emergencies may cause new shutdowns. Also nuclear fission is a temporary expedient, since we have only enough fuel to power these plants for about thirty years, and then even more dangerous breeder plants must be used to increase our supply of nuclear fuel.

The products of nuclear fission are highly dangerous, and if they escape into our air or water, they will last MANY THOUSANDS of years. Plutonium 239 has a half-life of 24,000 YEARS. This means that if you put one pound of plutonium into the atmosphere today, one-half pound will still be there in 24,000 years! So far we still do not have an adequate means of disposing of nuclear power plant wastes which will add up to tons of lethal material in a very few years. The whole of written human history has only lasted for 10,000 years, so how can we guarantee that we can guard these nuclear wastes for thousands of years to make sure they do not contaminate the earth, its air and its water?

What happens if a truck or train carrying nuclear wastes or fuels has an accident?

What happens if an earthquake damages a plant in California? At present, the San Onofre plant is built to withstand an earthquake force of 1/2 G (1/2 the force of gravity). The February 1971 earthquake in Los Angeles was measured at a force of 1 G—twice the capacity of the San Onofre plant. What would happen if a nuclear power plant were near the epicenter of a major quake?

We believe a five year moratorium on nuclear fission power plant construction is only a minimum requirement when we are talking about earthquakes and 24,000 years of radiation pollution.

The opposition claims that removing the lead from gasoline in four years will make it impossible for you to drive your cars which are presently in use. THIS IS NOT TRUE.

The standards proposed by Proposition 9 are identical to the standards proposed by the Environmental Protection Agency. The State of California has also proposed the same standards, but they would allow five years to phase them in instead of four.

What will this do to your car? You will need a tuneup of your engine in which the mechanic will retard the spark and possibly change the spark plugs on your car. In some cases, you will have to put in a thicker head gasket to reduce the compression ratio slightly. (The costs of all this are $3.50 for a head gasket and about two hours labor—top price, maybe $20.) However,

EXHIBIT 11-4 *(continued)*

since most cars are phased out of service after five years, it has been estimated by the California Air Resources Board, that 85 to 95 percent of the cars on the road in 1976 will have been produced since 1971, and all these cars will operate on lead-free gasoline.

LEADED GASOLINE CONTRIBUTES SUBSTANTIALLY TO THE HIGH LEVEL OF ATMOSPHERIC LEAD AND CONSTITUTES AN EXTREMELY SERIOUS HEALTH HAZARD.

Lead is a toxic element which can produce liver, kidney and brain damage and deterioration of the central nervous system. Children are especially susceptible to lead poisoning; among them mental retardation and other signs of central nervous system involvement are common. The California State Air Resources Board Standard is 1.5 micrograms per cubic meter of air. Los Angeles has the highest concentration of lead in the air of all major American cities, 5.7 micrograms per cubic meter on the average. A concentration of lead in the air in L.A. County as high as 71.3 micrograms per cubic meter has been recorded during a peak traffic period. This is 47 times the California standard!

PESTICIDES

Opponents say we will have epidemic diseases and termites if we do not use the types of pesticides banned by Proposition 9. THIS IS NOT TRUE.

These persistent pesticides like DDT have only been in existence for about 30 years, yet the epidemics the opponents predict such as malaria or yellow fever have been unknown in California for many years prior to the introduction of these pesticides. However, should such an epidemic or other emergency occur, the legislature may, by four-fifths majority vote, authorize the use of such pesticides. Legislatures can and have acted quickly in emergencies, so this seems to be a reasonable precaution against such disaster.

We now know the devastating side effects of persistent chemical pesticides and herbicides on the reproductive systems of certain sea and bird life, and most scientists who have studied the problem agree that the dangers to man are such that banning of such pesticides is mandatory. Some of the herbicides being used in California have already been banned for use in Viet Nam by our military because they cause birth defects in children. The Environmental Protection Agency of the U.S. government has already recommended a complete ban on DDT and other persistent pesticides because they are not needed in the United States, and their dangers are well known.

The opposition claims we are banning the only known pesticide for termite control. THIS IS NOT SO. Diatumaceous earth is a safe and acceptable substitute and is widely used by exterminators today.

FLEXIBILITY

They say the law is inflexible and cannot be changed except by very difficult processes. THIS IS NOT TRUE.

The law can be made stricter at any time by the legislature or any pollution control agency which has that power today. If this law is not tough enough, we can make it tougher. However, we know how former pollution laws have been weakened through the influence of the big polluters. Therefore, the legislature is forbidden from weakening the law—from inserting loopholes which are the cause of so much pollution today.

In an emergency, the legislature can act as shown above in the case of pesticides, and it seems unlikely that any legislature would not respond to a genuine emergency. Other provisions can be changed at the next election either through the referendum or the initiative --the same processes we are using to pass it. And of course, we expect the polluters to challenge some provisions in the courts. We expect to win most of these challenges, but this is another method for adjusting or modifying the law.

PENALTIES AND INCENTIVES

The Clean Environment Act encourages a firm to clean up its pollution by a series of penalties and incentives. After a firm has been found to be violating pollution standards, it may be fined 0.4 percent of its gross sales for the previous year, each day it continues to pollute. For Standard Oil of California this would amount to approximately $18,000,000 per day. This type of penalty should get the polluters attention, unlike current penalties which may run $500 or $1,000 which are frequently assessed today.

However, our purpose is not to put Standard Oil or anyone else out of business. We want to clean up pollution. We believe no polluter will want to pay these fines and will therefore file a writ of compliance showing the steps he is taking to clean up his mess. As soon as he has done this, the fines will stop.

The polluter will then have a certain specified length of time to comply with the pollution laws. After he has complied, 75 percent of the fine he paid will be refunded. That should be a good incentive to comply quickly. The remaining 25 percent will be kept to pay for administering pollution laws, research into pollution problems, etc.

THE COST OF CLEANING UP AND MORE IMPORTANT--THE SAVINGS!

Since businesses and governments have no other money than what they receive from we the people as consumers and as taxpayers, we will ultimately bear the costs of cleanup. However, the National Wildlife Federation has estimated that the costs of cleaning up will be smaller than the costs we are now incurring from the pollution itself.

	Total for U.S.	Our share as Head of Family
Air & Water pollution damages	$28.9 billion	$481
Gross savings from cleanup (by 1976)	$22.2 billion	$370
Minus-cost of cleanup	$10.2 billion	$170
Net annual savings	$12.0 billion	$200

SOURCE: National Wildlife, Vol. 10, No. 2, Feb.-Mar., 1972, pp. 14-15.

With these facts, doesn't it make sense to vote for Proposition 9? Let's show the polluters they don't own California . . . we do! Let's clean up and make California a healthy and a beautiful place to raise our children.

VOTE YES FOR A CLEAN ENVIRONMENT. VOTE YES ON PROPOSITION 9.

EXHIBIT 11–5

The following people have endorsed the Clean Environment Act (Proposition 9):

The opponents of the Clean Environment Act (Proposition 9) plan to spend millions of dollars to discredit it.
Don't be fooled. Thousands of responsible Californians have already endorsed the Clean Environment Act as a sensible solution to a deadly problem.
For more information about the Clean Environment Act, contact:

People for the Clean Environment Act
3456 W. Olympic Blvd. Los Angeles, CA 90019 (213) 731-8321
Edwin A. Koupal, Jr., Executive Director   Margaret Clergy, Treasurer

The following are against it:

OIL COMPANIES.
POWER COMPANIES.
BIG INDUSTRIAL POLLUTERS.
THE CHEMICAL INDUSTRY.
Etc.

EXHIBIT 11–6

YOU CAN GIVE OUR CHILDREN TOMORROW

Vote Yes on
Proposition 9
Tuesday, June 6, 1972

fact:
During smog alerts our children are kept off the playgrounds, while industry is allowed to continue emitting poisonous gases into our air.

Proposition 9 would close each source of industrial pollution exceeding permitted levels during a first stage smog alert.

This is only reasonable. Industry must be held accountable for its own pollution. The government provides tax incentives and low interest bonds for installation of pollution control equipment. Industry can well afford to clean itself up.

We must clean up too. Sulfur in diesel fuel means sulfuric acid in our lungs. Lead in our gasoline means lead in the air we breathe. Lead can produce liver, kidney, and brain damage and mental retardation in children.

We CAN restrict sulfur content in diesel fuel without causing disruptions in the trucking of goods and services. This fuel is currently available. It is a matter of industry's willingness to provide it for a larger market.

Unleaded gas is also available. By 1976 most cars will be able to run on unleaded gas; the remaining few will need only minor adjustments. Everyone agrees that lead must be taken out of gasoline. Proposition 9 does it.

fact:
A nuclear accident from one nuclear power plant would release radiation equal to 100 Hiroshima-type atomic bombs.

Would you fly in an airplane that had never been tested? The emergency cooling systems in these nuclear power plants have NEVER BEEN TESTED. A mockup test done by the Atomic Energy Commission failed completely.

The risks are so great that insurance companies will not cover your home or your life in the event of a nuclear accident.

The nuclear power plants that NOW exist have already produced 100 million gallons of lethal, radioactive waste. It will remain highly toxic for thousands of years. No SAFE place has been found YET to dispose of this waste.

Brownouts? Only if you believe the power companies' projection that our power needs will double in 8.10 years. We don't. Remember, the power companies are in the business of creating a market for their service.

Proposition 9 calls for a five year ban on the construction of nuclear fission power plants—time to study SAFE means of meeting our power needs. Ralph Nader applauds this provision.

fact:
Many of the public officials we rely on to enforce our anti-pollution laws receive their paychecks from the same industrial polluters they are supposed to regulate.

Proposition 9 will make this illegal by providing conflict of interest clauses.

By including class action suits in its provisions, Proposition 9 finally gives citizens the right to protect themselves against environmental destruction. Concerned citizens have been trying for years to obtain this legal authority only because our government is reluctant to take its own agencies to court in matters of pollution.

Proposition 9 also protects people from dangerous, long-lived pesticides and herbicides. It bans a select list that are known to cause birth defects, cancer, and even death in man. Safe alternate methods to control pests and weeds do exist. Also, biological pesticides are proving to be an even more direct and economical approach to the problem.

fact:
Smog costs the average American family an additional $268 a year: unnecessary doctor bills; extra car repairs, lost property values and higher food prices.

Why does every discussion about pollution always center on what it would cost industry to clean up, and not on what it costs every one of us to live in it?

It would actually cost us less to clean up NOW than to continue living with pollution.

Pollution control is a new industry creating many new jobs: designing, building, installing, and maintaining pollution control equipment.

Leonard Woodcock, president of UAW, predicted that "loss of jobs" would be nothing but a threat — a "game plan" used by industry to fight new pollution legislation. He argues forcefully that the working man's best interests could only be served by a total clean up of the environment. It is the working man who works in the filth and then goes home to the smoggiest part of the city where he raises his children. THESE CHILDREN DESERVE A BETTER LIFE. WE ARE ENTRUSTED WITH THEIR FUTURE. WE CAN'T LET THEM DOWN.

A partial list of the corporations that have contributed more than $1,000,000 to defeat Proposition 9, The Clean Environment Act. Original copy on file with the Secretary of State, Sacramento, California.

STANDARD OIL COMPANY OF CALIFORNIA $40 000 00
GENERAL MOTORS 25 000 00
FORD MOTOR COMPANY 25 000 00
AMERICAN CYANAMID 25 000 00
GULF OIL CORP 25 000 00
PACIFIC GAS & ELECTRIC 20 000 00
BRAND OIL COMPANY 65 830 00
SOUTHERN CALIFORNIA EDISON COMPANY 25 000 00
KAISER INDUSTRIES 50 000 00
BANK OF AMERICA FOUNDATION 6 000 00
GENERAL ELECTRIC CORP 25 000 00
MONTROSE CHEMICAL CORP 25 000 00
E I DUPONT de NEMOURS & CO 25 000 00
STAUFFER CHEMICAL CO 25 000 00
CELANESE CORP 25 000 00
U S BORAX & CHEMICAL CORP 10 000 00
AMOCO CHEMICALS 5 000 00
PACIFIC TELEPHONE 15 000 00
F M C CORPORATION 25 000 00
ETHYL CORPORATION 15 000 00
CORPORATION ENGINEERING CO 15 000 00
BECHTEL CORPORATION 25 000 00
TEXACO INC 5 000 00
POWERINE OIL COMPANY 5 000 00
McGRAW EDISON COMPANY 2 000 00
WESTINGHOUSE ELECTRIC CORP 25 000 00
PACIFIC LIGHTING CORP 15 000 00
LOS ANGELES CLEANING HOUSE ASSOCIATION 20 000 00
ALLIS CHALMERS 10 000 00
AERO JET GENERAL CORPORATION 10 000 00
MONSANTO COMPANY 10 000 00
ROHM & HAAS COMPANY 5 000 00
HERCULES INC 10 000 00
LEHMAN BROS 10 000 00
BABCOCK & WILSON 5 000 00
U S STEEL CORP 5 000 00
FIRESTONE TIRE & RUBBER 7 500 00
B F GOODRICH COMPANY 5 000 00
FIRESTONE TIRE & RUBBER 8 545 00
KOPPERS CO INC FOREST PRODUCTS DIVISION 5 000 00
HEGGLADE MARGULEAS TENNECO INC 5 000 00
CONSOLIDATED FREIGHTWAYS 5 000 00
P P G INDUSTRIES INC 10 555 00
THE ATCHISON TOPEKA SANTA FE RAILWAY SYSTEM 16 926 25
CALIFORNIA LAND TITLE ASSOCIATION 15 000 00
GENERAL TIRE & RUBBER COMPANY 2 250 00

The California Medical Association says:

"We are living in a state of chronic and increasing emergency due to pollution."

The problems grow worse while the legislators refuse to act and our pollution control boards refuse to effectively regulate industry.

And who suffers? We do!

The question is not whether we clean up our environment but when. The longer we wait the more difficult, the more expensive, and the more disruptive it's going to be. We must act now by voting yes on Proposition 9.

By tackling pollution today, it will be easier, cheaper, and much less chaotic.

The facts are frightening.

Cancer mortality rates are 25% higher in polluted areas than in areas of relatively clean air. Crop losses due to smog drive food prices up. Our very health, economic security, and well-being suffer. Yet big business would have us believe that we must not act in haste — that they too want to fight pollution but that this is not the time nor the way to do it. If we wait for them it will never be time.

The same vested interests who have for years been lobbying against environmental legislation in Sacramento are now pouring hundreds of thousands of dollars into a campaign against Proposition 9.

Isn't it sad that money can buy your vote?

Your vote is your voice! Stand up and be heard!

Limited funds have restricted us to one newspaper ad. If you would like further information on Proposition 9 please call the number below. Help us spread the word by circulating this ad to all your friends and neighbors.
Additional funds will help us even now to buy radio and television spots
Enclosed is $ _____

Name _____
Address _____
City _____ State _____ Zip _____

People for The Clean Environment Act
Margaret Cheap, Treasurer
3456 West Olympic Boulevard, Los Angeles, Calif. 90019 / 731-8321

Some of the thousands of responsible Californians who endorse Proposition 9:

National Health Federation
Federation of American Scientists,
Los Angeles Chapter
Los Angeles County
Democratic Central Committee
California State
Environmental Quality Study Council
Congressman Jerome B. Waldie
California Federation of Teachers,
AFL-CIO
Virginia W. Taylor,
San Diego Republican Central Committee
Friends of the Earth
Carol Burnett
Nanette Fabray
Burt Lancaster
Jack Lemmon
Eddie Albert
Walter Matthau
Carl Reiner
Robert Wise
U.S. Senator Mike Gravel
Protective Council of C.A. Senior Citizens
Congressman Augustus Hawkins
Bryan C. Crafts,
Vice-President Young Men's of United Presbyterian Church
Donald Freeman,
Chairman of Chairman
Michael Peters, M.D.,
Head Department Medicine Granada Hospital
Richard Ross, M.D.,
Former Medical Association Head
Alex Sweeten, Jr.,
President Pacific Southwest Metal Council
Rabbi Albert M. Lewis, D.D.,
Temple Beth Hillel
Fortney (Pete) Stark,
Congressional Candidate
David Seiden, Pres. A.F.T.-AFL-CIO
Congressman Ronald V. Dellums

EXHIBIT 11–7

On June 6th, pollution will be up for re-election.

While the politicians hem and haw, the people of California can cast a powerful vote against pollution on June 6th, by voting "yes" on the Clean Environment Act.

Passage of the Clean Environment Act will give California a group of tough, effective anti-pollution measures that the legislature can't water down and the environmental control agencies will have to enforce.

More than 500,000 Californians signed petitions to put the Clean Environment Act on the ballot, an unprecedented show of grass-roots strength. It's the first time in history that a grass-roots initiative has made a statewide ballot.

So if you get mad when the politicians you've elected won't vote against pollution, remember June 6th. That's the day we all go over their heads and vote pollution out of office.

Provisions of the Clean Environment Act

1. Phases out lead in gasoline.
2. Authorizes shutting down of flagrant industrial polluters.
3. Bans offshore oil drilling.
4. Prohibits construction of new nuclear power plants for 5 years.
5. Restricts manufacture, sale and use of DDT.
6. Forbids conflict of interest by enforcement officials.

For more information, contact People for the Clean Environment Act, 3456 W. Olympic Blvd., Los Angeles, CA 90019.

Prepared in the interest of a clean environment by Hall/Butler/Blatherwick, Inc., 3345 Wilshire Blvd., Los Angeles. Art Direction by Tom Kelly/Written by Al Maleson. Engraved by Mitchell & Herb Engraving Co.

Support the Clean Environment Act.

EXHIBIT 11–8
PEOPLE'S LOBBY TELEVISION COMMERCIAL: "CANDICE BERGEN"

*Video
Frame*

A, B, C

Audio
This was a very special place to grow up.
Animals, trees, clear view of the city.

D

Now the city is hardly ever in view and
when it is, there's a cloud of smog around it.

E

Like most Californians I care about the effects of pollution on our lives. . . . Now we
have an alternative . . . Prop. 9, The Clean
Environment Act, will appear on the ballots
on the June 6 election.

F

Dr. Irving F. Fengelsdorf (Ph.D. in Chemistry from University of Chicago) will answer
some basic questions about Prop. 9.

G

The opposition to Prop. 9 says that the
transportation system will cease to run and
that 100,000 jobs will be lost because the
Act proposes the banning of diesel fuel.

H

It is technically feasible to produce alternatives to diesel fuel. If pressed by law, the oil
companies could do so. The courts will give
the companies enough time.

J

The opposition claims that if Prop. 9 is
passed and the use of lead-based gasoline is
banned, most cars in California will be inoperable.
Within four years 85% of all cars on the
road will be able to operate on low lead gas.

K

Prop. 9 will ban the use of persistent pesticides such as DDT.

At this time we find traces of DDT on every
continent . . . on birds in the arctic. We
don't know the effects yet, but laboratory
tests on birds and animals show that DDT
can cause cancer. There are alternatives,
both chemical and non-chemical, to DDT.

M

The opposition states that the proposed 5-year moratorium on nuclear power plants
will be counterproductive, forcing us to rely
on our depleting supplies of conventional
fuel.

Join me and thousands of other Californians
on June 6 in voting yes for Prop. 9.

O

More Jobs, Better Health, Stronger Economy. Yes on 9.

EXHIBIT 11–8 *(continued)*

*Video
Frame*

A

B

C

Paid for by PEOPLE FOR
THE CLEAN ENVIRONMENT ACT

Audio
Our pollution control laws aren't being enforced.

Politicians don't like to get tough with the big polluters because the big polluters finance their campaigns.

That's why 1/2 million California voters worked to put the Clean Environment Act on the ballot.

Take politics out of pollution. Vote for Prop. 9.

EXHIBIT 11–9
PEOPLE'S LOBBY TELEVISION COMMERCIAL: "CARTOON"

*Video
Frame*

Audio
Background music

A

B

C

EXHIBIT 11–9 (continued)

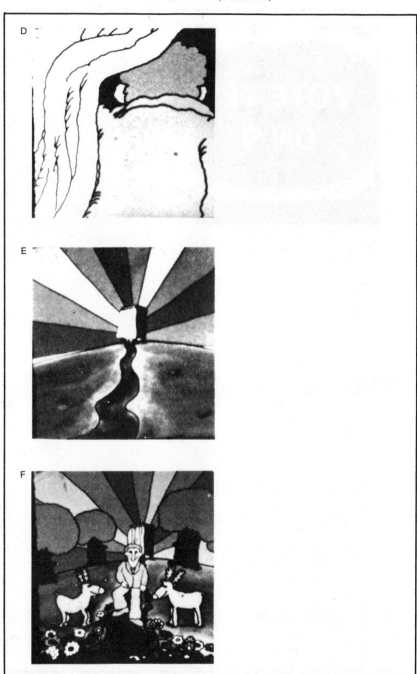

EXHIBIT 11–9 *(concluded)*

G

WHITAKER & BAXTER

The formation of the opposition group came about primarily as a consequence of Whitaker & Baxter's apprising various corporations and industry groups of the potential dangers to the industry and economy of California if Proposition 9 were enacted. An example of the corporate initiative and activity in the formation of the opposition can be found in the memo by James L. Wanvig addressed to Otto Miller (Exhibit 12–1). Included in this memorandum was a "Preliminary Plan of Campaign Against the People's Lobby Initiative Submitted by Whitaker & Baxter," dated June 1, 1971 (Exhibit 11–10).

EXHIBIT 11–10
PRELIMINARY PLAN OF CAMPAIGN AGAINST THE PEOPLE'S LOBBY
INITIATIVE SUBMITTED BY WHITAKER & BAXTER, JUNE 1, 1971

The People's Lobby initiative constitutes one of the gravest threats to the well being of the people of California yet devised.

The measure synthesizes into legislative form one of the most acute issues of this era—the balancing of the environment in which we live with the fuel, food, fiber and energy essential to life itself.

The People's Lobby initiative proposes to resolve the issue by:
1. severely restricting the fuels and sources of energy available to the people in their homes and businesses; and
2. eliminating and limiting the chemicals which can be introduced into the ecocycle in the production of food and fibre.

This truly is an issue the people must decide and it must truly be a people's campaign to determine how much people are willing to endure in loss of jobs, higher prices, and less of the niceties of life to enhance the environment.

Obviously, there must be a balance between need and nicety—between a pastoral society and industrial-service society.

The question the people of California must decide at the June 6, 1972, ballot—or at any statewide special election called in the interim—is whether the People's Lobby initiative provides that balance.

The measure does not provide the balance if viewed rationally and, in our opinion, will not be accepted by the electorate if the issues are properly and effectively posed.

The considerable danger is that the measure will not be dealt with effectively but will be cast in the light its promoters intend as a great environmental test between the people and the business and industrial "despoilers" of our land, a crusade which could be joined with near religious fervor and which would have but one outcome.

In short, the campaign against the People's Lobby initiative must not be spearheaded *publicly* by business and industry. *It should be publicly launched by responsible conservationists, by academicians, labor spokesmen, leaders of the Democratic Party* and joined at the appropriate time in the appropriate fashion by business, industry, agriculture, and the Republican Party leadership.

This strategy insures greater credibility to the thesis the People's Lobby initiative is so extreme, so destructive of people's lives, that responsible environmentalists are embarrassed by it and urge its defeat.

Time is of the essence if the strategy is to be employed successfully.

A public citizens committee must be formed and announced quickly under the

EXHIBIT 11–10 (continued)

leadership of men known to be Democratic conservationists, highly respected scientists and academicians, and key labor leaders of the state to create the people against the People's Lobby posture essential to this campaign.

Then membership should be quickly built throughout all spectrums of society —through the hundreds of responsible and powerful statewide organizations of every type.

The committee should take its detailed, thoughtful, well-prepared case to the media—broadcast and print. It should seek out every forum, every potential ally, every potential resource, to be brought to bear in reaching the public generally.

A public committee of this type, a campaign based on the strategy proposed, can be most effective only if the utilities and the oil industry—the businesses most directly affected by the initiative—take direct control of the direction of the campaign, rather than have a dozen or more well-meaning groups take the lead and in the doing create a big business versus people's issue which can only be self-defeating.

The involvement of the principal oil companies and the principal utilities— and the other affected businesses and industries which should be added to the support base—is not a public involvement. Rather, in a non-publicized sense, it is a means of directing the campaign under the aegis of a public citizens committee as outlined. In the doing, total control of the public campaign strategy and direction is maintained.

In the weeks immediately ahead, while the citizens committee is being formed there are several critical research projects which should be launched:

1. The initiative itself must be analyzed fully by each company affected so that the limitations it would impose are susceptible to lay interpretation. What plants would be affected? What fuels would be restricted or eliminated? What would happen to cost of operation? What truly happens to the availability of energy for domestic, industrial and business use? What about steel plants? Borax plants? Etc., ad infinitum.
2. What existing federal and state regulations are presently in play and what conflicts are posed between existing federal and state law and regulation with the strictures of the People's Lobby initiative?
3. Intensive opinion research must be undertaken to test public attitudes on all relevant matters and to test the public validity of arguments to be set forth in the course of the campaign.

This data must of necessity be funneled to a central point for effective usage and working with assigned industry personnel, the campaign managers—whose responsibility it will be to translate the myriad data to clearly understandable public terms—should provide that service.

The campaign managers also should contract for the required analysis of existing federal and state regulation and law as it applies to the initiative. They also should devise and be responsible for the intensive public opinion research and testing.

In a framework of time the campaign should be viewed as follows:

1. Announcement of the public citizens committee by the week of June 21, 1971. The committee will be expanded obviously right up to election day.
2. An immediate start on industry research, to be completed preliminarily within 30 days.
3. An immediate start on matching federal and state regulation to the initiative to be completed within 30 days.
4. Structure of the public opinion survey to test voter attitudes and campaign arguments for placement into the field within 30–45 days, conclusion to be within 60 days of placement in the field.

EXHIBIT 11–10 (concluded)

5. Compilation of an initial fact sheet for early use with media and state and local organizations. All media and all principal organizations should be contacted both by mail and in person with emphasis on securing the endorsement of every possible endorsing entity by March 1, 1972.

Assuming a special statewide election is not called prior to June, 1972—in which event timing and effort would have to be revised drastically—the goal of the campaign between the present and March 1, 1972, should be to try to win the campaign, insofar as that is possible, before advertising media must be committed.

The reason for this, of course, is that the greater the degree of success prior to the use of paid media, the greater the prospect for conducting the campaign at a cost far below the sums required for intensive 90-day, all-out media-supported campaigns.

In summary, so long as qualification of the People's Lobby initiative is an unfortunate fact—its existence should be viewed as an opportunity.

The opportunity is to join one of the most important issues confronting the country in an affirmative, not defensive, stance.

Stated in simplest terms, there is an opportunity here to secure a public expression of support for the desire of people to have the light go on when they throw the switch or to buy an apple free of worms—all in keeping with the acknowledged desire for the cleanest environment possible consistent with life on earth.

That expression of support at the polls, an expression directly achievable in legislative bodies at any level, should provide a true measure of what people want in life. It is a catalyst around which responsible alternatives can be sought and achieved in legislative halls on the many similar issues existent and on which decisions must be reached.

Based on the above, we recommend:

1. Creation of a small steering committee which would not become public composed of the delegated spokesmen for the principal utilities and oil companies.
2. Approval of campaign underwriting by this committee.
3. Creation of a broadened, non-public finance committee to raise the requisite campaign budget.
4. Retention of campaign management which will bring forth the effort subject to steering committee approval.
5. Approval of a preliminary campaign budget to finance all phases of the campaign until March 1, 1972, in an estimated amount of $600,000.
6. Submission of and approval of a paid media budget for the period of time from March 1, 1972, to June 6, 1972, to be submitted by January 1, 1972, at which time the effectiveness of the preliminary campaign can be judged and an intelligent media budget devised to fit existing circumstances.

Whitaker & Baxter, long established in San Francisco, is a public relations and campaign management firm that provides services for groups and candidates both in California and throughout the nation. In addition to conducting an actual issue or election campaign, Whitaker & Baxter serves as a type of monitoring agency for its clients: "We alert our clients to any issue that we think may be of consequence to them. We have monitored for all types of clients and maybe one in one hundred times something will come of an issue we notice, but at least our clients are aware of the issues that are developing and won't be surprised in mid-stream." Furthermore, Whitaker & Baxter pays detailed attention to the specifics of any campaign they manage. "We do our own writing, all our own production for all media types, our own news writing. We oversee our own organization department, our own press department, our own mail department. This is a little unusual. Most firms don't do this, but we feel that if we do it here, we are doing it as we want it done. We feel that we are more competent as a result of our experience in getting this done right," Whitaker explained. Consequently, the firm usually limits itself to two or three undertakings at any one time.

The actual operation of a campaign involves an extensive publicity effort aimed at reaching every segment of the public. While mass media advertising is an important part of any campaign, Whitaker & Baxter also relies on a personal contact to reach its intended audience.

> We run a total publicity campaign to overly simplify it. We do not deal with paid media alone but try to take our issue to the public through every existing forum. That might be a panel show, a talk show, a rotary club meeting, wherever we can go. If we have something of sufficient consequence we call a press conference.

Planning and organizing the campaign

Whitaker & Baxter based its plan on the premise that business and industry must not publicly lead the campaign. It saw "considerable danger" in letting the campaign become a "test between the people and the business and industrial 'despoilers' of our land" as "its promoters intend." The proposed strategy was to be as follows:

1. Organize a citizens' committee led by Democratic conservationists, scientists, academicians, and labor leaders.
2. Through a steering committee, maintain "nonpublic" direct control of the campaign by the "affected businesses and industries," particularly the utilities and principal oil companies.
3. Use the steering committee to raise the required campaign budget.
4. Generate the research and data necessary to launch an effective campaign.

The plan was accepted. The opposition group was called Californians Against the Pollution Initiative (CAPI). Its address was 870 Market Street, San Francisco—which is also the address of Whitaker & Baxter. There were four co-chairmen of CAPI: Dr. Emil M. Mrak, chancellor emeritus, University of California, Davis; Joseph J. Diviny, first vice-president, International Brotherhood of Teamsters; Dr. J. E. McKee, professor of environmental engineering; former member of the Advisory Committee on Reactor Safeguards, Atomic Energy Commission; and Myron W. Doornbos, president, Southern Council of Conservation Clubs. These were the men who were to be visible to the public. They were chosen to lend credibility to the effort. For example, Dr. Mrak had headed the Mrak Commission, which had reported on the carcinogenic threat of DDT.[11]

Financing the campaign

The position of chief fundraiser for CAPI was held by J. Simon Fluor, honorary chairman of Fluor Corporation. Mr. Fluor and other fundraisers managed to raise $1.5 million. The petroleum and chemical industry accounted for 40.5 percent of the total contributions, followed by utilities, with 10.5 percent; automotive, 7.9 percent; and transportation, 4.9 percent. These amounted to a total of 63.8 percent of all contributions, and reflected the goal of Whitaker & Baxter in their preliminary plan—to maintain "direct control."

The figures somewhat understate the total amounts raised for the campaign to defeat Proposition 9. For example, Gulf Oil Corporation contributed $25,000 to CAPI, but also spent an additional $27,181 conducting its own campaign. Bechtel Corporation is another example: It contributed $25,000 to CAPI, yet records of the California secretary of state show a total expenditure of $65,391.04. Bechtel reported that of this additional $40,366.04, $25,000 was paid to Stanford Research Institute, and $14,541.04 was paid to Kaiser Industries Corporation for Bechtel's portion of newspaper advertising costs.

The campaign strategy

The first step in the development of a campaign strategy was to hire the firm of Kahl Associates, research consultants in government and public affairs from Washington, D.C., to do a thorough analysis of the technical, legal, and political aspects of the Clean Environment Act initiative as it was drawn.[12] Based on their analysis, Kahl Associates suggested that a successful campaign strategy should have the following elements:

1. It should emphasize the broad character of the opposition to Proposition 9 by seeking and publishing the endorsement of influential people from all segments of the California population. This would also mean that business would keep a low profile, and People's Lobby would be projected as an extremist group with little serious public support.
2. It should hammer home the point that the initiative was poorly drafted

---

[11] William Ristow, "The Old Coalition," *San Francisco Bay Guardian*, April 27, 1972.
[12] Kahl Associates, *Policy Analysis of the California Pollution Initiative*, p. 2.

and if enacted would not only do the cause of "environmental improvement" irreparable harm, but would also be highly damaging to the economy of California and would result in unemployment and economic stagnation.

3. Campaign leaders should communicate with opinion leaders and the news media to enlist their support for further disseminating the CAPI viewpoint and opposition to the initiative.

4. It should launch an effective media campaign to persuade the people to vote against the passage of Proposition 9.

The preliminary plan called for the creation of a citizens committee to run the campaign while its "control" remained with business and industry. The citizens committee was organized so that CAPI was able to enlist the support of a large number of conservationists, labor leaders, and politicians. One of their primary efforts was launched in the direction of the Sierra Club, the most prestigious conservation organization in the United States. In the political arena CAPI was instrumental in getting Lieutenant Governor Ed Reinecke to send a memo dated March 28, 1972, on state stationery, to editors, publishers, and station managers throughout California. The memo follows exactly a pamphlet printed by CAPI entitled "How the Pollution Initiative Affects You" and calls the initiative "an irrational doomsayer's approach." Labor also turned out to be a staunch ally of the opposition. The second largest single contributor to the campaign was the Construction Industry Advancement Fund, which gave $50,000. The California Labor Federation, AFL-CIO, adopted a statement on March 9, 1972, calling for a No vote on Proposition 9.[13] Altogether, according to Mr. Whitaker, CAPI received some 2,300 No endorsements on Proposition 9.

CAPI set up a speaker's bureau to provide speakers to fraternal organizations, college and university groups, women's organizations, and local chambers of commerce to explain the defects in the initiative and how it would affect them. They also prepared an elaborate kit for members of the news media and made regular follow-ups. The cornerstone of this direct mail campaign was a beautifully produced 16-page black, red, and yellow pamphlet entitled "How the Pollution Initiative Affects You." The pamphlet stated that if Proposition 9 were enacted:

1. You will not be able to provide yourself and your families with the necessities of life.
2. You can be turned in by a neighbor—and arrested—if you fail to throw away a can of ant or other insect poison.
3. You may be forced to junk your relatively new car.
4. You may have to go back to the scrub board and laundry tub for washing clothes.
5. Your very life will be endangered. Epidemic diseases such as typhoid

---

[13] "News," California Labor Federation, AFL-CIO, March 9, 1972, p. 1.

fever, malaria, yellow fever, and encephalitis . . . will no longer be subject to effective control.

6. When hundreds of thousands of people lose their jobs because plants are shut down, . . . it is the working people—white collar, blue collar, small owners, minorities—who are directly affected. The odd combination of wealthy "ecology" extremists and commune-living drop-outs who find the Pollution Initiative groovy are relatively unaffected.

7. The people of California can distinguish between motherhood and suicide.

This was a major piece in the CAPI program. Over 825,000 copies were mailed. The philosophy of emphasizing the adverse effects of the passage of Proposition 9 was best summarized by Mr. Whitaker:

> The major thrust of the entire effort was to deal with the issue in terms of what it meant to individual people and then trying to take them through it in terms of personal consequences to them. It meant the Initiative should be postured not as a proposal but as a fact and what the consequences would be under those circumstances.

CAPI received widespread support in terms of public and media criticism of the initiative as a poorly written law that on balance would do more harm than good. In addition to the neutral position taken by the Sierra Club, the western regional office of the Audubon Society also came out in opposition to Proposition 9. Most major newspapers in California opposed the passage of Proposition 9 on the grounds that it would be a bad law, thereby lending credibility to CAPI's arguments.

CAPI realized that People's Lobby had made great progress with students on the various campuses in the state and had presumably gotten many endorsements. To counter the influence of People's Lobby, CAPI picked three students, one from UCLA, one from UC, and one from Stanford, all recent graduates. They were brought in and exposed to the CAPI viewpoint, material, and arguments, and asked to go home with the material and develop an approach to argue the CAPI position with students.

> We sent them to every campus in the state, to every student newspaper, and they did truly a superb job. People's Lobby had claimed to have the endorsement of a whole series of universities and colleges. These kids found out that wasn't true. As a consequence, we felt that there was greater understanding about our position on the college campuses.

Mrs. Koupal offers the following explanation:

> We made the ballot over one year prior to the election. We immediately went out and organized on all the campuses in the state and got endorsements of many of the student body groups and various officers. CAPI explains that they discovered we didn't really have those endorsements.
>
> Demonstrating how very naive and inexperienced we were, we did not realize that these student body groups change office and elect every semester. Our endorsements (which were real and in writing) were moot by election time.

The media campaign

Prior to March 1, 1972, the bulk of the campaign was aimed at enlisting supporters for a No vote. In addition to the pamphlet, CAPI distributed "Voters Arguments Against Proposition 9" (Exhibit 11–11). Over 1.6 million copies of the two promotional pieces, the basic pamphlet and Voters Arguments were distributed. There were about fifty other promotional pieces, of which over 800,000 copies were distributed. In addition, thousands of leaflets were produced and mailed by supporting organizations.

In the two months immediately prior to the election, heavy use was made of outdoor advertising, particularly transit posters and 7-sheets. Transit posters were mounted on the sides of 605 buses and streetcars in nine metropolitan areas. Two painted billboards were positioned for maximum visibility by the heavy traffic crossing the San Francisco–Oakland Bay Bridge. The final form of outdoor advertising used was "7-sheets," or compact sidewalk posters (Exhibits 11–12, 11–13).

EXHIBIT 11–11

Responsible Conservationists
Urge
Vote NO
on
Proposition No. 9

Following is the official text of the
VOTERS ARGUMENT
AGAINST
PROPOSITION NO. 9

which will be distributed by the Secretary of State of California before the June 6 election.

Your job, your future, your ability to provide the basic necessities of life for your family, depend on the defeat of Proposition No. 9, the Pollution Initiative, at the June 6 election.

Proposition No. 9 is so extreme, so unworkable, so devastating in its adverse effects on the day-to-day living problems of every Californian, that its enactment would set back the cause of environmental improvement for years to come.

TRANSPORTATION BREAKDOWN

One innocent-sounding section alone —limiting the content of sulfur in diesel fuel to 0.035 per cent—would virtually bring the economy of California to a halt.

Most trucks, trains, and transit buses operate on diesel fuel. Except for a very small amount of scarce, imported fuel, the sulfur content of diesel fuel available today is many times the amount allowable under Proposition No. 9.

It would take an undetermined number of years and enormous capital outlay to build refineries capable of producing such fuel in quantity.

This simply means that if Proposition No. 9 were enacted, the vast majority of trucks and trains that transport food and other basic necessities of life to all Californians would cease to run.

Diesel-powered transit buses would be retired from service, forcing a heavier reliance on private automobiles—thus **increasing** the pollution problem, instead of reducing it.

SEVERE UNEMPLOYMENT

Lost jobs in the transportation industries would number in the hundreds of thousands. The additional unemployment in industries and businesses idled because of a transportation breakdown would be staggering.

EXHIBIT 11–11 (continued)

PESTICIDE PARANOIA

Proposition No. 9 would ban a long list of pesticides used in the production of food, in the control of epidemic diseases and for the destruction of household pests. For some uses, including termite control, there are no known substitutes. For many uses, allowable substitutes are less effective, must be applied more often, are highly dangerous to handle, and are toxic to pets and birds and beneficial insects such as bees.

POOR AUTO PERFORMANCE

Proposition No. 9 phases out lead in gasoline in four years. Federal proposals would phase out lead, but over a longer period of time, making allowance for the driveability of cars presently in use. Under Proposition No. 9 many, possibly most car owners, would be stuck with cars that could not be driven effectively, if at all.

CLEAN POWER BANNED

For five years, Proposition No. 9 bans construction of nuclear power plants, the only major source of **clean** electric energy, thus forcing heavier reliance on generating plants powered by air-contaminating fossil fuels. Again, Proposition No. 9 would **increase** pollution, instead of reducing it.

In every area covered by the Initiative, increasingly strict anti-pollution regulations are being enforced by local, state and federal agencies. These regulations can be adjusted if proved unworkable or counter-productive.

Proposition No. 9's complex, arbitrary regulations would be frozen into law. For all practical purposes, even in the face of dire economic or epidemic emergency, none of its provisions could be changed except through time-consuming court challenges and the lengthy and cumbersome process necessary to bring such a change before the people for a vote.

Vote NO
on Proposition No. 9

Signed:
DR. J. E. McKEE, Professor of Environmental Engineering; Former Member, Advisory Committee on Reactor Safeguards, Atomic Energy Commission
MYRON W. DOORNBOS, President, Southern Council of Conservation Clubs
JOSEPH J. DIVINY, First Vice-President, International Brotherhood of Teamsters

CALIFORNIANS AGAINST THE POLLUTION INITIATIVE

870 Market Street, San Francisco, CA 94102
1127 Wilshire Boulevard, Los Angeles, CA 90017

Co-Chairman:
DR. EMIL M. MRAK, Chancellor-Emeritus, University of California, Davis

EXHIBIT 11–12

many bugs in Prop. No. 9

VOTE NO ON NO. 9

CALIFORNIANS AGAINST
THE POLLUTION INITIATIVE

LOSING YOUR JOB WON'T SOLVE POLLUTION

EXHIBIT 11–13

> # Losing your job won't solve Pollution!

Vote NO on No. 9

CALIFORNIANS AGAINST THE POLLUTION INITIATIVE

During the three-week period before the election, both radio and television were used extensively to reach the voters (Exhibit 11–14). A series of five filmed TV spots dramatizing the main arguments against Proposition 9 were produced and aired. In all, 1,788 were run by twenty-nine television stations in the San Francisco–San Jose, Sacramento–Stockton, San Diego, and Los Angeles markets during the three weeks, and in both the Fresno and the Bakersfield markets during the final week. Three radio spots were taped and placed with 215 stations during the final two weeks. The total of spots run was 8,099.

During the last two weeks before election day, outdoor advertising was augmented by a statewide newspaper advertising program. Five 3-column by 14-inch ads were placed in 111 dailies on the following schedule:

YOU AND YOUR CAR (Exhibit 11–15)	May 22
FRAUDULENT WAY (Exhibit 11–16)	May 24
THE SACRED MOSQUITOES (Exhibit 11–17)	May 26
TRUCKS AND TRAINS (Exhibit 11–18)	May 30
RATIONING ELECTRIC POWER (Exhibit 11–19)	June 1

Two of these ads, "Trucks and Trains" and "The Sacred Mosquitoes," were placed in 465 weekly papers on the publication date nearest May 24 and

EXHIBIT 11–14
TEXT OF TELEVISION AND RADIO COMMERCIALS*

30-SECOND TV

Video	*Audio*
People walking in lighted city street—then the lights go out (blackness, shadowy forms)	Announcer (voice over): Who wants darkened city streets at night?
Nuclear power plant by ocean—sparkling blue sky	Proposition 9 would cause severe power shortages in California by stopping construction of clean nonpolluting nuclear power plants for five years.
Woman scrubbing clothes with scrubboard in old-fashioned laundry tub	Who wants to go back to the scrubboard?
Family huddled around fireplace—candles for light	Or depend on the fireplace to heat their home?
Card: Vote NO on No. 9	Vote NO on Proposition 9.
	The preceding announcement sponsored by Californians Against the Pollution Initiative.

20-SECOND TV, NO. 1

Video	*Audio*
Beautiful blue sky	Everybody is in favor of clean air—but losing your job won't solve the pollution problem.
Breadline—or unemployment line	
Train coming to a halt (or derailed?)	Proposition 9 would halt virtually all train and truck transportation of food and other products in California—throwing millions of people out of work.
Truck stopped at a crossing signal	
Card: Vote NO on No. 9	Vote No on 9.
	The preceding announcement sponsored by Californians Against the Pollution Initiative.

60-SECOND TV

Video (film or animation?)	*Audio*
Beautiful blue sky	Announcer (voice over): Everybody is in favor of clean air but losing your job won't solve the pollution problem.
Breadline—or unemployment line	
Train coming to a halt	Proposition 9 would halt virtually all train and truck transportation of food and other products in California—throwing millions of people out of work.
Truck stopped at a crossing signal	
Empty stocks in a supermarket	And you would be unable to provide the basic necessities of life for yourself and your family.
Lighted city at night—then blacked out	Electricity blackouts won't solve the problem either. Proposition 9 actually would *increase* pollution—not reduce it—by banning construction of *non-polluting* nuclear power plants for five years.
Mosquitoes, termites, etc. (buzzing background sound)	Banning pesticides that protect your home from termites and protect *you* from epidemic diseases such as malaria won't solve the problem either.

* Radio commercials were the audio portion of TV commercials.

EXHIBIT 11–14 *(continued)*

Card: Vote NO on No. 9	Proposition 9 is *no way* to combat pollution. Vote No on 9.
	The preceding announcement sponsored by Californians Against the Pollution Initiative.

10-SECOND TV SPOT

Video	*Audio*
Card: Vote NO on No. 9	Announcer (voice over): Losing your job won't solve the pollution problem. Vote NO on Proposition 9.
	The preceding announcement sponsored by Californians Against the Pollution Initiative.

20-SECOND TV SPOT, NO. 2

Video	*Audio*
Mosquitoes, termites, etc. (buzzing background sound?)	Announcer (voice over): Who wants to bring back malaria?
Card: Vote NO on No. 9	Proposition 9 would ban pesticides that protect your food supplies, protect your home from termites and other pests, and protect *you* from epidemic diseases.
	Vote No on 9—there are too many bugs in it!
	The preceding announcement sponsored by Californians Against the Pollution Initiative.

May 31, respectively. On the final weekend prior to election day, a 5-column, 17-inch ad displaying a sampling of the individuals and organizations endorsing the No-on-9 campaign was run throughout the state.

The effectiveness of this massive media effort was measured at the ballot box on June 6, 1972. Proposition 9 lost by a 2 to 1 margin. CAPI was criticized by People's Lobby and some other groups for using scare tactics in advertising campaigns and for projecting the opposition as weird and irrational people.

A particularly glaring example was the ad entitled "The Sacred Mosquitoes of California." A spokesman for Whitaker & Baxter, the public relations and advertising firm which prepared the advertisement, conceded it "[was] in error." His firm used as source material a 1970 publication issued by a fruit and vegetable growers association. The ad shouldn't have included "typhoid," which is caused by bacteria transmitted in contaminated water, but should have said "typhus" instead. (Typhus, however, is caused primarily by insanitary living conditions and is transmitted by body lice, according to medical sources.)

When asked whether such scare tactics were not in fact debasing the process of public communication and creating more public misinformation, Mr. Whitaker commented:

EXHIBIT 11–15

You and your car

You may not love it as much as you used to, but are you ready to junk it?

The old love affair with the automobile has cooled off a bit, because everybody now realizes that most of our smog problem comes right out of our cars' exhausts.

What's being done about the problem? Plenty.

The State of California requires that cars be equipped with smog control devices now. A new Federal law requires that auto manufacturers—by 1975 and 1976—must equip all new cars with **super devices** that reduce pollutants by 90 per cent from present levels.

Lead is being phased out of gasoline—not because it contributes to smog (it doesn't)—but because the smog control devices won't work with leaded gas.

These tough measures will have a real impact on the smog problem in the years immediately ahead—and that's welcome news for every Californian.

BUT—does this mean you should junk your present car? Or be unable to run it without damage to your motor?

Proposition No. 9 on the June ballot asks you to do just that.

Not content with what the State and Federal governments are doing about auto-caused smog, the sponsors of Proposition No. 9 want to do more. Their idea of **more** is to phase lead out of gasoline **completely** at the time new cars equipped with the super smog devices are on the market.

Proposed Federal regulations allow a small amount of lead content to take care of the needs of older cars. But under Proposition No. 9, if you can't afford to buy a brand new car, you've had it!

Not only that, but Proposition No. 9 also places limits on **other** ingredients in gasoline. The Technical Advisory Committee of the State Air Resources Board states that the "combination of these separate requirements is questionable on a techincal basis" and that "it is doubtful whether all manufacturers can meet these requirements."

That means that even if "legal" gasoline would operate your car without damaging it, it would be in short supply and very likely rationed. And all for no purpose!

Proposition No. 9 contains another little "goodie", too. If, even without your knowledge, the smog control device on your car isn't working properly, you would be fined .1% of your annual gross income **every day** until it was fixed!

Let's attack the smog problem intelligently. The Proposition No. 9 way is just plain absurd—and would cause severe economic problems for middle and low-income Californians.

Vote NO on Proposition No. 9

CALIFORNIANS AGAINST THE POLLUTION INITIATIVE

870 Market Street, San Francisco, CA 94102
1127 Wilshire Boulevard, Los Angeles, CA 90017

MYRON W. DOORNBOS, President, Southern Council of Conservation Clubs
Co-Chairman

EXHIBIT 11-16

The Fraudulent Way To Combat Air Pollution

Air pollution is of vital concern to every man, woman and child in California.

Fortunately, a great deal is being done about it — by regulatory agencies at every level of government.

Every county in the state now has an Air Pollution Control Board, with powers to enforce standards for emissions of air contaminants, and to shut down plants that don't meet them.

Ten years ago, in Los Angeles County, 50 per cent of all air pollutants (other than from natural sources) came from industrial plants and businesses. Today, the Air Pollution Control Board has succeeded in reducing industrial air pollution to the point that such sources now contribute only about 10 per cent.

But the sponsors of Proposition No. 9, on the June 6 ballot, say that the Pollution Control Boards aren't tough enough. They want to make it much more difficult for industrial plants to stay in business.

For example, Proposition No. 9 would require that, whenever a smog alert is called, certain plants must shut down — regardless of whether or not the particular types of emissions from those plants are contributing to the smog problem.

But even if they succeeded in closing down **all** industrial plants **permanently** — with all the unemployment problems that would result — 90 per cent of the air pollution would remain — because **90 per cent** of the smog problem is caused by automobile exhausts.

Hopefully, increasingly restrictive California automobile emissions standards and Federal requirements for highly advanced smog control devices will substantially reduce smog in the next few years.

But the sponsors of Proposition No. 9 contend the problem is so serious that drastic steps must be taken **right now.** If so, why didn't they put up for voter approval a requirement that when a smog alert is called, all autos must be off the streets within two hours, with tough penalties for violators?

That would be the only way to effectively reduce smog, **right now.**

Proposition No. 9 is a fraud. It would cause widespread unemployment, but it wouldn't reduce air pollution, in any effective way.

Vote NO on Proposition No. 9

CALIFORNIANS AGAINST THE POLLUTION INITIATIVE

870 Market Street, San Francisco, CA 94102
1127 Wilshire Boulevard, Los Angeles, CA 90017

MYRON W. DOORNBOS, President, Southern Council of Conservation Clubs
Co-Chairman

EXHIBIT 11-17

The Sacred Mosquitoes of California

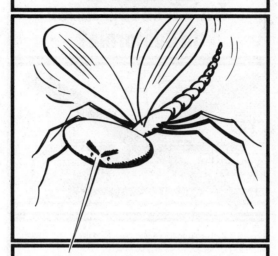

Who wants to bring back typhoid? Or malaria? Or encephalitis? Only people who love mosquitoes.

The sponsors of Proposition No. 9 on the June 6 ballot must love mosquitoes—also termites, cockroaches and silverfish. Because Proposition No. 9 makes illegal the use or possession of a long list of chemicals, including the only effective pesticides for controlling various pests.

They must hate bees, though. Because the substitute pesticides that could still be used, though far less effective for many purposes, are death on bees. They're also dangerous to humans and pets.

If Proposition No. 9 passed, you could be arrested for having on your premises a can of insect spray you'd purchased some time ago if it happened to contain one of a long list of suddenly illegal ingredients.

A university scientist could be arrested for experimenting with any of these banned chemicals in a laboratory research project.

What kind of sense does all this make?

Like most things about Proposition No. 9, it doesn't make any sense at all.

It doesn't make sense to risk the resurgence of epidemic diseases that have been kept in control for so many years that most of us have virtually forgotten they ever existed.

It doesn't make sense to risk the destruction of forests and agricultural crops.

It doesn't make sense to prohibit scientists from experimenting to develop new knowledge in the field of pest control.

It doesn't make sense to forbid the use of the only known effective means of protecting your house from termite infestation.

Proposition No. 9 is senseless—and very dangerous.

There's good in most religions, and harm in some. The protected, "sacred cows" of India have contributed to that country's abject poverty for centuries. It would be the height of folly to yield to the fanatics who, in their zeal for a new "religion," would inflict on all of us the "sacred mosquitoes" of California!

Vote NO on Proposition No. 9

There are too many bugs in it!

CALIFORNIANS AGAINST THE POLLUTION INITIATIVE

870 Market Street, San Francisco, CA 94102
1127 Wilshire Boulevard, Los Angeles, CA 90017

DR. EMIL M. MRAK, Chancellor-Emeritus, University of California, Davis
Co-Chairman

EXHIBIT 11–18

Would you vote to Stop all Truck and Freight Train Transportation in California?

You certainly wouldn't if you happen to be one of the 1,000,000 Californians who work directly in the transportation industry! You'd lose your job within a few days after election.

And if you think about it for a minute or two, you realize that no matter what you do for a living, you'd be in serious trouble.

Businesses of all kinds would no longer be able to market their products.

Farm crops would rot in the fields and on the trees.

Unemployment would reach staggering proportions.

You wouldn't be able to provide yourself and your family with the basic necessities of life!

Nobody in his right mind would vote "yes" on such a stupid, vicious proposal. Yet that's what you're being asked to do when you go to the polls on June 6 to vote on Proposition No. 9 — the Pollution Initiative.

Down in the fine print, Proposition No. 9 contains an innocent-sounding provision limiting the content of sulfur in diesel fuel sold for use in internal combustion engines in Califorina to .035 per cent.

The limit now in effect is .5 per cent — 14 times as much!

The very small amount of diesel fuel now available that would meet this ridiculous requirement is insufficient even to fill the needs of public transit buses, which run on the lowest sulfur content diesel now in production.

If Proposition No. 9 should pass, the next day the great majority of trucks and diesel-powered freight locomotives would have to stop running — because there would be no "legal" fuel available to operate them!

It would take an undetermined period of time — two years? — six years? — nobody knows for sure, before refineries could be adapted at enormous expense to produce diesel fuel in the quantity needed to meet our transportation needs.

Knowing the facts, nobody in his right mind would vote for Proposition No. 9.

LOSING YOUR JOB WON'T SOLVE POLLUTION!

And voting for Proposition No. 9 won't solve pollution. The Technical Advisory Committee of the Air Resources Board of California reports that even if the sulfur content of diesel fuel required by Proposition No. 9 could be achieved, it would reduce sulfur-dioxide emissions in Los Angeles County by only three-tenths of one percent! What a price you're being asked to pay to accomplish virtually nothing!

Vote NO on Proposition No. 9

CALIFORNIANS AGAINST THE POLLUTION INITIATIVE

870 Market Street, San Francisco, CA 94102
1127 Wilshire Boulevard, Los Angeles, CA 90017

MYRON W. DOORNBOS, President, Southern Council of Conservation Clubs Co-Chairman

EXHIBIT 11–19

What Happens When You Have to Ration Electric Power?

For three weeks in February, electric power was rationed in England because of a shutdown of coal supplies to fuel generating plants. The headlines tell the story:

'Guard your house against thieves' warns Yard chief

LONDON STREET BLACKOUT

Schools shut, chicks die as siege begins

Woman dies as power cut candle starts fire

Commuters face 50% cut in train services
By Staff Reporters
Southern Region's train services may be cut by half from Monday.

Evening Standard

Crisis news stuns the Commons

ALL BRITAIN ON HALF TIME

Thousands more laid off as power crisis tightens grip

'Millions to be laid off'

No more baths
The 120,000 citizens of Ipswich, Suffolk, were asked by town officials yesterday to take no more baths while the power emergency lasts, because of pumping station problems.

Disillusioned hens
Power cuts have caused millions of hens to reduce their laying, by removing the bright lights which fool birds into thinking it is perpetually spring.

Sugar ration starts —beer threatened

Where to expect the cuts today

A short period of electric power rationing almost wrecked England's economy.

Can you imagine the effect that **permanent** power rationing—with recurring brownouts and blackouts—would have on the people of California?

IT COULD HAPPEN HERE!

Proposition No. 9, on the June 6 ballot, would ban for five years construction of nuclear power plants, including those now being built.

If our normal power needs could be met at all, they would have to be met by increased reliance on fossil fuel burning steam generating plants, which emit pollutants into the air. Nuclear plants, by contrast, are a **clean** source of electric energy.

Thus, Proposition No. 9, which is promoted by its sponsors as an anti-pollution measure, would **increase** air pollution instead of reducing it. At the same time, it would force upon all Californians the insane risks involved in rationing electric power: widespread unemployment, darkened city streets, the loss of such labor-saving devices as electric stoves and washing machines.

DON'T BLACKOUT YOUR FUTURE!

Vote NO on Proposition No. 9

CALIFORNIANS AGAINST THE POLLUTION INITIATIVE
870 Market Street, San Francisco, CA 94102
1127 Wilshire Boulevard, Los Angeles, CA 90017

DR. EMIL M. MRAK, Chancellor-Emeritus, University of California, Davis
Co-Chairman

Whitaker: It may have been a function of the need to simplify issues in a 30-second or 60-second time constraint. When you go to a play, if it is dull, you are going to fall asleep and you won't pay any attention to it. The same is true when you are trying to command people's attention in any other way. You have to be able to hold their attention, and that means it should be colorful, it should be lively, it should be sad, it should be something that takes it out of the ordinary.

Sethi: Isn't there then a danger that by resorting to that sort of effect, exaggeration and overdramatization, there might be a tendency to degenerate the issues into very simplified notions and miseducate people? It seems to me this is especially important in the case of "idea" advertising where one of the perennial complaints by business has been a lack of understanding on the part of the news media of complex economic and technological issues. The result has been that business's position and viewpoint on these issues is either misrepresented or completely ignored.

Whitaker: . . . You cannot launch a campaign of this type three weeks before the election with a series of catchy, colorful spots. You couldn't hope to win. You launch this by doing the massive kind of research and in-depth studies of the issue that it requires to isolate the elements—good and bad—within it so that you can discuss them. You take that documentation to people and organizations who will sit and take the time to go through the whole problem. . . . Once you have established, and we term this an organizational base, once you have established that, then you can go out and begin to do your job publicly, issue by issue by issue, in publicity, in news conferences, in mailings of materials. By the time you get down to the last two or three weeks, of course you are down to the refined, last extract of issue with which you can deal in thirty to sixty seconds.

THE OUTCOME: EVALUATION BY THE PARTICIPANTS

In discussing the outcome of the campaign, Mr. Whitaker said: "They [People's Lobby] had a bad issue. That's the major thing. It's fatal if you have an organized opposition." Mr. Whitaker further observed: "If they [PL] had drafted it better, it would have meant a better initiative from their point of view. However, if they really were serious about all these specific standards for pollution abatement, they would have lost anyway. It just would have been more difficult." The remainder of the arguments in terms of why People's Lobby lost and CAPI won could be summarized in terms of money, emotionalism, and inexperience in organization and campaigning on the part of People's Lobby, and the political muscle of big business employed by CAPI.

Money

According to the late Mr. Koupal, money was *the* reason PL lost the campaign. Koupal maintains that because of the lack of money, they could not do sufficient audience research or buy enough advertising to gain effective audience reach or frequency in their ad campaign. The author suggested to Mr. Koupal an alternative way of looking at equalizing resources between the two opposing groups would be to look not at campaign expenditures but the total effort expended by each group regardless of whether they were purchased or received in kind through volunteer help. The following dialog is illustrative of PL's viewpoint:

> **Sethi:** It seems to me that by limiting campaign expenditures in monetary terms, you would be putting at a competitive disadvantage those groups or causes which may be unpopular at a given point in time and therefore may not be able to attract volunteer help. For example, you seek to limit expenditures on advertising and put restrictions on total spending because you cannot attract big contributors to your cause. Yet you do not see anything wrong in using 10,000 volunteers because they are available to you. Why shouldn't the opposition charge you with taking unfair advantage because you would not limit the use of volunteers, and also would not let them *buy* help for their cause which your 10,000 volunteers provide to you?

> **Joyce and Edwin Koupal:** Volunteer help cannot be equated with money because people are taking part in the political process. Money, on the other hand, is used to manipulate people against their self-interest.
>
> Moreover, the idea that people going door to door wins campaigns is absolutely outrageous and absurd, particularly in the case of initiatives. The real way initiative campaigns are won or lost is by turning the minds of opinion leaders. You don't need a whole lot of people to go to opinion leaders.

Emotionalism

Joyce Koupal stated that emotionalism and inexperience could also be attributed some of the responsibility for the failure of the PL campaign. To generate support for the initiative, it was necessary that people have a chance to consider the proposition rationally and feel safe about it. Therefore, a quiet campaign was desirable from the viewpoint of People's Lobby. According to Joyce Koupal:

> Anybody who is trying to kill an initiative or stop it would create a controversy and make outrageous claims so that there is a huge battle going on. Psychologically, when people get involved in controversy and are faced with uncertainty, they take to status quo—and will stay with what they have. We did everything wrong in the campaign for the Clean Environment Act. All the things, the confrontations and the charges and countercharges, were the wrong tactics for us to use. They [CAPI] were absolutely delighted that we were doing these things.

Edwin Koupal added that PL advertised emotionally instead of institutionally. Instead of carrying out a campaign, they concentrated on answering CAPI's charges. Thus PL got on the negative side instead of getting on a positive thrust. Mr. Whitaker of CAPI also agrees to the introduction of emotionalism on the part of the Koupals in the campaign.

Based on their experience with the Clean Environment Act initiative, People's Lobby developed a campaign strategy that led to success in a campaign to pass the Political Reform Act Initiative in 1974. This strategy was outlined in a PL publication as follows:

1. A well-drafted document is hard to fight. Draw in people who know the field. Seek advice from expert attorneys.
2. Timing is important from both practical and political standpoints.
3. Secure a broad base of support at the very beginning. Get all endorsements in writing. Get to opinion leaders.
4. Carefully evaluate potential opposition.
5. Dry up the money sources of the opposition. Never let them get off the ground.
6. Keep the opposition "off balance."
7. Keep controversy at a minimum—NEVER DEBATE.
8. If a legal dispute arises—settle in court.
9. Set up your own opinion polls. They clearly define the strong and weak areas in your campaign.
10. Distribute literature wisely. Look for opportunities to piggyback your material with candidates and get on state mailers. People's Lobby used this method to send over 5 million pieces of 'YES ON 9' literature.[14]

Mr. Whitaker, however, does not see the success of People's Lobby in the Political Reform Act Initiative in quite those terms: He attributes PL's success to the failure of the opposition. "The [People's Lobby] would have lost on the Political Reform Act if there had been any intelligent campaign against it." He comments, "I think people, good people, who were just as disgusted with the whole Watergate mess as the supporters of the Political Reform Initiative, did not want to get involved in opposing an issue where in the public mind they could be accused of defending excesses—and they walked away from it. That was a mistake, in my opinion, but that is the reason they weren't there."

Another reason for the failure of the Proposition 9 campaign was attributed to arm-twisting by politicians in power who were opposed to it. According to Mr. Koupal:

With us it was a one-to-one form of persuasion for the votes. With them it was arm-twisting every inch of the way all over the state. They even applied pressure from the labor unions on the candidates so they would withdraw their endorsements.

People's Lobby contended that all the facilities of the State of California were pitted against them. Whenever they made a statement on pesticides or some other aspect of agriculture, the Agriculture Department would come up with a big promotional program indicating that the state was

---

[14] *The Political Reform Act*, p. 7.

already working on it, had thought of it in the first place, or that the PL's program was unworkable and PL's statements had no scientific proof.

It should be stated to the credit of the Koupals and People's Lobby that many of the sections contained in the Clean Environment Act have subsequently passed into law. DDT was banned shortly after the CEA was defeated. Persistent chlorinated hydrocarbons have also been banned. EPA is phasing lead out of gasoline, and the California Air Resources Board is now working up to mandatory in-stack monitors in industrial stacks. The conflict of interest sections were enlarged upon and passed into law by the Political Reform Act of 1974, which People's Lobby drafted and qualified and helped to pass. On the debit side, the initiative to control and regulate the construction of nuclear power plants was defeated by a 2 to 1 margin by the voters of California in June 1975.

SELECTED BIBLIOGRAPHY

Bird, Allen W. II; Goldman, Thomas W.; and Lawrence, Keith D. "Corporate Image Advertising: A Discussion of the Factors that Distinguish Those Corporate Image Advertising Practices Protected under the First Amendment from Those Subject to Control by the Federal Trade Commission." *Journal of Urban Law* 4 (1974): 405.

Bigelow v. Virginia. 95 S.CT. 2222 (1975).

Blumberg, Phillip I. "The Politicization of the Corporation." *The Business Lawyer,* July 1971, p. 1551.

"Community, Privacy, Defamation, and the First Amendment: The Implications of *Time Inc. v. Hill." Columbia Law Review* 67 (1967): 926.

Cooper, George C. "The Tax Treatment of Business Grassroots Lobbying: Defining and Attaining the Public Policy Objectives." *Columbia Law Review* 68 (1968): 801.

"Corporate Freedom of Speech." *Suffolk University Law Review* 7 (1973): 1117.

Council on Economic Priorities. "Corporate Advertising and the Environment." *Economics Priorities Report, September–October 1971* 2 (New York, October 1971): 28.

Darling, Harry L. "How Companies Are Using Corporate Advertising." *Public Relations Journal,* November 1975, pp. 26–29.

"Developments in the Law, Deceptive Advertising." *Harvard Law Review* 80 (1967): 1004, 1032–33, 1063–1101.

"The Excesses of Proposition 9." *San Francisco Examiner,* March 19, 1972, p. 2-B.

"Freedom to Advertise." Editorial, *The New York Times,* June 16, 1972.

Gwyn, Robert J. "Opinion Advertising and the Free Market of Ideas." *Public Opinion Quarterly,* summer 1970, pp. 246–55.

Lilliston, Lynn. "One Man's Family in Pollution War." *Los Angeles Times,* July 30, 1971, p. 4.

Ludlam, Charles E. "Abatement of Corporate Image Environmental Advertising." *Ecology Law Quarterly* 4 (1974): 247–78.

Neckritz, Alan F., and Ordower, Lawrence B. "Ecological Pornography and the Mass Media." *Ecology Law Quarterly* 1 (1974): 374.

O'Toole, John E. "Advocacy Advertising Shows the Flag." *Public Relations Journal,* November 1975, pp. 14–15.

Sethi, S. Prakash. *Advocacy Advertising and Large Corporations.* Lexington, Mass.: Heath, 1977.

Webster, G. D. "Deductibility of Lobbying and Related Expenses." *American Bar Association Journal* 42 (1956): 1975.

12 Children's television, advertising, and programming

When and how children should be protected from undesirable communication

*The biggest big business in America is not steel, automobiles or television. It is the manufacture, refinement and distribution of anxiety. . . .
Logically extended, this process can only terminate in a mass nervous breakdown or in a collective condition of resentment. . . .*

Eric Sevareid

On October 31, 1974, the Federal Communication Commission (FCC) issued its long-awaited policy statement outlining the commission's position on TV commercials and programs aimed at children.[1] The report was made in response to a petition by Action for Children's Television (ACT) seeking imposition of certain restrictions on TV commercials aimed at children and also adoption of certain guidelines for television programming for children. This statement was the latest salvo in a continuing battle among the broadcast media, the advertisers, parent groups and other industry critics, and various government agencies concerned with the quality and quantity of television programming and advertising directed primarily at children. Moreover, the controversy is not confined to the United States, but is being debated with varying degrees of intensity in every coun-

---

[1] Federal Communications Commission, *In the Matter of Petition of Action for Children's Television (ACT) for Rulemaking Looking Toward the Elimination of Sponsorship and Commercial Content in Children's Programming and the Establishment of a Weekly 14 Hour Quota of Children's Television Programs,* Docket No. 19142, October 31, 1974.

try where television stations carry commercials and where television is a mass media and a major source of public entertainment.

ISSUES FOR ANALYSIS

The case raises major issues of public policy that encompass not only the relationship between the advertiser, the consumer, and the buyer of a given product, but the "responsible" use, however determined, of publicly owned airwaves, and the protection of a particularly vulnerable population group. Among the many questions that should be analyzed are these:

1. Do children, as a specific group, need government protection or representation of their interests as far as television programming or advertising are concerned? As a specific group, do children have developmental characteristics that require special attention? What is the evidence that children's behavior has been adversely affected by the existing nature of television programming and advertising? To what extent should parents be expected to assume responsibility for protecting children from programs and commercials they consider undesirable?

2. How should the FCC fulfill its obligation in protecting the public interest while at the same time protecting the rights of speech of an advertiser and the freedom of the broadcaster to develop content without unnecessary regulation and outside interference? How might one define the public interest in these circumstances?

3. What are the responsibilities of a broadcaster and advertiser outside the area of seeking a maximum viewing audience for the former and influencing favorably the largest number of viewers toward its products for the latter? What other considerations should be relevant in developing program content and advertising themes to reduce public discontent? To what extent do traditional marketing and competitive factors limit the freedom of advertisers and broadcasters to consider these factors?

4. What is the record of self-regulation on the part of industry in improving program content and preventing exploitation of children through television commercials? What are the relative merits of the arguments advanced by the industry and its critics to support their respective viewpoints?

5. If it is considered necessary that a significant change be made in current practices in children's programming and advertising, how might these changes be brought about? What relative roles should be assumed by the industry, the advertising agencies, the broadcasters, the parents, the FCC and other regulatory bodies, and other public interest groups? How and why would these changes bring about a better

serving of children's interest? What are the drawbacks in such a proposal? What steps can be suggested to bring about implementation of such a proposal?

6. What is the experience of other countries in regard to regulation of programming and advertising for children on television? What lessons can be drawn from these experiences?

DEFINING THE PROBLEM

The law considers children to be entitled to special protection because of their immaturity and inexperience. For example, contracts made by minors are not legally binding, and both tort law and criminal law require different standards of behavior for children.[2] This special protection extends to children in their relationship to television. The 1974 FCC "Children's Report and Policy Statement" emphasized that special treatment should be accorded to children. Because of their immaturity and their special needs, children require programming designed specifically for them. Accordingly, the FCC expected television broadcasters, as trustees of a valuable public resource, to develop and present programs that will serve the unique needs of a child audience.

> Children, like adults, have a variety of different needs and interests. Most children, however, lack the experience and intellectual sophistication to enjoy or benefit from much of the non-entertainment material broadcast for the general public. We believe, therefore, that the broadcaster's public service obligation includes a responsibility to provide diversified programming designed to meet the varied needs and interests of the child audience.[3]

Concern for the effect of TV on children has long been of interest to other public bodies as well. For example, early in 1950 the Midcentury White House Conference on Children and Youth studied this issue; the harmful effects of television were looked at in the Senate judiciary committee's study of juvenile delinquency; and in 1969 the Department of Health, Education and Welfare studied the relationship between television viewing and behavior. A more recent study (1975), "Broadcast Advertising and Children," was done for the subcommittee on communication of the House of Representatives.[4]

---

[2] Marjorie S. Steinberg, "The FCC as Fairy Godmother: Improving Children's Television," *UCLA Law Review* 21 (1974): 1302.

[3] Federal Communications Commission, *In the Matter of Petition of Action for Children's Television (ACT)*, p. 7.

[4] R. L. Shayon, *Television and Our Children*, 1951; U.S. Congress, Senate, *Hearings on S.R.274 Before the Subcommittee to Investigate Juvenile Delinquency of the Senate Committee on the Judiciary, The Effects on Young People of Violence and Crime Portrayed on Television*, part 16 (88th Cong., 2nd sess., 1965); U.S. Congress, Senate, *Hearings on S.R.48 Before the Subcommittee to Investigate Juvenile Delinquency of the Senate Committee on the Judiciary, The Effects on Young People of Violence and Crime Portrayed on Television,*

The problem, however, is not the concern for protection, but what constitutes children's television programs, and how to define offensive program content, misleading and deceptive advertising, and the degree of protection necessary for children in different age groups.

Children's viewing of television

Children constitute a significant portion of the viewing audience in general, and are majority viewers in certain specific time slots. According to the 1976 Nielsen index, American children watch an average of four hours of television a day. The report further states that in homes with preschoolers, the television is on for fifty-three hours per week, ten hours more a week than in the average home. The high school student will have seen almost 22,000 hours of television, and an estimated 350,000 commercials.[5]

A children's program is defined in a proposal by six consumer groups, including the council on Children, Media, and Merchandising and Action for Children's Television, as "a program for which children comprise over 50 percent of the audience," and a family program as "a program for which children comprise over 20 percent but not more than 50 percent of the audience."[6] This definition, however, is at variance with those used by different industry groups for the purposes of monitoring children's advertising. The National Association of Broadcasters defines a children's commercial as "any commercial designed primarily for children which the advertiser or agency by their media buying patterns or merchandising goals place in children's programs in order to reach an audience composed primarily of children."[7]

The Council of Better Business Bureaus and the regulatory agency, the Children's Review Unit of the National Advertising Division (NAD), define

---

part 10 (87th Cong., 2nd sess., 1963); U.S. Congress, Senate, *Hearings on S.R.62 Before the Subcommittee to Investigate Juvenile Delinquency of the Senate Committee on the Judiciary, Television and Juvenile Delinquency* (84th Cong., 1st sess., 1956); Rubenstein, Comstock, and Murray (eds.), *Television and Social Behavior: A Technical Report to the Surgeon General's Scientific Advisory Committee on Television and Social Behavior* (1972); U.S. Congress, House, Committee on Interstate and Foreign Commerce, Subcommittee on Communication, *Broadcast Advertising and Children* (93rd Cong., 2nd sess., 1975).

[5] Joann S. Lublin, "From Bugs to Batman, Children's TV Shows Produce Adult Anxiety," *The Wall Street Journal*, October 19, 1976, p. 1. Also see Joan Barthel, "Boston Mothers Against Kidvid," *The New York Times Magazine*, January 5, 1975, p. 1; Colman McCarthy, "A Diet of TV Food Ads," *Washington Post*, December 18, 1973, p. 8; and Robert Berkvist, "Can TV Keep Giving Kids the Business?" *The New York Times*, May 12, 1974, p. 1, for other figures on the amount of television that children view. Another fruitful source here is Federal Trade Commission, *Petition to Issue a Trade Regulation Rule Governing the Private Regulation of Children's Television Advertising*, Appendix III, Exhibit U, number 1.

[6] "ACT Says Stations Aren't Living Up to Rules on Ads in Children's TV: Stations Say Group is Way Off Base," *Broadcasting*, December 22, 1975, p. 28.

[7] Federal Trade Commission, *Petition to Issue a Trade Regulation Rule*, Appendix II, Exhibit E.

children's advertising as that which is "broadcast in children's programs and programs in which audience patterns typically contain more than 50 percent children."[8] This definition would not include commercials which are shown on eight out of ten shows most watched by children, for the FCC report on children's television stated that children formed a substantial segment of the audience on weekday afternoons and early evenings as well as on weekends.

In terms of program content, one area of concern is the amount of violence in children's programs. Recent studies indicate that the incidence of violence on Saturday morning children's television has increased. One study conducted by the Media Action Research Center of Setauket, New York, found that in the 1975–76 season, an act of violence occurred for every 2 minutes of programming, in comparison to one act of aggression every 3½ minutes in 1974–75. A 1967–75 study by George Gerbner and Larry Gross found a drop in violence during the "family hour," the first two hours of prime time, but "a sharp increase in violence during children's (weekend daytime) programs in the current season." A 1973 study showed that 60 percent of programs directed to children contained "moderate" to "much" violence. If children watched primarily programming oriented toward them, they would be exposed to about twenty-one hours of violent programming per week.[9] Studies on the effect of viewing violence on children's subsequent aggressive behavior, however, have produced inconclusive results. What constitutes violence, and what level of depiction of violence, however defined, should be tolerated because it conforms to the reality of contemporary society within which children must grow and adapt remains a matter of controversy.

The presentation of different racial groups and sex roles on television programs has also been studied. The Media Action Research Center's report on the 1974–75 season showed that sex role bias on television shows was still high, with males accounting for 72 percent of all roles, 59 percent of these being white males. Eighty-two percent of all characters were white, and there were almost no performances by minorities.[10]

Commercials on children's television programs

The quantity of commercials and the types of products advertised on children's television programs is another area of contention. Since 1974,

---

[8] Children's Review Unit, National Advertising Division, Council of Better Business Bureaus, Inc., "Children's Advertising Guidelines," *News From NAD*, June 1975, p. 2.

[9] Lublin, "Bugs to Batman," p. 1; and "Evidence on TV Violence Is 'Cause for Concern,'" *ACT News* 4 (spring 1975): 6. Also see Susan E. Harvey, Robert N. Liebert, and Rita W. Loulos, *The New Children's Television: A Profile of the 1974–1975 Season* (New York: Media Action Research Center, 1975), and "Summary of Violence Profile No. 7: Trends in Network Television Drama and Viewer Conception of Reality, 1967–1975" (Philadelphia: Annenburg School of Communications, 1976).

[10] Steinberg, "FCC as Fairy Godmother, p. 1301.

commercial time on Saturday and Sunday mornings has been reduced from 16 minutes to 9½ minutes; 9½ minutes of commercials per hour is normal in adult prime time television. The most heavily advertised products on children's "prime time" (Saturday and Sunday mornings) are "foods such as cereals, desserts, pastas, artificial drinks, gums, candies, and snacks; toys, such as dolls, racing cars and games; and occasional clothes, shoes, and school materials."[11]

When considering the top 40 children's television programs shown before 9 p.m., a report covering the period September 23, 1974, to October 13, 1974, showed that there were 67 drug commercials, the most advertised product being Geritol, with 13 commercials; 36 household chemical or aerosol product commercials, with Lysol as the most advertised; 10 aerosol personal care products; and 3 other hazardous products (Bic Butane Lighter and Wilkinson Bonded blades).[12] As is apparent from the commercials, the programs with the largest child audiences are indeed not those aired on Saturday and Sunday morning; nor do these programs have more than 50 percent of the viewing population composed of children. The top program, by audience size, is Emergency, which is shown at 8 p.m. and attracts an audience of 8.7 million children. Of the top 40, only 17 have an audience over 50 percent children, and only 18 are shown on Saturday and Sunday mornings.

INDUSTRY GROUPS

The business and industry groups involved in the children's television issue are the broadcasters, the advertisers, and the advertising agencies. The two major industry organizations are the National Association of Broadcasters (NAB) and the Association of National Advertisers (ANA).

National Association of Broadcasters (NAB). NAB is a voluntary organization, comprising only 58 percent of all broadcasters. However, NAB asserts that since non-NAB members carry commercials and programs that are code-approved, an estimated 85 percent of all programs and commercials have been subjected to code approval. In its regulations of children's advertising, the NAB code has forbidden advertising of health aids (such as vitamins) to children; forbidden some advertising that blurs the distinction between the commercial and the program; has created guidelines for toy advertisements; and has regulated timing and amounts of "nonprogram" material, reducing commercials to 9½ minutes per hour on children's weekend programs.[13] Since the efforts of the Code Authority are

[11] Federal Trade Commission, *Petition to Issue a Trade Regulation Rule,* p. 8. Also see Robert B. Choate, "The Sugar-Coated Children's Hour," *Nation,* January 3, 1972, pp. 146–48.

[12] Federal Trade Commission, *Petition to Issue a Trade Regulation Rule,* Appendix II, Exhibits E and F.

[13] Television Information Office of the National Association of Broadcasters, *Children, Television and Broadcast Regulation* (New York: Television Information Office of NAB, September 1974), pp. 4, 7.

reviewed only by the NAB's Television Board of Directors, no advertisers, sponsors, or consumers have any influence on the code's operation. The Code Authority is dependent on the fees paid by its member stations, and it has no power to enforce compliance.

Association of National Advertisers (ANA). The ANA is comprised of between 50 to 60 companies that advertise to children, and whose ads make up 80 percent of children's television network advertising. Although the ANA has a set of Children's Advertising Guidelines, no regulatory agency reviews advertisements or enforces the code. According to Peter Allport, president of the ANA, "Were we to have sanctions, competitors would be regulating the activities of their competitors. Even if this were legal, which I do not believe it is, we would consider it unethical."[14] In his testimony before the FCC, Allport stated that the ANA guidelines were designed to be just that—guidelines—and were not intended to be a set of rigid structures or traffic rules covering the second-by-second development or content of a commercial.

The formation of a self-regulatory organ sponsored by advertisers which would be more effective than the ANA code began in 1971 through the combined efforts of the ANA, the American Advertising Federation, the American Association of Advertising Agencies, and the Council of Better Business Bureaus. This organization is made up of the National Advertising Review Council (NARC), the National Advertising Review Board (NARB), and the National Advertising Division of the Council of Better Business Bureaus (NAD).

NARC, which is composed only of the chairmen and presidents of the four sponsoring groups, is an administrative body that appoints the members and chair of the NARB, establishes the rules for the operation of self-regulatory actions, and establishes new programs. The NARB is the appeals body of the organization. It consists of a chair and 50 persons, 30 of whom are from advertisers, 10 from advertising agencies, and 10 from the public. The NAD is the investigative body. It receives complaints from outside sources such as consumers, Better Business Bureaus, or government agencies, and initiates complaints through its own monitoring of advertisements. After receiving the complaint, it asks for substantiation from the advertiser, and then closes the case if the substantiation is adequate or if the advertiser agrees to alter the advertising. If no agreement is reached, the case can be appealed to the NARB. If the NARB upholds the NAD, the case goes to the FTC.[15]

In 1974, concern over the children's advertising issue caused another body to be created. In June, the Children's Advertising Review Unit be-

---

[14] Federal Trade Commission, *Petition to Issue a Trade Regulation Rule*, p. 15. See also ANA, Inc., "Children's Television Advertising Guidelines," adopted May 31, 1972, by ANA Board of Directors.

[15] U.S. Congress, House, Hearings Before the Subcommittee on Communications of the Committee on Interstate and Foreign Commerce, Statement by Roland P. Campbell on "Self-Regulation of Children's Advertising" (93rd Cong., 2nd sess., July 15, 1975).

came a separate unit within the NAD. This unit judges ads not only on their truthfulness but also on their fairness to a child's perception. The advertising, however, is regarded as being children's advertising only when it is shown on programs where children constitute more than 50 percent of the audience, or when the shows are clearly addressed to children 11 and under.[16]

Public interest groups

The two most active public interest groups working for regulation and improvement of children's television are Action for Children's Television (ACT) and Council on Children, Media and Merchandising (CCMM).

ACT, organized in 1967 by Peggy Charren of Boston as a group concerned about the quality of children's television, was incorporated in 1970 as Action for Children's Television. Six years after its formation, it was described as having "grown from a kaffeeklatsch of concerned mothers to a 3,000-member national organization with prestigious support (the American Academy of Pediatrics, American Library Association, American Dental Association) and a fair measure of clout with the powerful moneyed and established broadcasting and advertising industries."[17] ACT describes its aims and objectives as:

> To encourage and persuade broadcasters and advertisers to provide programming of the highest possible quality designed for children of different ages;
>
> To encourage the development and enforcement of appropriate guidelines relating to children and the media;
>
> To encourage research, experimentation and evaluation in the field of children's television[18]

The broadcast industry has regarded the ACT with suspicion, criticizing ACT's petition to the FCC as "unlawful, unviable, and uninformed."[19] ACT's demands were also seen as too radical.

The Council on Children, Media, and Merchandising (CCMM) was founded in 1970. Headed by Robert Choate, it has been a participant in the FCC and FTC proceedings that affected children's television advertising. Choate has concentrated on fighting the advertising of products he considers to be potentially harmful to children—heavily sugared food, candy, soft drinks, vitamins, over the counter drugs, and household products. CCMM is funded partly from foundation grants and partly from

---

[16] Children's Review Unit, "Children's Advertising Guidelines," p. 2.

[17] Liz Roman Gallese, "Consumers Advocate Better Children's TV, Get Some Concessions," The Wall Street Journal, August 5, 1974, p. 1.

[18] Action for Children's Television, "ActFacts: A History and Chronology of Action for Children's Television" (Newtonville, Mass.: Action for Children's Television, n.d.).

[19] "No Support for Adless Kid Shows," Broadcasting, April 6, 1970, p. 48.

Choate's private funds. CCMM has also formed another organization, On Second Thought, which produces public service announcements on such topics as nutritional education and dental care for children. On Second Thought is based in Washington and is also sponsored by such other groups as the Consumer Federation of America, the Society for Nutrition Education, and the National Council of Negro Women.

Like ACT, CCMM has also resorted to legal and regulatory avenues to accomplish its objectives. CCMM's major action was in 1974, when it filed a petition before the FTC to issue a trade regulation rule governing the private regulation of children's television advertising (see the section on "Reform Proposals"). Along with other public interest groups, CCMM has also found FCC's policy statement unsatisfactory and is continuing its efforts to bring about substantive changes in children's television programming and advertising practices. CCMM has worked with the Food and Drug Administration on issues relating to food labeling, ingredients, and additives. In addition to its legal actions, CCMM also works with private organizations.

Children's Television Workshop (CTW) is another group with nationwide impact. Located in New York City, this nonprofit corporation is the producer of such well-known children's educational programs as "Sesame Street" and "The Electric Company," which are broadcast on public television. Joan Ganz Cooney is the Workshop's executive director, and Lloyd N. Morriset, president of Markle Foundation, is its chairman.[20] CTW continually researches and evaluates its programs to ascertain how to teach most effectively and how to avoid anything that might be harmful to children.

The Media Action Research Center, Inc. (MARC) is also a nonprofit organization involved in studying the effects of media on our society. The scientific director of MARC, Robert M. Liebert, is a child psychologist and is on the faculty at the State University of New York at Stony Brook. Liebert has created 30-second spots for television that present children with nonviolent alternatives for problem-solving.[21] MARC has also done "content analyses" of Saturday morning children's television for both the 1974–75 and 1975–76 seasons. The analyses covered amounts of violence, positive social behavior, sex role bias, and other aspects of programming.[22]

Still other groups act on the local level. In the San Francisco Bay area, the Committee on Children's Television (CCT), founded in 1971 and headed by Sally Williams and Neil Morse, became involved in changing

---

[20] George Gent, "New 'Sesame Street' Corporation Plans Older Children's Series," *The New York Times,* April 8, 1970, p. 87. See also G. Lesser, *Children and Television: Lessons from Sesame Street,* (New York, 1974); Evelyn Kaye, *The Family Guide to Children's Television* (New York, 1974), pp. 34–35.

[21] Caryl Rivers, "What Sort of Behavior Control Should TV Impose on Children: Violence or Harmony?" *The New York Times,* August 18, 1974, p. 15.

[22] U.S. Congress, House, "Broadcast Advertising and Children."

children's television. The CCT developed "station consultation teams," groups of community members concerned about children's television, who meet with the broadcasters of local stations to provide them with information and encourage them to improve their programming for children. The CCT has also produced bilingual public service announcements on nutrition, consumerism, recreation programs, and racial pride.[23]

Regulatory agencies

The two federal government agencies involved in the children's television issue are the Federal Communications Commission (FCC) and the Federal Trade Commission (FTC).

The Federal Communications Commission (FCC) is composed of seven commissioners appointed for seven-year terms by the president of the United States, with the advice and consent of the Senate, with one member of the commission being chosen by the president as chair; its enabling legislation allows it to "perform any and all acts, make such rules and regulations, and issue such orders, not inconsistent with this chapter, as may be necessary in the execution of its functions." In most cases, Congress gave the FCC the freedom to use its own discretion, and all specific powers granted to the FCC should be exercised "as public convenience, interest, or necessity requires."[24] Section 315 of the Communications Act contains a clearer definition of the public interest, the "fairness doctrine." This section clearly authorizes the FCC to interfere with program content, requires broadcasters to provide "equal time" to political candidates, and "to afford reasonable opportunity for discussion of conflicting views on issues of public importance." The FCC's power to enforce its regulations revolves around its ability to grant and revoke licenses. In performing this function, the FCC monitors the operations of broadcasters and issues policy statements to explain the FCC's view of its role and the broadcaster's responsibility.

One of the FCC's sensitive areas has been the problem of regulating programming without coming into conflict with the First Amendment's protection of freedom of speech. Although the broadcasting medium's unique nature as a limited resource gives grounds for some differences in

---

[23] Committee on Children's Television, *CCT Newsletter*, Fall 1975, p. 6; and Committee on Children's Television, Inc., "What Is CCT?" n.d.

[24] For a discussion of the scope of the FCC's activities in general and children's television in particular, see Marjorie Steinberg, "The FCC as Fairy Godmother"; Acard Brinton, *The Regulation of Broadcasting by the FCC: A Study in Regulation by Independent Commissioners* (Cambridge, Mass.: Harvard University Press, 1962); Henry Geller, *A Modest Proposal to Reform the Federal Communications Commission* (Santa Monica, Calif.: The Rand Paper Series, April 1974); Newton Minnow, *Equal Time: The Private Broadcaster and the Public Interest* (New York: Atheneum, 1964); Roger Noll, Merton Peck, and John McGowan, *Economic Aspects of Television Regulation* (Washington, D.C.: The Brookings Institution, 1973).

its protection by the First Amendment, Congress has expressly prohibited "censorship" by the FCC. Thus, "in applying the public interest standard to programming, the Commission walks a tightrope between saying too much and saying too little. In most cases it has resolved this dilemma by imposing only general affirmative duties. . . ."[25]

Although the FCC has always called for programming that would serve all substantial groups in the community, children were not recognized as one of these "substantial groups" until the commission's 1960 "Report and Statement of Policy Re: Programming." In this report, programming for children was listed as one of fourteen "major elements usually necessary to meet the public interest, needs, and desires of the community."[26] However, the FCC made it clear that decisions about programming were left to the licensees. The 1960 policy statement added another provision about programming content: "Broadcast licensees must assume responsibility for all material which is broadcast through their facilities . . . with respect to advertising material the licensee has the additional responsibility to take all reasonable measures to eliminate any false, misleading, or deceptive matter. . . ."[27] Thus, under its mandate to protect the public interest, the FCC requires the licensee to exercise a minimum level of judgment to avoid deceptive advertisements.

The Supreme Court's decision in the *Red Lion Broadcasting Co. v. FCC* was a landmark case in giving the FCC power to control programming. Not only did this decision reaffirm the commission's fairness doctrine, but it went even further by stating: "It is the right of the viewers and listeners, not the right of the broadcasters, which is paramount."[28] In its 1974 "Children's Television Report and Policy Statement," the FCC commented on the *Red Lion* decision: "This language, in our judgment, clearly points to a wide range of programming responsibilities on the part of the broadcaster."[29] However, this Supreme Court decision must be balanced against the FCC's history of reluctance to make affirmative rulings.

Although the FCC is the major government agency that handles broadcasting, the Federal Trade Commission also has regulatory power. The FTC is composed of five commissioners appointed by the president with advice and consent of the Senate for seven years. With its basic function to prevent "unfair methods of competition" and "unfair or deceptive acts or practices in commerce," the FTC is concerned with false and misleading advertising, and thus with the broadcasters who depend on advertising as

---

[25] *Banzhaf* v. *FCC*, 405 F. 2nd 1082. Also see *Children's Television Report and Policy Statement*, FCC-74-1174, 24950, Docket No. 19142 (released October e1, 1974).

[26] *Children's Television Report*, p. 6.

[27] Susan Scott, "Children's Television Advertising: The Reluctant Evolution of New Standards for Industry. Self-Regulation" (unpublished paper, Boston University, December 1975).

[28] *Red Lion Broadcasting Co.* v. *FCC*, 395 U.S. 367 (1968), p. 390.

[29] *Children's Television Report*, p. 7.

their sole economic support. While the original legislation prohibited only "unfair methods of competition," the Wheeler-Lea Act of 1938 provided that any unfair or deceptive act or practice in commerce, regardless of its effect on competition, is unlawful. This amendment protects consumers from all deceptive advertising.[30] The FTC is also responsible for creating legislation against unfair practices not previously been declared illegal. The FTC's Bureau of Consumer Protection examines and initiates action in cases of deceptive advertising. The commission may settle cases through administrative action, by public hearings leading to cease and desist orders, and finally by bringing the case to court, depending on the compliance of the accused.

The FCC and FTC have worked with some cooperation in the area of advertising and issued liaison statements in 1957 and 1972.[31] The 1972 statement specified the areas of responsibility for each agency. The FTC "will exercise primary jurisdiction over all matters relating to unfair or deceptive advertising in all media," while the FCC "will continue to take into account pertinent considerations in this area in determining whether broadcast applications for license or renewal of license shall be granted." The FCC furthermore stated: "The commission cannot require licensees to stop broadcasting commercial announcements on the grounds that they are materially deceptive. The announcements are the subject of an FTC proceeding. That agency has primary jurisdiction and qualifications in the area."

PROPOSALS FOR CHANGES IN CURRENT REGULATORY PRACTICES

The major thrust for reform in current regulatory practices, both at the FCC and the FTC level and in the industry's self-regulatory practices, have come from ACT and CCMM.

Revised guidelines for television programming for children

In 1970, ACT filed a petition before the FCC requesting that the agency adopt rules for specifying quotas for children's programs on television and also the elimination of sponsorship and commercial content in children's programming. In particular, the petition asked that the following rules be implemented by the FCC:[32]

---

[30] Wheeler-Lea Act, approved March 21, 1938, 52 Stat. III (1938), amending FTC Act, quoted in Walter B. Emery, *Broadcasting & Government: Responsibilities and Regulation,* 1971, p. 73.

[31] FCC Public Notice No. 41503, February 21, 1957 (22 FCC 1572); and FTC, "FCC in Liaison Agreement on Ads," April 27, 1972.

[32] The following is from *Children's Television Report and Policy Statement,* pp. 1–2.

1. There shall be no sponsorship and no commercials on children's programs.
2. No performer shall be permitted to use or mention products, services or stores by brand names during children's programs, nor shall such names be included in any way during children's programs.
3. Each station shall provide daily programming for children and in no case shall this be less than 14 hours a week, as a part of its public service requirement. Provision shall be made for programming in each of the age groups specified below, and during the time periods specified.

Preschool; ages 2–5	7 A.M.–6 P.M. daily
	7 A.M.–6 P.M. weekends
Primary; ages 6–9	4 P.M.–6 P.M. daily
	8 A.M.–8 P.M. weekends
Elementary; ages 10–12	5 P.M.–9 P.M. daily
	9 A.M.–9 P.M. weekends

The FCC accepted ACT's petition and on January 26, 1971, issued a wide-ranging inquiry into children's programming and advertising practices. The FCC asked for comments on these proposed rules and on certain general questions:

1. What types of children's programs not now available do the parties believe commercial TV stations should present?
2. To what extent, generally and with respect to particular programs and types of programs, does "children's programming" have benefits to children beyond the fact that it holds their interest and attention and thus removes the need for other activity or parental attention?
3. What, generally speaking, is a definition of "children's programming" which could serve for the Commission's use in this connection? To what extent do children, particularly in the higher age groups mentioned by ACT, view and benefit from general TV programming?
4. What restriction on commercials short of prohibition—e.g., on types of products or services, what can be said, number, divorcement from program content, etc.—would be desirable? Comments should take into account in this connection the provisions of the NAB Television Code and its guidelines.
5. To what extent should any restriction on commercial messages in children's programs also apply to such messages adjacent to children's programs?[33]

Comments in support of the ACT petition were filed by, among others, Council on Children, Media, and Marketing; Foundation to Improve Television; Broadcasting and Film Division of the National Council of the Church of Christ in the U.S.A.; the American Library Association; the Pittsburgh Area Pre-School Association; the Ambulatory Pediatric Association;

---

[33] *Notice of Inquiry and Notice of Proposed Rule Making in the Matter of Action for Children's Television* (Docket 19142), P&F Radio Reg. paragraph 53:391 at 395 (1971).

the Association for Childhood Education; the American Friends Service Committee; and the National Organization for Women.

Revision of private regulation of children's television advertising

In 1973, Lewis Engman, chairman of the Federal Trade Commission, initiated a Children's Television Advertising Project with representatives from the broadcasting, advertising, and sponsoring industries and from six consumer groups. These groups were the Association of National Advertisers; the Leo Burnett Company; the American Advertising Federation; the Council of Better Business Bureaus; the American Association of Advertising Agencies; the National Association of Broadcasters; Action for Children's Television; Council on Children, Media and Merchandising; Consumers Union; Consumer Action Now; and the FCC chairman's office. The purpose of their discussion was to develop and implement a workable code for the regulation of children's television advertising.

The deliberations of these groups culminated in a petition by CCMM, ultimately denied, before the Federal Trade Commission to issue a trade regulation rule governing the private regulation of children's advertising. Among other things, the petition asserted that:

1. The National Association of Broadcasters Code Authority and the Council of Better Business Bureau's Children's Advertising effort purport to protect children from fraud, deceit and mismanagement, but *in themselves* are guilty of being fraudulent, deceitful and misrepresentative.
2. The NAB and CBBB codes governing children's advertising are poorly enforced, and in any case, the largest children's audiences are found viewing programs outside the times—Saturday and Sunday mornings— when the codes and guidelines are really operative.

CCMM's petition asks the FTC to promulgate the following trade regulation rule:

It shall be considered an unfair and deceptive trade practice if:

(1)   Any private organization purports to regulate, restrain or guide television advertising to children under 12 by saying or implying that such advertising has been held up against some standard or guideline and found to be acceptable unless:
A.   Such organization has published a standard to regulate, restrain or guide such advertising;
B.   The scope, extent, purpose and daily operations of the regulating and restraining are clearly made known and documented to the public;
C.   The coverage of the effort includes the 35 most child-watched television programs aired nationally before 9:00 P.M. and the advertising adjacent thereto;

D. The coverage of the effort also includes advertising in any single television market when the following minimum audience is anticipated:

Total available local TV households	Critical child audience levels
Over 1,000,000	Over 100,000
999,999 to 500,000	Over 50,000
499,999 to 200,000	Over 20,000
Under 200,000	Over 10,000

E. Monthly public reports on the regulating/restraining activity are made available to the public;

F. Films, storyboards and scripts of all advertisements under consideration are kept so as to provide reasonable access to the public.

(2) Any private organization purports to regulate, restrain or guide television advertising to children under 12 (applicable as defined in subparagraph "C" and "D" above) by saying or implying that such advertising has been held up against some standard or guideline and found to be acceptable if it includes advertising of hazardous products unless the advertising of such hazardous products is made subject to the following requirements:

A. A substantial portion of the audio and visual time spent in advertising the product shall be devoted to warnings of product hazard;

B. Any advertising of hazardous products to children shall include in its warning, material reflective of and consistent with any product hazard warnings which appear on the product, package or label, but shall not be limited to those products which have an explicit warning to children on the label.

C. The wording of product hazard warnings shall be subject to the approval of the FTC in consultation with the appropriate Federal agency responsible for regulating the safety of the product itself i.e.: with the Food and Drug Administration for drug products, the Consumer Product Safety Commission for hazardous products under its jurisdiction, etc.)

In the alternative, petitioner requests that if the FTC is unable to adopt part (2) of the Rule proposed above, it shall adopt the following alternative Rule:

A. It shall be considered an unfair and deceptive trade practice if any private organization purports to regulate, restrain or guide television advertising to children (as part of an audience defined in "C" and "D" above) by saying or implying that such advertising has been held up against some standard or guideline and found to be acceptable if the organization permits the advertising of hazardous products.

In a further alternative to the above, petitioner requests that if the Federal Trade Commission is unable to adopt the foregoing rules, it adopt the following rule:

A. It shall be considered an unfair and deceptive practice for any television advertiser to advertise a hazardous product

1. On any of the 35 most child-watched television programs aired nationally before 9:00 P.M.; or

2. On any television program when the local audience in a stated market area exceeds the following number of children:

Total available local TV households	Critical child audience level
Over 1,000,000	Over 100,000
999,999 to 500,000	Over 50,000
499,999 to 200,000	Over 20,000
Under 200,000	Over 10,000

Petitioner further requests that this petition be published within 30 days in the Federal Register, opened for public comment and that action then be taken rapidly, preferably within 60 days. Since 10 months of negotiation and nearly four years of legal activity have occurred on children's advertising at the Commission, and all interested parties have had an opportunity to express themselves and most have done so, it should be possible to expedite Commission action on this proposed Trade Regulation Rule.

The two petitions became the subject of intense debate and controversy among various industry organizations, public interest groups, the news media, and even the general public. The arguments for and against the adoption of these rules reflect the nature of general debate among those who seek greater regulation of programming and commercial content of children's television, and those who seek to maintain the status quo or even advocate further relaxation of current regulatory practices. These arguments are summarized in subsequent sections, as are the disposition of the two petitions by the FCC and the FTC and the reaction of the various groups to the decisions made by the two commissions.

REGULATION OF CHILDREN'S TELEVISION PROGRAMMING AND ADVERTISING

The FCC involvement

Interest in the children's advertising issue was focused by the ACT petition to the FCC on January 26, 1971. The FCC's "Notice of Inquiry and Notice of Proposed Rule Making in the Matter of Action for Children's Television," which had asked for comments on the proposed rules and questions, drew over 100,000 letters and supporting petitions, the majority of which supported ACT.[34] In July 1972, Alan Pearce, communications

---

[34] Steinberg, "FCC as Fairy Godmother," p. 1293.

economist for the FCC, filed a report entitled, "The Economics of Network Children's Television Programming." The study showed an extremely high degree of concentration in the advertising market for children's television. Kellogg, Mattel, and General Mills accounted for 30 percent of total revenues from children's shows. Concentration by product was also high, with cereals, toys, vitamins, over the counter drugs, food, candy, and beverages dominating the market. These findings indicate that network weekend children's television is a specialized market aimed at a particular group of consumers.[35]

Pearce investigated the costs and revenues of network children's programming and found that most weekend television programs cost between $10,000 and $11,000 per half-hour, assuming that each program is shown six times over a two-year period, excluding market potential for syndication. Programming costs of around $250,000 per hour were average for first showings of network prime-time children's television. In investigating the impact of a reduction in commercial time on network profits, it was found that a 25 percent reduction would result in a reduction of $6.3 million in profits for CBS, leaving that network a profit of $10 million from children's television. NBC's profit would be reduced from $3.7 to $1 million, and ABC's would be reduced from $7.2 to $3.5 million. But these calculations show what would happen in the worst possible case. Although the ACT demand for fourteen hours per week of quality children's programming would have an immediate cost impact, the costs could be amortized over a long period of time. For example, Disney films for children have had a long-term payoff because the early films still make a profit every time they are shown. The second ACT proposal, that there be no commercial sponsorship of children's programs, would cause serious financial loss to all three networks. Pearce's analysis of the final ACT request, that for age-specific programming, concludes: "It *might* be possible to program to age-specific groups and also make money."

Following the release of this report, the FCC convened hearings in October 1972 and January 1973. The different points of view on this issue were represented by panels, with Lee Polk, former head of children's programming for National Educational Television, as facilitator. The panelists were divided on the fundamental question of what television for children should be, although most agreed that the status quo is necessary in order to finance children's television. They also agreed that some measure of control was necessary to correct abuses. Supporters of industry warned that controls might impinge on the First Amendment protection of freedom of speech, and that if advertising were cut back, there would be no money available to improve programming.

The FCC took no immediate action. In May 1974, the new chairman,

---

[35] Federal Communications Commission, *The Economics of Network Children's Television Programming*, a report by Alan Pearce, July 1972.

Richard E. Wiley, in an address before the Atlanta chapter of the National Academy of Television Arts and Science, suggested some reforms. Wiley emphasized the need for a reduction of commercials on children's programs and questioned why the NAB Code had reduced commercial time from 16 to 12 minutes per hour on children's weekend programs when adult prime time had only 9½ minutes per hour; he also said that he favored the elimination of practices "which tend to blur the distinctions between programming and advertisements." Finally, he wanted more balance between animated and live action shows on Saturday and Sunday morning.[36]

Despite his statement that, "in my opinion, the time has now come for commission action," Wiley subsequently had several meetings with NAB officials in an attempt to substitute self-regulation for FCC regulation. On June 24, 1974, the NAB Code Board convened. As *Broadcasting*, an industry magazine, reported, "The question to be decided, it was privately admitted, is how far self-regulation must go to deter Mr. Wiley from proceeding with government rule making."[37] The new code did in fact fulfill most of Wiley's requirements. It called for:

1. A substantial reduction in the amount of advertising time permitted on children's programs (including a phaseout of weekend morning commercials to 9½ minutes per hour by December 31, 1975);
2. Clear separation between program content and advertisements;
3. Banning the advertising of supplemental vitamin products;
4. Tightening policies excluding the advertising of nonprescriptive medications;
5. Strengthening the standards relating to safety;
6. Requiring audio and video disclosure when items such as batteries are needed to operate a toy.[38]

On October 31, 1974, the FCC issued its "Children's Television Report and Policy Statement," the result of four and a half years of research and discussion. In the report, which is based on an attempt to balance the commission's obligation to the public with its fear of overregulation, the FCC addressed the various issues raised by the ACT petition. Although the FCC agreed that broadcasters "have a special obligation to serve children," what this obligation meant in concrete terms was not revealed. On the issue of the amount of programming for children, the report stated: "While we are convinced that television must provide programs for children . . . we do not believe that it is necessary for the Commission to prescribe by rule the number of hours per week to be carried in each category." In

---

[36] "Wiley Says FCC's Coming Close to Action on Children's Advertising, Programming; He Lays Blame on Broadcasters for Inertia," *Broadcasting*, May 27, 1974, p. 6.

[37] "TV Code Board Set to Convene for Fast Action on Self-Regulation," *Broadcasting*, June 24, 1974, pp. 38–39.

[38] National Association of Broadcasters, *Code News* 7 (June 1974): 6.

place of these rules, "we do expect stations to make a meaningful effort in this area." On guidelines for educational programming, the commission believes that "stations' license renewal applications should reflect a reasonable amount of programming which is designed to educate and inform. . . ." In response to the ACT request for age-specific programming, the report states: "While we agree that a detailed breakdown of programming into three or more specific age groups is unnecessary, we do believe that some effort should be made for both preschool and school-aged children." In regard to the lack of children's programs during the week, the commission advises: "Although we are not prepared to adopt a specific scheduling rule, we do expect to see considerable improvement in scheduling practices in the future."

The area of advertising practices is treated in a similar manner. In place of making its own rules to restrict commercials, the FCC notes that the NAB has amended its code to limit nonprogram material on children's shows to 9½ minutes per hour on weekends and 12 minutes per hour on weekdays. The only specific rule set out by the FCC in this area is the decision to amend the renewal form so that licenses must list the number of minutes of ads in each hour of children's programming. These data will be used to determine the effectiveness of self-regulation. The report does take a stand on the issue of young children's inability to distinguish between commercials and programs. The commission insists that "basic fairness requires that at least a clear separation be maintained between the program content and the commercial message. . . ." However, the FCC feels that in this area the NAB's newly amended code, which now requires a separation device, is sufficient.

The FCC stance regarding the issue of children's television is summed up by the concluding statement that "[television cannot] live up to its potential in serving America's children unless individual broadcasters are genuinely committed to that task, and are willing—to a considerable extent—to put profit in second place and the children in first."

The FTC involvement

In October and November 1971, the FTC held hearings on the impact of advertising on consumers that included discussion of children's advertising. Subsequently, ACT filed a petition with the FTC to prohibit the selling of vitamin pills to children on television, and filed another petition in December to prohibit selling toys to children. In March 1972, ACT petitioned the FTC to prohibit selling edibles to children on television. The next month it filed specific complaints against three drug companies. The FTC did not act on any of these petitions.

This lack of action continued until August 1973, when Lewis Engman, appointed the new chairman of FTC, immediately began working on the children's advertising issue. In October 1973, Engman convened the Children's Television Advertising Project mentioned earlier. It created a code that reduced commercials on children's programs to 6 minutes per hour, banned premiums, and forbade selling edible products containing over 15 percent sugar by net weight or 35 percent by dry weight.[39]

After ten months of discussion, the broadcasting industry finally revealed its counterproposal. It would create a new children's unit in the National Advertising Division of the Council of Better Business Bureaus, and use the old Association of National Advertisers' code as its initial review standard. Neither the FTC nor consumer groups were satisfied with this.[40] As Peggy Charren asserted, the guidelines are so vague that "advertisers could make any commercial in the world."[41] In response to industry's inaction, Engman warned: "I intend to recommend to the Commission enforcement guides banning the advertising of premiums to children on television."[42] In June 1974 the NAB issued its new code, which seemed to satisfy the FTC.

Although in June the commission issued a proposal for premium guidelines which stated that advertisers should not "promote a product or service by referring to an offer of a premium such as a prize, toy, game, or other promotional device having significant appeal for children under 12 years of age and unrelated to the merits of the product or service being promoted," it took no further action.[43] In December, Engman indicated that self-regulation had been satisfactory. He stated that although "government wheels grind slowly," the creation of the National Advertising Division of the Council of Better Business Bureaus "is an encouraging procedural development," and that "I have also been pleased with the NAB's actions with respect to the advertising of vitamins to children and the use of simultaneous audio and video disclosures in toy advertising."[44]

Six months later, J. Thomas Rosch, director of the FTC Bureau of Consumer Protection, said that advertising is moving in a direction "satisfactory to the commission."[45] At that time the FTC was requesting bids to study the effect of the hero on children, and had also granted $100,000 to the National Science Foundations's research project on the effect of ad-

---

[39] Federal Trade Commission, *Petition to Issue a Trade Regulation Rule*, Appendix II, Exhibit C.

[40] "Children's Ad Plan Draws Heavy Fire," *Broadcasting*, May 27, 1974, p. 39.

[41] Ibid.

[42] Lewis Engman, "Address on Children's Television Advertising," speech before the 1974 Annual Convention of the American Advertising Federation, Washington, D.C., June 3, 1974, quoted in Federal Trade Commission, *Petition to Issue a Trade Regulation Rule*, Appendix II, Exhibit C.

[43] "FTC Is Seen Ending Bid to Halt TV Ads of Product Premiums Aimed at Children," *The Wall Street Journal*, December 13, 1976, p. 2.

[44] Federal Trade Commission, *Petition to Issue a Trade Regulation Rule*, Appendix IV, Exhibit X.

[45] "It's Show and Tell During Workshop on Children's TV," *Broadcasting*, June 9, 1975, pp. 32–37.

vertising in general on children. In regard to children's commercials on television shows not in children's prime time, Rosch said there was not enough evidence to support bans of certain ads at these other times.

In 1976 the FTC seemed to have stopped even its attempts to regulate premiums. A *Wall Street Journal* article stated: "Now, a substantially changed commission is expected to announce fairly soon that it's abandoing efforts to write general premium guidelines. . . . (this) reflects the preference of the commission's current chairman, Calvin Collier, for dealing with any premium abuses on a case by case basis." Collier's statements support this expectation:

> With available research on the effects of children's advertising on behavior—particularly commercial behavior—still cloudy, general pronouncements in the context of rule making are difficult to make and even more difficult to defend. . . . It is far easier to observe that children are especially vulnerable than it is to design a clear set of rules that protects against the varieties of deception or unfairness that may seize upon those vulnerabilities.[46]

AREAS OF DISPUTE ON PROGRAMMING AND ADVERTISING FOR CHILDREN'S TELEVISION

Violence

The major criticism of children's television, that it is too violent, is based on the premise that children will learn and imitate violent behavior. A large body of evidence purports to support the critics. The Surgeon General's report on this topic, for example, is a 2,500-page compendium of research.[47] In support of their petition to the FCC, the ACT and its supporters cited additional research supporting the claim that violence on television affects children.[48]

Broadcasters and proponents of the broadcasting industry concede the

---

[46] "FTC Is Seen Ending Bid," *The Wall Street Journal,* December 13, 1976.

[47] For the entire Surgeon General's report, see *Television and Social Behavior: A Technical Report to the Surgeon General's Scientific Advisory Committee on Television and Social Behavior,* Rubenstein, Comstock, and Murray (eds.), 1972. For an annotated bibliography of research on children and television, see W. Schram, J. Lyle, and E. Parker, *Television in the Lives of Our Children,* 1961, pp. 297–317.

[48] Foundation for Character Education, *Television for Children;* A. Stein and L. Friedrich, "Television Content and Young Children's Behavior," Pennsylvania State University, NIMH Contract No. HSM 42, 70, 6k, 1971; "Wasteland Revisited: A Report on the Failure of Commercial Television to Serve Children of the Bay Area," no author or date given; Albert Bandura, "Imitation of Film Mediated Aggression Models," *Journal of Abnormal and Social Psychology* 66 (1963): 601–7; Heller and Polsky, "Television and Violence," *Archives of General Psychiatry* 24 (1971): 279; Larson, Gray, and Fortis, "Goals and Goal Achievement Methods in TV Content: Model for Anomie?" *Sociological Inquiry,* spring 1965, pp. 180–96; Siegal, "Film Mediated Fantasy Aggression and Strength of Aggressive Drive," *Child Development* 27 (1956): 365.

fact that there might be some relationship between televised violence and aggression, but most deny that the evidence is clear enough to warrant FCC action. In comments filed in response to the FCC's "Notice of Inquiry" on the subject of children's television, CBS stated: "Here there is no societal—or even commission—consensus as to the nature, the type, or the extent of the danger, much less the appropriate remedy or limitation."[49] To show the ambiguity of the evidence, industry groups have criticized the research on this subject.[50] Finally, in response to ACT's petition, opponents presented research findings which indicated that observing television did not affect the aggressive behavior of children.[51]

One of the studies supporting the broadcasters' position was commissioned by ABC. An independent research organization surveyed 10,000 children between 8 and 13 years old to determine the effect of viewing violence on a child's attitudes and behavior. The report, published in 1976, stated that "under certain conditions, and depending on the types of violence portrayed, exposure to televised violence is capable of producing increased inclination toward aggression in children." However, the report also asserts that "it was not possible to determine a casual relationship between 'inclination toward aggression' and actual aggression." The report concluded that "the inclusion of commercials breaks the concentration of the boys, and dampens the buildup of excitement."[52]

Some supporters of the broadcasters' point of view felt that violence on television could be helpful to children. The NAB Television Code says: "Children should also be exposed, at the appropriate times, to a reasonable range of the realities which exist in the world sufficient to help them make the transition to adulthood." In addition to the ambiguity of the evidence relating to the effects of violence, another major difficulty any FCC action on this issue faces is the problem of trying to administer a rule that attempts to define and restrict violence. What levels or sorts of violence are harmful to children? Even if some precise standards of acceptable and unacceptable "violence" were set up, how could they be administered with any degree of objectivity or fairness? How could conflicts with the First Amendment be avoided?[53]

The difficulty of defining violence has led to another issue, that of de-

---

[49] Federal Communications Commission, Comments on *Matter of Action for Children's Television*, Docket 19142, Columbia Broadcasting Systems, Inc., quoted in Steinberg, "FCC as Fairy Godmother," p. 1299.

[50] Steinberg, "FCC as Fairy Godmother," p. 1297. For a general criticism of these studies, see N. Morris, *Television's Child*, 1971, pp. 104, 113.

[51] L. Berkowitz, *Aggression: A Social Psychological Analysis*, 1962; S. Feshback and R. Singer, *Television and Aggression*, 1971; J. Klapper, *The Effects of Mass Communication*, 1960; Oppenheim and Vince, *Television and the Child*, 1960; Heffner, "Television: Friend or Foe?" *Teaching and Learning*, vol. 17, 1964.

[52] Lieberman Research, Inc., *Overview: Five Year Review of Research Sponsored by the American Broadcasting Co., September 1970 through August 1975*, New York 1976, 40 pp.

[53] Steinberg, "FCC as Fairy Godmother," pp. 1303, 1319.

termining the amount of violence to which children are actually exposed. According to the study by the Media Action Research Center, in the 1975–76 season an aggressive act occurred for every 2 minutes of Saturday morning programming. Dr. George Gerbner, with his colleague, Dr. Larry Gross, under a grant from the National Institute of Mental Health, found that in 1975 there was "a sharp increase in violence during the children's [weekend daytime] programs in the current season, and an even larger two-year rise in violence after 9 p.m."[54] However, industry supporters suggest that amounts of violence have been overestimated. Gerbner suggests a reason for the difference between his findings and the beliefs of the broadcasters by asserting that CBS's definition of violence "differs in important respects from ours. They qualify 'violence' by 'intentional' and 'serious' types, and limit their study to prime time."[55]

Amount, scheduling, and quality of children's programs

Critics of children's television are concerned with the scarcity, poor scheduling, and low quality of children's television. In their comments to the FCC, ACT and its supporters argued that not enough child-oriented programming was being offered, and the schedule of what was offered neglected weekday viewing times. Although independent stations offered some children's shows during the week, these were usually syndications of network reruns. The lack of weekday children's programs, according to ACT, led children to watch programs not designed for them and less suitable for them.

Another ACT Petition was concerned with the lack of age specificity in current programming for children. In trying to attract as large an audience as possible for their children's programs, the broadcasters, according to ACT, would direct children's shows to the entire age range of 2 to 12 years. In order to hold the interest of such an age range, the shows emphasized loud, fast, crude, and violent action.

The other major area of dispute was over the low quality of the programs offered. In their comments to the FCC, ACT and its supporters contended that current shows were weighted toward violence, sexism, and racism, with little informational or educational programming. Although they felt that television had the capacity for being beneficial for children, too few programs fulfilled this potential. The previously cited study of the Media Action Research Center supported this claim.

Critics of children's television believe that children learn violence, sexism, and racism from these shows. Many psychological studies have shown

---

[54] Lublin, "Bugs to Batman," p. 29; George Gerbner, *Summary of Violence Profile No. 7: Trends in Network Television Drama and Viewer Conceptions of Social Reality 1967–75,* 1976, 15 pp.

[55] Gerbner, *Summary of Violence Profile No. 7.*

that children imitate the behavior of social models, including influential television characters. Children also pick up their ideas about the world from television. According to Charles Colderbolz, a University of Texas educational psychologist, "The ideas [youngsters] pick up tend to be even more stereotyped than what they actually see." Robert Liebert, child psychologist at State University of New York at Stony Brook, said: "If kids don't see a black or an Asian-American on the screen, then they form a world view in which these people don't exist." Liebert feels that children later develop racial prejudices out of ignorance.[56]

The broadcasters' disagreement with the critics' position is based primarily on changes that have been recently made in children's programming. In regard to the ACT charge that there is too little children's programming, particularly during the week, the NAB Television Code states:

> There is a wide range of programming which children find attractive—scattered in good measure throughout the week. There are programs that deal with history, government, and biography, with biology and astronomy, with the environment and animal life, and with the seas and the stars.[57]

For examples of weekday programming, NBC-owned stations pledged for the 1975 season to present a series of weekday specials starring Shari Lewis. For the same season, ABC continued its "ABC Afterschool Special," and CBS pointed to its Monday through Friday "Captain Kangaroo" series, in addition to its occasional specials such as the "Children's Festival of the Lively Arts."

Broadcasters also refute the critics' charge that there are no age-specific shows. As an example, the Group W network, long a leader in innovative programming, announced that for the 1975 season its stations will telecast a new daily half-hour series aimed at preschool children and their parents. However, broadcasters do not agree that age specificity is necessary for children's shows. In addition to citing the financial necessity of having the large audiences that make continuous programming possible, the broadcasters contended that an attempt to categorize programs into age-specific categories would involve endless disputes and the possible illegal interference of the FCC.[58]

---

[56] See Albert Bandura, "Vicarious Processes: A Case of No Trial Learning," in *Advances in Experimental Social Psychology*, ed. Leonard Berkowitz, vol. 2 (1965), pp. 1–55; Albert Bandura, "Influence of Models: Reinforcement Contingencies on the Acquisition of Imitative Response," *Journal of Personality and Social Psychology*, 1965, pp. 589–95; Robert Liebert, "Television and Social Learning: Some Relationships Between Viewing Violence and Behaving Aggressively," in *Television and Social Behavior*, vol. II, ed. E. Rubenstein, G. Comstock, and J. Murray (NIMH, 1971), pp. 1–42; S. Ball and G. Bogatz, *The First Year of "Sesame Street": An Evaluation*, 1970; James P. Flanders, "A Review of Imitative Behavior," *Psychological Bulletin*, 1968, pp. 316–77; Richard H. Waters, Marion Leat, and Louis Majei, "Inhibition and Disinhibition of Responses Through Empathetic Learning," *Canadian Journal of Psychology*, 1963, pp. 235–243. See also Lublin, "Bugs to Batman," p. 29.

[57] Television Information Office, *Children, Television and Broadcast Regulation,* p. 12.

[58] *Children's Television Report*, p. 11.

Broadcasters and proponents of industry also disagree with the complaints about low quality. In their 1974 comments to the FCC, the industry contended that the then-current programming covered a broad range from entertainment to education and information. In disagreeing with the ACT belief that informational programming should have a larger place in children's programming, the broadcasters said that all television was informative and horizon-broadening, and asserted that television helped produce the informed child of today. Not only did the broadcasters feel that entertaining shows had educational potential, they also insisted that children were entitled to enjoy programs for their sheer entertainment value. Broadcasters also brought up the recent changes in children's programs as an answer to ACT's criticisms about quality. Among the changes made in the 1974–75 season were the elimination of the "larger than life hero," the replacement of some animated shows with live action shows, the addition of educational shows, and the creation of specials for young viewers. Broadcasters also assert that they are toning down violence, racism, and sexism.

Finally, broadcasters emphasize the prosocial messages children learn from current television shows. According to the Television Information office, one show, "Fat Albert," "isn't a teacher, but millions of youngsters empathize with him as he struggles with the value conflicts and peer-group problems that confront kids today." Another show, "Harlem Globetrotters Popcorn Machine," was the subject of a research study by Dr. Jerome Klapper, director of CBS's Office of Social Research. This study showed that, on the average, 87 percent of 680 children interviewed received prosocial messages from watching this show. According to the broadcasters, more research is being done to try to merge prosocial content and entertainment.[59]

Commercialization

The commercialization of children's television is one of the largest areas of controversy. ACT's original petition to the FCC asked for the removal of all commercials from children's television. The basis of this position is ACT's belief that until broadcasters are free from commercial pressure, children's television will never be responsive to the needs of the child rather than to the pressure of the advertisers.

ACT gives many reasons for the belief that commercialization causes children's shows to be of lower quality. It attributes the violence on children's shows to the broadcasters' desire to attract the entire child audience. Because advertisers prefer adult consumers as an audience, children's shows are offered only when there is no large adult audience

---

[59] "It's Show and Tell During Workshop," p. 37. See also Television Information Office, "Broadcast Self-Regulation," p. 18.

available—Saturday and Sunday mornings. Until government action was threatened, there were 16 minutes per hour of commercials on children's shows, compared to 9½ minutes per hour on adult prime time, and there were often veiled commercials in the program itself. Finally, critics contend that advertisers influence program content in a number of ways, not just in causing broadcasters to emphasize violence. ACT asserts that the programs support the messages of the commercials by promoting materialism.

The harmful effects of commercials. Not only does commercialization have a bad effect on the quality of the programming, but the commercials themselves abuse children. According to Warren Barren, associate director of Consumer's Union: "Advertising to children constitutes an unfair trade practice because young children have not yet developed the mental skills needed to handle repetitive and persuasive sales messages. Nor have they accumulated the experience that can help them evaluate these messages."[60]

In support of this claim, much research has been done on the inability of children to cope with television advertising. Dr. Richard I. Feinbloom, medical director of the Family Health Care Program of Harvard Medical School, challenged the propriety of directing advertising to children: "An advertisement to a child has the quality of an order, not a suggestion. The child lacks the ability to set priorities, to determine relative importance, and to reject some directives as inappropriate."[61] This naivete toward commercials makes the child an ardent lobbyist for the advertising industry in the home. According to one study,

> Mothers surveyed indicated that because their children ask for specific products and brands, they spend an average of $1.66 more on weekly shopping. This "child power" adds at least $30 million weekly—$1.5 billion annually—to grocery retail sales—just to make Junior happy.[62]

Junk food and hazardous products. Some consumer groups claim that persuasive techniques which overwhelm their vulnerable audience are directed toward teaching behavior harmful to children. According to Robert B. Choate, chairman of CCMM, the largest category of advertisers to children are food companies, and the foods most advertised are the highly sugared foods with little nutritional value. Choate reports that many nutritional experts believe the patterns laid down in the earliest years shape a person's food habits through life. Thus, early exposure to a barrage of advertising for junk foods may have a bad effect on general health for the

---

[60] Warren Barren, speech before the International Festival of Children's Television, April 1974, in *ACTfacts*, p. 7.

[61] Richard I. Feinbloom, letter submitted by ACT to the FTC for its hearing on the "Impact of Advertising on Consumers," November 1971.

[62] Melvin Helitzer and Carl Heyel, *The Youth Market: Its Dimensions, Influence, and Opportunities for You*, 1970.

rest of life. Choate suggests that commercials' bad influence can be seen in the widespread malnutrition in America today, and cites the Department of Agriculture's evidence of the decline in the nation's eating habits between 1955 and 1965.[63]

Another area of concern about children's television is the advertising of potentially hazardous products on or near shows that children watch. Choate summarized his concern in a petition to the FTC:

> Evidence shows that children in great number are placed in dangerous circumstances by ingesting drugs and other hazardous products. . . .
>
> Evidence shows that advertising enhances the acceptability of commercial products.
>
> Evidence shows that advertising of these products is found adjacent to or within many of the television programs watched by large numbers of children.[64]

The broadcasting industry feels that critics have exaggerated the harmful effects of commercials, if any, and that commercials serve a necessary function which should not be curtailed by legislation. Their two major arguments against the restriction of commercials are based on the freedom of speech guaranteed by the First Amendment and on the financial structure of the industry.

Since the ACT petition in 1970, broadcasters have fought a possible ban on commercials on children's television by claiming the protection of the First Amendment. According to one broadcasting company executive, "Adoption of the proposed rules would constitute an unauthorized assumption of power by the commission and would result in an unconstitutional infringement of the rights of broadcasters."[65] At hearings about this issue before the FCC in 1972, Commissioner Benjamin Hooks stated that in regulating one aspect of broadcast content, the FCC would make a precedent that it might use in the future to control other aspects. This would constitute a violation of the First Amendment and an intrusion of government into private spheres.

The second major argument of the broadcasters is based on profitability. As a spokesperson explained at the 1972 hearings, if there is no income from the shows, the broadcasters will merely put something together to fill the requirement. If there is no profit, then there is no competition and quality will suffer. Thus, without commercials not only would there be no motivation to create good children's programs, but there would be no funds available to create the expensive shows that ACT desired. The 1973 cutback of commercial time from 16 to 12 minutes per hour on weekend

---

[63] Federal Trade Commission, "Petition to Issue a Trade Regulation Rule," Appendix II, Exhibit P, pp. 11–14; Choate, "The Sugar-Coated Children's Hour," p. 146.

[64] Federal Trade Commission, "Petition to Issue a Trade Regulation Rule," Appendix III, p. 7.

[65] "No Support for Adless Kid Shows," *Broadcasting,* April 6, 1970, p. 48.

morning children's shows did indeed show a loss of profit, as the broadcasters predicted. Where in 1970 CBS made a profit of $16.5 million on Saturday morning shows, in 1973 it was making a $2 million profit. NBC director of children's shows William Hogan said NBC showed only a "marginal profit" in this time slot, and ABC's Saturday morning profits dropped from $7 million in 1970 to $2.5 to $3 million in 1973.

If commercials are further restricted or banned entirely, broadcasters contend that children's shows can exist only if there is revenue from other sources. However, as the FCC "Children's Television Report" said in summarizing the broadcasters' position, the plan of having commercial support of programs is seen as "the only workable one, as subject to adequate safeguards, and consistent with the profit motive implicit in the American system of broadcasting."[66]

Positive aspects of commercials. In addition to expressing these positions, the broadcasters combatted the critics' complaints about the harmful aspects of commercials. According to the FCC summary of the broadcasters' position, the industry saw commercials as informative and possibly valuable to children, rather than deceptive and unfair as the critics claimed. The "Children's Advertising Guidelines" of the ANA assert:

> Advertising directed to children, for products and services which are used or consumed by children, is appropriate in a society and economy such as ours. Such advertising serves to bring information to children and helps prepare them for maturity.

To the charge that advertising teaches children harmful nutritional habits or causes them to use dangerous drugs or household products, the broadcasters contended that the effects of commercials on children have been exaggerated. Broadcasters also argued that self-regulation standards have made commercials completely unobjectionable. For example, in response to the nutrition issue, one step has been "the display of juice and milk in cereal commercials and the announcement that the product is 'part of a nutritionally balanced breakfast.'" In addition to praising the safeguards on commercials, the broadcasters assert that it is ultimately the parent who must keep a child from harm.

The industry's final support for its position came from a survey by Roper Associates commissioned through the Television Information Office to discover public attitudes toward television. In November 1972, Roper asked a nationwide cross-section of adults if they thought it was "All right to have commercials in children's programs." Of the total, 62 percent of parents said "Yes": 58 percent of those with children under 6, 62 percent of those with children under and over 6, and 64 percent of those with children between 6 and 16. Roy Danish, director of TIO, said of these results:

---

[66] *Children's Television Report*, Appendix A, p. 40.

It is fair to say that the public does not share the views of those critics who see advertising to children as a threat to the moral fiber of the nation. In fact, most viewers seem to recognize television commercials for what they are: an acceptable means of selling goods and supporting innovative and costly programming.[67]

SELF-REGULATION: SUCCESS OR FAILURE?

Before the ACT petition to the FCC, industry self-regulation was centered in the NAB Code Authority and the ANA guidelines. The movement toward further self-regulation was gradual. In 1970 the NAB made its code more stringent by issuing some guidelines for toy commercials. A year later, the NAB made several other changes, such as not allowing hosts on children's programs to sell products, and cutting the number of commercials on weekend programs from 16 to 12 minutes per hour. These changes were to be effective in 1973. Consumer groups were dissatisfied with these efforts, since not only was the code voluntary, but the changes, which would not be implemented for two years, would still keep the commercial level above the 9½ minutes per hour of adult prime time.

In 1973 FTC chairman Lewis Engman established task forces to form new standards for children's television. In response to the code drawn up by six consumer groups, the industry presented its counterproposal. It would use the already-existing ANA guidelines as a basis for establishing a Children's Advertising Review Unit of the National Advertising Review Board/National Advertising Division (part of the Council of Better Business Bureaus), which would clear ads voluntarily submitted by advertisers. Since the ANA code was subjective and nonspecific, and since the procedure depended on voluntary submissions, the proposal was rejected by consumer groups and by Engman.

On June 27, 1974, the NAB announced a new and more stringent code. Commercials would be cut to 10 minutes per hour after December 31, 1974, on children's weekend programs and then to 9½ minutes by the end of 1975. Weekday programs, now showing 16 minutes of commercials per hour, would be cut to 14 minutes at the end of 1974 and to 12 minutes at the end of 1975. The new code would also ban vitamin ads and over the counter drug ads to children. Host selling and other techniques that blur the distinction between program and commercial were also forbidden. After this new code was put into effect and the Children's Advertising Review Unit established, Engman and the FCC took no further legislative action.

The Children's Advertising Review Unit is the major administrative body for industry self-regulation. The first step in its establishment was

---

[67] Television Information Office, "Growing Majority Believes Commercials OK in Children's TV," July 22, 1974, p. 1.

the issuance of a new set of standards in June 1975: the Children's Advertising Guidelines. These guidelines are a revised version of the ANA code. Some of the differences between the two are a clause asking that commercials promote good nutrition and a series of guidelines about premium advertising. In addition to rulings on nutrition, premiums, and instructing children to pressure their parents to buy, the new guidelines forbid advertising medicines, drugs, vitamins, or any product not intended for their use to children. Commercials may not show children in unsafe actions; they may not mislead children as to the proper use of the item or the actual makeup of the item; and hard-sell techniques are forbidden. These rulings cover all advertising directed primarily to children aged 11 and under, and television programs with children as over 50 percent of the total audience.[68]

The NAD then retained a committee of seven consultants, experts on children's perceptions and behavior. Meetings with these consultants led to the modification of the Children's Advertising Guidelines and gave CARU information about new research and positive goals for children's advertising.

To fulfill its function, CARU set up monitoring and review procedures. As of July 15, 1975, 500 commercials had been voluntarily submitted by advertisers, a regular monitoring schedule was established, and over 2,000 announcements had been videotaped for future review. CARU had received 125 letters from the public regarding children's advertising, of which a small number that dealt with deceptive, misleading, or unfair advertising was acted upon. The remainder, dealing with nonfulfillment of orders, defective products, or the propriety of advertising to children at all, were either referred elsewhere or "duly read and answered but not pursued." Twenty-six inquiries into advertising were begun, 6 of which were based on consumer complaints, and 20 of which were based on CARU's own monitoring system. By July 1975, 19 inquiries were resolved. Seventeen of them resulted in "modification or discontinuance of the questioned advertising." The remaining two were dismissed after substantiation by the advertiser. None of these cases was appealed to the National Advertising Review Board.[69]

CARU has done other work in the area of children's advertising. It has had occasional meetings with consultants and supporters to share information on new research and attitudes toward children's advertising. The organization has also developed twelve television announcements for child consumer education called Junior Consumer Tips. Roland P. Camp-

---

[68] U.S. Congress, House, Committee on Interstate and Foreign Commerce, Subcommittee on Communications, *Hearings on Broadcast Advertising and Children*, statement of Roland P. Campbell, "Self-Regulation of Children's Advertising," July 15, 1975.

[69] Campbell, "Self-Regulation of Children's Advertising," p. 19.

bell, vice-president of the Better Business Bureau, feels that CARU's program has shown the success of self-regulation:

> Successful advertising, by definition, is designed to encourage a desire for the advertised product on the part of the consumer. In the case of child consumers, so long as there is advertising there will be attempts on the part of children to influence purchase. Our program is designed, not to thwart this purpose, but to ensure that advertising directed to children does not mislead the child or use unfair means to encourage his interest in the advertised product.[70]

Other industry supporters agreed. Jerome Lansner, assistant director of the NAB Code Authority, asserted that "self-regulation has responded positively and reasonably to public interest issues," concluding that "broadcast self-regulation is second to none."[71] The Television Information Office of the NAB asserted that a look at the success of NAB self-regulation shows that "broadcasters working independently and through their support of the [NAB] Television Code make a continuing and demonstrably effective effort to meet the needs of all their viewers, with special consideration for the youngest."[72]

Despite industry claims, consumer groups and other individuals are highly critical of the effectiveness of self-regulation. One of the most vocal critics is Robert Choate, chairman of CCMM. In March 1975, CCMM filed a petition with the FTC which called for the abandonment of self-regulation and the adoption of tight federal controls. Choate's complaint is primarily based on the grounds that current regulations do not define children's television advertising in a realistic way. The 1974 NAB code defined such a commercial as a "commercial designed primarily for children," and the CBBB code defined children's commercials as those which appear when children are more than 50 percent of the audience. However, according to Choate, "Eight of the ten television programs most viewed by children are not the subject of these private regulatory guidelines." In addition, these definitions confine self-regulation to Saturday and Sunday mornings, ignoring the majority of the shows children watch in the afternoon and evening.

Therefore, hazardous household products and over the counter drugs, which a Consumer Product Safety Commission report shows constitute a serious danger to children, can be advertised on shows a great number of children watch. There are three loopholes in the industry code which, according to Choate, allow any hazardous product to be advertised to children:

---

[70] Ibid., p. 23.
[71] "It's Show and Tell during Workshop," p. 36.
[72] Television Information Office, *Children, Television and Broadcast Regulation.*

1. The commercial was not designed primarily for children.
2. The sponsor's merchandising goals did not include children.
3. The program adjacent to the commercial may have a large child audience but is not "primarily designed for children."

This, Choate asserts, is a "Catch 22" situation, since the advertiser can claim that because the product advertised was hazardous, it was not directed to children and thus not subject to the guidelines.

Choate also complained about the workings of the Children's Review Unit. According to Choate, Emilie Griffin, director of CARU, refused to screen for Choate a number of commercials he was concerned about. Although Griffin said that complainants were free to comment on the basis of storyboards, she did not say where they were available to the public. Griffin also stated that since CARU only reviewed commercials where the child audience exceeded 50 percent, she had no over the counter drug ads available. In response to Choate's request to see specific ads, Griffin asserted that NARB files were not complete and did not contain many of these ads. This indication that CARU efforts are half-hearted and insufficient is another sign to Choate that self-regulation is not successful.

ACT has reached a similar conclusion. It asserts that not only do the broadcasters not obey the code rulings, but the codes themselves do not go far enough in restricting the number and type of commercials shown to children. In proving this point, in 1975 ACT commissioned two studies supervised by Dr. F. Earle Barcus, a professor of communications research at Boston University, to show that television stations are not adhering to industry guidelines. One report claimed that five commercial stations in Boston "regularly" exceeded the NAB ceiling of 10 minutes of commercials per hour on Saturday and Sunday mornings. The second report asserted that six out of ten independent stations around the country exceeded the 14 minutes per hour of commercials allowed by the NAB Code in the Monday through Friday, 3 to 6 p.m. time period. Many of the stations involved, however, claimed that ACT had misinterpreted the code or made other mistakes, such as confusing programs designed for children with off-network reruns which children watch.[73]

Dr. Barcus and Peggy Charren asserted that the two reports revealed still other prohibited advertising practices, such as the fact that almost half the commercials directed to children were for cereals, candies, and sweets. They also found that in the report on the ten independent stations, "less than one hour out of the thirty hours studied was locally originated programming," and that nearly two-thirds of independent programs contained violence and three-tenths were "saturated in violence." Peggy Charren summed up ACT's position:

---

[73] "ACT Says Stations Aren't Living Up to Rules on Ads in Children's TV; Stations Say Group Is Way Off Base," *Broadcasting*, December 22, 1975, pp. 28–29.

The studies negate the argument of the FCC's policy statement on children's television that self-regulation is an adequate solution to the problems of children's television. These analyses of advertising and programming practices prove that broadcasters have not yet made a commitment to the health and well-being of children.[74]

Pursuing this position, in September 1976 ACT again asked a federal appeals court to ban commercials on children's programs. Earle K. Moore, ACT representative, claimed that despite self-regulation codes, children still cannot distinguish between ads and entertainment, and understand modern advertising techniques which cause them to put pressure on their parents. Moore also asserted that although a 1971 survey showed that 82 percent of children's programs carried violence, "there's more violence today in children's TV programming than there was in 1971." Henry Geller, another ACT representative, contended that self-regulation had been approved by the FCC so as not to cut industry profits. According to Geller, despite the fact that in 1975 the networks made a profit of $314 million, the commission has told the industry it may continue to "make a buck" on 4- and 5-year-olds. Thus, for ACT, industry self-regulation is a travesty, a façade that keeps the FCC and FTC quiet and allows the industry to make huge profits.[75]

Consumer groups are not the only critics of self-regulation. Donald H. McGannon, chairman of the board and president of Group W (Westinghouse Broadcasting Company), is another. In 1970 Group W developed special restrictions for children's programs and advertising. For example, commercials in children's programs are restricted to 3 minutes per half-hour and 6 minutes per hour, and these commercials are clustered at beginnings and ends of programs. Group W's policies also forbid, in children's "prime time," host selling, hard-sell techniques, and promos (promotional announcements) for programs not suited for children. These standards were instituted because Group W felt the NAB code did not go far enough. In fact, Group W resigned from the NAB Television Code in 1969 as a gesture of protest.

In June 1975, McGannon spoke before a House of Representatives committee on the subject of broadcast advertising and children. He presented a position somewhere between the consumer groups and the industry, saying:

> While I am sorry to report that self-regulation has not been truly effective to date, I do not favor additional federal regulation. I say this not only because of the inherent constitutional problems, but also because in the long run I believe it would be counter-productive.[76]

---

[74] Ibid.

[75] "Suit Seeks Ban on Children's TV Ads," *The Recorder,* September 15, 1976, p. 1.

[76] U.S. Congress, House, Committee on Interstate and Foreign Commerce, Subcommittee on Communications, *Hearings on Broadcast Advertising and Children,* statement of Donald H. McGannon, July 14, 1975.

McGannon felt that the government should act as a catalyst to make broad-casters "understand their responsibilities to the public." In this area, FCC action has not been sufficient: "While I credit the chairman [of the FCC], the industry did not fully respond. The limitations are not tight enough and it is taking too long to implement them." In regard to violence on TV, McGannon also thought that self-regulation had been ineffective: "The industry should deeply regret what occurred last season. The quantum of violence and the percentage of action formats reached an all-time high—and next season doesn't promise to be any better." However, despite these indications of failure, McGannon concluded: "I repeat my conviction that [self-regulation] can succeed when and if the industry wants it to."

EPILOGUE

The FCC's "Children's Television Report" in 1974 was the last major government action on the issue of children's television. However, as indicated earlier, this report made no specific rule recommendations for children's television, leaving this responsibility to industry self-regulatory mechanisms. Since that time, the industry has maintained its self-regulatory code and machinery with few changes beyond that of creating the "family hour" in 1975. This addition to the code provided for two hours of programming for a "general family audience" from 7 to 9 p.m.[77] Consumer groups and other critics, disappointed with the FCC report and the FTC's lack of action, continue to claim that self-regulation has failed, and to petition the government for legal action on this issue. In September 1976 ACT petitioned a federal appeals court to ban commercials on children's television, the same demand as in their 1970 petition to the FCC.

Apparently children's television has become a dead issue for government agencies. In response to the 1976 ACT suit, the FCC asserted that industry self-regulation had already considerably improved children's programming, and that the commission felt this was the best course. The FTC has also refrained from legislating on any aspect of this issue. In December 1976, The Wall Street Journal saw the FTC as "about to back off from an initiative once seen as evidence of a tougher consumer-protection stance: its proposed guidelines against television advertising of product premiums aimed at twelve year olds." Calvin Collier, the 1976 chairman of the FTC, said about this issue: "General pronouncements in the context of rule making are difficult to make and even more difficult to defend."[78]

In 1977 the FCC again evinced interest in the broadcasting industry, this time taking a broad look at the practices of television network programming. This inquiry was in response to critics who claimed that CBS, NBC,

---

[77] "Cleaning Up TV for the Kiddies," The Wall Street Journal, April 25, 1975, p. 8.

[78] "Suit Seeks Ban"; Burt Schorr, "FTC Is Seen as Ending Bid to Halt TV Ads of Product Premiums Aimed at Children," The Wall Street Journal, December 13, 1976, p. 2.

and ABC exercise unfair control over national television. John Schneider, president of CBS, said: "No need for such an inquiry has been demonstrated, and we believe none exists," a statement with which the other networks agreed.[79] It is not known yet whether this inquiry will have any effect on the children's television issue.

SELECTED BIBLIOGRAPHY

Action for Children's Television. Testimony of Action for Children's Television Inc., before the Federal Trade Commission, November 10, 1971.

Atkin, Charles. "Survey of Pre-adolescent's Responses to Television Commercials." In Effects of Television Advertising on Children. East Lansing: Michigan State University, 1975, #6.

Atkin, Charles. "Parent-Child Communication in Supermarket Breakfast Cereal Selection." In Effects of Television Advertising on Children. East Lansing: Michigan State University, 1975, #7.

Atkin, Charles. "Survey of Children's and Mother's Responses to Television Commercials." In Effects of Television Advertising on Children. East Lansing: Michigan State University, 1975, #8.

Blake, Richard A. "Children's TV: Ethics and Economics," America, October 21, 1972, pp. 308–11.

Caron, Andre, and Ward, S. "Gift Decision by Kids and Parents," Journal of Advertising Research 15 (August 1975): 15–20.

Goldberg, Marvin E., and Gorn, Gerald J. "Children's Reaction to Television Advertising: An Experimental Approach." Journal of Consumer Research 1 (September 1974): 69–74.

Gorn, Gerald J., and Goldberg, Marvin E. "Children's Television Commercials: Do Child Viewers Become Satiated Too?" Working Paper. Faculty of Management, McGill University, Montreal, Canada, 1976.

Head, Sydney W. Broadcasting in America: A Survey of Television and Radio, 2nd ed. Boston: Houghton Mifflin, 1972.

Melody, William. Children's Television: The Economics of Exploitation. New Haven: Yale University Press, 1973.

Melody, William, and Ehrlich, G. "Children's TV Commercials: The Vanishing Policy Options." Journal of Communications 24 (autumn, 1974): 13, 25.

U.S. Congress, Senate, Committee on Commerce. FTC Oversight Hearings. Washington, D.C.: U.S. Government Printing Office, March 14, 1974.

Ward, Scott, and Wackman, Daniel. "Children's Information Processing of Television Advertising." In New Models for Mass Communications Research, ed. P. Clark. Santa Monica, Calif.: Sage Publications, 1973.

---

[79] "FCC to Probe Accusations That Networks Exercise Unfair Control of TV Programs," The Wall Street Journal, January 17, 1977, p. 10.

PART IV

MARKETING IN THE LESS DEVELOPED COUNTRIES

13 Marketing of infant formula foods in less developed countries: Responsibility in the sale and promotion of certain products in poorer countries

Third World babies are dying because their mothers bottle feed them with Western style infant milk. Many that do not die are drawn into a vicious cycle of malnutrition and disease that will leave them physically and intellectually stunted for life.

Mike Muller[1]

It has long been recognized by medical science that the ideal feeding for infants is human milk. When mothers cannot or choose not to breast feed, an alternate source of nutrition is required. SMA and S-26 infant formulas are well-balanced formulas, providing optimum nutrition for normal infants.

American Home Products Corporation[2]

On September 27, 1976, the Sisters of the Precious Blood, a Roman Catholic religious order, filed suit in U.S. District Court against Bristol-Myers company, a large multinational drug and food-processing corporation based in New York City. The action sought by the Sisters was to require the management of Bristol-Myers to correct false and misleading statements made in the company's 1976 proxy statement concerning the extent and nature of its marketing practices in less developed countries, specifically with reference to its handling of baby food formulas marketed principally under the brand names Enfamil and Olac. The Sisters owned 500 shares of Bristol-Myers common stock.

To simplify what is in fact a very complex issue, the Sisters hold that

---

[1] Mike Muller, *The Baby Killer,* 2nd ed. (War on Want, May 1975), p. 2.

[2] *Sisters of the Precious Blood, Inc.,* v. *Bristol Myers Co.,* 76 Civ. 1734, U.S. District Court, S. District of New York, "Memorandum of Law in Opposition to Defendants' Motion for Summary Judgment."

baby food formulas are inferior to natural breast feeding for infants, and that the use of such formulas leads to less healthy children. The suit states:

> The primary conditions which contribute to the dangers associated with bottle formula feeding fall into five general categories: (1) a sanitary water supply for mixing formula (or facilities to boil the water or funds to buy sanitary water); (2) proper hygiene with respect to bottles and nipples; (3) income sufficient to support the greater cost of formula feeding compared to breast feeding and avoidance of stretching the formula and undernourishing the infant; (4) availability of refrigeration to preserve mixed formula; and (5) suffcient availability of medical personnel for proper guidance.[3]

It is, then, the entire broad issue of selling such products in poorer nations that is being attacked. The Sisters are concerned that such practices do not contribute to healthy babies, that mothers are being "pressured" into buying the product through advertising and promotional campaigns that do not have the real interests of the babies or mothers in mind, and that the corporations engaged in marketing the products are motivated by one overriding factor: to earn a profit, regardless of its source.

ISSUES FOR ANALYSIS

The case of the *Sisters of the Precious Blood* v. *Bristol-Myers, Inc.*, involves a number of substantive issues that confront not only modern large corporations and the societies in which they operate, but the individual actors in these two interacting spheres as well: the corporate managers who determine and implement policy, and citizens who live in a world in which corporations, to a greater degree than ever before, dominate our way of life.

1. What ethical bounds should inhibit a corporation's choice of products? To what extent, if any, is a company responsible for the improper use of its products?
2. To what extent should a corporation use advertising and promotional tools to increase sales? What about the corporation's obligation to promote only those products it knows will be used in an approved manner? If competitors are manufacturing and promoting a product in a certain way, and doing it successfully, how should this affect a company's decision to enter the market and utilize similar tactics? Does a firm have an obligation not to undertake the manufacture and promotion of a product without any specific governmental or legal sanctions restricting its use?
3. If there is a demand for a product, should not this be the ultimate court in the corporation's decision to undertake its manufacture?
4. Should there be a government-directed choice of products a private corporation can manufacture? If not, why not? If, for example, baby

---

[3] Ibid., p. 6.

food formula was indeed judged to be harmful to children from poorer countries, why shouldn't the government force it off the market?

5. What does "corporate social responsibility" mean? How does it relate to the concept of shareholder democracy? How can it be implemented? What is the legitimate role of the nonshareholding public in this area of controversy?

6. Some legal scholars have argued that managements control their corporations through their control of the proxy machinery. However, as is evidenced in this case, certain pressure groups have also begun to resort to this mechanism. Their purpose is not only to bring certain issues before the stockholders, but through mass media, before the public at large. *(a)* Is the use of proxy machinery, as exemplified by the Sisters' action against Bristol-Myers, a good way to bring grievances to the surface? What other options are available to these groups? *(b)* How might a large company best deal with such groups and their actions?

The issues on which the suit brought by the Sisters hinge are thus several and significant. In order to deal with them in an enlightened and reasonable manner, it will be necessary to trace the development of their emergence as a subject of public debate and controversy. The first, and perhaps the key issue at stake, is the argument surrounding the nutritional value of baby food products when compared to the mother's natural supply of milk. This medical factor, however, is inextricably bound up with the problem of poverty in less developed countries.

GROWTH OF THE CONTROVERSY

Infant formula food was developed in the early 1920s as an alternative to breast feeding. Sales rose sharply after World War II and hit a peak in the late 1950s, following the 4.3 million births in 1957.[4] However, birth rates began declining in the 1960s, and by 1974 the annual number of births had declined to 3.1 million. This low birth rate caused a steep downturn in baby food formula sales.

The major American and foreign companies engaged in the manufacture and marketing of infant formulas are Abbott Laboratories, which produces Similac and Isomil infant formulas through its Ross Laboratories division; American Home Products, which produces SMA, S-26, and Nursoy infant formulas through its Wyeth Laboratories; Bristol-Myers, which produces Enfamil, Olac, and Prosobee through its Mead Johnson division; Nestlé Alimentana, S.A., a Swiss multinational; and Unigate, a British firm. In their search for business, these milk companies began developing markets in Third World countries where population was still expanding, since

---

[4] Robert J. Ledogar, "U.S. Food and Drug Multinationals in Latin America: Hungry for Profits," LDOC, North America, Inc. New York, 1975, p. 128.

the baby food markets in developed countries has witnessed a gradual decline because of declining birth rates.

American Home Products showed international sales increases in 1973, with approximately $60 million in foreign sales of SMA and S-26. Bristol-Myers showed an increase in international sales from just over $100 million in 1968 to a record high of $400 million in 1974. The annual reports of both companies showed that infant formula was one of the most important parts of international sales. Nestlé Alimentana has an estimated $300 million in worldwide sales of infant foods, and is heavily involved in marketing in less developed countries.[5]

The Sisters' suit against Bristol-Myers was actually part of a much broader assault on the manufacturers of infant formulas sold in Third World nations. In March 1974, a report entitled *The Baby Killer* was issued by a British relief organization called War on Want. It discussed the nutritional impact of formula feeding and criticized the promotional practices of such producers as Nestlé and Unigate. Public interest groups in Switzerland, France, and Germany also became interested in this subject, and began investigating the activities of Nestlé. A Swiss group published a translation of *The Baby Killer* under the title *Nestle Totet Kinder* (Nestlé Kills Babies) and was sued for criminal libel by the company. Nestlé won the suit and the defendants were sentenced to the nominal fine of 300 Swiss francs each. At the same time, the court told Nestlé to "carry out a fundamental reconsideration of its sales techniques in less developed countries," and emphasized that the "verdict is not an acquittal of Nestlé."[6]

The World Health Assembly, the governing body of the World Health Organization (WHO), adopted a resolution on May 23, 1974, which asserted that misleading promotion of baby foods had contributed to the decline of breast feeding, and urged countries to take legal actions in this area. Later in 1974, the World Food Conference adopted a resolution recommending that governments actively support breast feeding. The UN, whose Protein Advisory Group (PAG) had sponsored one of the earliest forums on the baby formula problem in 1972, sponsored another seminar in November 1974 for industry, UN, and government representatives, as well as nutrition experts. Recommendations were adopted to form an international industry council to establish a code of ethical advertising and promotion practices. As a result, an International Council of Infant Food Industries (ICIFI) became active and a code went into effect on September 1, 1975. This code required, among other things, that all product labels state that breast milk is the most desirable food for infants.[7]

In the United States, concern over this issue was manifested in 1975

---

[5] Ledogar, *Hungry for Profits,* pp. 128–29.

[6] "The Infant Food Industry," *The Lancet,* September 4, 1976, p. 503.

[7] Ann Crittenden, "Baby Formula Sales in Third World Are Criticized: Products Held Unnecessary for Nutrition of Infants," *The New York Times,* September 11, 1975, pp. 51, 61.

when members of the Eco-Justice Task Force of the Interfaith Center on Corporate Responsibility (ICCR), representing over twenty-five church groups with a combined investment portfolio of several billion dollars, sought marketing information from the three leading American infant formula manufacturers—American Home Products, Abbot Laboratories, and Bristol-Myers. And in San Francisco the Beech-Nut Baby Foods Company was sued by Public Advocates, Inc., because of alleged "scare tactics" used in a letter sent directly by the company to more than 760,000 American mothers of infant children.

This widespread assault, which crosses national boundaries, is an attempt to enforce a policy of social responsibility on those corporations selling baby food formulas to mothers of infant children in the poorer, less developed countries. It is aimed at all large corporations involved in the industry, and apparently will not stop until these firms either radically alter their marketing practices for baby food products or else cease and desist in their manufacture.

NUTRITIONAL ASPECTS OF THE CONTROVERSY

The World Health Organization, the American Academy of Pediatrics, the American Public Health Association, and other medical authorities all agree that human milk is the best food for most infants.[8] No infant formula has any similarity to a yellowish fluid called colostrum which mothers produce for the first few days after childbirth. Colostrum is rich in antibodies which work locally, protecting the child from allergies, infections, and other diseases. In addition to providing protection from various infections, human milk has several other unique qualities. It is substantially higher in cholesterol content than any infant formula. Research studies indicate that a moderate amount of cholesterol in infancy helps in establishing mechanisms to metabolize cholesterol later in life, helping to prevent arteriosclerosis. The protein found in human milk is more easily digested than the usual protein in infant formula. Taurine, an amino acid which is important in the transmission of nerve impulses, is practically absent in infant formula. Furthermore, only human milk contains lipaze, an enzyme which increases the availability of free fatty acids.[9]

Infant formula

Recently, commercial formulas have been modified to more closely simulate human milk. The protein level in infant formula has been re-

---

[8] Citizens' Committee on Infant Nutrition, *White Paper on Infant Feeding Practices* (Washington, D.C.: Center for Science in the Public Interest, December 1974), p. 2.

[9] For various studies dealing with the infection-resistance properties of mother's milk, see Citizens' Committee on Infant Nutrition, *White Paper;* "Is Breast Feeding Best for Babies?," *Consumer Reports* 42 (March 1977): 152–57; Muller, *The Baby Killer;* Ledogar, *Hungry for Profits.*

duced, and the ability of the infant to use vegetable oil fat in infant formula is about the same as that for fatty acids in human milk. Infant formulas also try to simulate the mixture of minerals and vitamins in human milk, as well as human milk's lactose content and electrolyte and osmolar loads. The caloric distribution, low curd tension, and high level of fatty acid are also comparable to human milk.[10]

Some doctors believe that the production of infant formula foods is important because a significant number of infants may have special problems where mother's milk may not be suitable. A common use for these "sick baby formulas" is with infants who have gastrointestinal illnesses or nutritional problems. "Well baby" formulas may also be necessary for the many mothers who cannot nurse because of physiological difficulties, illness, or work schedules. According to the infant formula industry, mothers who are taking certain drugs which can be absorbed by the infant should also not nurse.

Some recent studies have reported high levels of polychlorinated biphenyls (PCBs) in breast milk. These chemicals are potentially poisonous substances which have been used industrially and have contaminated soil, water, air, and food. Although no evidence of PCB poisoning in infants has yet been reported, experimental studies are still being conducted to determine its effect. This discovery of PCBs in human milk has led many mothers to prefer formula feeding.

Growth in infant formula sales in less developed countries

A variety of studies point to an increasing trend toward bottle feeding in less developed countries (LDCs). For example, in the last twenty years, the rate of breast feeding in Chile has fallen from 95 to 6 percent, and the length of the nursing period has shrunk from over a year to less than 2 months. Similar findings were reported from Jamaica, Nigeria, Rhodesia, East and West Africa, the Middle East, Pakistan, and Puerto Rico. In all these countries, breast feeding showed a similar declining trend.[11]

Three important environmental factors, according to most observers, account for the shift toward bottle feeding in the LDCs. These are the sociocultural changes in developing countries, the changing attitudes of health workers and health institutions, and the promotional activities of infant formula manufacturers.

The sociocultural factors influencing changes in feeding infants can be understood primarily in terms of urbanization, which causes Westernization of social mores and a need for mobility for employment. Since high-

---

[10] Bristol-Myers Company, "The Infant Formula Marketing Practices of Bristol-Myers Co. in Countries outside the U.S.," August 7, 1975, p. 4.

[11] Muller, The Baby Killer, p. 4; "The Baby Food Tragedy;" The New Internationalist, August 1973, p. 9.

income groups, in imitation of Western practices, are the first to use infant formula, bottle feeding comes to represent a high-status modern practice. Low-income groups tend to follow suit. The breast has also come to be viewed primarily as a sex symbol, which leads to embarrassment in using it for nursing, and to a fear that nursing will make the appearance of the breast less desirable. Finally, there is the convenience aspect. Since most places of employment do not provide facilities for a nursing woman, bottle feeding of the infant may become a necessity for a working woman.

Health professionals, including doctors, nurses, and clinic workers, as well as the policies of the hospitals and clinics themselves, often act wittingly or unwittingly to endorse the use of infant formula. Although much of this activity originates in the promotional efforts of baby food formula manufacturers, to the mother the endorsement may appear to come from the health professionals themselves.

On the upper rung of the medical profession are the doctors, the majority of which have learned Western practices of infant feeding. Students in the medical school at Kuala Lumpur, Malaysia, for example, received no instruction about breast feeding.[12] Mothers interviewed in different studies indicated that their doctor recommended bottle feeding or gave them a prescription for infant formula. Mead Johnson, Nestlé, and other companies provide preprinted prescription slips for this purpose.[13]

Nurses and social workers who staff hospitals and clinics may also encourage the use of bottle feeding. In many hospitals, newborn babies are routinely bottle fed whether or not the mother plans to breast feed later. Hospitals and clinics receive free samples of infant milk and special plastic milk bottles which nurses distribute to mothers. These nurses may also distribute "vaccination cards" that advertise infant formulas, and baby care booklets that recommend bottle feeding.

INDUSTRY PROMOTION PRACTICES

Many observers claim that the infant formula industry's promotion is overly aggressive and has contributed to the decline of breast feeding. The industry itself, however, feels that its promotion is generally responsible and performs a valuable function.

Description

One of the major forms of promotion used by baby food companies is the information booklet. Some typical titles are *The Ostermilk Mother and*

---

[12] B. Vahlquist, "Occurrence of Nutritional Anemia in Children," in *Causes and Prevention of Nutritional Anaemias*, ed. G. Blix (Symposium of Swedish Nutrition Foundation, 1968), pp. 36–46.

[13] Ledogar, *Hungry for Profits*, p. 141.

Baby Book; Caring for Your Baby, published by Ross Laboratories; and *A Life Begins,* published by Nestlé. These booklets are distributed free in maternity wards of public hospitals, clinics, doctor's offices, and by nurses. The booklets provide information on prenatal and postnatal care, with special emphasis given to discussing how babies should be fed. Many of these books, directed to illiterate or semi-literate women, use pictures to show correct or incorrect feeding methods.

Some baby food booklets, usually earlier versions, described and illustrated bottle feeding without mentioning breast feeding. However, as public concern over the possible harmful effects of bottle feeding rose, promotional booklets began to discuss breast feeding and to recommend "mixed feeding," in which the bottle would be used as a supplement to breast milk. Examples of this type include Nestlé's *Your Baby and You,* which suggests "an occasional bottle feed . . . if you cannot breast-feed Baby entirely yourself."[14]

In discussing the use of supplements for feeding the baby, these booklets often emphasize reasons to discontinue or diminish breast feeding. Nestlé, for example, in *A Life Begins,* asserts that bottle feeding must be substituted for breast feeding if the mother is ill, if her milk is insufficient for the baby or of "poor quality," or if the mother's nipples crack or become infected. These booklets also suggest that breast feeding should be diminished to include solid food in the baby's diet. The *Ostermilk Mother and Baby Book* advises introducing solid foods for babies a few weeks old or even earlier, while Cow and Gate suggests feeding its brand of cereal to the baby at two to three months.[15]

Companies also promote their products through advertisements in magazines and newspapers, on radio and television, and through loudspeaker vans. As with the baby care booklets, early advertisements usually did not mention breast feeding. Poster advertisements, often exhibited in hospitals and clinics, showed how to prepare baby formula, but gave only minimal attention to breast feeding. Many advertisements after the 1970s, however, either stated that breast milk was best, or recommended "mixed feeding." For example, in Nigeria, all Nestlé radio ads began with the quote, "You should always breast feed your baby, but if you can't, then use . . ."[16] In addition, poster series began to include an entire poster devoted to showing breast feeding. Magazine and television advertisements also reflected this change.

One of the most widespread promotional techniques is the distribution of free samples and the offer of free gifts to users or potential users of baby food formula. These usually take the form of samples of formula or free feeding bottles, and may be handed out by nurses and salespeople at hos-

---

14 Ledogar, *Hungry for Profits,* pp. 133–34.

15 Ibid., p. 142.

16 "The Baby Food Tragedy," *New Internationalist,* pp. 10–11.

pitals, clinics, or in the home. A survey in Ibadan, Nigeria, found that 9 percent of the mothers surveyed had received samples. These had been given in equal proportion to more affluent mothers and to those who could not afford baby food formula. A spokesman from Nestlé admitted that sampling in the Philippines cost about 4 to 5 percent of turnover.[17] Free gifts are less often used as an inducement to buy.

The infant food formula companies' promotion of their products through the medical profession has already been discussed. In general, all promotional methods such as booklets, free samples, posters, and salespeople are also used in the hospitals and clinics. In addition, the use of milk nurses and milk banks also functions to associate baby food formula with the medical profession. Mothercraft nurses or milk nurses are fully or partially trained nurses hired by infant food formula companies. The milk companies train these women, primarily in "product knowledge." Most nurses are paid fixed salaries plus a travel allowance, but some may receive sales-related bonuses. Some hospitals allow milk nurses to speak to mothers in maternity wards or clinics; other nurses visit mothers in their homes. In some isolated areas, milk nurses also make formula deliveries. A 1974 study conducted by the Caribbean Food and Nutrition Institute found that Mead Johnson, subsidiaries of Nestlé, Glaxo, Ross Laboratories, and Cow and Gate all employed milk nurses in Jamaica. Mead Johnson employed twelve.[18]

Milk banks, usually set up in hospitals and clinics that serve the poor, are sales outlets for commercial infant food formula. These banks sell formula at reduced prices to poorer mothers. For example, at the milk bank at Robert Reid Cabral hospital in Santo Domingo, a pound tin of Nestlé Nido is sold for 90 cents, a 40 percent discount off the regular $1.50 price; Nestlé Nan is sold for $1.35, a 33 percent discount off the regular $2 price. Milk banks do not sell to mothers who can afford the regular prices.

Criticisms

All forms of promotion used by infant formula companies have been criticized. In general, critics claim that most forms of advertising are misleading or use hard-sell techniques to turn mothers away from breast feeding.

Mothers reading the baby care booklets will be led to believe that bottle feeding is as good or better than breast feeding. Even if the booklet directly states "breast feeding is best," critics assert that the overall impression is still misleading. Critics also disapprove of the new trend in these books toward promoting "mixed feeding," or the early introduction

---

[17] Muller, *The Baby Killer*, pp. 11–12.
[18] Ledogar, *Hungry for Profits*, p. 137.

of solid food. According to La Leche League International, an organization that promotes breast feeding,

> . . . the supplementary formula is one of the greatest deterrents to establishing a good milk supply, and frequent nursing is one of the greatest helps. You see, the milk supply is regulated by what the baby takes. The more he nurses, the more milk there will be. If he's given a bottle as well, he'll gradually take less and less from the breast, and the supply will diminish.[19]

In addition, the use of a bottle and overdiluted formula, even as a supplement, can still cause infection and malnutrition in the infant.

Critics' objections to other media promotion are similar to their objections to the booklets. They feel that even with minor changes admitting the superiority of breast milk, media promotion remains essentially misleading in encouraging mothers to bottle feed their children. A survey on infant feeding practices in Ibadan, Nigeria, revealed that of the 38 percent of 400 mothers who remembered having seen ads for formula, the majority recalled statements that the formula gives infants strength, energy, and power; none remembered having heard that breast milk is better for babies. In Nigeria, when ads for Ovaltine included the picture of a plump, smiling baby, observers noted there was a trend for mothers to feed their babies Ovaltine and water as a supplement.[20]

Critics believe that free samples of baby food formula and feeding bottles, as well as free gift gimmicks, are a direct inducement to bottle feed infants. The widespread distribution of these items shows an unethical lack of concern for informing mothers about the superority of breast feeding or for determining whether mothers have the economic ability to buy infant formula after the first samples.

Critics find the promotion of infant formula through the distribution of free samples and literature or the display of advertising posters in hospitals and clinics especially dangerous. Dr. D. B. Jelliffe, head of the Division of Population, Family, and International Health at UCLA, called these promotional techniques "endorsement by association" and "manipulation by assistance." Jelliffe, along with many other critics, feels that the companies providing hospitals and clinics with free samples, information on new developments in infant formula, and a barrage of advertisements influence health care workers to become favorable to and to promote bottle feeding to their patients. The critics furthermore believe that because mothers see posters and receive informational booklets and free samples at hospitals and clinics, they come to believe that the health profession endorses bottle feeding. Thus, this type of promotion works two ways in influenc-

---

[19] *The Womanly Art of Breastfeeding*, 2nd ed. (Franklin Park, Ill.: La Leche League International, 1963), p. 54.

[20] "Baby Food Tragedy," *New Internationalist*, p. 10; Muller, *Baby Killer*, p. 10.

ing both the beliefs of professionals and the beliefs of mothers about the value of bottle feeding.[21]

The use of milk nurses also receives its share of criticism. Observers charge that the use of uniforms conceals the fact that the "nurses" are essentially salespeople who act to encourage mothers to bottle feed. Critics also assert that some nurses are paid on a sales-related basis, causing them to be even more eager to push for sales. In support of this belief, critics quote an industry man who said, "Some nurses will be paid a commission on sales results in their area. Sometimes they will also be given the added stick that if they don't meet those objectives they will be fired."[22]

Critics believe milk banks are used by companies to expand sales by encouraging bottle feeding in the poor while still retaining their higher income level market. But the discount prices of the formula are still beyond the economic means of the people at whom the milk banks aim. For example, a milk bank in Guatemala City sells Nestlé products for $1 per tin, an 80 cents to $1 discount from the regular price. A tin lasts only a few days when properly prepared. However, since the women buying milk there generally have household incomes of between $15 and $45 per month, most buy fewer tins and dilute them. This starts the baby on a cycle of malnutrition and disease.

Industry response

Infant formula companies claim that all their promotion practices are justifiable, and many of them benefit consumers. Their basic claim is that, in general, infant food formula is marketed to doctors or health care professionals, rather than to individual buyers. Nestlé asserts that any mass media marketing they do use is primarily intended to cause mothers to ask their doctors about the product. Wyeth Laboratories states that "It is Wyeth's policy not to promote these products [infant formula] directly to lay persons, although Wyeth representatives do conduct courses on prenatal and postnatal care. . . ."[23]

According to the companies, baby care booklets are primarily educational pamphlets covering all aspects of child care. As an example, the companies mention the value of their new policy of discussing the importance of breast feeding in educational literature. The baby care literature provided by Bristol-Myers states: "Your milk is best for your child, yet circumstances often prevent a mother from breast feeding her child. In which case you must resort to milk similar to yours."[24] Wyeth Laboratories summed up its policy as follows:

---

[21] Muller, *Baby Killer,* p. 8.

[22] Bristol-Myers Company, "The Infant Formula Marketing Practices," p. 13.

[23] American Home Products Corporation, "Optimum Infant Nutrition."

[24] Mead Johnson, "Enfamil: A Well-Balanced Infant Formula for Your Baby," p. 2.

The milk of a healthy mother is the ideal food for her offspring, being nutritionally superior, free, readily available and requiring no preparation. However, a prepared formula should be available for those occasions when through sickness, lack of lactation, nipple problems, etc., such formula is essential for the survival of the baby. . . .[25]

Companies feel that free samples are a service to the medical profession, as well as being a good promotional technique. A Nestlé spokesman said: "Where the local medical profession wants samples, we give them. Don't forget, hospitals are short of money; many have given up the habit of buying because milk is supplied free of charge by the companies."[26]

As suggested earlier, the companies believe that promoting their products to the medical profession educates and informs doctors about the different aspects and uses of different formulas. This education is important, since it is the doctor, rather than the mother, who should make the final decision on whether the mother should bottle feed. Bristol-Myers states: "Only the physician has the scientific training to determine whether breast feeding, bottle feeding, or a combination is in the mother's and infant's best interest."[27] According to a Nestlé spokesman, promotion through the medical profession by supplying milk banks, free samples, and information about bottle feeding at hospitals allows mothers who choose to bottle feed to have at least some medical guidance and supervision.

Formula companies also believe that milk nurses have a valuable function. Nestlé asserts that the nurse acts as a detailman to inform doctors about products, and to give needed advice to mothers at the same time. Bristol-Myers stated that their nurses are like Public Health nurses in American municipalities, since the nurses work with physicians, hospitals, local health authorities, and patients. In describing the functions of the nurses, Bristol-Myers emphasized that their nurses are registered, not assigned sales quotas or compensated on a commission basis, and provide the service free of charge. In addition, Bristol-Myers declares that the nurses' primary function is to help mothers in carrying out the doctor's instructions, whether or not this includes bottle feeding. Finally, according to the company, Bristol-Myers nursing services are offered only where they are needed; at this time in only 9 of the 36 countries where the infant formula is marketed. The code of marketing ethics to which Abbott Laboratories subscribes has similar provisions about their nurses or salespeople. The functions of their "paramedical personnel," according to Abbott, "are to develop product understanding, to render services that facilitate applica-

[25] American Home Products Corporation, "Optimum Infant Nutrition."
[26] Muller, *Baby Killer*, p. 12.
[27] Bristol-Myers, "The Infant Formula Marketing Formula," p. 14.

tion of our products, and to make available other health care aids, without attempt to incur obligation for services."[28]

Infant formula companies see milk banks as an example of their public responsibility. Since these banks sell baby food at substantially lower prices, the companies believe that poorer mothers can buy sufficient quantities of formula for their infants without making too great a sacrifice. Milk banks are usually associated with a hospital or clinic, thus providing formula under medical supervision.

BOTTLE FEEDING IN DEVELOPING COUNTRIES

Bottle feeding was originally developed for countries that were technologically and socioeconomically advanced. This background is reflected in the fact that bottle feeding, under optimal conditions requires the user to be literate enough to read the instructions and figure out the correct amount of formula for babies of different ages; to have the equipment necessary to sterilize the bottle and the water; to have a refrigerator to store excess quantities of formula; and to have the funds necessary to buy sufficient amounts of the formula. Instruction booklets issued with infant formula generally require all these items. Observers of the users of baby food formula in developing countries have found discrepancies between the ideal situation and the real one.

The necessary items for sanitary conditions—that is, pure water, equipment for sterilizing water and bottles, and refrigeration—are lacking in many areas where baby food formula is used. The suit against Bristol-Myers submitted affidavits that described conditions in eighteen countries where Bristol-Myers formula is marketed. In a typical example, an affidavit asserted that in low-income areas in Mexico, ". . . sanitary water is not available, nor do people generally sterilize water. There is almost a total lack of refrigeration and drainage, while trash removal and sanitation are deficient or non-existent." This description also held true for the Dominican Republic, Jamaica, St. Vincent, the West Indies, Haiti, and many other countries.

In countries with low literacy rates, the instruction booklets issued with baby food formula may not be read by mothers. Dr. David Morley, a reader in tropical child health at the University of London and an authority on child malnutrition in developing countries, asserted that in the poorer parts of developing countries, "Many of [the] mothers to whom these bottles are given are illiterate, and even if they *could* read they would often not understand the complex instructions with mathematical mea-

---

[28] Ross Laboratories Division of Abbot Laboratories, "International Code of Marketing Ethics with Reference to Infant Feeding," undated.

surements."[29] The practices of formula companies support this assertion that baby formula is marketed to illiterate or semi-literate mothers, since many of the labels or instruction booklets use line drawings and pictures to show the right and wrong way to prepare formula.

The cost of baby formula is a much higher percentage of a family's total income than in developed countries. A 1970 PAG manual states that the cost of artificial feeding in the United Kingdom ranges from 2.1 percent of the minimum wage per week to feed a 3-month-old baby to 3.3 percent of the minimum wage per week to feed a 6-month-old baby. In Nigeria, however, it ranges from 30.3 to 47.1 percent, and in Egypt from 40.8 to 63.3 percent (see Exhibit 13–1).[30] Studies have shown that because of lack of money, formula will be diluted to make it last longer.[31]

EXHIBIT 13–1
COST OF ARTIFICIAL FEEDING IN SOME COUNTRIES
AND PERCENTAGE OF MINIMUM WAGES

Country	Minimum wage per week (U.S. $)	Cost at 3 months per day (U.S. $)	% of wage	Cost at 6 months per day (U.S. $)	% of wage
United Kingdom	$39.20	$0.84	2.1%	$1.30	3.3%
Burma	5.01	0.53	10.6	0.81	16.2
Peru	5.60	0.84	15.0	1.30	23.2
Philippines	9.69	1.67	17.2	2.59	26.7
Indonesia	5.60	1.05	18.8	1.62	28.9
Tanzania	7.62	1.57	20.6	2.44	32.0
India	4.62	1.05	22.7	1.62	35.1
Nigeria	5.18	1.57	30.3	2.44	47.1
Afghanistan	2.80	1.05	37.5	1.62	57.9
Pakistan	5.18	2.09	40.3	3.23	62.4
Egypt	4.09	1.67	40.8	2.59	63.3

Accurate information on wages and costs of food is difficult to find. Here they are expressed at U.S. $ for comparative purposes. It is assumed here that the artificial food, a full-cream modified milk, supplies the infant's total daily need for food.

The information in this table comes from a joint seminar held on March 24, 1970, at the London School of Hygiene and Tropical Medicine (UNICEF/WHO course for senior teachers of child health and students taking their postgraduate diploma in nutrition). Reprinted from the *Protein Advisory Group Manual on Feeding Infants and Young Children*, PAG Document 1.14/26, December 1971.

[29] "The Baby Food Tragedy," *The New Internationalist*, p. 23.

[30] Muller, *The Baby Killer*, p. 7. Another study based on June 1970 retail prices in Jamaica, West Indies, found that it would cost about $2.75 a week to feed an infant artificial food for the first six months of life. In 1972, 40 percent of those Jamaicans who had jobs were earning $11 per week or less. See John McKigney, "Economic Aspects," in *The Uniqueness of Human Milk*, eds. D. B. Jelliffe and E. F. P. Jelliffe, Symposium reprinted from *The American Journal of Clinical Nutrition* 24 (August 1971): 1009.

[31] A 1969 study in Barbados found that 82 percent of mothers surveyed answered that a one-pound can of powdered milk would feed a 2- to 3-month-old baby five days to three weeks. The correct length of time was four days. *The National Food and Nutrition Survey of Barbados*, Scientific Publication No. 237 (Washington, D.C.: Pan-American Health Organization, 1972).

The lack of proper hygenic conditions, the "stretching" of formula to make it last because of insufficient funds, and the illiteracy of many users contribute to what has been called the "cycle of malnutrition." In one description of this cycle, when the mother dilutes the infant formula, the baby does not get the required amount of calories, proteins, or other essentials. Consequently, the baby begins to lose weight and to shrivel up, a condition called *marasmus*. Since a child suffering from marasmus becomes increasingly susceptible to infection, the unsanitary conditions under which the formula is made usually results in the child contracting gastroenteritis. Because of diarrhea, the child is able to use even less of the formula given him. This results in further malnutrition, and often death.[32]

Several studies have shown that unsatisfactory bottle feeding practices have resulted in an increase in severe malnutrition and diarrheal diseases in infants, and at an increasingly young age (see Exhibit 13–2). One study found that over the last twenty years, the decline of breast feeding has caused the average age of children with severe malnutrition to drop from 18 to 8 months in some parts of the world.[33] Another study reported that deaths from malnutrition peak statistically for children as young as 3 to 4 months. This study also showed that in 35,000 childhood deaths investigated, nutritional deficiency was the most important contributor to death in the first year of life, and that nutritional deficiency in every community studied was "less frequent in infants breast fed and never weaned than in infants who were breast fed not at all or for only limited periods."[34] However, no wide-ranging authoritative study has yet been made on this issue. Information on the social consequences of bottle feeding are, in general, confined to individual case studies, research projects in a few individual cities and areas, and eyewitness reports. .

Industry response

Although in general the baby formula companies do not deny that many of these problems occur, they say they are doing everything possible to prevent these results. Companies say they are directing their promotion to health professionals or higher-income groups, not promoting in the poorest countries, and doing everything in their power to make sure mothers are able to prepare the formula properly. In regard to the problem of possible overpromotion, David C. Cox, president of Abbott's Ross Laboratories, stated: "I don't know anybody in the industry who's not sensitive to this charge and worked to eliminate it. We have eliminated most of the

---

[32] "The Baby Food Tragedy," *The New Internationalist,* p. 10.

[33] Alan Berg, *The Nutrition Factor* (Washington, D.C.: The Brookings Institution 1973), p. 95.

[34] Cited in Ledogar, *Hungry for Profits,* p. 130.

EXHIBIT 13–2

A. INFANT DEATHS FROM NUTRITIONAL DEFICIENCY AS UNDERLYING OR ASSOCIATED CAUSE ACCORDING TO BREAST FEEDING, IN TWO AGE GROUPS, IN 13 LATIN AMERICAN PROJECTS: JAMAICA

Project	Breast fed never weaned			Breast fed one month or longer			Breast fed less than one month			Not breast fed		
	Deaths	Nutritional deficiency		Deaths	Nutritional deficiency		Deaths	Nutritional deficiency		Deaths	Nutritional deficiency	
		No.	%		No.	%		No.	%		No.	%
Total	1,405	479	34.1	2,286	1,124	49.2	2,384	1,191	50.0	1,916	986	51.5
28 days–5 months	74	17	23.0	103	39	37.9	51	17	33.3	60	19	31.7
6–11 months	15	4	26.7	203	24	46.3	18	8	44.4	17	13	76.5

B. DEATHS FROM DIARRHEAL DISEASE AS UNDERLYING CAUSE ACCORDING TO BREAST FEEDING OF INFANTS' DYING AT 28 DAYS–5 MONTHS OF AGE IN 13 LATIN AMERICAN PROJECTS: JAMAICA

Project	Breast fed never weaned			Breast fed one month or longer			Breast fed less than one month			Not breast fed		
	Deaths	Diarrheal disease		Deaths	Diarrheal disease		Deaths	Diarrheal disease		Deaths	Diarrheal disease	
		No.	%		No.	%		No.	%		No.	%
Total	1,405	446	31.7	2,286	1,175	31.4	2,384	1,292	54.2	1,916	991	51.7
Jamaica	74	18	24.3	103	36	54.4	31	19	37.3	60	29	48.3

Source: Sisters of the Precious Blood, Inc. v. Bristol-Meyers Co., 76 Civ. 1734 (MP), p. 8.

abuse. It's just not enlightened free enterprise to sell products that don't help people."[35] A spokesperson for Nestlé agreed that they try to control their promotion so as to avoid the "cycle" of malnutrition, since "It is very bad advertisement for our product if it happens with our product. So we would like to control the consumption to those people who can afford our product. It's good business to do so."[36]

The most detailed response to the charges of critics can be found in Bristol-Myer's report, "The Infant Formula Marketing Practices of Bristol-Myers Company in Countries Outside the U.S." (Appendix A). In response to the charge that marketing practices have contributed to malnutrition and infant mortality in developing countries, Bristol-Myers compared its 1974 international Enfamil and "sick baby" formula sales with a study reported in a December 1974 *PAG Bulletin*. This study used 71 indicators of general development to place fifty countries into 12 development groups and 5 levels ranging from least developed to developed. Bristol-Myers found that the company did not market infant formula in the "least developed" countries; that less than one-third of sales came from the lower areas of the "other developing" countries, and in these countries 55 percent of sales were for "sick baby" formula; and that more than 75 percent of Enfamil sales came from the more developed countries. Bristol-Myers also pointed out that "sick baby" formulas were required in all parts of the world.

A second charge from the critics was that lack of hygenic conditions, illiteracy, and poverty contributed to the malnutrition which results from the misuse of formula. To this charge Bristol-Myers replied that its "well baby formula products are neither intended for, nor promoted into, markets where chronic poverty or ignorance could lead to product misuse or harmful effects." One way of preventing such misuse by the lower sectors of more developed countries is by pricing formula out of the reach of the poorer classes. In addition, Bristol-Myers makes every effort to ensure that the formula is properly used. For this purpose, the company provides multilingual instruction books with diagrams and pictures, premeasured scoops to help in using the right amounts of formula, and advice nurses for individual assistance in the use of formula.

SOCIAL ACTIVISM AND THE INFANT FORMULA: MANUFACTURERS IN THE UNITED STATES

The interaction of manufacturers and social activist groups on this issue has suggested that many corporations, concerned about their image as socially responsible citizens, are willing to make some concessions to the concerns of stockholders. Naturally, this attitude is not held universally.

---

[35] Crittenden, "Baby Formula Sales in Third World," *The New York Times*, p. 51.
[36] Muller, *Baby Killer*, p. 13.

The three major cases initiated by the Interfaith Center for Corporate Responsibility, National Council of Churches, New York, show a range of corporate response.

American Home Products

Initial discussions between American Home Products and ICCR resulted in the release of some marketing information. However, when American Home Products would not release all the requested information, the church group filed a resolution to be included in the upcoming proxy statement. American Home Products decided the day before the proxy was to be printed to furnish the information, and the resolution was dropped. American Home Products also agreed to send a report to its shareholders which stated that many authorities believe misuse of infant formula in developing countries is a serious health hazard; that the company promotes breast feeding, although formula should be available for mothers who cannot or do not choose to breast feed; that the company's policy is to promote formula to medical professionals and not directly to the consumer; and that Wyeth, the American division of American Home Products, is the U.S. member of an international steering committee whose purpose is to develop a voluntary code of promotional practices.

Abbott Laboratories

Abbott Laboratories held meetings with ICCR for a year and a half and released most of the requested information. However, because Abbott would not furnish all the information, a shareholder resolution was filed by the church groups. The proposal received only 2 percent of the vote, and the Securities and Exchange Commission rules require that 3 percent of the vote be received for the resolution to be resubmitted. Despite this success, Abbott has since added a research specialist on the Third World to its staff whose function is to investigate possible abuses of formula promotion.

Bristol-Myers

Bristol Myers declined to cooperate with ICCR, and one shareholder, Sisters of the Precious Blood, filed a shareholder resolution in 1975 that asked for the information to be released. This resolution received 5.4 percent of the vote, allowing it to be reintroduced at the following year's annual meeting. In August 1975, Bristol-Myers released a report entitled "The Infant Formula Marketing Practices of Bristol-Myers Co. in Countries outside the United States." However, the Sisters of the Precious Blood were not satisfied with the candor, accuracy, or completeness of the information in the report. The Ford Foundation and the Rockefeller Foundation, large stockholders, also expressed their concern. With this support, the Sisters submitted a second proposal for the 1976 proxy statement.

When the 1976 proxy was printed, the resolution of the Sisters was opposed by a statement entitled "Management's Position." The Sisters declared that the information in this statement was false and misleading to the shareholders, and subsequently they sued Bristol-Myers for a new solicitation and meeting where Bristol-Myers would correct its misstatements (see Appendix B).

THE SISTERS OF THE
PRECIOUS BLOOD v. BRISTOL-MYERS
The Sisters' case

The Sisters' suit against Bristol-Myers was based on their claim that Bristol-Myers violated Section 14(a) of the Securities Exchange Act and Rule 14a-9 promulgated under that act. These rules, according to the Sisters, barred Bristol-Myers from soliciting proxies in opposition to the Sisters' shareholder proposal by using false or misleading statements. The Sisters claim that Bristol-Myers made such false or misleading statements and omissions in the statement entitled "Management's Position," which was printed in opposition to the Sisters' proposal in the 1976 proxy statement. According to the Sisters, the "Management's Position" statement was false and misleading not only by claiming that the earlier Bristol-Myers report was accurate and "fully responsive" to the concerns expressed in the 1975 shareholder resolution, but also by repeating the false and misleading conclusions contained in the Bristol-Myers report.

The conclusions in the report which were repeated in "Management's Position" and singled out by the Sisters as false include the following:

2. that the company [Bristol-Myers] does not sell infant formula products in the least developed countries of the world and has only one-third of its sales in the lower category of developing countries, with more than half of this amount being in the "sick baby" formulas so urgently needed in these countries.
3. That the company's infant formula products are neither intended nor promoted for private purchase where chronic poverty or ignorance could lead to product misuse or harmful effects;
4. that as a matter of policy the company's infant formula products are marketed through professional medical personnel and not directly to the consumer.

In response to these assertions, the Sisters submitted affidavits from Jamaica, the Dominican Republic, Venezuela, Guatemala, Mexico, Trinidad, Haiti, St. Vincent, Peru, Barbados, Republic of the Philippines, Malaysia,

Indonesia, Thailand, Singapore, Nigeria, Ethiopia, and Sudan which, according to the Sisters, "make it abundantly clear that Bristol-Myers was simply not telling the truth" in their proxy statement.

The Sisters hoped to win several important points from their suit. They sought, among other things, a declaration that the proxies Bristol-Myers obtained by its "Management's Position" statement were invalid; a new shareholder meeting; a new resolicitation of proxies for which Bristol-Myers would disclose its past fraud and correct the fraudulent statement.

Bristol-Myers' case

Bristol-Myers based its case on its belief that the Sisters had not been able to show sufficient injury caused by Bristol-Myers' statement in the proxy either to make any claim under Section 14(a) of the Securities Exchange Act, or to fulfill the "irreparable harm requirement" needed for court action.[37] Furthermore, Bristol-Myers claimed that "relief" the Sisters sought in their suit was abstract and academic. First, the Sisters wanted a special stockholder meeting to vote on a resolution which, as Bristol-Myers points out, was already defeated in the 1975 and 1976 votes. Second, according to Bristol-Myers, not only could no stockholder meeting be held before its next annual meeting in April 1977, but the company had already consented to have the resolution offered again at that meeting.

Since the relief the Sisters sought was academic, Bristol-Myers believed their suit was intended to be part of a publicity campaign on the subject of bottle feeding, rather than a serious attempt to get judicial relief for injuries. This "publicity campaign" aspect of the Sisters' suit is suggested by the large number of affidavits and exhibits filed to show that Bristol-Myers' proxy statement was false and misleading, even though Bristol-Myers did not address these issues in its defense but preferred to argue the case on other grounds. Although Bristol-Myers did not want to fight the case on the issue of whether or not its position statement was false, the company nevertheless denied the Sisters' charges. However, Bristol-Myers also asserted its belief that any trial based on this issue would take years to resolve, considering the fact that evidence and witnesses would be needed from at least twelve countries on four continents and on remote islands. In May 1977, the court accepted Bristol-Myers' request for summary dismissal on the grounds that the Sisters had not suffered "irreparable harm" or financial loss. The Sisters are planning to appeal this decision.

---

[37] *Sisters of the Precious Blood, Inc.* v. *Bristol-Meyers Co.,* 76 Civ 1734 (MP) U.S. District of New York, "Reply Memorandum of Defendant Bristol-Myers Co. in Support of its Motion for Summary Judgment," unpaginated.

APPENDIX A: THE INFANT FORMULA MARKETING PRACTICES OF BRISTOL-MYERS COMPANY IN COUNTRIES OUTSIDE THE UNITED STATES*

INTRODUCTION

Inquiries on overseas infant formula marketing

During the past three years, Bristol-Myers, like other companies in the infant formula business, has received inquiries about the impact of its infant formula operations on infant nutrition in many of the world's least developed and developing nations. Bristol-Myers infant formula products are manufactured by the company's Mead Johnson Division and marketed overseas by its International Division. Both divisions are wholly owned by Bristol-Myers.

The number of inquiries has been relatively small—no more than a handful each year. Yet the nature of these inquiries has been a matter of profound concern to Bristol-Myers. Stimulated by articles in magazines and newspapers about the overseas infant formula industry in general, recent inquiries have questioned the ethics and morality of the company's marketing program.

The origin of the inquiries

How have these questions come about? Many owe their origin directly or indirectly to publications and statements by the Protein Advisory Group (PAG) of the United Nations.

An interdisciplinary committee of internationally recognized experts, the PAG advises the United Nations and its agencies on technical, economic, educational, social, and related aspects of global malnutrition, particularly in infants and children. Since its inception in 1955, the PAG has emphasized protein-calorie malnutrition as a primary and continuing threat to the health and survival of infants and young children in developing countries.[1]

Bristol-Myers has long been, and will continue to be, allied with the PAG. Its Mead Johnson vice-president, Nutritional Science Resources, has often been called to advise this body. He is also technical advisor to the

---

* Bristol-Myers Company, 345 Park Avenue, New York, New York 10022, August 7, 1975.
[1] PAG Bulletin 4 (December 1974): inside cover.

U.S. delegate to the Codex Committee on Foods for Special Dietary Uses, which sets standards for milk-based and nonmilk-based infant formulas, for canned baby foods, and for cereal-based processed foods for infants and children. Mead Johnson's extensive research and food technology data have been made available to both committees. Mead Johnson's representative has also worked with the PAG committee that drafted PAG Statement No. 23, "Promotion of Special Foods (Infant Formula and Processed Protein Foods) for Vulnerable Groups." This statement contains:

1. Recommendations to governments and UN agencies.
2. Recommendations to pediatricians and other physicians caring for children.
3. Recommendations to industry.

Recommendations to industry are:[2]

1. Food industry leaders should be constructively involved in solving the special nutritional problems of vulnerable groups, particularly in developing countries.
2. The importance of breast feeding should be stressed in employee training, and personnel should be instructed to avoid sales and promotional methods that could discourage appropriate breast feeding.
3. Industry should train its personnel adequately about local public health norms, needs, and regulations in implementing national food and nutrition policies.
4. Industry should emphasize that the immediate postpartum period and the hospital nursery are not appropriate for any promotion of infant foods to others than medical professionals.
5. To minimize misuse, industry should stress the importance of unambiguous, standard directions for reconstituting dry or liquid infant formulas. The needs of illiterate as well as literate persons should be considered in label design. Labels and product literature should foster hygienically oriented practices, such as use of boiled water and proper cleaning of utensils.
6. Industry should actively consider developing and producing supplementary foods and infant formulas that do not require reconstitution or can be made palatable by boiling only.

Bristol-Myers endorses the PAG's overall work and goals. Yet, a distinction must be made between the work of the organization and the activities of a few individual members. In recent years, some of them have granted interviews to reporters, or have themselves written articles related to infant feeding practices in overseas markets.

---

[2] Protein Advisory Group of the United Nations System, "Promotion of Special Foods (Infant Formula and Processed Protein Foods) for Vulnerable Groups," *PAG Statement*, No. 23 Rev., November 18, 1973, pp. 5–6.

Sometimes, these articles have been misleading. And they have been titled, written, and illustrated in such a way that objective conclusions are difficult, if not impossible.

In one newspaper article, for example, a nutritionist associated with the PAG advised readers that the result of bottle feeding with powdered infant formula is a "wizened, shrunken baby."

The 1975 proxy proposal

Understandably, such efforts raised questions and concerns in the minds of some Bristol-Myers stockholders. As a result, the Sisters of the Precious Blood Generalate of Dayton, Ohio, and the St. Walbury Monastery of Benedictine Sisters of Covington, Kentucky, requested that the 1975 proxy statement include a proposal relating to the company's infant formula marketing practices. The action was coordinated by the Interfaith Center on Corporate Responsibility (ICCR), a sponsored related movement of the National Council of Churches, New York.

The sponsors offered to withdraw their proposal if the company would agree to mail all stockholders a report on its infant formula activities in overseas markets.

At that time, the company did not feel there was sufficiently widespread public concern to warrant such a report. But the company did promise the ICCR representatives that all requests would be dealt with individually, as in the past.

The purpose of this report

While stockholders rejected the proxy proposal, Bristol-Myers now believes there is evidence of sufficient concern to make this information public.

The following report describes the history of the infant formula business and the role of the company's Mead Johnson and International Divisions in this business. It will also respond to issues raised by stockholders, the Protein Advisory Group, and others.

MEAD JOHNSON & COMPANY: A PIONEER IN THE IMPROVEMENT OF INFANT NUTRITION

The development of infant formula products

. . . in 1911 Mead Johnson became the first U.S. manufacturer of infant formula carbohydrate modifier—a mixture of dextrins and maltose that was trademarked Dextri-Maltose.

The company continued to pioneer in research and production of unique infants' and children's special nutritional products—such as standardized cod liver oil, oleum percomorphum, Pablum cereals, Vi-Sol drops, and chewable vitamin products—as well as formulas for infants with normal and special needs.

Large numbers of infants have special nutritional requirements—as many as 10 percent in developed countries like the United States and probably a similar number in less developed countries. Their special needs may be due to:

1. Malabsorption problems—celiac disease, cystic fibrosis, pancreatic insufficiency.
2. Lactose intolerance.
3. Inborn errors of carbohydrate metabolism—galactosemia.
4. Inborn errors of amino acid metabolism—phenylketonuria, tyrosinemia, homocystinuria.
5. Low birth weight or prematurity.
6. Intestinal resection during early infancy.

These infants may not survive, or may not develop normally, when fed breast milk or breast-milk-type formulas for normal infants. To survive, these infants need special formulas—formulas with no cow's milk, with no lactose, with special fats or carbohydrates, or with protein hydrolysate or amino acid mixtures.

The results of Mead Johnson research

Mead Johnson scientists have directed much of their infant nutritional research efforts toward special formulas, sometimes called "sick baby" formulas, over the past fifty years. Results have been impressive:

1921: Casec. Concentrated protein preparation for supplementary infant feedings. For simple, mild diarrheas; for supplementing breast feeding or infant formulas when added protein or calcium is desirable.

1923: Protein Milk. Acidified milk high in protein and low in lactose, with specially modified curd. For patients with celiac syndrome (particularly in the early stages of dietary management); for infants with cystic fibrosis of the pancrease; for infants with diarrhea or other gastrointestinal disturbances.

1925: Alacta. Powdered milk high in protein and low in fat for use in infant formulas. For infants who need a moderately low-fat milk; for premature infants, particularly those with lower birth weights; for full-term infants with poor tolerance or poor absorption of fat, as in digestive disturbances, malnutrition, or febrile illnesses.

1929: Sobee. The first soy-based infant formula; a pleasant-tasting milk substitute. For infants allergic to milk; for infants with a family history of allergy; for infants with galactosemia.

1936: Olac. Infant formula exceptionally generous in protein, supplying fat as corn oil. For bottle feeding of infants—full-term and premature —who need a high-protein formula; for infants with poor tolerance of milk fat; for supplementary use with breast feeding.

1942: Nutramigen. The first protein-hydrolysate-based infant formula; a hypoallergenic formula supplying protein nutrients in hydrolyzed form. For infants sensitive to intact proteins of milk and other foods; for infants with severe or multiple food allergies; for infants with persistent diarrhea or other gastrointestinal disturbances; for maintenance of nutrition during test or elimination diets; for infants with galactosemia.

1950: Probana. Infant formula containing protein milk, protein hydrolysate and banana powder. For use in celiac syndrome, including those with cystic fibrosis of pancreas (mucoviscidosis), gluten-induced enteropathy or "idiopathic" celiac disease; for diarrhea, in both acute and recovery stages; for other conditions involving steatorrhea or poor absorption of fat or protein.

1958: Lofenalac. Low phenylalanine formula powder. For infants and children with phenylketonuria.

1965: ProSobee. The first nutritionally complete soy-isolate formula for infants, a milk substitute. For infants allergic to milk, for infants with a family history of allergy; for infants with galactosemia.

1966: Portagen. A nutritionally complete infant formula containing medium-chain triglycerides (a special type of fat) and free of lactose. For use in the nutritional management of infants and children who do not efficiently digest conventional food fat or absorb the long-chain fatty acids. (Impaired fat absorption—steatorrhea—may be a nutritional problem in the following clinical conditions: pancreatic insufficiency, bile acid deficiency, intestinal resection, lymphatic anomalies.)

1971: Pregestimil. Glucose, medium-chain triglycerides, protein-hydrolysate formula providing all major nutrients in the simplest, most easily absorbable forms. For infants and children with disaccharidase deficiency or malabsorption problems; for carbohydrate digestive problems, for food allergies, for chronic nonspecific diarrhea, for cystic fibrosis, for fat malabsorption, for complications of intestinal resection, and for idiopathic defects in digestion or absorption.

Other special formulas are Acidolac, Alacta with Dextri-Maltose, Lonalac, and Premature Formula. Brand names of these products are probably unfamiliar to those outside the pediatric field—unless they are parents of a child whose survival or growth depended on them.

These are not prescription products, but Mead Johnson has, however, marketed them to medical doctors or to hospitals, for administration to infants in the hospital or after discharge. Overseas, the mother whose child requires a "sick baby" formula most often obtains it from pharmacies, from her baby's physician, or from International Division nurses if this service is available.

Enfamil and Enfamil with Iron are the two major products for healthy full-term infants. Enfamil provides levels of protein, fat, carbohydrates, and ash similar to those in breast milk, as well as all vitamins and minerals known as essential to infants. Enfamil With Iron is an infant formula with supplemental iron. This formula is primarily indicated for infants with risk of iron deficiency, offspring of anemic mothers, infants of multiple births, and infants with low birth weights.

Both Enfamil formulas truly meet the definition of infant formula in Food and Drug Administration regulations 21 CFR 125.5 (e) : "A food which purports to be or is represented for special dietary use solely as a food for infants by reason of its simulation of human milk or its suitability as a complete or partial substitute for human milk."

The manufacture and marketing of infant formula products

. . . At Mead Johnson, significant results have evolved from the company's approach to the market through research. Mead Johnson research has provided quality "well baby" products and a broad range of special or "sick baby" formulas to decrease infant mortality and support the development of nutritionally handicapped infants. Its research has also achieved the worldwide respect and confidence of the medical profession and of nutritionists. This permits Mead Johnson to market its products effectively through the medical profession.

ISSUES AND COMMENTS: INFANT FORMULA SALES IN INTERNATIONAL MARKETS

The present issues relate to the industry as a whole rather than to Bristol-Myers. The company is not engaged in deleterious or unethical practices. Nor has there been evidence raised to suggest that it has been. However, a few companies operating in worldwide infant formula markets have been open to such criticism.

It is not the role of Bristol-Myers to defend the industry, but the following comments should place the company's marketing approach in proper perspective with respect to these issues.

Issue

There are "serious setbacks in infant mortality and malnutrition rates" in less developed countries where Bristol-Myers markets infant formulas.[3]

---

[3] Investor Responsibility Research Center, "Infant Nutrition, Breast Feeding and Formula Promotion Practices: Bristol-Myers Co., *IRRC Analysis*, No. 5, March 24, 1975, pp. 5–11.

Comment

Bristol-Myers markets infant formulas in 36 countries outside the United States, and the spread of its infant formula sales through these 36 countries has been analyzed.

A study reported in the *PAG Bulletin* (December 1974) provided a useful tool for this analysis.[4] Using 71 indicators of general development, the PAG study placed 50 countries into 12 homogeneous development groups. The PAG then placed these countries in five levels and assigned them descriptive classifications shown in Exhibit A–1.

EXHIBIT A–1

Level	Groups	Classification
I	1, 2, 3	Least developed countries
II	4, 5, 6	Other developing countries
III	7, 8	
IV	9, 10	Developed countries
V	11, 12	

Volta, Niger, and Ethiopia, the least developed countries, are placed in group 1. At the opposite extreme are the United States, Australia, and Canada, placed in group 12.

Bristol-Myers' total 1974 International Enfamil and special "sick baby" infant formula sales were analyzed in relation to the PAG development groupings and definitions (see charts on the following pages). Three categories were set up for this analysis:

Category A. Included are eight countries where Bristol-Myers markets infant formula. These eight are all included in PAG groups 8–12. People in this category of countries could best use, desire, and afford premium-quality infant formula products.

Category B. Included are 28 countries where Bristol-Myers markets infant formula. PAG classified seven of these countries in groups 4–7; the remaining twenty-one were not included in the PAG study. Taking a conservative approach, the latter twenty-one countries were placed in groups 4–7. However, many of these countries—New Zealand, Ireland, and Puerto Rico, for example—would probably qualify for groups 8–12. The populations in this category may have less capability for using and purchasing Enfamil-type formula products.

Category C. Groups 1–3 are the "least developed" countries. Bristol-Myers does not market infant formulas in these locations.

---

[4] Economic and Social Policy Department, United Nations Food and Agricultural Organization, "Review of Indicators of General and Agricultural Development," *PAG Bulletin* 4 (December 1974): 9.

Total Enfamil and special infant formula sales were then expressed in terms of percentages for each category. Results are shown in Exhibits A–2 and A–3.

EXHIBIT A–2
INFANT FORMULA SALES BY
BRISTOL-MYERS COMPANY INTERNATIONAL DIVISION

			Percentage of international division total formula sales		
	Categories	State of development	Enfamil	Special formula	All formula
A.	Groups 8–12 8 international markets	"Developed countries" and top "other developing countries"	77%	60%	70%
B.	Groups 4–7* 28 international markets	Remaining "other developing countries"	23	40	30
C.	Groups 1–3†	"Least developed countries"	0	0	0
	Total		100%	100%	100%

* 21 of the countries in this group were not covered in the PAG study. Although they include countries such as New Zealand, Ireland, and Puerto Rico, they have been arbitrarily placed among the remaining "other developing countries."
† The company does not market infant formula in these countries, although two shipments totaling $47,000 were sold to private distributors in Sudan and Ethiopia in 1974. This constitutes approximately 1/10 of 1 percent of total international infant formula sales.

EXHIBIT A–3
INFANT FORMULA SALES BY
BRISTOL-MYERS COMPANY INTERNATIONAL DIVISION

			Percentage of each category's formula sales		
	Categories	State of development	Enfamil	Special formula	All formula
A.	Groups 8–12 8 international markets	"Developed countries" and top "other developing countries"	64%	36%	100%
B.	Groups 4–7* 28 international markets	Remaining "other developing countries"	45	55	100
C.	Groups 1–3†	"Least developed countries"	0	0	0

* 21 of the countries in this group were not covered in the PAG study. Although they include countries such as New Zealand, Ireland, and Puerto Rico, they have been arbitrarily placed among the remaining "other developing countries."
† The company does not market infant formula in these countries, although two shipments totaling $47,000 were sold to private distributors in Sudan and Ethiopia in 1974. This constitutes approximately 1/10 of 1 percent of total international infant formula sales.

This analysis produced the following conclusions or inferences about Bristol-Myers' overseas infant formula sales:

1. We do not market infant formula products in the "least developed" countries.

2. Less than one third of sales come from the lower categories of the "other developing" countries. In these countries, 55 percent of Bristol-Myers' sales consist of special "sick baby" formula products—and 45 percent of Enfamil.

3. More than three-fourths of Enfamil sales come from the more "developed countries."

4. "Sick baby" infant formulas are needed more than Enfamil in the "developing" countries, although the need for special formula products is evidenced in all Bristol-Myers international markets.

5. In each country, regardless of overall level of development, one segment of the population has sufficient affluence to seek medical services and to demand and pay for top quality products. It is believed that this segment accounts for essentially all Enfamil sales in the "developing" countries.

6. Enfamil is not marketed in groups 1–3 (the "least developed" countries)—most often cited as placed where infant formula marketing abuses occur.

The results of this analysis are not surprising when viewed in relation to the development and positioning of Mead Johnson business and products over the past fifty years.

Its "well baby" formulas are of premium quality and are not designed for mass markets. They are premium priced and most likely to be used by those who can pay premium prices.

At the same time, its "sick baby" formulas are required in all parts of the world when an infant's development, or life, depends on nourishment that cannot be supplied by mother's milk or simulated mother's milk formulas.

Physicians make frequent urgent requests for special formula products in countries where Bristol-Myers does not have a market position. In such instances, products are dispatched in sufficient quantity to meet the emergency. A sourcing arrangement is then established to meet ongoing requirements. This is done on a social-service—rather than on a commercial—basis.

There well may be "serious setbacks in infant mortality and malnutrition rates" in some developing countries where Bristol-Myers markets infant formulas. But Bristol-Myers is confident that these conditions do not stem from the company's products or practices—and that its infant formula products contribute to reduced morbidity and mortality rates in countries where they are available.

Issue

The combination of infant formula products and "consumer ignorance, lack of sanitary facilities and chronic poverty may be contributing" to these setbacks, because infant formula is not used properly.[5]

Comment

Bristol-Myers' "well baby" formula products are neither intended for, nor promoted into, markets where chronic poverty or ignorance could lead to product misuse or harmful effects. Relatively high prices make it unlikely that Bristol-Myers' infant formula products would be affordable, accessible, or desirable for such consumers. Local government and medical authorities have expressed appreciation for contributions of the company's local managers to upgrading infant health and nutrition in their communities or countries.

Issue

Bristol-Myers is involved in formula promotion programs "which are misleading consumers" and it is important for the company to help solve, rather than create, problems of hunger and malnutrition.[6]

Comment

The company denies this categorically. There is no evidence to support the "belief" that the company is misleading consumers. The company believes that it has been, and will continue to be, a prominent force in resolving hunger and malnutrition problems. The following should be noted:

Advertising practices. Bristol-Myers does not use consumer mass-marketing techniques to sell infant formulas in overseas markets. The company's product positioning does not lend itself to mass media advertising (radio, television, newspapers, or magazines), and country managers have been instructed against its use. An isolated instance of such advertising in the past was stopped. Billboard advertising is not used. Limited advertising in professional medical journals is used.

Promotional practices. Pediatricians and other medical professionals are the primary audience for Mead Johnson's technical promotional literature. The company believes the physician—not the producer of infant formula products—should advise the mother about her infant's feeding and health care.

Only the physician has the scientific training to determine whether

---

[5] IRRC, pp. 5–11.
[6] Ibid.

breast feeding, bottle feeding, or a combination is in the mother's and infant's best interest. If bottle feeding is recommended, the physician is best able to determine what kind of formula is required. All formulas in the line are treated as ethical pharmaceutical products.

Mead Johnson provides the physician with literature that accurately defines each product's ingredients, nutrient content, proper use, capabilities and limitations.

Nursing services. Critics have described nursing services as "dressing sales girls in nurses' uniforms to give their pitch an appearance of nutritional counseling."[7]

Bristol-Myers' International Division sponsors nursing services in nine of the thirty-six countries where its infant formula products are marketed. Nursing services are instituted only when a need exists, and they must first be sanctioned by the local medical community.

A basic qualification for employment in the Bristol-Myers-sponsored nursing services is registration as a nurse. In most countries, this is the SRN (state registered nurse) degree. Over one-fourth of the nurses also have SCM (state certified midwife) degrees. Additional requirements may be imposed by local management. In Hong Kong, for example, all nurses in the program must themselves be mothers.

Nurses in the Bristol-Myers-sponsored programs wear the badges and uniform of their profession. They are salaried Bristol-Myers employees. They are not assigned sales quotas nor are they compensated on a commission basis.

Although their efforts are concentrated on services related to maternal and infant health, duties of all Bristol-Myers nurses can be likened to Public Health nurses in many U.S. municipalities. These nurses work with physicians, with hospitals where mothers deliver, with local health authorities, and, on request, with patients in their homes both before and after birth. Their primary function is to assist mothers in carrying out physician's instructions on their babies' care and feeding, whether they breast feed or bottle feed. If infant formulas are used, nurses can show mothers how to prepare them properly and provide instructional literature. Nurses also respond to emergency or special requests by mothers or physicians.

The nursing service is free of charge to all and is not contingent on the purchase of Mead Johnson infant formula or related products. Bristol-Myers' management is convinced that the nursing service is a logical adjunct to the International Division's business and compatible with the markets in which the company is engaged.

Issue

The description of Enfamil as "nearly identical to mother's milk."[8]

---

[7] P. West, "Bottle Formulas Not Good?" *The North Virginia Globe,* March 1974.
[8] IRRC, pp. 5–16.

Comment

Bristol-Myers agrees completely with the medical profession that mother's milk is the "standard" for infant nutrition. But the medical profession long ago recognized that substitutes for breast milk can, and in some cases must, be used. For instance, infant formula should replace breast feeding when the mother cannot nurse, or if she is taking certain drugs—anticoagulants, antibiotics, narcotics, amphetamines, phenobarbital, thiouracil—that can harm the infant by being absorbed through mother's milk. Therefore, the natural scientific objective has been to develop substitutes that emulate mother's milk as closely as possible.

The statement that Enfamil is "nearly identical to mother's milk in nutritional breadth and balance" is based on its caloric distribution, protein level, protein quality, low curd tension, easily absorbed fat, high level of essential fatty acids, lactose content, and electrolyte and osomolar loads similar to those in human milk. Formulas made by diluting evaporated milk with carbohydrates and water were the main kind of feeding until the 1950s. The statement "infant formula nearly identical to mother's milk" informs the physician that Enfamil is a breast-milk-type formula and *not* a modified evaporated-milk-type formula. It also means Enfamil provides the essential nutrients present in breast milk.

Antibodies present in colostrum cannot be provided in infant formulas. Colostrum is produced for the first five or six days of lactation, and some scientific evidence indicates that it may provide a source of antibodies that may protect infants against disease. Some physicians consider this a valid reason for encouraging breast feeding for the initial days of the baby's life. However, mother's milk and Enfamil are quite comparable in supporting the growth and development of infants.

Issue

The absence of any reference to breast feeding in the advertisement reproduced in the IRRC Analysis No. 5.[9]

Comment

The advertisement in question appeared in the March 5, 1975, *American Baby Magazine,* designed for United States readership. It has not been used in overseas publications. In fact, no direct advertising of infant formula products is carried out in international markets.

The broader implication, however, is that Bristol-Myers discourages the mother from breast feeding. This is not the case. Literature distributed by Mead Johnson to physicians and mothers provides much information on breast feeding. Statements from such literature indicate that:

---

[9] Ibid., pp. 5–11, 5–12.

1. The mother is encouraged to consult her physician for guidance: "You and your doctor will decide the best way for you to feed your baby— breast feeding or bottle feeding."[10]
2. The mother is provided with separate breast-feeding instruction books, or breast feeding is covered in one section of multipurpose books: "Breast feeding is a natural act, but a few pointers may yet be in order. In each instance the doctor will advise you whether and how to breast feed your baby." (Four paragraphs on breast feeding follow.)[11]
3. The physician may leave the alternative to the mother: "Your milk is best for your child, yet circumstances often prevent a mother from breast feeding her child. In which case you must resort to a milk similar to yours."[12]

Issue

"To minimize misuse, industry should give special attention to the importance of unambiguous and standard directions for reconstituting formulas from dry or liquid preparations for feeding young infants. The needs of illiterate as well as literate persons should be considered in designing labels. Labels and product literature should foster hygienically oriented practices such as the use of boiled water and the proper cleaning of utensils.[13]

Comment

Even though it is not required in many countries, Mead Johnson formula products throughout the world are labeled in accord with the U.S. Food and Drug Administration's labeling regulations for such products. These include a complete list of all ingredients, as well as the nutrients provided by the products. In addition, the label of each infant formula product (powder, concentrate or ready-to-use liquid) contains complete and explicit directions for the correct storage, preparation and use of the product. Directions follow current recommendations of pediatricians, public health officials, and consumers.

Label space limitations, due to government nutrition-labeling requirements, usually preclude the use of legible diagrams on the can. This problem is met by supplying physicians, hospitals, and nursing services with printed literature to supplement the complete instructions printed on each can. The literature uses diagrams, pictures, and the printed word to detail the preparation (including sterilization), storage, and use of formula prod-

---

[10] Mead Johnson, "A Mother's Guide During Pregnancy and After Baby Is Born," p. 38.
[11] Mead Johnson, "Mother and Child Care," p. 12.
[12] Mead Johnson, "Enfamil: A Well-Balanced Infant Formula for Your Baby," p. 2.
[13] PAG, "Promotion of Special Foods," p. 5.

ucts. Feeding record cards are also provided. Measuring scoops are enclosed in formula powder cans to aid in measuring the correct amount of the product.

Labels are printed in several languages besides English. Instructional literature is available in a wide range of languages, including English, Italian, Greek, Slovack, Lebanese, Spanish, German, Turkish, French, Chinese, Thai, Swedish, Vietnamese, and Arabic. Every avenue has been taken to provide the literate user, of whatever nationality, with detailed printed instructions, both on the can and through supplementary materials.

Bristol-Myers' infant formula products are not marketed to marginal-income or illiterate families. Special formula infants in such families will, of course, be under a physician's care.

APPENDIX B: 1976 PROPOSAL OF PLAINTIFF, *SISTERS OF THE PRECIOUS BLOOD* v. *BRISTOL-MYERS,* 76 CIV. 1739 (MP), PP. 15–18.

Stockholder proposal—Infant formulas

The Sisters of the Precious Blood of 4000 Denlinger Road, Dayton, Ohio 45426, who own 500 shares of Common Stock, the St. Walburg Monastery of Benedictine Sisters of Covington, Kentucky, of 2500 Amsterdam Road, Covington, Kentucky, who hold of record, 200 shares of Common Stock, the United Church Board of World Ministries, of 475 Riverside Drive, New York 10027, who own 3,110 shares of Common Stock, and the Franciscan Sisters of Perpetual Adoration, St. Rose Convent, 912 Market Street, La Crosse, Wisconsin 54601, who own 2,300 shares of Common Stock, have informed the Company that they, or any of them, intend to present to the meeting the following resolution:

> WHEREAS the sale of infant formulas in developing countries may be linked to rising rates of malnutrition and infant mortality.
>
> WHEREAS the users of such formula who have abandoned breast feeding are sometimes unable to economically afford sufficient quantities of formula and/or do not have access to the necessary sanitary conditions for the use of such formula.
>
> WHEREAS the report made available to stockholders last year did not sufficiently disclose needed information.
>
> THEREFORE, BE IT RESOLVED that the shareholders request the Board of Directors to provide a full, written report to the shareholders within four months of the date of the 1976 annual meeting, containing the following information, provided that information (directly) affecting the competitive position of the company may be omitted, and further provided that the cost of preparing this report shall be limited to an amount deemed reasonable by the Board of Directors.

I. *Sales and Market Share Information*
  1. A list of all countries in which our Company either markets or distributes infant formulas.
  2. A chart by country of the total amount of formula marketed and/or distributed, including both sales and free samples.
  3. A chart by product (Enfamil, Olac, etc.) and country of our Corporation's share of the infant formula market.
  4. A chart of the sales and earnings by product and country of our Corporation's infant formula(s). Compare these amounts to the amount of total sales by the Mead Johnson Division for each country.
  5. Describe any contractual or special arrangements with government agencies for distribution of infant formulas (well and sick baby) within health care facilities.
  6. Given current policies, what is the projected market growth rate by region, i.e., North America, Europe, Caribbean, Latin America, Africa, Asia.
II. *Sales Promotion Policies*
  1. Describe our Company's methods of insuring that sales are limited to families that can afford to use the product properly. Include any market research that identifies the economic status of potential customers and the current strategies for exploiting these markets.
  2. List by country (a) the amount of free samples distributed and (b) the amount of money spent on advertising in medical and trade journals. Attach samples of advertising and other promotional material.
  3. Indicate whether our Company sponsors (a) pediatric and other professional conferences, (b) community activity which involves product promotion. If so, describe such activities.
  4. A chart by country of the number of "mothercraft" personnel, including wage scale, fringe benefits and methods of remuneration.
  5. Describe this year's training literature for "mothercraft" and other promotional personnel including the description of instructions to potential customers about the expense and the proper amount of infant formula needed for good nutrition.
III. *Nutritional Information and Research*
  1. Describe our Company's latest research comparing our infant formula with maternal milk.
  2. State whether or not our Company has plans to develop nutritional supplements for lactating mothers.

They submit the following statement in support of this resolution:

While management's issuing of a report was a welcome first step, we believe it failed to answer important questions raised in last year's shareholder resolution. Several doctors as well as lay specialists have indicated (both publicly and privately to management) that the report distorted important facts concerning the sales and promotion of Bristol-Myers formulas.

The report obscured in which developing countries Bristol-Myers markets. Several leading specialists noted that Olac, a Bristol-Myers infant formula, was listed as a sick-baby formula in the report, although it is widely marketed in the Caribbean in the same manner as a well-baby formula. A full examination is needed. A new report that corrects discrepancies and provides information for shareholders to evaluate our Corporation's policies is imperative.

Management's position

At the 1975 Annual Meeting, stockholders were asked to consider a resolution requesting the company to issue a report with respect to its infant formula business. That resolution (sponsored by two of the four sponsors of the 1976 resolution) was based on the same premise contained in the 1976 resolution that "the sale of infant formulas in developing countries may be linked to rising rates of malnutrition and infant mortality."

Despite the fact that the resolution was defeated by a 94.6 percent vote, the company did prepare the requested report which was summarized in the company's Quarterly Report mailed to all stockholders in July 1975. In addition, the full report was offered, without cost, to any stockholder requesting it. Only 43 requests have been received and, including requests for multiple copies, fewer than 200 copies of the report have been sent.

Briefly, that report stated

1. That as a result of over fifty years of nutritional research, Mead Johnson had developed quality products for the normal infant and a broad range of special or "sick baby" formulas to decrease infant mortality and support development of nutritionally handicapped infants;
2. That the company does not sell infant formula products in the least developed countries of the world and has only one-third of its sales in the lower category of developing countries, with more than half of this amount being in the "sick baby" formulas so urgently needed in those countries;
3. That the company's infant formula products are neither intended nor promoted for private purchase where chronic poverty or ignorance could lead to product misuse or harmful effects;
4. That as a matter of policy, the company's infant formula products are marketed through professional medical personnel and not directly to the consumer.

The company believes that the premise on which the resolution is based is faulty in that the latest available statistics show a decline in worldwide rates of infant mortality and malnutrition. Moreover, the company has already taken responsible steps to provide the answers to the questions raised by the proponents of the resolution. The report is totally responsive to the concerns expressed both in the 1975 and 1976 resolutions, and despite the assertions made in the supporting statement above, accurately reflects company policy and practice in the marketing of infant formulas.

In addition to preparing the report, company representatives have had several meetings with representatives of the proponents and other interested organizations, and the company has made its nutritional scientists available for dialogue with experts outside the company. Finally, the company has recently reaffirmed and strengthened the principles outlined in the report in a comprehensive policy statement issued to its international management. The company, therefore, believes that no purpose will be served by a further report in this area.

The Board of Directors of Bristol-Myers recommends a vote AGAINST the proposed resolution.

SELECTED BIBLIOGRAPHY

Citizens' Committee on Infant Nutrition. *White Paper on Infant Feeding Practices.* Washington, D.C.: Center for Science in the Public Interest, December 1974, 17 pp.

Crittenden, Ann. "Baby Formula Sales in Third World Are Criticized: Products Held Unnecessary for Nutrition of Infants." *The New York Times,* September 11, 1975, pp. 51, 61.

"Is Breast Feeding Best for Babies?" *Consumer Reports* 42 (March 1977): 152–57.

Protein Advisory Group of the United Nations System. "Promotion of Special Foods (Infant Formula and Processed Protein Foods) for Vulnerable Groups." *PAG Statement,* No. 23, revised November 28, 1973.

Index

This book has been set in 10 and 9 point Optima, leaded 2 points. Part numbers and titles are 36 point Lubalin Extra Light. Chapter, reading, and case numbers are 60 point Lubalin Extra Light. Section, chapter, reading, and case titles are 30 point Lubalin Extra Light. The size of the type page is 28 by 47 picas.